Creative
Drama
in the
Classroom

FOURTH EDITION

Nellie McCaslin

CREATIVE
DRAMA *in the*
CLASSROOM

Longman New York & London

TO ELIZABETH FLORY KELLY

whose years of dedicated service, enthusiasm, and
perseverance have helped to further our goals in child drama
and theater for children and young people.

Creative Drama in the Classroom
Fourth Edition

Longman Inc., 95 Church Street, White Plains, New York 10601
Associated companies, branches, and representatives
throughout the world.

Copyright © 1968, 1974, 1980, 1984 by Longman Inc.

Developmental Editor: Gordon T.R. Anderson
Editorial and Design Supervisor: Russell Till
Design: Antler & Baldwin, Inc.
Manufacturing and Production Supervisor: Ferne Y. Kawahara
Composition: Jay's Publishers Services, Inc.
Printing and Binding: The Alpine Press, Inc.

Library of Congress Cataloging Publication Data

McCaslin, Nellie.
   Creative drama in the classroom.

   Bibliography: p.
   Includes index.
   1. Drama in education.   I. Title.
PN3171.M25 1984   371.3'32   83-11293
ISBN: 0-582-28508-9

MANUFACTURED IN THE UNITED STATES OF AMERICA
9 8 7 6 5 4   87 88

Contents

Foreword

"Creative Drama?" the dean repeated several times, rolling the words on his tongue, trying them on for size.

Once long ago while attempting to explain the values of creative drama to a school administrator, I was asked a question intended to undermine my hopes of teaching a course in this subject and to send me in quick retreat so the dean could get on with his work.

"Tell me, Professor Swortzell," the dean smiled with that superior superciliousness for which some members of his profession are famous, "is there such a thing as *non*creative drama?"

"The term 'creative drama' is redundant to be sure," I blurted back, "but necessary in order to emphasize the link between drama and the creative development of the participants."

"You really should give the term some thought," he smiled, half in jest, half in disinterest. "It does your work disservice."

Ignoring his attempt to sidetrack my purpose in being there, I kept talking. Enough information was soon imparted to win his interest and eventually his permission to implement the course. But the term "*non*creative drama" stuck in my mind and has haunted me ever since. It was only a joke, and not a very good one at that, I tell myself. And it came from someone almost ingorant of the field. A dean! Forget it.

Yet the term has persisted in my thinking because the question itself persists: Can drama be *non*creative?

Of course, as practiced by well-intentioned but undertrained teachers, or experienced by well-entertained but unchallenged students, the possibility exists that little or no creative development can take place. I have seen one session in which *nothing* happened, the only creation being my rising ire at the ineptitude of the leader to seize creative opportunities by listening and relating to her group, to recognize her cues, and to respond as she should know how. But today with numerous college courses in both theory and methods of creative drama, with frequent workshops conducted by leaders prominent in the field (including many by the author of this book), with increased meetings at regional and national conferences providing opportunities to see demonstrations, to exchange ideas, and to solve problems, *non*creative drama is disappearing. And with it is disappearing my fear that that dean of long ago might have made a valid point beyond his feeble joke that drama is inherently creative and does not need to advertise itself as such.

Clearly, this new edition of *Creative Drama in the Classroom* is testimony enough to convince even a dean that *creative* belongs beside *drama* in describing our field. Just look at the enormous range of interests and activities discussed and illustrated here: dramatic play; pantomime; improvisation; building of plays; use of poetry, speech, and storytelling; drama as a teaching tool—to name but a few. Yes, the field is becoming increasingly creative, and no better evidence for that development exists than the evolution of this very book.

After reading the manuscript of this, the fourth edition, I went back to the first and systematically traced changes and developments from 1968 to 1984. The initial appearance, critically praised and widely adopted in college courses, consisted of 165 pages in a small format that offered ten chapters and largely centered upon *creative dramatics,* a term then in popular use. The book was written, according to the preface, largely as response to questions and discussions with students and teachers interested in including creative dramatics in the classroom and was intended as a "simple guide for the inexperienced leader or classroom teacher." By 1974, the book had grown to twelve chapters and 236 pages in a large volume that included an important new chapter entitled "Experiments in Learning," demonstrating that what was effective in the classroom could also take place effectively in camps, community centers, libraries, special programs, and teacher training. Creative drama had moved well beyond the schools and into the community. The third edition boasted still more additions into a still larger format of fourteen chapters and 280 pages. For the first time, a splendid use of photographs offered visual proof that creative drama could take place anywhere (school, theatre, university, church, federal government programs, or in just an empty space) and with anyone (the gifted, the mentally retarded, the emotionally disturbed, the physically handicapped, the culturally and economically disadvantaged, and in bilingual education). Creative drama was everywhere winning new recognition, and the three editions of this textbook attested to the progress of this form of drama as a burgeoning creative force.

Now in the latest edition the book and the record of creative drama together become even more impressive. Not only are two entirely new chapters provided, but also materials are added throughout on a great variety of subjects such as participation theatre, developmental drama, drama-in-education, poetry and dance, sound and motion, playwriting with young people, arena staging, professional organizations, and research. The new chapters demonstrate an openness to all forms of theatre including areas once considered to be specialized, such as puppets and mask making. And the author takes a giant step forward for the field when she acknowledges that performance deserves a place in creative drama. There will be those who disagree, but in my opinion this is long overdue recognition of one logical outcome of the craft. I cannot agree more with her conclusion that "performance must not be exploitation but it should likewise not be refused when the players are ready for it, which sooner or later, they will be." Professor McCaslin puts a stamp of approval on an issue that too long has been debated in print rather than tested in performance where its values are best proved and where creative drama, I submit, can acquire new significance.

My applause also cites the importance the book gives to creative drama as an opportunity for independent thinking, along with a corollary freedom for collective and group development of ideas. Young people today especially need such experiences if they are to arrive at attitudes and opinions of their own rather than those dictated by trends and fashions, by mass media, and by special interest and pressure groups operating both at home and abroad. Creative drama represents an ideal forum for democratic as well as creative expression.

"It seems to me, as it seems to many artists right now, that an effort is being made to put creative work and workers under wraps. Nothing could be more dangerous to Democracy." You may be surprised to learn that these words were written by Tennessee Williams, some forty years ago. Even then they seemed relatively unusual for him because he seldom voiced political points of view or crusaded causes except to defend fellow artists or to advocate advances in human understanding and compassion. They were uttered as an outcry against conformity, a danger he saw as repressive and noncreative, and which he feared if not opposed would result in a time when "nobody in America will ever be really young any more and we'll be left standing in the dead center of nowhere."

And though Williams's remarks were aimed against the totalitarianism of the Fascist and Communist states in particular, they also were directed at America itself—and especially at that portion of America which in reactionary panic to outside threats moves toward "forms of controlled thought and feeling." Control to him was the greatest evil of all, the one to which artists should devote their full energies in combat.

Williams singled out our community theatres as one important place to foster the creative spirit in this country. He challenged them to make a difference in the lives of their spectators. This would happen, he insisted, only if they created a special kind of theatre, which he defined as: "something wild, something exciting, something that you are not used to."

Today a renewed insistence upon conformity, ultraconservatism, and control appears to command parts of the land, once again threatening creative work and workers. Now in fact we find many creative workers no longer under wraps but excised altogether from community theatres, libraries, museums, recreational centers—yes, even from classrooms where they can make the most difference. It is time, as this book appears anew to advance our field, to sound Williams's alarm again and to meet his challenge.

Creative Drama in the Classroom with its expanding riches offers a multitude of methods and materials for parents and professionals to put to use for the purpose of making a difference in the lives of participants. The theories and activities advocated here foster individual expression of thought and feeling, and by eliminating *non*creativity they diminish the chances for conformity and control. They give us one tested means to create for people of all ages something they are not used to, something wild and exciting—something called creative drama.

And what a wonderful redundancy that term is, if we make the most of it in the classroom and everywhere else we practice it.

Lowell Swortzell

Professor of Educational Theatre
The School of Education, Health,
Nursing, and Arts Professions
New York University

Preface

*T*he opportunity to prepare a new edition of a textbook is both a welcome and a challenging responsibility: welcome because one knows a need has been met, challenging because a new edition implies new content and significant change. This immediately raises the questions: What have I to say that I have not said before? What of importance has taken place in the years since the last edition? Has my point of view been changed or modified in any substantive way?

Like most authors, I suppose, I think of a dozen things I wish I had included as soon as a manuscript is out of my hands. The case of *Creative Drama in the Classroom* has been no exception. With each edition I have felt the familiar pangs of regret at having omitted a point or example I wish I had included. Therefore it is with pleasure that I greet this opportunity to update the text yet once more, knowing full well, however, that I shall undoubtedly experience the same frustration once the final proof is in.

One of the dangers inherent in preparing a new edition is the temptation to include more than the stated content. No book can be all things to all persons, and a text that goes far beyond its original purpose runs the risk of superficiality. I hope I have avoided this pitfall even though I have added material that does not fall precisely within the original definition of creative drama. My rationale was that this new material meets many of the same educational goals that creative drama does and could therefore extend and enrich the experience. Also, in the past few years we have become freer in our exploration of content and form. Different themes, mixed media, additional goals, and new uses of drama have taken us beyond the previously accepted boundaries of our discipline.

The sixteen years that have passed between the first and fourth editions have brought many changes and advances in drama and theatre education. Probably no other comparable period in the history of arts education in our country has witnessed so much excitement, controversy, interest—and discouragement. Whereas there has been notable progress in program development and acceptance of the arts in the curriculum, the budgetary cuts of the early eighties on all levels have substantially reduced and, in some cases, wiped out fine programs. There is cause for elation when we see what can be done, but there is cause for dismay when we see what these cuts have destroyed. Nevertheless, solutions are being found: new ways of working when the old no longer serve or, more accurately, are no longer there. Adversity and dissatisfaction force an evolution of our practices Can we reach our goals by other routes? What are these routes? Perhaps we should ask what, in fact, are the goals of the eighties?

In the preface to the two earlier editions, I said that this text had been written in response to questions from students and teachers regarding the use of creative drama in schools and recreational programs. Some of those questions had arisen in university classes; others, in workshops and at professional conferences. During the sixteen years since the original publication, I have visited many more schools and college campuses and have participated in numerous meetings. I have led workshops in creative drama and have been a consultant to groups establishing arts programs. My many discussions with students, teachers, and administrators have been convincing proof of a deep and urgent need for the arts in our society, a need greater today in many respects than at any other time. These discussions have, at the same time, disclosed some remarkably good work being carried on in every region of the country. Some of it is being done by specialists; some, by generalists—classroom teachers who are frequently unaware of their own ability to guide children to a fulfillment through creative expression. New leadership has emerged in the past decade, and some strong and effective influences are revitalizing our efforts.

In the earlier editions I made mention of the increasing number of workshops being offered under a variety of sponsorships. One important difference is that today many of these workshops are made possible through funding programs of government agencies and private foundations. Some consist of a single session or meeting. Others are planned as a series, ranging from as few as three meetings to all-day sessions over a period of one to three weeks. Some are long-term residencies. Often these workshops are focused on a single topic or theme, such as drama therapy, drama as a teaching tool, drama in the language arts program, drama in human relations (using drama/theatre as techniques), and playwriting for young people, to mention only a few. There are also in-service courses for teachers, conducted along more academic lines, which are organized to include participation, demonstration, discussion, and the opportunity for reading in the field.

It has been my experience that the majority of those who enroll in such workshops or classes have had little or no previous training. Participants are eager to learn, but many express feelings of inadequacy, often despite years of successful classroom teaching. Frequently asked questions are: What exactly is creative drama? How should I start? Where should it be introduced? Is it the same as role playing? What material is available? Don't I need a background in theatre? What is the difference between creative drama and drama-in-education, as practiced in England? What is T.I.E.?

The questions are legitimate. At the same time, I am aware that many of those who question their own qualifications have the primary requisites: the desire to learn, a respect for the contribution of children, and an appreciation of theatre as an art form. Without these basic attitudes, it is doubtful whether satisfying results can ever be achieved; with them, there is every likelihood of success.

Few teachers or students have had sufficient experience in the performing arts to feel secure in the beginning. On the other hand, many who have studied formal theatre techniques have had no experience with children. There is little doubt in my mind that the creative teacher will find his or her own way sooner or later, but if the following chapters hasten the process by offering a point of view and a way of working, they will have served their purpose.

This textbook is intended as a guide for the inexperienced leader or classroom teacher—the nonspecialist—who wants to initiate dramatic activities but who needs some practical help in getting started. It has, therefore, been conceived from a point of view toward drama education rather than toward organizing material along specific age or class levels. Moreover, I believe, the philosophy to be essentially the same for all, regardless of the age or grade level of the participants. Indeed, recent workshops for senior adults have proved that creative drama techniques, as used with children, are equally effective in working with this older age level.

My own experience with teachers has convinced me of their awareness of the interests, tastes, and backgrounds of their pupils. What they seek is guidance in the planning of simple activities and the adaptation of material for use in creative drama and language arts classes. With that in mind, therefore, this text was written.

The contents include a rationale for creative drama with specific objectives and values, some suggestions for pantomime and improvisation, discussion of play structure, and presentation of the simple basic procedures involved when a class wants to share a play with an audience. While this is not intended to be a book on play production, it recognizes the fact that groups occasionally want to put on a play, and when that happens, new problems are posed. Suggestions for solving the problems are not meant to encourage performance for an audience, but rather to help make the transition from process to presentation easier. Indeed, a major reconsideration in preparing this new edition has to do with the question of performance. As I reread the three earlier editions, I realized that a change in my own thinking has been taking place over the past few years. While I am still firmly convinced that process is of greater value than product for students and that young children should not be pushed into performance, I believe we have disregarded the fact that the theatre is a performing art and therefore performance (product) is the natural outcome of the process. In our desire to prevent the boredom of long rehearsals and the wooden presentations of the past, we have taken an arbitrary stand against communication with an audience, when children may be actually needful of that experience.

Let me repeat, however, that very little creative drama ever reaches the performance level, but when it does, it should be recognized as growth and therefore supported. Not supported with publicity, the featuring of star performers, and endless practicing for perfection, but with realistic goals, which include understanding, sincerity, and a modicum of performance skills, resulting in satisfaction for actors and audience alike. In short, although performance must not be exploitation, it should likewise not be refused when the players are ready for it, which, sooner or later, they will be.

This fourth edition includes two new chapters, which, I hope, will increase its usefulness. One is a chapter on puppets and masks. The opportunities puppets and masks afford for relevant extensions of creative drama warranted more space than was given them in the third edition. The variety of kinds of puppets and simple methods of construction should enable any teacher to make use of them as means, if not as ends, in their own right. Mask making is also popular with children and serves therapeutic as well as educational purposes.

A new chapter has also been added on the use of alternative spaces for the teaching of drama. The desire for after-school and Saturday classes, and the lack of facilities have prompted some leaders to look elsewhere for places in which to work and perform. They have found them in nontraditional locations, resulting often in the enrichment of our aesthetic education. Because of the imaginative use that is being made of libraries, museums, and churches, among various other social and cultural institutions, I have included a brief discussion on how drama is being and can be handled outside the classroom.

In addition, I have expanded in this fourth edition on the ways in which drama is being used for educational purposes, differentiating between education *in* the arts and education *through* the arts. The former, often referred to as aesthetic education, has different goals from drama-in-education but a curriculum can and often does support both, particularly in the elementary school. More space has been given to the discussion of theatre-in-education and children's theatre. Playwriting for children, a new thrust in education along with contemporary themes, and the value of drama/theatre for teaching English as a second language are included in this edition. Special and therapeutic uses of drama, a relatively new field in the sixties, is now receiving long overdue attention; although a text on creative drama cannot treat this field in any depth, I have described some of the new practices and recent literature that is available for those who are interested in the subject. All of us deal with the exceptional student every day of our lives, therefore it is hoped that this further information may be of value.

Numerous new activities, stories, and poems throughout the text have been included in an effort to enrich the content. Again, a conscious decision was made to emphasize practicality rather than theory. The limitations of space as well as purpose necessary in a textbook preclude extensive discussion of theory; what theory is included is therefore implicit, serving as a guideline for material that has been carefully chosen. It is my belief that a good experience in drama and theatre, regardless of the raison d'être, enhances the quality of human life, and it is to this end that I am most deeply committed. To bring as much satisfaction and joy as possible into the lives of *all* children is our ultimate common goal.

The bibliography has been revised and updated. Familarity with the literature in the field will not only help to build a better background for the teacher, but should strengthen his or her own perception and awareness of the values of drama. The teacher can then begin to devise original techniques, geared not to an arbitrary age or grade level, but to individual circumstances.

A word concerning the problem of the use of the generic pronoun "he" in the text. I recognize that our field is now represented by both men and women; however, the constant repetition of "he or she" is awkward, whether in reference to teachers or students. After careful consideration, the decision was made to avoid this awkwardness through alternating the use of "he" and "she," by using "he" in one paragraph or set of examples and "she" in the next.

Again, I must acknowledlge the inspiration that has come from my many friends and colleagues in the United States and abroad. In the earlier editions I mentioned the names of persons to whom I felt particularly indebted. The list has expanded to the point that it would be literally impossible to name them all. I can only say that their thinking and their work have continued to shape my own views as their writing has contributed to our field. I should like to express particular appreciation, however, to those persons who are pioneering in the newer areas of drama therapy and drama in special education. Although teachers of the arts have long recognized the value of drama for handicapped persons, little had been done to provide opportunities for this group. The federal legislation in the midseventies forced us to take a closer look at our offerings in the arts and their availability to the handicapped. The lacks that were revealed have resulted in a number of new programs and improved facilities; most important, however, has been a heightened awareness of the needs of handicapped persons.

I must once again express my gratitude to friends and colleagues across the land, who responded to my call for photographs of their work. I cannot thank them enough for their generosity. The pictures they sent not only enhance the book but add another dimension in showing the reader some of the approaches and types of work being done in different regions and schools.

My thanks also go to those teachers who continue to raise the questions I am attempting to answer. Their desire to learn has stimulated my own further thinking, and their observations have caused me to reconsider and modify some of my earlier views.

Finally, I want to extend my special appreciation to Nancy Swortzell for her helpful suggestions in the revision of the text, to Lowell Swortzell for his foreword to the fourth edition, and to Daty Healy for her careful and critical reading of each chapter of the book. Once again, my deepest gratitude must go to Gordon T.R. Anderson, whose editorial guidance has made the preparation of the manuscript a pleasure.

Nellie McCaslin
New York City

Acknowledgments

"The Little Scarecrow Boy" by Margaret Wise Brown. From *Fun and Frolic*, revised edition, by Margaret Wise Brown, published by D.C. Heath and Co., 1955. Copyright by Margaret Wise Brown.

"The Snow Walker" by Farley Mowat used by permission of The Canadian Publishers, McClelland and Stewart Limited, Toronto. From *The Snow Walker* by Farley Mowat. Copyright © by McClelland & Stewart Ltd., 1975. By permission of Little, Brown and Company in association with the Atlantic Monthly Press.

"I have two selves" from *Puppetry in Early Childhood Education* by Tamara Hunt and Nancy Renfro. Reprinted by permission of the authors.

"Bread and Honey" from *Bread and Honey* by Frank Asch. Reprinted by permission of the author.

"The Magic Stones" by Aviva Layton. From *Magook #5*, copyright © 1979 by Magook Publishers Ltd. Reprinted by permission of Magook Publishers Ltd.

"The Old Man and the Goombay Cat" by Kitty Kirby. Copyright © by Kitty Kirby. By permission of the author.

Yoshiki Uchida, "The Wise Old Woman," in *The Sea of Gold and Other Tales.* Copyright © 1965 Yoskiko Uchida. Reprinted with the permission of Charles Scribner's Sons.

"Jump and Jiggle" frcm *Another Here and Now Storybook* by Lucy Sprague Mitchell. Copyright 1937 by E.P. Dutton & Co., Inc. Renewed, 1965 by Lucy Sprague Mitchell. Reprinted by permission of the publisher, E.P. Dutton, Inc.

"Merry-Go-Round" by Dorothy Baruch. Permission granted by Bertha Klausner International Literary Agency, Inc.

"Halloween" from *Children's Literature for Dramatization: An Anthology* by Geraldine Brain Siks. Copyright © 1964 by Geraldine Braine Siks. Reprinted by permission of Harper & Row, Publishers, Inc.

"Sing a Song of Seasons" by Alice Ellison. Copyright © 1964 by Alice Ellison. From *Children's Literature For Dramatization: An Anthology* by Geraldine Brain Siks. Reprinted by permission of Alice Ellison Brain.

"Imaginings" by J. Paget-Fredericks. From *Green Pipes* by J. Paget-Fredericks, published by The Macmillan Company, 1929.

"Some One" by Walter de la Mare. Reprinted by permission of The Literary Trustees of Walter de la Mare and The Society of Authors as their representative. representative.

"Mobile" from *All Day Long* by David McCord. Copyright © 1965, 1966 by David McCord. By permission of Little, Brown and Company.

"The Negro Speaks of Rivers." Copyright 1926 by Alfred A. Knopf, Inc., and renewed 1954 by Langston Hughes. Reprinted from *Selected Poems of Langston Hughes,* by permission of the publisher.

"The Old Wife and the Ghost" by James Reeves (1952). Reprinted by permission of Oxford University Press.

"The Creation" from *God's Trombone* by James Weldon Johnson. Copyright 1927 by The Viking Press, Inc. Copyright renewed 1955 by Grace Nail Johnson. Reprinted by permission of Viking Penguin Inc. CAUTION: Any public reading of "The Creation" will require the further permission of the Estate of James Weldon Johnson. Please address all inquiries to Viking Penguin Inc., 40 West 23rd Street, New York, N.Y. 10010.

"The Night the Elephants Marched on New York" from *Seven Sound and Motion Pictures* by Joanna H. Kraus. Reprinted by permission of New Plays, Inc., Rowayton, Conn.

"Rimouski" from *In One Basket* by Shirley Pugh. Copyright © 1972 by Shirley Pugh. Reprinted by permission of Anchorage Press of New Orleans.

Creative
Drama
in the
Classroom

1

Creative Drama: An Art, a Socializing Activity, and a Way of Learning

In the sun that is young once only,
Time let me play and be
Golden in the mercy of his means.
                    DYLAN THOMAS

Play

The phenomenon of play has fascinated philoso-phers, educators, psychologists, and anthropologists through the ages. Studies reveal a persistent search for the meaning of play and its role in life, civilization, and culture. Theories range from its being an expression of surplus energy, a means of relaxation, and an escape from reality to a concern with its importance in the develop-ment of higher intelligence and the learning process. Psy-chologists have viewed play as a way of working through

2   *Creative Drama:* A socializing activity.
                    "Children building a magic wall."
                    (*Courtesy of Milton Polsky, photo-*
                    graph by Ann Raychel.)

unconscious pressures; some have discerned a close relationship between play and the creative process, signifying that art is actually one aspect of play. Regardless of theory, however, there is consensus on play as being a profoundly important activity in the process of human development. According to Richard Courtney, whose scholarly work on the subject encompasses all areas, "Play initially, and the arts subsequently, develop imaginative constructions whereby people function in the world. The arts are expressions of imagination through which the personality develops, and upon which cognitive and abstract ways of working with the environment are built."[1]

Primitive societies released this impulse to play through tribal expressions of hope, joy, fear, desire, sorrow, hatred, and worship. What primitive people felt strongly, they danced or mimed. From their sacred play came ritual; poetry, music, and dance were a part of their play. Philosophy and wisdom found expression in words.

In ancient Greece religious celebration resulted in contests, and these contests gave birth to dramatic forms or plays. As highly organized as they were later to become, these contests could be considered the creative expression of the people, from whose ranks individual playwrights emerged. During the Middle Ages, drama had its rebirth in the Church. Authorship of the scripts is unknown, but there is proof that the performers were amateurs, whose participation was voluntary. Professionalism had no part in these plays, which served a religious and educational purpose. The involvement of the audiences was probably great as they responded to the dramatization of the Bible stories and moral tales as enacted by their neighbors. In every period of history, play has served a significant purpose, interpreting and affecting the lives of the people. "We have to concede, therefore, that civilization is, in its earliest phases, played."[2]

According to the author of this statement, our modern adult preoccupation with making a business of play has resulted in its decline, and this decline is man's loss. True play does not know professionalism, for it is a voluntary activity, based on, but different from, the business of everyday life. Joy and freedom are the hallmarks of play, with the rules and limits established by the players.

True play, though free, creates order—indeed, *is* order. Whereas people may play alone, one of the basic characteristics of play is the teamwork involved; through play, the participants are drawn closely together. Huizinga notes that dressing up is often an element of play, though it is not always included and is not necessary. Examples of play may be found in all countries of the world, at different periods in history and on every age level. Play is

---

1. Richard Courtney, *Re-Play: Studies of Human Drama in Education* (Toronto: The Ontario Institute for Studies in Education, 1982), p. 157.

2. J. Huizinga, *Homo Ludens, A Study of the Play Element in Culture* (Boston: Beacon Press, 1955), p. 14.

inherent in human beings, and the child early manifests an impulse to engage in it.

One has only to watch a group of children playing in an empty lot or a playground to accept the truth of these observations. The child plays almost as soon as he moves, and through his playing, he learns. In his dramatic play the three- or four-year-old tries on the roles of those about him; he observes their activities and learns by pretending to be and do. He enters the various worlds of his family and neighbors, interpreting and reenacting. First he observes; then he responds, repeating in play what has made a strong impression on him in his life. Not unlike primitive man, the young child expresses his feelings through movement and words, creating more complex situations as he grows older, with the boundaries stretched but the rules still clearly established. By the time he is ready for school he has learned much about the world he lives in, and a large part of his learning has come about through his play. As Winifred Ward observed, "Drama comes in the door of every school with the child."[3]

The impulse to play, if encouraged, can become a continuing way of learning, a medium of expression, and eventually an art form. Many teachers have realized the potential of play and have made drama an integral part of their programs. Some have rejected it on the grounds that it is frivolous and therefore unrelated to serious learning. The fact that the child gives it her most serious attention escapes their notice; she is made to feel that play is unworthy and therefore something to be left outside the schoolroom door. When this happens, the joyful and creative element of her free play is extinguished, perhaps never to be rekindled. Other teachers, and it is to them that this book is addressed, ask how they can keep the play impulse alive, that it may enhance learning and thus enrich the lives of their pupils.

Jon and Rumer Godden,[4] in their recollections of a childhood spent in India, speak with feeling of play, its magic and privacy. When asked, as they often were by their parents, what they were playing, the reply was generally "nothing." "Or, if that were too palpable a lie, we would give a camouflage answer like 'Mothers and Fathers,' which we never played or, with us, another improbable play, 'Shops.' . . . Yet if we had told what we were playing no one would have been much the wiser, because our plays were like icebergs, only three-tenths seen, the rest hidden, inside ourselves. It was what we thought into our play that made its spell."

Games, sports, and ritual are closely related to play. Whereas sports are like theatre and are designed for an audience, games and drama exist for the participants. Theatre games, about which we hear so much these days, were created for the actor, not for the audience. A sport is held in a particular place; a game, wherever players may assemble. As to ritual, it may be defined as the

---

3. Winifred Ward, *Drama With and For Children*, Bulletin 30 (Washington, D.C.: U.S. Department of Health, Education, and Welfare, 1960), p. 1.

4. Jon and Rumer Godden, *Two Under the Indian Sun* (New York: Knopf, 1966), p. 55.

observance of a set form or series of rites. We think of the ritual as having religious significance, but it is more inclusive than that. The repetition of an act or set of acts is also ritual. This is important to remember when working with children, for their games assume a ritualistic form. Movement and chants play an important part in them. By beginning a creative drama class with the familiar—movement, rhythms, songs, or group games which all know—the leader is using ritual to draw the members together and make them comfortable.

Educational Objectives

One of the most frequently stated aims of education today is the maximal growth of the child both as an individual and as a member of society. In order to achieve this aim, certain educational objectives have been set up. Although these objectives vary somewhat, there is general agreement that knowledge, skills, and appreciation of the arts are essential. The modern curriculum tries to provide for each child to:

1. Develop basic skills in which reading, writing, arithmetic, science, social studies, and the arts are stressed;
2. Develop and maintain good physical and mental health;
3. Grow in his ability to think;
4. Clarify his values and verbalize his beliefs and hopes;
5. Develop an understanding of beauty, using many media including words, color, sound, and movement;
6. Grow creatively and thus experience his own creative powers.[5]

Although other objectives are mentioned, these six are most frequently listed in the building of programs designed for today's world and the complex problems life offers.

The most enthusiastic proponent of creative drama would not go so far as to claim that its inclusion in the curriculum will ensure the meeting of these objectives. On the other hand, many objectives of modern education and creative drama are unquestionably shared. Among the shared objectives are:

1. Creativity and aesthetic development
2. The ability to think critically
3. Social growth and the ability to work cooperatively with others
4. Improved communication skills

5. Robert S. Fleming, *Curriculum for Today's Boys and Girls* (Columbus, Ohio: Charles E. Merrill, 1963), p. 10.

5. The development of moral and spiritual values
6. Knowledge of self

Before discussing creative drama in greater detail, some definitions are in order. The terms *dramatic play, creative dramatics* or *creative drama* (now the preferred term), *play making, children's theatre,* and *role playing* are used, often interchangeably, though they have quite different meanings. A definition of terms will clarify the meanings as they are used in this text.

Definitions

Dramatic Play

This is the free play of the very young child in which she explores her universe, imitating the actions and character traits of those around her. It is her earliest expression in dramatic form but must not be confused with drama or interpreted as performance. Dramatic play is fragmentary in nature, existing only for the moment. It may last for a few minutes or go on for some time. It may even be played repeatedly, if the interest is sufficiently strong, but when this occurs, the repetition is in no sense a rehearsal. It is, rather, the repeating of a creative experience for the pure joy of doing it. It has no beginning and no end, and no development in the dramatic sense.

Dramatic play may be as simple as Susan's passing of imaginary cookies to a guest when her mother is entertaining a friend at tea. The two or three minutes of spontaneous pantomime are indeed dramatic play since they involve stepping into the role of the mother and performing an often observed activity. Susan has seen how a hostess behaves and is taking advantage of an opportunity to slip into the role to see what it is like to be "mother" and do as she does.

Dramatic play may, on the other hand, follow the pattern of six-year-old Erma, who was the youngest child on the street and, therefore, the last to go to school. She had heard about teachers and lessons and longed for the day when she, too, could pack up her books in a bag and trot off after breakfast with the other boys and girls to the elementary school. When the time came, her curiosity may have been satisfied, but her fascination became even more intense. According to her family, she would return every afternoon and set up her own class in the dining room. Whether the others joined her or not, she would play for an hour or more with an improvised desk and a blackboard. She assumed, in turn, the various roles of principal, teacher, boys, and girls. Most often, however, she would be the teacher who called the roll, disciplined the children, and, to the great amusement of her mother and older sister, reenacted everything that had taken place during the day. This situation held

Dramatic play.(Courtesy of Rachael Carr, photograph by Edward Kimball.)

her interest for three years, though the content varied according to her daily experiences. Other parents have described similar preoccupations, some lasting for an extraordinarily long time, until the interest waned and another took its place.

It has been stated that "dramatic play helps the child develop from a purely egocentric being into a person capable of sharing and of give and take."[6] Certainly this is true of the two examples cited. In both instances the mother accepted the play without interference, letting it continue with neither impatience nor the kind of amused attention that might have caused self-consciousness. In dramatic play the child creates a world of her own in which to master reality. She tries in this imaginative world to solve real-life problems that she has, until now, been unable to solve. She repeats, reenacts, and relives these experiences. In the book *Understanding Children's Play,* the authors observe that through this activity the child is given an opportunity to imitate adults, encouraged to play out real-life roles with intensity, to dramatize

6. Ruth Hartley, Lawrence K. Frank, and Robert M. Goldenson, *Understanding Children's Play* (New York: Columbia University Press, 1964), p. 19.

relationships and experiences, to express his own most pressing needs, to release unacceptable impulses, to reverse the roles usually taken, to try to solve problems, and to experiment with solutions. If encouraged, by providing the place, the equipment, and an atmosphere in which the child feels free to express himself, dramatic play is a natural and healthy manifestation of human growth.

According to Richard Courtney, "Play is the principal instrument of growth. Without play there can be no normal adult cognitive life; without play, no healthful development of affective life; without play, no full development of the power of will."[7]

Marie Winn writes in her book, *The Plug-in Drug,* that the child can work out difficulties through play, assuming the roles of the adults in his life, redressing grievances and reenacting scenes that have caused distress. "In play he can expose, and perhaps, exorcise, fears that he cannot articulate in any other way; more important, perhaps, is the opportunity imaginative play affords the child to become an active user rather than a passive recipient of experience."[8] In our TV world, this is an important contribution.

One of the most delightful and understanding treatments of the subject is to be found in Virginia Glasgow Koste's *Dramatic Play in Childhood: Rehearsal for Life.* In this book she offers three main reasons for valuing play:

> That is the time when most people are most expert and constant in playing; that is the time when they most freely externalize their playing so that it is possible to see and hear it; and that is the time when the power of play as a means of growth and accomplishment can most effectively be nurtured for a stronger rising generation of adults.[9]

The text is rich with examples of children at play. Though she purposely eschews the scholarly approach, Koste presents effective evidence of learning, imagination and social growth. Valuable insights are to be found in this early stage of human development, which is preparation for the next—creative drama. That it is also the root of drama and theatre is an obvious conclusion.

Creative Drama and Play Making

The terms *creative drama*[10] and *play making* may be used interchangeably since they refer to informal drama that is created by the participants. As the

7. Richard Courtney, *Play, Drama and Thought* (New York: Drama Book Specialists), p. 204.

8. Marie Winn, *The Plug-in Drug* (New York: Viking, 1977), p. 95.

9. Koste, Virginia Glasgow, *Dramatic Play in Childhood: Rehearsal for Life* (New Orleans: Anchorage Press, 1978), p. 6.

10. Definition of creative drama accepted by the Children's Theatre Association of America in 1977: "Creative drama is an improvisational, nonexhibitional, process-centered form of drama in which participants are guided by a leader to imagine, enact, and reflect upon human experiences. Although creative drama traditionally has been thought of in relation to children and young people, the process is appropriate to all ages."

name *play making* implies, this activity goes beyond dramatic play in scope and intent. It may make use of a story with a beginning, a middle, and an end. It may, on the other hand, explore, develop, and express ideas and feelings through dramatic enactment. It is, however, always improvised drama. Dialogue is created by the players, whether the content is taken from a well-known story or is an original plot. Lines are not written down or memorized. With each playing, the story becomes more detailed and better organized, but it remains extemporaneous in nature and is at no time designed for an audience. Participants are guided by a leader rather than a director; the leader's goal is the optimal growth and development of the players.

The replaying of scenes is therefore different from the rehearsal of a formal play, in that each member of the group is given an opportunity to play various parts. No matter how many times the story is played, it is done for the purpose of deepening understanding and strengthening the performers rather than perfecting a product. Scenery and costumes have no place in creative drama, although an occasional property or piece of a costume may be permitted to stimulate the imagination. When these are used, they should not be considered mounting or production. Most groups do not feel the need of properties of any kind and are generally freer without them.

The term *creative drama* is used to describe the improvised drama of children from age five or six and older, but it belongs to no particular age level and may be used just as appropriately to describe the improvisation of high school students. The young adult is more likely to label it *improvisation,* which indeed it is, but the important distinction to keep in mind is that it has form and is, therefore, more structured than dramatic play. At the same time, it is participant centered and not intended for sharing, except with the members of the group who are not playing and are, therefore, observers rather than audience.

The word *drama* is also used to mean literature. In the present context, however, it is used to mean a play that is developed creatively by a group, as opposed to one that abides by a written script. When dialogue is written by either teacher or children, it automatically ceases to be spontaneous drama, although it may, indeed, be a fine example of creative writing. This occasionally happens, and when it does, the results may be doubly rewarding. Nevertheless, whether simple or elaborate, if the play is to be properly described as creative drama, it must be improvised rather than written.

Children's Theatre

The term *children's theatre* refers to formal productions for children's audiences, whether acted by amateurs or professionals, children or adults, or a combination of both. It is directed rather than guided; dialogue is memorized, and scenery and costumes usually play an important part. Since it is audience centered, it is essentially different from creative drama and dramatic play. The child in the audience is the spectator and the benefits derived are aesthetic.

What does a child gain from attending good children's theatre? She gains much. First of all, there is the thrill of watching a well-loved story come alive on a stage. There is the opportunity for a strong, vicarious experience as she identifies with characters who are brave, steadfast, noble, loyal, beautiful. Emotions are released as she shares the adventure and excitement of the plot. And, finally, she learns to appreciate the art of the theatre if the production is tasteful and well done.

We are speaking now of the child in the audience, not the child in the play. While there is much that is creative and of value for the performer, it is generally agreed that participation in creative drama is far more beneficial than public performances for all children up to the age of ten or eleven. Occasionally, there is an expressed desire "to put on a play," and when this comes from the children themselves, it is probably wise to grant the request. There are times, to be sure, when sharing is a joy and a positive experience, but is to be hoped that formal play production would be infrequent. Certainly, if it is done, the production should be simple and all precautions taken to guard against the competition and tension that so often characterize the formal presentation of a play. For junior and senior high school students, however, a play is often the desired culmination of a semester's work. To deprive students of the experience would be to withhold the ultimate satisfaction of communicating an art.

Some leaders in the field believe that any performance in front of an audience is harmful because it automatically interferes with the child's own free expression. I should agree up to a point, but the theatre is, after all, a performing art; and when the audience is composed of understanding and sympathetic persons, such as parents or members of another class, performance may be the first step toward communicating a joyful experience. Without question, however, very young children should not perform publicly. Those in the middle and upper grades may not be harmed if their desire and the right occasion indicate that the benefits outweigh the disadvantages. A performance is a disciplined and carefully organized endeavor, involving a variety of skills that children of elementary school age do not and should not be expected to possess.

I am not speaking here of the professional child actor, who, most educators agree, is in grave danger of being damaged by exploitation and the pressures of performance. The same dangers, however, are present whenever children are used for ends other than their own growth and development. When children are trained rather than guided, praised extravagantly instead of encouraged, or featured as individuals rather than helped to work cooperatively with others, they risk losing all the positive aspects of the experience. Ironically, this leads to poor theatre as well, for ensemble, that most desirable quality of good theatre, is achieved through the process of working together, not by featuring individual players.

Role Playing

The term *role playing* is used most often in connection with therapy or education. It refers to the assuming of a role for the particular value it may have to the participant, rather than for the development of an art. Although all art may be considered to have certain curative powers, it is not the primary purpose of either creative drama or theatre to provide therapy or make use of drama to solve social and emotional problems. Role playing is what the young child does in his dramatic play, it is true, but it is also a tool used by psychologists and play therapists.

Acting is, in a way, an extension of dramatic play. According to Richard Courtney, "Play, acting and thought are interrelated. They are mechanisms by which the individual tests reality, gets rid of his anxieties, and masters his environment."[11]

Drama therapy is similar to role playing in its stated purpose. Its use assumes a problem, for which this type of treatment is indicated. Physically handicapped, mentally retarded, emotionally disturbed, and culturally disadvantaged children may derive great benefit from its use, provided the therapy is in the hands of a competent and sensitive therapist. The distinction between role playing and therapy, therefore, consists more of degree than of kind. *Role playing* may be considered preventive, in that it provides an opportunity for all children in a group to develop sensitivity toward the feelings of others and encourages changes of attitude through understanding. *Therapy* is the dramatic technique used for its curative power in helping a patient to solve problems that frighten, confuse, or puzzle her. "It is in itself both a form of comfort and reassurance, and a way of moving on toward new attitudes about these things."[12]

New Techniques in Drama and Theatre Education

Although the following techniques have been in use in England since the mid-sixties, they are only now becoming generally known and accepted in this country. The terminology, however, is not always clearly understood here nor indeed is it always used to mean the same thing; therefore I am defining the more common terms in order that references in later chapters will be understood.

Participation Theatre

This is a technique, originated by Brian Way in England, which permits the audience to become vocally, verbally, and physically involved in the produc-

11. Richard Courtney, *Play, Drama and Thought,* p. 177.
12. Peter Slade, *Child Drama* (London: University of London Press, 1954), p. 119.

tion.[13] Children are invited to suggest ideas to the actors from time to time during the enactment of a play. Frequently the audience, if not too large, is invited to come into the playing area to assist the cast in working out these ideas. Skillfully handled, this can be an exciting technique.

Of course, all theatre involves participation the moment the attention is captured. An audience feels, thinks, laughs, applauds, and occasionally speaks out; in our time, unlike earlier periods, adult audiences are expected to sit quietly whether the performances pleases them or not. The child audience, however, less inhibited and unschooled in these conventions, wants to do more, to become actively engaged as it suspends all disbelief. It identifies with the protagonist and participates in the action to the extent that conditions and authority permit. The younger the audience, the more natural the involvement. The point to be made here is that the Brian Way Method offers a new approach to children's theatre by combining the formal with the informal in its attempt to establish a closer relationship between actor and audience. The line commonly drawn between creative drama and children's theatre disappears as the spectator becomes participant.

Developmental Drama

The term, developmental drama, has been used primarily by Richard Courtney in Canada. Although one occasionally finds it in the literature here, Courtney's definition is the best and clearest we have.

> Developmental drama is the study of developmental patterns in human enactment. Drama is an active bridge between our inner world and the environment. Thus the developments studied are both personal and cultural, and each is in interaction with the other. These studies overlap with other fields: with psychology and philosophy on a personal level, and with sociology and anthropology on a cultural level. Despite the use of these allied fields, however, the focus of study within developmental drama is always the *dramatic act.* From these theoretical considerations, implications can be drawn for specific practical fields.[14]

13. Brian Way, *Audience Participation* (Boston: Baker Plays, 1981). In this book Way begins with a description of his study of the child audience. Based upon his observations, he tells how he developed a play structure in which spaces were left open for audience input and actual physical participation. This meant, first of all, reducing the size of the audience to a managable group of no more than two hundred and fifty persons, preferably seated in the round. Next was the training of his actors to handle the technique: how to invite children's responses, how to involve them in the action, and how to get them back into their seats when their part in the play was finished.

Lifting the barrier between actors and audience removed the controls that exist in the theatre, however, and it had to be replaced by a sense of security on the part of the actors, and an involvement in the *play,* not in the *release* from restrictions on the part of the audience. While the Way method might be summed up in the single word, *trust,* its success depends on experience in a theatre where periodically actors and audience merge. Participatory theatre has been most successful with younger children, though a skilled, experienced company can provide a rich and meaningful experience for any age level.

14. Richard Courtney, *Re-Play,* p. 5.

Drama-in-Education

D.I.E. (Drama-in-Education) is the use of drama as a means of teaching other subject areas. It is used to expand children's awareness, to enable them to look at reality through fantasy, to see below the surface of actions to their meanings. The objective is understanding rather than play making, although a play may be made in the process. Attitudes rather than characters are the chief concern. Exponents of DIE say that this technique can be used to teach any subject.

Classroom teachers find it a valuable tool for involving children in the study of a topic. Rather than dramatizing a story or developing a play, children project themselves into a dramatic moment of the topic at hand (i.e. a mine disaster, a strike, a gold rush, an election, etc.); from there they go on to examine and learn more about the topic. They *become* the persons in the situation as they study it. The teacher brings in source materials and guides the study. A play may result but it is not the purpose of this use of drama.

Theatre-in-Education

T.I.E. (Theatre-in-Education) is a British concept which differs from traditional children's theatre in its use of curricular material or social problems as themes. Performed by professional companies of actor-teachers, it presents thought-provoking content to young audiences for educational purposes rather than for entertainment. Obviously it must entertain in order to hold their attention but that is not the primary purpose. The intent is to challenge the spectator and push him or her to further thinking and feeling about the issue. John O'Toole describes it as follows:

"T.I.E. (Theatre-in-Education) was conceived as an attempt to bring the techniques of the theatre into the classroom, in the service of specific educational objectives . . . its aim was more than to be entertaining and thought-provoking, or to encourage the habit of theatre-going. . . . First, the material is usually specially devised, tailor-made to the needs of the children and the strength of the team. Second, the children are asked to participate; endowed with roles, they learn skills, make decisions, and solve problems, so the programs' structures have to be flexible . . . to respond to the children's contributions within the context of the drama and still to uphold the roles. . . . Third, teams are usually aware of the importance of the teaching context, and try to prepare suggestions for follow-up work, or to hold preliminary workshops for classroom teachers. . . ."[15]

In order to accomplish these aims T.I.E. members are Equity actors and certified teachers.

---

15. John O'Toole, *Theatre-in-Education* (London: Hodder and Stoughton, 1976), preface, p. vii.

Special Techniques
The following terms are used in referring to special techniques used by some teachers of creative drama.

Side Coaching   This is a technique practiced by some teachers as a way of encouraging and strengthening players. The teacher offers suggestions from the sidelines in order to keep the improvisation going.

Teaching In-Role   The teacher takes an active part in the drama in order to deepen and extend the belief in established circumstances. This technique breaks the division between leader and group, but is not necessarily continued after the group is going well.

Parallel Work   All students work at the same time, doing the same thing in different groupings (i.e., individual, pairs, two or more groups) in order to give everyone an equal opportunity for active simultaneous involvement. With all students participating there are no spectators.

Values in Creative Playing

Television has made us a nation of spectators. Children view it from infancy, and surveys reveal that they spend more hours in front of the screen each week than they spend in school. The current craze for video games has intensified this situation; therefore it is more important than ever that we make opportunities available for children to experience participation in the arts. Creative drama is an ideal form for this participation, with its inclusion of the physical, mental, emotional, and social abilities of the participant.

There is general agreement among teachers of creative drama that important values can be gained from creative playing. Depending upon the age of the children, the particular situation, and the orientation of the leader, these values may be listed in varying order. It is the contention of this book, however, that in spite of these differences, certain values exist in some measure for all, regardless of age, circumstances, or previous experience. To be sure, the activities must be planned with the group in mind, and the emphasis placed upon the needs and interests of those involved. The five- or six-year-old needs and enjoys the freedom of large movement and much physical activity, but this should not deny a similar opportunity to older boys and girls. Adult students in early sessions also gain freedom and pleasure when given an opportunity to move freely in space.

The ten- or eleven-year-old enjoys the challenge of characterization and often creates with remarkable insight and understanding. The young child, however, can also create on his level, though he cannot be expected to compete with children who are older. In other words, it is not a question of assigning different values to various age levels; it is a matter of accepting basic values that exist on all levels, varying more in degree than in kind. Specifically, these values may be listed as follows:

An Opportunity to Develop the Imagination

Imagination is the beginning. In order to work creatively, it is necessary, first of all, to push beyond the boundaries of the here and now, to project oneself into another situation, or into the life of another person. Few activities have greater potential for developing the imagination than play making. Little children move easily into a world of make-believe; but as we grow older, this amazing human capacity is often ignored, or even discouraged. The development of the imagination to the point where the student responds spontaneously may take time, in some cases, but it is the first step toward satisfying participation.

The sensitive teacher will not demand too much in the beginning but will accept with enthusiasm the first attempts of the beginner to use her imagination to solve a problem. Once the player has had the fun of seeing, hearing, feeling, touching, tasting, or smelling something that is not there, she will find that her capacity grows quickly. Holding the image until she can do something about it is the next step, but the image must come first. Through drama, the imagination can be stimulated and strengthened to the student's everlasting pleasure and profit. We learn through experience. Unless we want a child to experience everything—which is, of course, impossible—we are obliged to give up the idea except by way of theatre. Through participation in drama and vicariously through attendance at plays, we can provide realistic experiences in acceptable and exciting ways.

An Opportunity for Independent Thinking

A particular value of creative playing is the opportunity it offers for independent thinking and planning. Although the drama, both informal and formal, is a group art, it is composed of the contributions of each individual, and every contribution is important. As the group plans together, each member is encouraged to express his own ideas and thereby contribute to the whole. The leader recognizes the part each child plays and the value that planning has for him. If the group is not too large, there will be many opportunities before the activity is exhausted. Thinking is involved in such questions as: Who are the characters? What are they like? What part do they play? Why do they behave as they do? What scenes are important? Why? How can we suggest this action or that place?

The evaluation that follows is as important as the planning: indeed, it is preparation for a replaying. Children of all ages are remarkably perceptive, and their critical comments indicate the extent of their involvement. A well-planned session in creative drama provides exercises in critical thinking as well as an opportunity for creativity.

Freedom for the Group to Develop Its Own Ideas

It has just been stated that through creative drama an individual has a chance to develop and grow. This is also true of the group, in which ideas are explored, evaluated, changed, and used. As a group of any age works together under sensitive and skilled leadership, the members learn to accept, appreciate, and stimulate each other. Every teacher has experienced a group in which the dynamics were such that all seemed to produce more because of their association. This is not to say that creative drama is a magic formula for successful teamwork, but it unquestionably offers a rare opportunity for sharing ideas and solving problems together. The formal play, whatever problems it may pose, cannot offer a group this same challenge. The written script imposes a structure in which free improvisation has no place. There are values in formal production, to be sure, but the major emphasis is on the product, rather than on the participants.

The strength, incidentally, that is acquired through this kind of planning and playing together is a valuable asset when, at some later date, the group decides to give a formal play. Far from limiting the players, improvisation strengthens techniques and builds individual and group rapport.

An Opportunity for Cooperation

When a group builds something together, it is learning a valuable lesson in cooperation. Social differences may be forgotten in the business of sharing ideas and improvising scenes. Teachers who guide children in creative drama cite numerous examples of social acceptance based on respect for a job well done and the bond that develops from the fun of playing together. As an illustration, Jack entered a neighborhood class in drama that several of his third-grade schoolmates attended. It was obvious that he was an outsider, and the leader despaired of his ever becoming a part of the group. For the first three or four sessions, he contributed nothing and was chosen by no one, regardless of activity.

Then one day the children were dramatizing the story of *The Stone in the Road.* They wanted a farmer, to drive along the road with a donkey cart. Several attempted to pantomime the action, but each time the children insisted that "he didn't look like he was really driving." Suddenly Jack, who had been sitting on the sidelines, put up his hand and volunteered to try it. The vigorous and convincing pantomime he created as he guided his cart around the stone astonished the class. His position in the group changed at that moment, and while he never became one of the leaders, he was accepted and often sought out. Working together in an atmosphere of give-and-take is an experience in democratic partnership; it provides an opportunity for the Jacks in a group to contribute their skills and have them accepted. Or, as a college student once put it, after her first experience of being in a play: "Now I know what John Glenn meant by 'we.' It was all of us working together who did it!"

An Opportunity to Build Social Awareness

Putting oneself in the shoes of another is a way of developing awareness and human understanding. By the time a player has decided who a character is, why she behaves as she does, how she relates to others, and the way in which she handles her problems, she has come to know a great deal about her. Even the very young or experienced player may glimpse insights that help her in her understanding of people and, therefore, of living. Both literature and original stories provide the player with this opportunity to study human nature.

In one class of ten-year-olds, the teacher began the morning by asking the children to think of someone they had seen on their way to school who had attracted their attention. It was suggested that the person should have interested them enough to become a character in a play. Immediately, every hand went up, and a variety of people were described. After a period of telling what they looked like, where they were, who they might have been, and what they were doing, the teacher asked the class to select three who would be good subjects for original stories. The class was then divided into three groups, six or seven in a group, and given an opportunity to make up a story centered around the person of their choice.

The first group decided upon the character Peter suggested—an old man whom Peter described sitting on the steps of his apartment building. The children decided the old man might have been a school janitor who, in his retirement, spent the morning watching the children go to school. Having reached this decision, it was no time at all until they had developed a plot in which the old man's memory of having once saved a child's life became a sudden reality: A boy had run across the street after his ball, and the old man, in an automatic reaction, had rescued him from being hit by a car. The story, with its throwback scene imposed on the present, was dramatic and exciting both to the players and to the rest of the class; more than that, however, was the warm and sympathetic portrayal of the old man. Two adults who were in the room that day have spoken many times of the scene. If the memory remained with the observers, is it not likely that the children, who created the play, must have grown in the process?

A Healthy Release of Emotion

Much has been said about the thinking, both creative and critical, that characterizes creative drama. Another value is of equal importance: the opportunity to feel and release emotion. As children grow up, the opportunity for emotional response is too often restricted to television and movies. While there is value in being a spectator, the deep involvement of active participation is lacking.

Control of emotion does not mean suppression of emotion. It means the healthy release of strong feelings through appropriate and acceptable channels. At some time or another, all people feel anger, fear, anxiety, jealousy, resentment, and negativism. Through the playing of a part in which these emotions are expressed, the player may release them and thus relieve tension. "By permitting the child to play freely in a setting of security and acceptance, we enable him to deal satisfactorily and healthfully with his most urgent problems."[16]

Better Habits of Speech

To many teachers, a primary value of creative drama is the opportunity it offers for training in speech. There is a built-in motivation for the player who wishes to be heard and clearly understood. Volume, tempo, and pitch, as well as diction, are involved in a natural way; no other form of speech exercise captures the player to the same degree or offers so good a reason for working on speech. The little girl who can barely be heard in a classroom recitation will be reminded by her fellow players to speak up or the lines will be lost. And the boy with the strident tone will also be told when his voice is too loud or inappropriate for the character he is portraying. Being, in turn, a giant, a prince, a king, an old man, or an animal, offers further opportunity for developing variation of tone and expression. In creative drama, the concern is less for a standard of speech than it is for audibility, clarity, and expression. While the teacher does not dwell on speech as the major objective, she can point out its importance, and the children will accept the validity of her suggestion.

16. Hartley, Frank, and Goldenson, *Understanding Children's Play,* p. 16.

Not only articulation but also vocabulary is served through this form of oral expression. Conceptual thinking and the cognitive aspect of language are encouraged when words are put into practical use. For the young child, the culturally disadvantaged child, or the student with a foreign language background, vocabulary can be built and distinctions in word meanings made clear through participation in creative drama. Even abstract learnings may come more readily when words are acted or shown.

A designer works with children. (*Courtesy of The Children's Theatre Company and School, Minneapolis; photograph by George Heinrich.*)

An Experience with Good Literature

The story one plays makes a lasting impression. Therefore, the opportunity to become well acquainted with good literature, through dramatizing it, is a major value—not that every story chosen will be of high literary quality. But many will be, and the leader usually discovers that these are the stories that hold interest longest. Both folk tales and modern tales provide fine opportunities for acting. Bruno Bettelheim has advanced powerful arguments for the folk and fairy tale, a genre that has in recent years been questioned as to its relevance for the modern child. In addition to the narrative interest of these tales, there are important psychological reasons why they continue to have value and why they should be used, though, of course, not to the exclusion of contemporary literature. A program that includes a variety of material helps to build appreciation and set a standard for original writing. Television shows and comic books attract temporary interest, but put beside a story that has stood the test of time, these rarely sustain attention. Believable characters, a well-constructed plot, and a worthwhile theme make for engrossing drama. What better way of discovering and learning to appreciate literature?

An Introduction to the Theatre Arts

Art is said to represent the human being's interpretation of life, expressed in a way that can be universally recognized and understood. The theatre offers many examples. While creative drama is primarily participant centered, like theatre, it deals with the basic conflicts in life and thus offers the young player her first taste of the magic and make-believe of the theatre. In her imagination, a chair becomes a throne; a stick, a wand; a change in lighting, a difference in time; and a character, a human being in whom she believes and with whom she can identify. Listening, watching, and becoming involved are required of the theatre audience. The child who is introduced to the theatre first through playing is going to look for more than superficial entertainment when she attends a performance. If we can visualize drama/theatre as a continuum, with dramatic play at one end and formal theatre at the other, we can follow a logical sequence leading from the child's earliest attempts at make-believe, to creative drama, to the finished product, in which there must also be belief.

Recreation

Implicit in everything that has been said so far, yet different and of value in itself, is the opportunity for recreation, or "re-creation," that drama/theatre affords. Under certain types of circumstances such as camp, community centers, after-school activity programs, and neighborhood clubs, the highest priority of drama may indeed be recreation. Drama is fun. It exists for the pleasure of the players and it expresses free choice. It may also, in time, lead to serious work or even a lifelong avocation. Many universities today have programs in leisure studies, in which the constructive use of our increased free time is the focus. The human impulse to play makes drama one of the most popular activities in a recreation program.

Creative Drama for the Special Child

Creative drama offers an opportunity for children with handicapping conditions to participate in a performing art. Because of its flexibility, drama can be a joyful and freeing adventure for groups of all ages. Special needs can be served by adjusting emphases and activities. Often the experience of participation in drama for these children serves to stimulate interest in other subjects and, in so doing, strengthens skills and awakens latent abilities.

Summary

Creative drama, whether in the classroom or in the camp or community program, may be regarded as a way of learning, a means of self-expression, a therapeutic technique, a social activity, or an art form. Children are helped to assume responsibility, accept group decisions, work together cooperatively, develop new interests, and—particularly in a classroom situation—seek new information. Drama is the most completely personal, as well as the most highly socialized, art form we have.

The values of informal play are many, and the leader will discover these and others as the group moves and grows. Not all the values listed will be manifested at once, or perhaps ever, for the creative process is slow and takes time to develop. Also, leaders do not all hold the same priorities. They arrange them according to their situations and interests. More will be said on this point later.

It is often observed that few persons perform on their highest level. This is true of the beginning player, child or adult, who, through shyness or actual fear, needs encouragement and acceptance.

The sensitive leader recognizes this and tries to create an atmosphere of mutual trust. In his acceptance of every child and what he has to offer, the leader has taken the first big step toward building self-confidence. Freedom will follow, learning will occur, and an ordinary room will become a place in which exciting things can happen.

2
Imagination Is the Beginning

*Imagination is but another name for absolute power
and clearest insight, amplitude of mind, and reason in
her most exalted mood.*

WORDSWORTH, **The Prelude**

*I*magination and creativity are two words we hear
a great deal these days. Whether we are able to define
them precisely, or whether we merely have a sense of
their meanings, we use them freely, and in regard to a
variety of people and a multitude of activities. While it is
not the purpose of this book to go into the subject in
either length or depth, the terms *imagination* and *creativity* have been used in describing the art of creative drama.
Therefore, some definition is required.

24

Encouraging dialogue through the puppet.
(*Courtesy of Tamara Hunt, University of
Hawaii at Manoa.*)

Imagination

The *fact* of imagination has long been recognized, but it is only recently that the *value* of imagination has been hailed. Shakespeare described imagination as the spark that makes man "paragon of animals." Today, not only the artist but also businessmen, scientists, military leaders, and educators describe imagination as the magic force that goes beyond the mastery of facts and techniques in the search for new ideas.

Suzanne Langer calls imagination ". . . probably the oldest mental trait that is typically human—older than discursive reason; it is probably the common source of dream, reason, religion, and all true general observation."[1]

John Allen in *Drama in Schools*, describes imagination as free flowing, open-ended, transformational. "Artistic discipline is a constraint—but here lies the paradox—only until the discipline has forced the material into its appropriate pattern; then there follows a sense of freedom and exaltation that is the ultimate reward of all artistic creation."[2] Thus can the trivial be transformed into the significant through a creative act, and the ordinary into something unique.

Creativity

Creativity may be defined in a number of ways. It may be thought of in terms of product or process, depending on whether we are concerned with the solution to a problem or the way in which the problem is solved. If creativity is interpreted as process, it is considered as a new way of seeing, a different point of view, an original idea, or a new relationship between ideas. Inventiveness and adaptation are often included in the thinking of those who believe creativity to be a way of working.

If, on the other hand, creativity is defined in terms of product, it is best illustrated by works of art (poems, stories, paintings, music, dance), scientific inventions, and new arrangements or designs. There has been great interest in the study and measurement of creativity in recent years, and a considerable body of data has appeared. One asssumption accepted by psychologists doing research is that creativity is not a special gift possessed by a fortunate few, but, rather, a human capacity possessed to some degree by everyone. It has been found, incidentally, that many individuals learn more if permitted to approach their studies creatively.

According to some authorities, the beginning of creative thinking may be found early in the life of the infant, in her "manipulative and exploratory

1. Susanne K. Langer, "The Cultural Importance of the Arts," in *Aesthetic Form and Education*, ed. Michael F. Andrews (Syracuse, N.Y.: Syracuse University Press, 1958), p. 6.
2. John, Allen, *Drama in Schools* (London: Heinemann Educational Books, 1979), p. 70.

activities."[3] In her awareness of human expression, gestures, and sound, the baby is first observer and then investigator. It is but a short step from here to her own experimentation, at which point she becomes creator. Drama, both informal and formal, is the artistic creation of human beings, based on their observation of human life—selected, arranged, and heightened.

The words *observer, investigator, creator* are of particular interest to the teacher of creative drama. One leader held a discussion on the subject of creativity and imagination with a group of eight-year-olds in a creative drama class. Their dialogue ran something like this:

TEACHER: What does creativity mean to you?
PATRICIA: I think it means to make.
DENISE: No, not to make. To make up.
TEACHER: Can you explain the difference?
KENNY: Well, if a man made a pair of shoes, he'd be creating.
TEACHER: Do you all agree with Kenny?
DENISE: No, I think only the first pair of shoes would be created. If the man made a lot of others like them, they'd just be made—not made up.
TEACHER: Then everything that's made is not created?
DENISE: (*sticking to her original point*) Only the things that aren't copied.
TEACHER: How do you feel about copying?
PATRICIA: You don't get any fun out of copying.
CATHY: I think it's all right to copy some things.
TEACHER: What kind of things, Cathy?
CATHY: Well, like good manners. And words. You wouldn't know what to do lots of times if you didn't have something to copy.
TEACHER: Then you don't think copying is always a bad thing to do? (*General agreement that it is not.*)
DENISE: Just the same, you shouldn't use somebody else's mind. You want a thing to be just yours.
ALAN: You have to know what to copy and what not to. Sometimes it's hard to know which is which.
TEACHER: How would you explain imagination? Dean?
DEAN: You think of something that isn't there.
TEACHER: Would anyone like to add to that?
BILLY: Yes, it isn't that it isn't there. It's more like you make yourself believe.
PATRICIA: You see, outside of you it isn't real. Inside your head, it's there.
TEACHER: Do you enjoy using your imagination?

3. E. Paul Torrance, *Creativity*, What Research Says Series (Washington, D.C.: National Education Association of the United States, 1963).

JOHN: Oh, yes. Because you can make anything happen.

PATRICIA: Sometimes they're silly things. What we do isn't always good.

TEACHER: What do you mean, "not good"?

PATRICIA: I mean, some children have better ideas than others.

TEACHER: But you still want a chance to try them all out?

DENISE: Oh, yes. It's better for an idea to be yours than good.

BILLY: I think using your imagination means being creative. It means making up something that wasn't ever there before.

The discussion went on like this for some time, but it was obvious that the terms *creativity* and *imagination* held real meaning for the children. Their observations—that it is important to have ideas and the freedom to try them out—are basic to good work in creative drama.

One of the most delightful views toward creativity was expressed by Professor Franz Cizek of the Vienna Schools of Arts and Crafts, in 1921. Although he was not referring to drama, his attitude is that of many successful teachers in any of the arts. The following "Conversation with Cizek" is included verbatim for its insight and relevance to this chapter.

"How do you do it?" we asked at last, when we had looked at some hundreds of the productions of Professor Cizek's pupils, each more delightful and original than the last.

"But I don't do," he protested with a kind of weary pity for our lack of understanding. "I take off the lid, and other masters clap the lid on—that is the only difference."

"Children have their own laws which they must needs obey. What right have grown-ups to interfere?"

"And do many of your children go in for art afterward?" we queried.

"Not as a rule. They go into all sorts of professions and trades. That's quite right. That's what I like. I like to think of art coloring all departments of life rather than being a separate profession."

". . . What a pity all children don't come to you."

"Yes, it is a pity," he assented, shaking his head rather mournfully. "There is so much of the summer and the autumn but the spring never comes again."[4]

Creativity refers both to the cognitive and the affective life and is the result of conscious and unconscious effort. In the anthology, *Essays on Creativity*, the point is made repeatedly that "ideas are born from stimulation from within and

4. Franz Cizek, in "Some conversations with Cizek," in *The Child as Artist,* booklet issued by the Children's Art Exhibition Fund, 1921.

without, but such stimulation must be grasped, filtered and used."[5] Working together, students and teacher can accomplish this to the satisfaction of all. A creative act does not happen once; it is an ongoing process, which with encouragement and guidance becomes a way of life. Rollo May puts the whole thing very simply when he says that creativity is the act of repatterning the known world into meaningful new configurations.

Beginning Exercises for Imagination

The first day the class meets, the leader will do well to begin with the simplest exercises in which imagination is involved. Regardless of age level, there must be an opportunity for the participants to go beyond the here and now, but they cannot, and should not, be expected to handle a story or create an improvisation. It is also wise to begin with the entire group, if space permits. This removes all thought of audience, thereby diminishing fear and self-consciousness.

How the leader begins will be determined by the age, experience, and number in the group, as well as the size of the playing space. If the group is fortunate in having a very large room, physical movement is an excellent opening exercise. Music or even a drumbeat will enhance the mood and help to focus the attention. One simple and very effective way of beginning is to have the group walk to the beat of the drum. As the group becomes more comfortable and relaxed, the beat can be changed: rapid, double time, slow, and so on. The participants, in listening for the change in beat, forget themselves and are usually able to use their entire bodies. Galloping, skipping, and hopping are fun for younger children, and good exercise for those much older. Adults find freedom and pleasure in physical movement, and when it is over sit down relaxed and better able to go on to the next assignment.

From the purely physical body movement, the teacher may move on to mood. For example, if the group has been walking to a beat, he may suggest that there is green grass underfoot. "How does it feel to you? Your feet are tired. Think what it is like to put them down on soft, cool grass. Take off your shoes. (Some will do so at this suggestion.) Walk on it. Feel it."

Soon the steps will become more flexible as the image of grass grows stronger. The teacher might suggest, next, that there is ice underfoot. "It is hard, slippery, difficult to walk on, dangerous." The movement usually changes perceptibly now as the participants imagine the difficulties of crossing an icy pavement. Muscles are tensed and bodies stiffen. It is here that one or two may lose their balance or even slip and fall down as they get into the spirit of the situation. The teacher's acknowledgment of their efforts offers encouragement

5. Stanley Rosner and Lawrence Abt, *Essays on Creativity* (Croton-on-Hudson, N.Y.: North River Press, 1974), p. 192.

Imagining costumes and props. (*Courtesy of The Paper Bag Players, New York.*)

and usually stimulates further invention. As participants imagine that they are running across hot sand, stepping over puddles, crossing a creek, wading through snow, each suggestion stretches the imagination a little more. When the exercise is over, most groups will have moved far from the first stiff, self-conscious steps without realizing when, or how, or even that they have done it.

Games known to all the participants might come next. Tossing a ball is a familiar activity, and the players by this time usually respond eagerly. The teacher may suggest that they are using a tennis ball, then a basketball, next a beach ball, or a ping-pong ball. The players experience little difficulty shifting from one ball to another and have fun showing its size and weight as they throw and catch it. Lively groups sometimes drop the ball, run for it, lose it, or carry the assignment much farther than the leader suggested. Favorite activities such as flying kites, jumping rope, playing hopscotch, and playing with jacks provide other opportunities for using the imagination. How long this goes on is best left to the discretion of the teacher, who can tell when the interest begins to wane.

A pantomime of seasonal sports might be the culmination of the various exercises and a means of tying them together. If the class is large, this may be the time to subdivide into smaller groups, with each taking a particular game or sport. However the teacher proceeds from here, he will find that imagination has been sparked and the next step will be easier. The chapter on movement includes a more detailed discussion of ways in which movement, dance, and mime can be used as both means and ends.

With the first meeting of any group the leader's goal is to create an atmosphere in which the players feel comfortable; the next step is to stimulate their imagination. There are various ways of doing this and each of us has his own favorite methods, but a good teacher is always looking for fresh ideas. Sometimes a nondramatic, quiet approach is preferable to physical activity. The following game was introduced by a drama teacher from Israel and I have used it successfully on several occasions with different age levels.

The class is seated in a circle on the floor. After introducing themselves, the students are asked to put some personal object in the center of the circle. (The more unusual the object, the better.) The teacher then goes around the circle, asking the players to try to remember to whom each object belongs and to return it to its owner. This is followed by each person's selecting another player's object and making up a story about it. Improvisations using the objects or stories told about them may follow, depending on time and interest. If the exercise simply stops with the stories, it will have given the class a chance to get acquainted before moving into active group work.

Another quiet exercise that captures the attention of most groups requires a blackboard and colored chalks. One student after another goes up to the board and puts a mark or drawing on it. When everyone has had a turn, second turns are taken. The size of the class determines whether or not there may be third and fourth turns. The mural created by the class is then described and interpreted. The more abstract it is, the more imaginative the interpretations will probably be. This activity may be a springboard to improvisation or may simply remain a means of drawing a group together. In either case, it is effective with both children and adults in engaging and holding the attention.

Sometimes an idea or activity that stimulates one group won't work with another. The leader should not be discouraged; try something else. Remember, this is the first time the class has met as a group and it takes some groups longer than others to become cohesive. Children's games can be used with most groups. Ones that any number can play and that are not too complicated, with the players entering at different times, are usually the best.

Fruit Bowl

This is a familiar game, which is adaptable to groups of all ages and abilities. It may be used as a warm-up or an activity while waiting for everyone to assemble. As the players enter the room, they are given names of a fruit to remember—say, "apple" or "banana." Players sit in a circle with the leader standing in the center. When she calls out "apple," all named apple change places; when she calls out "banana," those players change places. When she calls out "fruit bowl," everyone in the circle must get up and exchange places

The frog. (*Courtesy of Rachel Carr; photograph by Edward Kimball.*)

with someone else. The values are obvious: all players must move; there is no winning or losing; concentration is necessary; and the leader can expect total participation. Variations in the game can be made, but however it is played, the leader should always stop and turn to another activity or to the problem of the day before the players become bored.

Games are generally thought of as warm-ups or enjoyable activities. They are both of these and more, for they have other values. One is the framework for communication they provide a group. Another is the imposition of rules that develop discipline and self-control in the players. A third is the social nature of the game, especially important in drama, where interpersonal relationships are an integral element.

Deliberate brainstorming for ideas is often a successful way of starting a first session with older or more experienced players. Find out:

What interests them
What their concerns are
Whether there is a controversial subject they would like to explore

With young adults this may lead into explosive confrontation, but after working together on a topic for a while, they are usually receptive to suggestions and different ways of dramatizing it. It may even become the focus of an original play, continuing on for a number of class meetings.

Concentration

If imagination is the beginning, concentration—the capacity to hold an idea long enough to do something about it—must come next. It is not enough to glimpse an idea; the image must be held long enough for action to follow. Inexperienced players of any age may have difficulty here, for selfconsciousness and fear of failure are paralyzing and distracting agents. It is now that the teacher needs to encourage every effort, however small, in order to free the player of his self-doubt. This is difficult in some cases: the player may never have excelled at anything and so does not believe that he has anything worthwhile to offer. Many children, on the other hand, become involved easily. Concentration poses no problems for them because of their freedom from fear and their willingness to experiment.

Organization

Concentration and organization go hand in hand. Once the players are able to focus their attention on their material, they can get down to the business of organizing it. They have ceased to think about themselves and are ready to decide such things as who their characters are, what they are doing, and the overall form the improvision will take. If the group is working on a story, the organization will more or less follow the plot. The characters are related to a logicial sequence of events, and it is up to the players to decide how they will handle them.

If, on the other hand, the group is creating an original situation—pantomime or improvisation—a different kind of planning is involved. More guidance is required, since there is no structure to follow, but if children feel free to experiment, they come up with surprising and often delightful results. "Organization" does not mean the imposing of a conventional form, but, rather, an arrangement of parts or material so as to achieve order. Older groups, or groups that have had more exposure to television, movies, and theatre, are less inclined to experiment with organization although, with encouragement, they can be helped to find the challenge in "trying it another way." Organization is order, and until it exists in some form or another, the participants rarely find satisfaction in creative playing.

Self-Expression

So far, we have been talking about exercises that may or may not be expressive. Creative drama implies self-expression, hence the necessity of the participant's involvement beyond merely imitating an action. How does she feel when the kite soars high in the air? Who is winning the ball game? How do we know? How many jacks has she won? Does she enjoy picking flowers in the woods? What are her feelings as she fishes or rows her boat against a strong current? These are the kinds of questions we may ask as the players grow more confident.

We are not concerned with the quality of the child's performance yet; rather, we are concerned with his developing freedom and the ability to express himself. Each child has something to say, something that he alone can offer, provided he is given the opportunity and the encouragement. No one has put this any better than Hughes Mearns:

> You have something to say. Something of your very own. Try to say it. Don't be ashamed of any real thought or feeling you may have. Don't undervalue it. Don't let the fear of what others may think of it prevent you from saying it. Perhaps not aloud but to yourself. You have something to say, something no one in the world has ever said in just your way of saying it—but the thing itself is not half so important to you as what the saying will be to you.[6]

Communication

Although communication is the responsibility of the formal theatre, and therefore not our primary concern, there comes a time when the participants want to share their work in creative drama, and this sharing involves communi-

6. Hughes Mearns, *Creative Power* (New York: Dover, 1958), p. 259.

A striped box turns into a cat when the head is added. (*Courtesy of George Latshaw.*)

cation skills. It has been stated that, for the younger child, public performance is undesirable; for the older child, under the right conditions, it may do no harm. But unless the class is exceptionally small, there will be periods of time when some are observers and some are participants. It is to these periods that communication pertains. This is the audience that is not an audience in the usual sense. On the other hand, the observers want to see and hear, and they become deeply involved in the situation. The participant soon learns that she must move on to the next stage of development: that of making herself clear, of being heard and understood, and of being interesting—in short, of communicating.

Communication comes about quite naturally in the discussion periods that follow each playing. One procedure, used successfully by many teachers, is the playing, discussing, replaying method. Or, to describe it more fully, the teacher begins with the story or situation, which she either reads or tells to the group. This is followed by class discussion, in which the characters are enumerated and described, the plot is reviewed, and the scenes are planned. No matter how simple the situation, it is important that it be thoroughly understood before the first playing. The group will decide which characters are necessary to the plot, which ones may be eliminated, or whether others should be added. Often a story that is excellent to read takes considerable adapting to make it good drama.

When the teacher is sure that the group has all details well in mind, he is ready to suggest playing it. Asking for volunteers usually brings a show of hands from which the teacher will choose the first cast. The players come forward, while the rest of the class remain in their seats. After they have finished the scene, the teacher leads a general discussion. This evaluation period covers the plot and the way the children have handled it. The players themselves always have criticisms to offer, but the observers also have reactions to share. Children's criticism is honest and their observations are keen. Because the observers anticipate playing the story themselves, they are as deeply involved as the players. Such questions as these help to guide the discussion:

1. Did they tell the story?
2. Was anything important left out?
3. What did you like about the way they began it?
4. Did we understand the ending?
5. When we play it the next time, what might we add or leave out?

The questions are naturally more specific when we have a particular story in mind. There will be further discussion of characters, their relationships and motives, but these usually come after a second or third playing. Finally, when the teacher feels that a number of important points have been made and the class is growing eager to resume playing, a second group is given a chance to play the same scene. This group, having the benefit of observation and discussion, will probably succeed in developing more detail and clearer characterizations. This does not necessarily happen, for the first group to volunteer may have been the stronger.

At any rate, when the second cast has finished, a new evaluation period is in order. It is always interesting to hear the different kinds of comments that this second discussion evokes. A third playing, a fourth, even a fifth may follow, depending on the interest of the children and the length of the period. It is a good idea to take the cue from them as to when to move on to the next scene. As long as the scene holds their interest, they will continue to grow in their understanding of it. The teacher will become increasingly sensitive to their involvement as they work together.

As the group gains experience, its ability to communicate increases. Younger children, because of their more limited vocabulary, communicate more easily through body movement and facial expression. Older children are not only better able to express themselves verbally, but also enjoy improvising dialogue. The adult student, depending on his background and previous experience, will feel more comfortable in one medium or the other. If the teacher begins with movement and pantomime, however, she will find that dialogue flows easily once the player has overcome his self-consciousness.

Problems in Creative Playing

Sooner or later, the teacher of creative drama, or the classroom teacher who uses creative drama, is bound to encounter problems of one sort or another. They may be simple problems of time and space: periods that are too short; space that is inadequate; classes that are too large. These problems can be solved, though the solutions are not always easy. They call for adaptability and ingenuity on the part of the leader, and present difficulties that are discouraging and sometimes defeating. Other problems confronting the leader even under ideal circumstances, are the individual problems he finds in the group. Discipline has come to mean punishment in our society. This is not the original meaning of the word nor is it the sense in which it is used here. Rather, it signifies order or control, a control preferably of oneself.

It has been stated many times that self-consciousness is the greatest obstacle to creative playing. Self-consciousness, or fear, takes many forms. The shy child and the show-off are examples of the two forms in which self-consciousness is most frequently encountered in children. The insensitive child is also a problem, for he usually lacks friends and so finds it difficult to work cooperatively in a group. And, finally, there is the handicapped child, whose physical, mental, or emotional problems pose special difficulties for the leader.

We must keep in mind that in drama a player is exposing herself more than in any other art form or activity. Therefore, our handling of behavior problems implies awareness of their causes. Insensitivity on the leader's part can damage a player whose vulnerability is evidenced by a conspicuous form of behavior. There is great interest in drama as therapy at the present time, but this is a special field for which the average teacher—even the specialist in creative drama techniques—is not trained. Every teacher is aware of the therapeutic value of the arts, even though the primary purposes are educational, social, and aesthetic. But because there are, in every group, those children (or adults) who experience real difficulty in expressing themselves, consideration must be given to their problems. If the problem is severe, it should be handled by a therapist and not the classroom teacher; in many cases, an intelligent, sympathetic effort to build self-respect and bring fun into the lives of the players can go a long way toward solving problems.

Timidity

The timid child is the most common problem the teacher encounters, but one that creative drama can help. Such a child is usually quiet in a class, preferring to sit in the back of the room and let others do the talking. His fear of making a mistake, or even of being noticed, causes him to withdraw, even though down underneath he is eager to express his ideas and take part. He is usually not a happy child, for his feeling of inadequacy inhibits both expression and communication.

The little girl who never volunteers will need special encouragement to try doing a part, no matter how simple. The teacher who gives her this opportunity to show her peers what she can do may be taking the first step in helping her build a better self-image. If the child is successful, it will be less difficult for her a second time. The teacher will be wise to praise her warmly for whatever contribution she makes. Remember that, for the little girl, the very fact of getting up in front of the class is a big achievement.

There was eight-year-old Patty, who was referred to a Saturday-morning play group because of her excessive shyness. At first she took part only when the whole group was moving, and then because it would have been more conspicuous to remain seated than to get up with the others. After several weeks (probably five or six sessions), she did a pantomime of a child finding a kitten. Her honest joy and tenderness as she fondled its soft body drew spontaneous admiration from the other boys and girls in the class. This was the break-through. From that day Patty's eagerness to play was apparent. Her voice was small—inaudible at first—but grew stronger in proportion to her growing self-confidence. This was no sudden miracle; in fact, it took three years for the transformation to take place. Patty's feelings of inadequacy had been so deep-seated that many successes were necessary to convince her that she had something to offer that her peers would accept. She became not only one of the most vocal children in the group—she became an unquestioned leader. Whether she would have found her way anyhow, no one can say. Creative drama as a technique was deliberately used, and the change during her three years in the class was striking.

Exhibitionism

The show-off is just as much in need of help as the shy child, but he rarely elicits the same kind of sympathetic attention. His problem is also one of uneasiness, and in trying to prove his importance, he does all the wrong things. His behavior will range from monopolizing the class discussion to interfering with the work of the other children (pinching, pushing, interrupting). He may deliberately use a wrong word for the sake of a laugh. He is conscious of the effect he is having, and so has difficulty concentrating on what he is doing.

An example is John, a nervous little fellow of nine, with facial mannerisms and a habit of interrupting. John was accepted by the others: he amused them. For more than a semester John's work was erratic. He seemed unable to get involved in a part for more than a minute or two, and then he would look around the room to see what effect he was having on the rest of the class. There was no sudden or dramatic incident that effected a change; rather, it was a long period of working under the patient guidance of a teacher who took every opportunity to praise his honest expression and help him to find satisfaction in getting attention legitimately. By the end of a year, John was able to work cooperatively with the group much of the time and forego showing off. His problem was still not entirely solved, but he had learned something of the give-and-take of working together, and the pleasure of recognition that comes from work that is honest.

Arline was a high school student, whose weight problem caused her great embarrassment. She expressed this by comic behavior and exhibitionistic antics. For years Arline has been the class clown, deliberately tripping, using a wrong word or misunderstanding a simple question. In this way she made people laugh at what she did before they had a chance to laugh at the way she looked. Successful coping with her problem in this manner had created a behavior pattern that was hard to break. Through improvised drama, where there was no audience to impress, Arline gradually came to understand something of motivation and, finally, to trust and accept herself. True, the slapstick occasionally took place, but less and less often as the years passed and she was able to get the laughs for the right reasons. Beneath the clowning there was an intelligent, sensitive adolescent, who today is a successful educator. Undoubtedly there were other methods that could have been used effectively, but Arline liked theatre and elected to participate. It was obvious that through the use of creative drama she learned how to believe in herself and perhaps to lay the foundation for her future work in special education.

Sometimes the teacher may be forced to ask the disruptive child to go back to her seat. Not punishment, but the consequences of unacceptable behavior will teach her that creative dramatics demands consideration and teamwork.

Isolation

The isolate or loner is often a child who cannot relate to the group. He may work hard, have good ideas, and the ability to present them effectively, but always in isolation. It must be said that this is not necessarily a problem. Indeed, it may be indicative of superior talent and high motivation. Independence is a desired goal, whereas isolation, which is the result of an inability to relate to others, is a problem. Through movement and dance all members of a group are drawn together naturally; they discover the meaning of interdependence as well as individual effort. For the person who has real difficulty in relating to his or her peers, this is a natural way of becoming a part of the group.

Insensitivity

The insensitive player is similar to, but different from, the show-off in that she is usually rejected by the others and does not understand why. Her clowning brings no laughter, and she has great difficulty in making friends. She tends to reject the ideas of others and criticizes their efforts, often harshly. Playing a variety of roles may cause her to gain insights and develop an awareness of the feelings of others. Patient attention to her problem in human relations may, in time, help her to listen and learn to accept suggestions from her peers. Hers is a difficult problem, but once she has begun to feel some small acceptance, she will prefer belonging to going it alone. Again, we are not talking about the extreme personality disorder but about the human being who is experiencing difficulty in working cooperatively with others.

Distraction

Every teacher has experienced the easily distracted player—the one with imagination, interest, and enthusiasm, whose concentration is broken at any unexpected sight or sound. Often this is a hyperactive child but not always. I have had college students whose ability to remain involved in an exercise was so fragile that the slightest noise in the corridor or the appearance of someone at the door would destroy it. Unfortunately, this stops the other players, making it necessary to build back the situation, but rarely is the same degree or depth of involvement achieved that was present before the interruption.

Physical Handicaps

Children with handicaps need special attention. Moreover, their teachers need orientation to their special needs. While the classroom teacher may have a child who is crippled or who has a speech defect, she is not going to be equipped to practice therapy or given time for all the help these special children merit. If she has one or two children in a group who are handicapped, she will treat them essentially as she does the others. These children need sympathy, understanding, and encouragement. The teacher must know what can be expected of them and then try to adapt the activities to their capabilities. Often such a child will be in therapy, and if the teacher can work with the therapist, she will be able to receive helpful suggestions as to his approach.

For example, Marcia, who has a cleft lip and is seeing the speech therapist regularly, will benefit from an opportunity to use speech in a legitimate and pleasurable way. The teacher will not have the time to give her all the attention she needs, but in treating her like the others and encouraging her in her efforts, he will be contributing to her social growth and, in some measure, to her treatment.

It is a common phenomenon that the stutterer often speaks fluently when cast in a play. While there is no proof that acting ever cured a stutter, the child who tends to repeat, or whose anxiety causes him to stutter, often finds relief in speaking as someone else. Regular participation in either informal or formal dramatics may have a therapeutic effect in encouraging successful oral expression.

All people gain in self-respect when their ideas are accepted and put into effect. The child with a problem has a special need for acceptance, and the teacher tries to find the best way in which she can meet it. Creative drama provides an ideal opportunity to help the timid child overcome his inhibitions; provides the show-off with a better way of getting attention; guides the insensitive child to some awareness of the feelings of others; works with the handicapped to find her avenue of self-expression; and broadens the horizons of the disadvantaged. "How drama can be used today, how the play-acting impulse can be harnessed to help people grow, to develop greater sensitivity to themselves and to their fellow human beings, to become more spontaneous and outgoing, to discard old fears and insecurities, has attracted the interest of many who are working in the various fields of human relations."[7]

Today's children are subjected to pressures and demands, which, if not greater than in the past, are certainly new and different. Not only inner city children, but the children of affluent and suburban communities reflect the changes in values and mores. The pressures they feel often result in bizarre and unpredictable behavior, causing problems for teachers and creating difficulties when freedom is encouraged. The creative drama instructor is particularly vulnerable to these problems, for she is dealing with the emotional and social, as well as the intellectual, aspects of child development.

Although freedom is essential to creativity, it is often necessary to impose restraints in the beginning, or until children become more comfortable with the group and the leader. Social mobility, broken homes, television programs, the violence in our society, and economic problems are among the causes given for discipline problems. It is not the purpose of this text to explore the causes, but it is important for us to be sensitive to unusual behavior and to try to deal with it with understanding, compassion, and firmness. While we cannot accept certain antisocial behavior in a child, it is important for him or her to know and understand what is being rejected. In other words, we do not reject the *player* but we do reject behavior that interferes with the freedom of others to express their ideas and feelings. One person cannot be permitted to dominate the group, regardless of his needs.

Evaluating Children's Responses

A question that always comes up is how to evaluate children's responses. This is difficult to answer, for progress varies from one child to the next. The teacher has different expectations for each child and what may be extraordinary growth for one is scarcely an adequate performance for another. (The

7. Jack Simos, *Social Growth Through Play Production* (New York: Association Press, 1957), p. 16.

word *performance* as used here means work, not theatre performance.) Let me explain. The shy child, described earlier, may be a long time coming out of his shell; therefore the slightest offering he makes to the group—idea, vocal or physical expression, ease in working with peers—indicates growth. The overly aggressive child, who learns to harness her energy in deference to others, has also made progress. With the overcoming of individual problems, and every child has them, albeit less severe than the ones cited earlier, there has been progress. Beyond that, each teacher has social, intellectual and aesthetic goals he hopes will be met.

> Have the individuals in the class become a group, willing and able to work together? Is there easy give-and-take?
> Is each child an integral part of the group, sharing without fear or need to impress?
> Is there sincerity in the work?
> Is physical movement becoming freer, more expressive?
> Have verbal skills improved—speech, voice and diction, vocabulary, and the ability to express ideas orally?
> Depending on the focus, have other goals been met? Use of resource materials, integration of learnings, involvement in subject?
> Is there vitality in the group? Eagerness to begin; reluctance to stop at the end of the period?
> Does the noise level reflect activity, industry, enthusiasm?

The teacher may want to make "before and after" tapes of the class. These are often more revealing than the teacher's recollections, written notes, or check sheets in showing the progress made from the beginning to the end of the year. My own concern, however, is that no matter how valuable such records are—and there is value—there is also a danger of losing the spirit of creative drama in the quest for proof of its effectiveness. If evaluation can be done quietly, perhaps by student teachers or aides, it is a valuable record for the teacher, to be shared judiciously with staff and administration. The purpose of the class, however, determines the type and use of tests and measurements.

The Open Classroom

The open classroom, about which we have heard so much in the past few years, offers one of the best opportunities for small creative dramatics groups. Instead of classes of twenty-five to forty, so often found in the crowded city classrooms, this concept of learning provides both time and space for special interest groups. I have visited several open classes where small groups of children worked on favorite stories and theatre games under the guidance of assistants or student teachers majoring in the dramatic arts. In nursery school and kindergarten classes provision was made for dramatic play, and participation was encouraged. Pantomime claimed the interest of third-graders in one school, with twelve children participating at a time. Not only does the flexible physical arrangement of the open classroom accommodate the arts, but in working with fewer children at a time, the leader can accomplish more than is possible when the entire class is involved. The relaxed atmosphere also helps to free children who are intimidated by a more formal procedure. For the so-called normal child the open classroom encourages creativity and enterprise; for the child with a problem, however, it offers much more: time, space, more individual attention, and an opportunity to try out ideas in small groups. Although the open classroom is less popular today than it was ten years ago, it is still to be found, and it has great value for the teaching of creative drama.

Summary

To summarize, imagination is the spark that sets off the creative impulse. Concentration (the capacity to hold an idea long enough to do something about it) and organization (the design or arrangement of the parts) are necessary to satisfying self-expression. Communication—the bridge to others—comes last and is less the concern of creative drama than of the formal play.

In all creative work there are obstacles. These must be recognized and overcome. They may be problems of time and space, or the more difficult ones of human relations. The wise leader learns first to identify the problems and then to look for solutions. She will remember that she is neither therapist nor theatre director but teacher, guiding players, whatever their age, in the medium of informal drama. Brian Way has suggested the role of the teacher in these words:

> Schools do not exist to develop actors but to develop people, and one of the major factors in developing people is that of preserving and enriching to its fullest the human capacity to give full and undivided attention to any matter in hand at any given moment.[8]

Activities and exercises are suggested, not as ends in themselves but as means to self-expression and a springboard to other more extensive projects. Some prose and poetry are also included as illustrations of what can be used and how; with a point of view and a creative approach, it is hoped that the leader will be able to find additional materials relevant to his own and the group's interests and needs.

8. Brian Way, *Development Through Drama* (New York: Humanities Press, 1967), p. 15.

3
Movement, Rhythms, and Dramatic Play

*M*ovement is a natural response to a stimulus and therefore an important element of drama. Indeed, movement, dance, mime, and drama merge in the expression of feelings and ideas. Theatre began with movement; its origins were closely linked with religious and magical rites. Gradually the elements of conflict, character, plot, and dialogue were added. When this happened, the theatre as an art form was born.

Early human beings, in attempting to order their universe, explain natural phenomena, and pray to their gods, used rhythmic movement to express themselves; this, in time, became dance. An entire tribe might take part, or perhaps only the young men, or the most skilled of the dancers. As the movements were repeated, they became set and took on special meanings. These meanings were understood by both performers and spectators, and were taught to the young, thus serving an educative as well as a religious purpose.

44   A class in creative dance. (*Courtesy of Lucille Paolillo, The Children's Centre for Creative Arts, Adelphi University; photograph by George H. Meyer.*)

Every society has its rituals, and ritual and theatre are never far apart. Traditional garments, body paint, and masks are worn to enhance the performance. Though not theatre in our modern sense, these tribal dances are nevertheless closely akin to it in the use of body, voice, rhythm, and costume to help express strong feelings and ideas in a form the community understands.

As danced movement, therefore, drama is the oldest of the arts. Out of the rites and rituals of dance came myth; and out of myth, story or plot. It was but a short step from plot to play. The earliest theatrical performances in the Western world are generally believed to have taken place in Greece along the Aegean with the worship of Dionysus, the god of fertility. The chanting of a chorus with a leader developed into dialogue spoken by actors; by the fifth century B.C. the dramatic forms of comedy and tragedy had evolved. There were other forms of theatre before this, if theatre is defined as performance communicated through voice and action to an audience actively engaged in the experience. If, on the other hand, theatre is defined as including a body of dramatic literature, then the Greek theatre is the first and perhaps the greatest theatre known.

Children and Movement

Creative movement deals with the elements of dance but is more spontaneous. Children move naturally; by encouraging such movement, the teacher can help children to express themselves through physical activity, thereby creating their own styles of movement, gaining confidence in their bodies, and developing spatial awareness. It is easy to move from here to either dance or drama. Drama differs from dance because it involves a linguistic element; the older the players, the greater the dependence on words to communicate meaning. The teacher of creative drama hopes to develop ability and ease in the use of both verbal and nonverbal expression; starting early is an important factor in achieving these goals.

Like primitive man, the preschool child uses his body to express his strongest emotions and communicate his needs and desires. A child's posture, for instance, shows us how he feels, regardless often of what he may say. We read much about body language these days. This form of nonverbal communication includes any posture as well as reflexive or nonreflexive movement of the body that conveys emotion to the observer. Although most of this popular writing concerns the adult, the attitudes and feelings of children are just as clearly revealed by their movements and facial expressions. A leader can learn much about the members of a group of any age from the postures they assume, their ability to relax, and the use they make of the various parts of their bodies.

A young child tends to express physically what an adult states in words. For example, when asked how a horse moves, a small child is more apt to gallop than to describe the gait. Asked the height of a very tall person, he will stand on tiptoe to reach as high as he can. Although the majority of children walk before they can talk, this early use of the body to express emotions and describe or give information is a phenomenon common to most boys and girls, regardless of their linguistic development.

Rhythms classes for young children build on this natural impulse. What happens in the class is well described by an experienced teacher of rhythms and dramatic play. The children remove their shoes and stockings as they enter a gym or large, free, unencumbered space. Music is provided by a pianist or a recording, or "if we are lucky, it is music created by the children themselves." Then, as if by signal, the children respond to changing rhythms. If the music is fast, wild, free, so are their movements. If it becomes slower, quieter, softer, so will be their movements. The idea is for the children to listen to what the music says and then to transfer it into bodily activity. "To one child the rhythm may suggest the rhythm of a galloping pony; to another it may mean the branches of a tree buffeted in a wind storm; a third may think of the whirling arms of a threshing machine." The teacher does not suggest what the children should do, nor ask them questions but by watching, she is usually able to tell what is in the mind of each. In the middle grades rhythms may be based on units of study: Indians, Greek mythology, the great West, the jungle. "These are samples of the big rhythmic activities that appeal so strongly to growing, energetic youngsters."[1]

Children with language problems tend to find great satisfaction in movement. The physicality of dance/movement circumvents their disadvantages in verbal skills, thus providing another reason for its inclusion, particularly in the beginning. In addition to these conscious and unconscious expressions, however, there is the physical pleasure a child derives from moving, a pleasure that leads into play, dance, sports, and exercise for its own sake. Today, unfortunately, television constantly bombards the eyes and ears of children, giving information of all kinds, it is true, but at the expense of their movement experience and natural creative response. In bringing children indoors, they are made passive spectators rather than active participants in games and sports in open areas. Most children enjoy moving their bodies and discovering different ways of exploring a space. As they gain physical control, they prefer running to walking, and they enjoy finding new methods of locomotion that are energetic and fast. Running, skipping, galloping, hopping, jumping, leaping and rolling stretch the muscles and help the child to gain a mastery of her body as she tries out all the different things she can do with it. Because movement is so natural an expression, it is the ideal way of beginning work in creative drama. Experienced teachers of young children know this and will progress from rhythmic movement to dramatic play.

1. All the quotations in this paragraph are from *Rhythms by Mary Perrine,* as told to Henrietta O. Rogers (New Canaan, Conn.: The New Canaan Country School Monograph, Spring 1951).

Peter Slade uses the term *natural dance* to describe dance that is not tied to a set of rules or complicated techniques, but rather is improvised and personal in style. He further identifies it as the bridge between the primitive and the sophisticated, or between natural inclination and a disciplined art form.[2]

Elizabeth Polk, movement therapist and professor of dance at Adelphi University, places a special emphasis on skipping for young patients. She sees the skip as much more than alternating right and left hops; she describes it as "an upward movement, a joyous way of going places."[3] It begins with the jump; next the one-legged jump, which is a hop. If the child has a rhythmic sense, the hop easily turns into a skip. As to the value of the skip, she views it as twofold: coordination of movement and pride in achievement, which strengthens self-esteem. This achievement helps to develop the self-control and discipline that are needed in the classroom and in life.

Teachers and leaders of older groups find that their goals may be reached more easily and quickly if, instead of a verbal approach, they begin with physical activity. Actors call these activities warm-ups and declare them an effective way to relax and tone the muscles of their backs, legs, arms, and necks in preparation for a performance. Through rhythmic exercise a group can be drawn together and released in an objective and pleasurable way.

Rhythm, an element of movement, supplies structure and enjoyment. Rhythm is apparent in many of the games and chants of children and is the basis of music and dance. In fact, music and dance are frequently taught together through the medium of song, rhythm, and the employment of toy or rhythm instruments. This is called music-movement and is advocated by many educators. Dalcroze thought of using the body as a musical instrument by treating rhythm, with its roots in physical movement, as the organizer of musical elements.

Classes in movement are most successful when taught in a large room, where students have plenty of space in which to move freely. Too large an area, such as a gymnasium or a playground, on the other hand, presents problems; for large, unconfined space can lead to chaos, not freedom, dispersing the group rather than bringing it together. Therefore boundaries should be established and maintained.

Leotards, pants, jump suits, or comfortable old clothing of some kind should always be worn; rhythm sandals or bare feet prevent slipping on a hardwood floor. Piano accompaniment is an asset, if the leader can play or has an accompanist; if not, a drum is perfectly satisfactory. Later on, recorded music will help suggest mood and possible characterization. In the beginning, however, and for most purposes, percussion instruments are all the leader

---

2. Peter Slade, *Natural Dance* (London: Hodder and Stoughton, 1977).
3. Elizabeth Polk, *Teaching Children to Skip*, New York State Journal of Health, Physical Education and Recreation 29, no. 2 (June 1976): 2.

Students in The Children's Theatre Company's Conservatory School perform warm-up exercises. (*Courtesy of John Donahue, Minneapolis; photograph by George Heinrich.*)

needs to give the beat and suggest or change rhythms. One advantage of the drum, incidentally, is that it permits the leader to move about freely and watch the group. This freedom of movement is not possible while playing a piano or changing tapes and records.

In a movement class it is usually a good idea to begin work with the entire group, unless it is so large or the room so small that the participants bump into each other. In that case, the leader should divide the class into two parts, working first with one, then with the other, and alternating every few minutes so as to hold the interest of all. Beginning with a large circle, the leader should beat a good rhythm for walking. When all are moving easily and without self-consciousness, the beat can be changed to something faster, such as a trot or a run. Shifting the rhythm to a gallop, a skip, a hop, a jump, then back to a slow-motion walk is not only good exercise, but it holds the participants' attention as they listen for the changes. Depending on the pupils' ages, more complicated rhythms can be added. The participants themselves can take turns beating the drum or clapping new combinations. Why rhythmic movement first? According to Marjorie Dorian, teacher of dance and author of books on the subject, it encourages spontaneous movement within a disciplined framework. This is the goal of the teacher of creative drama as well as the teacher of dance.

The arts, through the common denominator of rhythm, can best be served by an introduction to rhythmic movement, both disciplined and expressive. Through rhythm the child experiences the dynamic changes of opposites: soft and loud, fast and slow, much and little: qualities that make us sensitive to everything around us. Through the measurement of time and space he becomes aware of the limitations that eventually give him strength to pursue other disciplines.[4]

As teachers, we have tended to think of creative drama as concerned primarily with developing intellectual and linguistic abilities, whereas we have thought of movement as concerned only with the control and use of the body. Actually, movement and body language are part of creative drama. It is the combined mental, physical, vocal, and emotional involvement that distinguishes creative drama from all other art forms and gives its special value.

Instruments

Although the drum is the most commonly used instrument when working on rhythms, there are other instruments that add variety and are not difficult to obtain. Some of these are triangles, bells, and gongs for metal sounds; sticks and castinets for wood sounds; and shaking instruments like maracas or gourds with pebbles inside. Imaginative leaders and groups will find or invent other instruments of their own. Actually, trying out different objects to discover what sounds they make is an exercise in itself and one most children enjoy.

One of the values of using different instruments is the discovery of the qualities of sound they produce. This in turn helps the student to feel the rhythm in a special way. For example, slow drumbeats might suggest waves washing up on the shore of a lake, whereas the sound of castinets might bring hailstones or raindrops to mind. In telling a story in movement, the use of several percussion instruments will stimulate the imagination, often giving different results from those obtained with the use of a single drum.

Records and tapes are excellent, of course; percussion instruments are recommended primarily because the teacher has complete control over them—stopping, starting, changing the rhythm, etc., according to the immediate need. The terms *legato* and *staccato* can be introduced at this time; they have special meanings, which describe rhythms clearly and, incidentally, add to a growing vocabulary.

Rhythmic Activities

The following activities are designed to help the student discover the drama in movement. In the early stages the leader works within the group, moving out when the participants are secure and able to move without her

4. Marjorie Dorian, *Ethnic Stories for Children to Dance* (San Francisco: BBB Associates, 1978).

support. She does not *show* the groups what to do, but she supports, in every way possible, honest effort, involvement, and the development of individual ideas.

1. Take the group on a journey over a desert, across a river, up a hill, over both smooth and rough ground, over slippery rocks, through tall grass, and into an open field. Vivid imaging stimulated by rhythmic accompaniment makes this a favorite game of young children and a challenge to older ones.
2. Have the group listen to different beats and then imagine what gaits or characters they suggest, which might be an Indian chief striding, an old man shuffling, a toddler, a young woman running for a train, a delivery boy with a heavy load, or a night watchman on his rounds. Try moving like these characters.
3. Do the same things with moods. Have the group first listen and then tell whether the beats sound happy, sad, proud, excited, sneaky, angry, or shy. Have the group move together to the same beats, expressing these moods.
4. "Snail" is a good beginning game for establishing a common rhythm. Have the group form a single file, each putting his or her hands on the shoulders of the person in front. The leader moves to the center of the room with the line following. Chanting "snail, snail, snail, snail," the group moves into a shell-like formation. When the players can move in no further, they reverse and move back into their original circle.
5. Rhythms can suggest people working or moving in unison. Try beats that describe the following: an assembly line, a marching band, robots, motorcycles, athletes warming up, workmen using picks, joggers, etc.
6. Not only young children but adult actors enjoy suggesting different animals through rhythmic movement. Try to find rhythms for the following:

horses	chickens	mice
cats	cranes	frogs
rabbits	kangaroos	sea gulls
snakes	monkeys	pigeons

7. An imaginative exercise that requires a little more experience is the creation of fantastic creatures. Ask the class to imagine strange or fanciful animals and then to show with their bodies what the animals are like. How do they look? What are they made of? What do they eat? How do they move? Breathe? Sleep? This exercise can be a source of fun and relaxation as well as a challenge.
8. The following is a quieting exercise to be used after vigorous movement. Sitting in a circle on the floor, the group creates different

rhythms and sounds. Clapping hands, snapping fingers, tapping knees, and brushing the floor softly with the hands are among the sounds that can be made in this position. Have each child put two, then three of these sounds together in a rhythmic sequence. The group listens carefully and tries to repeat the sequence.

From Rhythms to Dramatic Play

Dramatic play, the child's earliest effort to reproduce life situations and to try out the roles of others, is based on imitation. Through imitating the actions and behavior of those around him, the young child masters reality and gains self-confidence. Movement thus merges with improvisation, as the drama takes shape. Words, the last element to be added, will be scanty at first, for the vocabulary of the preschool child is limited. As a matter of fact, much older players in creative drama classes tend to say less than they have planned and feel. Sooner or later, however, the need for words is felt; when that moment comes, natural dialogue is born. This is the reason why movement is preferred to a verbal beginning for every age level.

Virginia Koste, in her book *Dramatic Play in Childhood, Rehearsal for Life,* observes that "Ironically one backlash of the creativity craze has been the neglect, the ignoring of imitation with all of its implications in human learning and art."[5] She urges us to restore imitation to its rightful place, for it is through observation and imitation that children learn. Knowledge of others and their ways of doing things enables children to invent new forms and create dramas and characters of their own. "Holding the mirror up to nature" is a necessary function; imitation is a fault only when it discourages inventiveness and encourages dependency and copying.

Observation and Imitation

Here is an exercise for observation and imitation that younger children enjoy. It is suggesting movement through the "—ly" game. The entire class can play it together, or one person can begin and the others follow his or her interpretation. In this way every child is assured of the opportunity to create a movement. Words used might be: *lazily, quickly, slowly, curiously, wearily, sleepily, noiselessly, loudly, angrily, happily, joyfully, thankfully, sheepishly,* etc. Incidentally, playing this game is also a way of learning new words.

Similar to this exercise is the beating out of rhythms. Each child beats a rhythm for the others to follow. After each has had several turns, variations of the game can be played. One child can go into the center and begin a rhythm,

5. Virginia Koste, *Dramatic Play in Childhood, Rehearsal for Life* (New Orleans: Anchorage, 1978), p. 19.

change it suddenly, and tap the one who will begin the next. This has endless possibilities and is an excellent exercise for encouraging close observation and imitation.

Movement Activities

In the preceding activities we were especially concerned with rhythms and the use of the body. All movement is concerned, however, with *where* and *how* the body is used:

A. *Where* the body moves refers to:
   1. Level (high, low, medium)
   2. Direction (forward, backward, left, right, in diagonals)
   3. Shape of the movement
B. *How* the body moves refers to:
   1. Energy (much or little)
   2. Time (sudden or sustained)
   3. Flow (free or tight)

The next group of exercises may be used to work on the *where* or the *how* of moving. Try the following to show *where* movement takes place.

Low movement: caterpillar, duck, seal, shallow pool of water, young plant emerging from the earth

High movement: airplane, high cloud, person on stilts, wire walker, kite

Horizontal movement: swinging bell, elephant's trunk, lion pacing in a cage, someone paddling a canoe, someone on a swing

Up-and-down movement: seesaw, plane, bird, bat, ball bouncing, elevator, falling star, Jack-in-the-box, rocket, piece of machinery

Try the following to show *how* movement takes place.

Fast movement: arrow, fire engine, express train, leaf in a storm, jet plane, speedboat, racehorse, top, skateboard

Slow movement: clock, farm horse, melting ice, tugboat, turtle, freight train pulling out of the station, movie in slow motion

Turning movement: curling smoke, merry-go-round, revolving door, spool of thread, figure skating, top

Strong, heavy movement: chopping wood, bulldozer, tank, stormy waves, digging in concrete

Soft, light movement: balloon, butterfly, flickering candle, soap bubble, kitten, kite, elf, leaf

Sharp movement: bucking bronco, cuckoo clock, cricket, grasshopper, juggler, woodpecker

Floppy, loose movement: clothes on a line, rag doll, mop, loose sail, straw hat blowing down the street, long hair blowing, flag in the breeze

Smooth movement: airplane, cat, fish swimming, syrup pouring, skating, rainbow forming, automobile on a throughway

Twisted movement: octopus, pretzel, knot, piece of driftwood, crumpled paper, tangled chain

Change in movement:
1. A candle standing tall and straight burns down to a pool of wax
2. A piece of elastic, stretched and then released
3. A paper drifting to the sidewalk, then picked up by a sudden gust of wind
4. A board slowly breaking away from the side of an old building, then falling off
5. A toy train moving rapidly, running down and stopping; then being rewound and repeating the sequence

The following images suggest being, using or doing, and feeling through movement.

Water

Being: bubbles, rushing water, rain, whirlpool, quiet pool, surf

Using: blowing bubbles, carrying water, hosing the lawn, water skiing, wading in shallow water

Feeling: weightlessness of floating, walking in water, walking against the tide

Fire

Being: bonfire blazing, forest fire raging, smoke puffing, match being lighted

Using: building a fire, putting out a fire, being warmed by a fire

Feeling: hot, warm, sleepy from a fire, choking from the smoke of a fire

Air

Being: soft summer air with only a slight breeze blowing

Using: pumping air into a tire, blowing up a balloon, breathing good, clean air

Feeling: warm air, cold air, polluted air, pleasant cool air

Try to suggest the following ideas in dance; then, in pantomime. They may be expressed quite differently or they may be much the same, depending on the one moving. Each student must move as he or she feels, for there is no right or wrong way. At this stage sincere involvement is the major goal.

1. Offering a prayer
   Giving thanks
   Asking for rain in a time of drought
2. Casting a magic spell on someone
   Being under a magic spell
   Trying to throw off a spell
3. Feeling frightened
   Investigating the cause of your fear
   Feeling relief at discovering that your fear was groundless
4. Feeling joyful
   Showing what has made you so happy
   Sharing your joy with others
5. Feeling very angry
   Showing what has made you so angry
   Resolving your anger by doing something about it

Now take one of the above ideas and combine the three parts of it so as to create a simple story.

Partner Activities

The activities so far have been planned for the whole class. Working in pairs or with partners is more difficult, because the movements must be synchronized. Try the following simple exercises as a starter.

1. Have each member of the group take a partner. Have them put their hands on each other's shoulders and then push to see who is the stronger. Working with a partner in this way helps the individual move from group work to individual work without feeling self-conscious.
2. Next try the theatre game of having one person lead another whose eyes are closed. Have the class walk around the room in pairs until all are moving easily together. Reverse roles and try it again.
3. Divide the group into pairs, with one person standing at each end of the room. To the beat of the drum, they:
   a. Walk toward each other, meet, and part
   b. Walk toward each other, meet, and clash
   c. Walk toward each other, meet, and go off together
4. Have one person begin a movement, and the partner pick it up and continue it.
5. Have one person begin to make or do something and the partner complete it.

Activities on a Theme

The activities that follow are different from the preceding in that they involve group cooperation. While simple in themselves, they become more complex in their dependency on interaction. Three themes are suggested but the children as well as the leader will think of others in which the entire class is asked to contribute to a single theme.

1. *The Old Men's Dance*   This is an actors' exercise that most children enjoy. The class is divided in half and placed in two lines facing each other. There may be music with a strong rhythm or a drumbeat as accompaniment. The person at the head of one line invents a step or movement of some part of the body. The person across from him repeats the step and adds one of his own. The second person in the first line repeats both movements and adds another. This continues until everyone in the class has contributed a step or movement to the dance. The larger the class, the more difficult it becomes to remember all the steps; but the exercise is a good warm-up for a group, as well as a good activity at the end of class, particularly when too little time is left to begin on new material.

2. *Building a Zoo*   This is fun for younger players. Each child creates a different animal in movement, eventually having them all move into imagined cages around the room. The teacher can be the zoo keeper, working "in-role" with the class.

3. *Making a Train, Being Ants, Being Boats*   Younger players enjoy this exercise. The problem here is one of precision. The players follow each other in a line, maintaining equal distances between themselves and the children preceding them. The leader (first car, ant, boat, etc.) determines the speed, direction, and rhythm.

Telling Stories in Movement

Pure dance has no describable story. Mime, on the other hand, uses movement to narrate or describe. Mime can range from the classic form that captures the essence of a person or action, to the imitative form that reproduces an action realistically and in detail. There is a trend at the present time to add sound to enhance the situation or help tell the story. This is a new direction in the art of mime, which requires as much skill as silent theatre. Indeed, all forms of movement and mime demand concentration, practice, and precision. In time, a personal style can be developed that characterizes the work.

Myths and legends lend themselves to mime and mimetic movement. They are generally simple in plot and deal with universal themes and feelings.

The wheel and the cobra. (*Courtesy of Rachel Carr; photograph by Edward Kimball.*)

The more complicated the narrative, the less easy it is to dance or mime, and therefore the greater the temptation to use words to explain it. Because of their simplicity the following stories can be told in dance, in mime or movement, or with improvised dialogue. Try telling them all three ways. Be sure that everyone is thoroughly familiar with the story before attempting to do anything with it. First beat a rhythm on the drum and have the entire group try telling the story in movement. Then, perhaps, individuals will have suggestions as to what more can be done with it.

SEWALI AND THE SNAKE

There was once in East Africa a brave young warrior named Sewali. He had heard tales of a great snake, Sesota, who killed and terrified his people, and he was troubled. One day Sewali went to the chief and told him that he wanted to go out and conquer the great serpent. The chief was pleased with Sewali, though he doubted that the young brave could overcome a monster that the strongest warriors had failed to capture. Nevertheless, he gave his permission for Sewali to go.

Sewali put a large jar on his shoulder and went into the jungle. When at last he reached the snake's cave, he took off his necklace and wrapped it around the neck of the jar. The great snake saw the sparkling beads of the necklace and was attracted to them. Cautiously he approached the jar. After a few minutes he glided inside it. Quick as a flash Sewali put the lid on the jar, thus imprisoning the snake. Then, dragging the heavy jar behind him, he returned to his village and proudly displayed his captive. All the people danced joyfully around the jar in celebration of Sewali's brave and clever deed, for they knew that this was the end of the feared Sesota.

THE SIX SONS OF ANANSI

The West African tales of Anansi the Spider make excellent material for both dance and dramatization. There are many of these stories, but one of the best known is the tale of Anansi's six sons.

Anansi was a clever trickster, whose popularity came from his ability to outwit others and thus help human beings. In this story, however, it is he who is in great danger, and his six sons come to his rescue. They are named See Trouble, Road Builder, River Drinker, Game Skinner, Stone Thrower, and Cushion.

Anansi was lost. First to discover it was his oldest son, See Trouble. See Trouble saw his father in grave danger across the river so he went to his brother, Road Builder. Road Builder quickly built a bridge across the river, but before Anansi could cross it, he was swallowed by a huge fish. This time River Drinker came to the rescue and drank all the water. This enabled Game Skinner to cut open the great fish and rescue their father. Before Anansi could escape, however, a huge falcon swooped down and lifted him high in the air. Then Stone Thrower threw a rock, hitting the falcon, causing him to drop his prey. Anansi fell to earth, landing on the body of his sixth son, Cushion, and thus was saved.

Anansi did not know to which son he should be most grateful, therefore he implored the God Nyame to reward the one who had done the greatest deed. Nyame could not decide, either, so he took the Globe of Light into the sky in honor of the six sons of Anansi, the Spider.

THE TURNIP

The old Russian folktale of pulling up the turnip can be told completely in movement. Although the tale is about individuals rather than groups, there are so many characters and the tale is so short that everyone in the class can have a turn. It is a very amusing situation, but also one that requires skill and control to prevent its becoming a series of pratfalls.

It was autumn and time for the turnips to be harvested. Grandfather went out to the garden and bent down to pull the first one. But this turnip was different from any turnips he had ever planted. It refused to come up! So, after trying unsuccessfully with all his might, he called his wife to help him.

When grandmother came out and saw what he wanted, she put her arms around his waist, and together they pulled and pulled. Still the turnip would not budge. Then granddaughter came out to the garden to see what was happening. Putting her arm around grandmother's waist, she pulled grandmother, who pulled grandfather, who pulled the turnip. But the turnip refused to come up.

(The story continues in this way with any number of characters included, each one pulling the one before him. Sometimes it is told with the granddaughter's dog pulling her and a beetle pulling the dog, followed by a second, third, and fourth beetle all pulling at the end of the line.)

Finally, when all pull together, the turnip comes up!

THE RAVEN TALES

The Raven stories of the North American Indians are excellent for either dance or improvisation on any age level. Raven was a creator of the world, but like Anansi, he was a trickster as well. Legends tell how Raven used his wits to defeat evil or greedy spirits and so help human beings in trouble. The story of how he stole the stars, moon, and sun, though complicated, can be cut down to the simple tale of a people rescued from living in darkness.

Raven, by changing himself from a bird into a human form, gained access to the house of the powerful chief, who kept the sun, moon, and stars in boxes under lock and key. Raven succeeded in persuading the unsuspecting grandfather to give him the box containing the stars. Stealthily, he took it out and tossed them to his people. But the stars alone did not give enough light, so Raven returned to the chief's house. Knowing where the boxes were hidden, he watched his chance; then, when no one was looking, he took the second box containing the moon. But it, also, gave too little light. Raven knew that the remaining box must contain the sun, so he went back for the third time to the chief's house and stole the sun.

One of the Raven legends has it that he came to the bank of a river and asked to be helped across with the heavy box, but the people refused assistance. Finally, angered and out of patience, he released the sun. The sudden burst of brilliant light terrified the people; those wearing the skins of animals fled into the forest where they became the "forest people." Those wearing garments made of sea animals dived into the water and were thereafter known as "sea people." Those clad in bird clothing flew into the air and became the "sky people." Thus the legend of Raven's theft continues on into an explanation of how the earth, sea, and sky people came to be.

Any part of this story, or several parts of it, can be told entirely in movement; it can also be told with sound added or played with simple dialogue. One program of Raven tales, developed by university students for children's audiences, began with an explanation of the totem pole, four of which were used to mark off the playing space. Then three of the Raven tales were played with choreographed movement and dialogue. The performers wore leotards and elaborate masks, which they put on and took off as they assumed the roles of the different characters.

Following the performance, the children in the audience were invited to participate in a variety of activities suggested or stimulated by the performance: improvisation, dance, and mask making. For the children who took part in these activities the afternoon provided rich experiences in theatre, folklore, and creative expression.

The leader can find other stories and discover what the group can do by using movement only to tell them. Nursery rhymes make good material for young children. For older children and adults, legends and myths suggest a variety of rhythms and movements. Modern situations are also good and may be preferred by older children.

THE PASTA POT

The old Italian tale of the witch and her pasta pot can be told in dance just as easily as with improvised dialogue. It is a simple story line.

The witch, Nona, had a magic pasta pot. One day, as she put the pot on the stove, her servant Anthony heard her chanting the words, "Boil and bubble, pasta pot. Make me some pasta, nice and hot." What Anthony did not see were the three magic kisses that Nona threw at the pot when she had eaten her fill.

Then, telling him to stay and guard the cottage, but not to touch the pot, Nona left. She had no more than gone out the door, however, when Anthony, eager to see if the magic worked for him, looked at the pot and chanted the words he had heard her say. No sooner were the words out of his mouth than the water began to boil and the pot to fill up with pasta. Anthony was greatly pleased with himself and ate heartily, but to his dismay the pasta continued to roll out of the pot. He couldn't stop it!

The neighbors, seeing the pasta rolling out the door of the cottage, rushed in to find out what was happening. They all tried to stop it but it only kept on coming. At this moment Nona returned. She threw three magic kisses in the direction of the pot and at once the pasta stopped. She gave Anthony a beating for disobeying her; then, seeing how frightened he had been, she forgave him. They and their neighbors joined together in a dance.

Players of any age will find this a humorous tale that can be handled in a variety of ways, depending on the interpretation. With the help of a drum and other instruments, children will find appropriate rhythms and movements by which to tell the story. Try out some movements. Decide what best expresses the old witch, Nona. How would Anthony move and show his feelings: curiosity, delight, dismay, helplessness, relief, enjoyment of the dance at the end? How would you suggest pasta boiling in a pot? Running over? Rolling out the door? What are the neighbors like? What are their feelings? Can you make up a group dance at the end? The players may want to use a folk dance here instead of creating one. There are many ways in which the story can be told and every group will find a way of its own.

Little children enjoy making up stories involving a variety of rhythms. For example, a story might go something like this: "I went for a *walk* in the park. It was a lovely morning and I *skipped* happily down a path. Soon I met an old man, *shuffling* along with a pack on his back. Next I met some pigeons *strutting* across the path in search of food." This can go on as long as you want, adding persons and animals with clearly observable gaits. The teacher, working with the children, suggests the rhythms with drumbeats. A little practice and the story will take on embellishments, providing a rich opportunity for imaginative ideas and ways of showing them.

THE STORY OF MA-UI

The Hawaiian Islands are rich in myths and legends, some of which offer excellent material for movement and creative dance. The Story of Ma-ui is one of them. Players of all ages will find ideas that can be expressed physically, perhaps even better than vocally—certainly, just as well. The story is simple and direct, with a theme reminiscent of folktales around the world.

There was a time, long ago, when the sun raced across the skies of Hawaii so rapidly that the fruit had no time to ripen on the vines and the fishermen could not catch any fish. The days were short and the nights were long. The earth was so cold and dark that plants froze on their stems. These beautiful islands, as we know them today, were inhospitable to life, and the people wondered how much longer they would exist or where they could go if they left. One day a small boy named Ma-ui decided that he would catch the sun and make it slow down. Then perhaps the plants and trees would have time to grow and mature, and the fishermen could wait for a catch before it was night again. He told his grandmother of his plan. At first she feared for his life and tried to dissuade him; but when he begged her not to stop him, she gave him a magic stick and a piece of rope and fearfully bade him goodbye.

The next day Ma-ui climbed to the top of Mt. Haleakala to wait for the sun to rise. The trip was long and hard, but at last Ma-ui stood where he could see the day break. When the first ray of the sun appeared on the mountaintop, Ma-ui jumped high in the air. Quickly he threw his rope around the ray and wrestled with it. Finally, with the help of his magic stick, he mastered it and tied it to the twisted trunk of a tree. Then he made it promise to slow down or he would not let it escape. The sun saw the magic stick in the small boy's hand and promised never to race across the skies over Hawaii again. From that day forth the flowers blossomed and the trees grew straight and tall. The fruit ripened on the vines and the fishermen had time to catch the fish so that the people had plenty to eat again.

Many different movements and rhythms can be found in this story. One way to begin is with a discussion of all the movements that are mentioned. Then the entire group can work on them together, using a drumbeat to set the rhythms. A warm-up composed of walking, running, jumping, stretching, curling up, falling, and rising might precede work on the story. Some of the rhythmic patterns that the group might try next are:

The sun, racing across the sky
The flowers, stretching and trying to grow, then wilting and withering
The fishermen, casting their lines and pulling them in as the sun goes down
The people, trudging back to their homes, exhausted and cold
Ma-ui, climbing the mountain and jumping to catch the sun's ray
The sun, slowing down in its course across the sky
The slower rhythms found at the end of the story

After the class has worked on the movements long enough to become free and thoroughly acquainted with the story, they will be ready to try playing it in its entirety. While the tale can be told in pantomime or improvised with spontaneous dialogue, *The Story of Ma-ui* can be beautifully conveyed through dance or simple creative movement. Older groups may want to add a Hawaiian dance at the end or to combine speech and movement. There is no best way of handling it; it was included in this chapter because it offers unusual opportunities for creative movement.

Summary

Movement—the basis of play, ritual, games, dance, and theatre—is a natural beginning for work in creative drama. Physically, the whole body is involved: torso, arms, legs, head, and neck. Through the use of the body, muscles are stretched and relaxed. Posture and coordination improve with regular exercise. Because the entire group can take part at one time, the possibility of self-consciousness is lessened. Persons of all ages and backgrounds usually find it easier at first to become involved through movement rather than through verbalization. This is particularly true of younger children, those for whom English is a second language, and persons with special problems and needs. Often in the rhythms and patterns of a child's movement the problems in his inner life are revealed. This is why movement and dance are recommended as treatment, serving both diagnostic and therapeutic purposes.

Imitation and observation are as much a part of movement as creativity. The leader encourages imagination but discourages the cliché. Through movement, therefore, children experience both discipline and freedom. By moving into the rituals of the group (and here the word *rituals* is used in its broadest sense), a feeling of belonging is engendered. Rhythm, that underlying flow and beat, captures the mover in what was described earlier as an experience both objective and pleasurable. Taught together, rhythms and dramatic play provide a sound foundation for acting. "Dance-drama" encompasses the disciplines of both arts and is, therefore, a powerful tool for creative expression.

4
Pantomime:
The Next Step

*P*antomime is the art of conveying ideas without words. Children enjoy pantomime, and for the young child this is an excellent way to begin creative drama. Since many of her thoughts are spoken entirely through the body, the five- or six-year-old finds pantomime a natural means of expression. Group pantomimes of the simplest sort challenge the imagination and sharpen awareness. In kindergarten, such basic movements as walking, running, skipping, and galloping prepare for the creative use of rhythms. Music can set the mood for people marching in a parade, horses galloping on the plains, toads hopping in a field, racing cars on a track, or children skipping on a fine autumn day. In other words, rhythmic movement becomes dramatic when the participant makes use of it to become someone or something other than herself.

Creative drama lesson at Kendall Demonstration Elementary School for the Deaf at Gallaudet College. (*Courtesy of Victoria Brown.*)

For older children and adults, pantomime is advocated because it encourages the use of the entire body and relieves the players of having to think of dialogue. Here, also, group pantomime should precede individual work. Familiar activities such as playing ball, flying kites, running for a bus, or hunting for a lost object get the group on its feet and moving freely. If the entire class works at one time, self-consciousness disappears and involvement is hastened. Fifteen or twenty minutes of this sort of activity, changed frequently enough to hold the group's interest, makes for relaxation and readiness to move on to a more challenging assignment.

Others for whom pantomime is especially satisfying are children who do not speak English and those with speech problems. Here the child who has an idea but not the words to express it, can convey his meaning, often very successfully, through body language. I have had speech-handicapped students of all ages present characters, stories, and ideas in pantomime with clarity and artistry. Another benefit, in addition to the obvious one of building self-confidence, is motivation for skill in the language arts. Having succeeded in sign language, the child is encouraged to express himself in words and writing as well. Pantomime, incidentally, has become a familiar art form in the past ten or fifteen years. One of the benefits of television is the opportunity it affords all persons to enjoy the performing arts, including skilled professional mime.

Class Size

While creative rhythms can be carried on successfully with any number, pantomime requires a group of no more than fifteen to twenty. If a class is very large, the teacher should make every effort to divide it so that half the group is involved with some other activity at that hour. Pantomime demands individual attention, and every child should be assured the opportunity of participation each time the class meets. This is true whatever the age level, for growth depends upon repeated experiences in exercises that increase in difficulty.

Length of Class Period

The length and frequency of class meetings depend upon the situation (school, club, or camp) and the age of the players. With very young children, daily experiences for ten to fifteen minutes are ideal, whereas for older children, two or three meetings a week for forty-five minutes or an hour work out well. With club groups, the meeting may be only once a week; this is less desirable but may be the only possible arrangement. High school students and young adults can be absorbed for as long as two hours, but in general more frequent meetings of shorter length are preferable.

In schools in which creative drama is a definite part of the curriculum, the teacher can look forward to regular meetings throughout the year. Where it is not, it will be up to the classroom teacher to introduce it whenever and however he can. He will probably use pantomime in connection with other subjects which, if imaginatively done, can be of value as a tool for teaching and a creative experience for the class.

Playing Space

A stage is generally used for formal rehearsals, whereas a large room is more desirable for creative drama. Little children enjoy moving all over the room and should be encouraged to do so. The younger the group, therefore, the larger the space required. If a large room is not available, a classroom in which all the chairs have been pushed aside will do. Space makes for freedom; a small or cramped area inhibits it. As was said in the preceding chapter, however, too large an area can present other problems, particularly for a beginning or uncontrolled group. Boundaries are needed, as the leader soon discovers; there is greater freedom where there are clear boundaries of both time and space than where neither exist. An auditorium with a stage and chairs is least desirable as a playing space for a beginning group of any age, since it inevitably leads to a concept of performance with stage techniques before the players are ready for it. Under any circumstances, seating children on the floor in a semicircle where all can see, hear, and be heard is the most satisfactory arrangement.

Imagination

Whatever the space, the teacher will try to see that it is kept uncluttered and that the players are seated in a circle or semicircle around it. Having engaged in rhythms and group activities, the players are now ready for pantomime. There are many ways of proceeding, but one that has proved effective is having the class handle a small, nondescript object (such as a small box or blackboard eraser) as if it were several different items. For example, the teacher calls six or seven players to the center, hands one the object and tells her it is a diamond bracelet, the most beautiful piece of jewelry any of them has ever seen. The teacher will then ask the players to:

1. Handle it.
2. Look at it.
3. React to it.
4. Pass it along to the next person.

When each has had a chance to handle and react to the object, the teacher may say that it is now a kitten with very soft fur. The same group again takes it and reacts to it. The next time, it may be a wallet—dirty and torn—with nothing in it. The fourth time it is passed, it becomes a knife, or a glass of water filled to the brim, or perhaps an old valuable manuscript. Each time it is handed around, the group invests it with more of the qualities of the suggested object. The idea, of course, is to stimulate the imagination and help the players realize that it is not the property used but their own imaginations that turn an eraser first into a bracelet, then a kitten, then a wallet, and finally a knife or a glass of water.

The observers are as interested as the players in the growing reality that develops. Depending upon the time at their disposal, the teacher may repeat the exercise with another group or move on to a new exercise. Some of the questions that might be asked of the observers are:

1. How did we know it was a bracelet?
   "One player held it so that the diamonds sparkled in the light." "John held it as if it were very expensive." "Linda tried it on." "Charles looked for the price tag."
2. Why did we know it was a kitten the second time the eraser was passed?
   "One stroked its head." "Another girl put it close to her cheek as if it were alive." "Barbara held its legs carefully when she gave it to Lois." "They all held it as if it were soft and round."

Questions put to the players might be:

1. What did the wallet look like to you?
   "It was dark green leather." "It was old and torn." "There was a faded snapshot in the front." "It had a hole in the bottom." "It was muddy because it had been lost in the yard."
2. You were careful not to let any of the objects drop, but you handled them differently. Why?
   "The bracelet was valuable." "I didn't want it to get broken." "The kitten was alive, and that made it different from all the others." "When I jiggled the glass, the water almost spilled."

Questions like these push the players to stronger visual images and greater power of observation.

Another exercise that serves to excite the imagination is the suggestion that a table in the middle of the room is covered with a variety of small objects. Each participant must go up and pick out one thing, showing, by the way he handles it, what it is. While this is an individual exercise, it can be done with several persons at once so that the attention is not focused on a single player. By having the rest of the class seated in a semicircle, some observers will see one player and some another. This is fun for all, and what self-consciousness may have existed in the beginning will soon be gone.

Concentration

Many children will be able to concentrate on the activities; but some, for whom this is the first experience of this sort, will not, so the next step is to work on "holding the image. One good exercise is to have the class hunt for a ring that has been lost. A few minutes of searching usually involves them in the assignment. If it does not, the teacher might actually hide a ring and ask them to find it. The reality that comes with the second playing demonstrates clearly the difference between pretending to hunt and really looking. Other good group exercises for developing concentration are:

1. Watching a plane come in
2. Looking at a funny movie
3. Smelling smoke in the woods
4. Listening for the lunch bell to ring

Sense Images

The class is now ready for some specific exercises involving the five senses. This might be introduced by a discussion of the ways in which we find out what is going on around us. We see; we hear; we touch; we smell; we taste. Individuals may do the following, using no props, but trying to "see" what is suggested.

1. Enter a very large room in which you have left your sweater.
2. Go into the dark closet to look for your sweater.
3. Go into your own room to get your sweater.
4. Try to find your sweater among a dozen in the locker room.

Exercises for the sense of hearing might include:

1. Hearing an explosion
2. Listening to a small sound and trying to decide what it is
3. Listening to a military band coming down the street
4. Hearing a dance orchestra playing a popular tune on the radio

Exercises for the sense of smell might include:

1. Coming home from school and smelling cookies baking in the kitchen
2. Walking in the woods and smelling a campfire
3. Smelling different perfumes on a counter
4. Smelling something very unpleasant and trying to decide what it is

Exercises for the sense of taste might include:

1. Eating a piece of delicious chocolate candy
2. Trying a foreign food that you have never tasted before and deciding you like it
3. Biting into a sour apple

Exercises for the sense of touch might include:

1. Touching a piece of velvet
2. Touching a hot stove
3. Touching or holding an ice cube
4. Touching or holding some sharp nails

These are only a few suggestions, and the leader will think of many more. Whatever is suggested, however, should always be within the experience of the players. Practice in actual hearing and observation is good exercise and may be introduced either beforehand or at any point that the teacher thinks it of value. For instance, the teacher might ask the players to:

1. Close your eyes for one minute and listen to all the sounds you can hear.
2. Go to one corner of the room and describe all the things that you see.
3. Touch one object and describe it as completely as possible.

What we are trying to do is to "lead children into experiences that will involve them in touching, seeing, tasting, hearing, and smelling the things in their world. We also want them to become involved in experiences that will lead to imagining, exploring, reasoning, inventing, experimenting, investigating, and selecting, so that these experiences will not only be rich in themselves but lead to personal creative growth."[1]

1. Earl Linderman and Donald W. Herberholz, *Developing Artistic and Perceptual Awareness* (Dubuque, Iowa: William C. Brown, 1964), introduction, p. x.

Performing an Action

There is no right or wrong order and no prescribed length of time the group should spend on one kind of exercise. Generally speaking, the older the players, the longer the attention will be sustained, but this does not always hold true. At any rate, a pantomime guaranteed to capture the interest of every player, regardless of age, is "making or doing something." In the beginning the teacher will offer suggestions, but later the players will have ideas of their own. Some good suggestions might be:

1. Setting a table
2. Baking a cake
3. Feeding your dog
4. Getting dressed
5. Doing your homework
6. Turning on a favorite TV program
7. Buying a pizza and taking it home
8. Riding on a crowded bus and going past your stop
9. Packing your backpack
10. Choosing food in a cafeteria

Again, let it be stressed that particularly in working with disadvantaged children, or with children in urban areas, the activities suggested should be those in their environments. "Washing clothes" rather than "fishing in a brook" is familiar to these children, and can, therefore, be easily imagined and acted. This, incidentally, also helps children to respect their own ideas and regard their own experiences more positively.

Pantomimes of actions will grow more complicated as the players put them into situations. The above might be inherent in such scenes as the following:

1. You are getting ready for a birthday party for your sister and must set the table. What are you going to put on it? Are there decorations? A cake? Favors? Presents? What dishes and silver will you use? Is it a surprise? Are you alone?
2. You are baking your first cake. No one is home, so you must read and follow the recipe yourself. What will you put in it? What utensils do you need? Is it a success?
3. You have a new puppy and have come home from school to take care of it. What do you feed it? How much? How big is he? What kind of dog?
4. You are getting up on a Saturday morning. Today it has begun snowing so you must dress to go out and play. What do you wear? Is it cold? Are

Adult Professionals from The New York Pantomime Theatre Demonstrate the Art of Mime to Children. (*Courtesy of Muriel Broadman and Mina Yakim.*)

you excited about it? Do you take time to comb your hair? Eat your breakfast?

5. It is after dinner and you have been told to do your homework. There is a television show you would like to see, but you know you should study. What is the assignment? Do you like the subject? Is it hard? Easy? Boring? What is the show you want to see? Is anyone else in the room? What do you finally do about it?

dumb →

needs speech

Mood and Feelings

Somewhere along the way, feelings have crept into the pantomimes so that a specific assignment on mood will not be appropriate. The teacher may want the group to talk about feelings first, or perhaps this will come about as a result of a particularly good job one of the players has done. The teacher might even ask the class what kinds of feelings they have experienced, and their responses will often include many more than she has anticipated. Anger, fear, happiness, excitement, pride, curiosity, vanity, anticipation, sorrow, and hatred are some feelings that seven- and eight-year-olds have enumerated.

This might be a time to break the class into groups of four or five, with each group taking one feeling to pantomime. Delightful results are always forthcoming when working on mood. One group showed excitement through a scene on Christmas Eve, when they crept downstairs to look at the tree and presents. Another asked if they could act out the story of *Pandora's Box* because it was such a good example of curiosity. Another group chose fear and set their scene in a tent at a summer camp. They were campers who heard a strange noise at night and imagined it to be a bear, but it was only their counselor coming back.

It soon becomes obvious that more than one emotion is usually involved in a situation of any length. Therefore, the next step will be to show change of mood. Situations like the following help the players to move from one mood to another.

1. You are a group of friends taking a hike in the woods. It is a beautiful day and you find strawberries and wildflowers. You stop to have your lunch, but when you are ready to move on, you discover that you have wandered from the path and are lost. Your happy mood changes to panic. Where are you? Should you go on or turn back? Is there any familiar landmark to guide you? Suddenly one of the girls finds a broken flower lying on the ground. As she picks it up, she realizes that it is on the path, and she must have dropped it when she looked for a picnic spot. Panic turns to relief as the group starts for home.
2. A group of boys discover a cave (or it could be the basement of an empty building). They go in, curious as to what they may find. One of them stumbles over a box. The boys open it and find money and jewels. Excitement grows as they realize they have found hidden treasure. Then they hear voices; men are approaching. Terrified, the boys hide. The men go past, not seeing them. The boys stuff a few coins in their pockets and run, escaping from danger.
3. A group of people get into an elevator in a big downtown building. Suddenly it stops between floors. Their poise turns to fear as the

operator pushes one button, then another, and nothing happens. Suddenly, she gets it started and the elevator moves, taking the passengers down to the ground level.

4. You are a group of children who come into your schoolroom one morning and find a monkey scampering about. First you are startled, then amused by his antics. Finally, the man who has lost him comes in and catches him, taking him away. You are sorry to see him go as he waves good-bye to you from his owner's shoulder.

5. You are going on a field trip to which you have looked forward for a long time. You get in the bus, but the bus will not start. After a few minutes, the driver lets you know that he cannot make it go, and so your trip must be postponed. Disappointed, you get out. Suddenly the engine starts. You turn around and see the driver motioning for you to get back in. Your happiness is great because you can now go after all.

6. You are sitting in a movie. First you are watching a very dull short subject. How do you feel when it seems to be going on forever? Then it changes to a hilariously funny cartoon. How do you react? At last, the feature begins and you are absorbed.

Mood can be created in countless ways, among them through the use of pictures, colors, light, music, and rhythms. The following ideas have been put into practice successfully with widely varying results.

1. The leader selects a picture or photograph that will evoke a strong emotional reaction. If the picture is realistic, the leader might, after all in the group have had a chance to look at it closely, ask such questions as: Who is in the picture? Why do you think she is there? What is she doing? What does she seem to be feeling? Why do you think she feels that way?

The discussion that results will lead into possibilities for pantomime or even improvisation, if the group is ready for it. A story can be built from the meanings and mood the children find in the picture. Instead of a composition in which persons are represented, however, a picture of a place may be shown. Country roads, city streets, the platform of a railroad station, a deserted house, a stretch of empty beach, woodlands—all are springboards if the mood evoked is one that kindles the emotions and arouses our curiosity. Where do you think this is? Why is no one around? What feelings do you have when you look at it? What is there about it that makes you feel this way?

After some discussion the leader will be ready to continue with questions leading to a scene laid in the place portrayed. Who might come along? Where is he or she going? Does he meet anyone? Anyone else? What do they talk about?

Do? Feel? In very little time most groups will people the canvas with characters, often involving them in an imaginative situation laid in the scene depicted. For example, a deserted house could take the group in several different directions. It might be the site of buried treasure (still a favorite theme of eight- to ten-year-old boys), important documents, or a fascinating archaeological discovery. It might, on the other hand, be the home a family has had to leave sorrowfully. Why? What has happened? Perhaps a son or daughter returns to say a last good-bye. Perhaps he or she meets a friend, finds something left behind, something meaningful. Or perhaps it is the home of a famous person, who has come back after an absence of many years to see his old neighborhood once more. Does anyone see him? Does anyone recognize him? What happens if they do? How does he feel about his home? The reception he is given? How do his old neighbors react?

2. Instead of a realistic painting, an abstract composition might be shown. Color, dark and light contrasts, design, the brush strokes—all will stimulate imaginative response. Not what the picture may *mean* but what it means to the viewer is the object of this exercise. Younger children tend to respond to the abstract composition more quickly than older players, perhaps because they do not feel the need for realistic detail and appreciate the fact that the artist's expression is direct and free like their own. Movement, rather than story, will usually be the reaction to this experience, although some children move naturally from physical movement into character.

3. As stated elsewhere, music is a powerful stimulus to creativity. Use of rhythms to suggest kinds of movement, characters, or animals is a popular and highly successful way of working. From this to the heightening of characterization is a natural next step. Actually, only the beat of a drum is necessary, although music, particularly if the leader is able to play the piano, can enrich the activity. Recordings of orchestral music are extremely effective means of establishing mood and may be used as we used pictures to stimulate the imagination, in a pattern of listening, reacting, responding. A leader with no formal background in music can guide the group, not in the sense of a lesson in music appreciation, of course, but in the sense of encouraging listening and imaginative response. Again, young children seem to respond more spontaneously to music than older children, who have learned to be concerned with structure, theme, and melody. Careful selection of the music to be used is necessary. Theareafter, the procedure is much the same as that followed with the pictures. How does it make you feel? Show us. Where are you? Who are you? Are there others with you? What might be happening?

To create a story from music takes time, but after several experiences in listening and responding the group will be ready to proceed with the creation of characters, an original situation suggested by the music, and perhaps some dialogue. Again, music is the way of inducing the flow of creative energy and, because of its abstract quality, may produce a mood more readily than other stimuli.

Characterization

Until now, we have been pantomiming activities and working to induce mood or feeling. The next step is characterization. Some participants will already have suggested characters different from themselves, but the teacher can use either the same exercises or new ones to start the group thinking in terms of characterization.

Again, situations involving groups are a good way to begin.

1. You are a group of people waiting for a bus on a city street. Each one of you will think of someone special to be: an elderly woman going to see her grandchildren, a businessman late for work, a girl on her way to high school, a blind man who needs help getting on the right bus, a young man beginning a new job, etc.
2. You are pilgrims who have gone to a shrine where, once a year, one wish is said to be granted. Decide who you are and what it is you want. You might be a crippled man who wants to walk again, a poet who wants very much to have her work published, a young mother who wants her sick baby to be cured. The teacher may wish to play with the group and be the statue at the shrine who indicates which wish is to be granted. This is a good situation to pantomime because it offers an opportunity to work on both characterization and strong motivation.
3. You are people in a bus terminal. Some of you are going on trips, others returning; still others are meeting friends or relatives. There may be a porter, a woman selling tickets, a man selling newspapers and magazines, etc. By your behavior, let us know who you are and how you feel as you wait for the buses to arrive and depart.

Some individual pantomimes stressing character are suggested:

1. You are a robber who is entering a house at night. While you are there, the people return unexpectedly. You listen and finally make your escape, having stolen nothing.
2. You are a neighborhood gossip. You have a party line, and one of your favorite pastimes is listening in on other people's conversations. This

afternoon you hear some very good news, some bad news, and then some remarks about yourself and your habit of listening in on your neighbors. How do you react? What do you do?

needs speech → 3. You are a child who has wanted a dog for a long time. One day you overhear your parents talking about it in the next room. Your mother does not want a dog, but your father thinks it is time you had one. They discuss reasons for and against it. How do you react to their arguments and what is the final decision?

seems difficult 4. Two of you will be a customer and a storekeeper in a shop in a foreign country. You do not know each other's languages. The customer decides, in advance, on three things he needs to buy and tries to convey what they are to the clerk, through pantomime. Who are you? What are the three things? How does it turn out? (This is an exercise that the entire class can do in pairs.)

Another exercise is to take one action and do it as three different people For example:

needs speech → 1. You go into a restaurant to order a meal. Do it as:
   a. A teen-aged boy who is very hungry
   b. A middle-aged woman who has very little appetite and sees nothing on the menu that she wants
   c. A very poor man who is hungry but must limit his choice to what he can afford
2. You are trying on dresses in a shop. Do it as:
   a. A very fat woman who has trouble being fitted
   b. A young girl, looking for a pretty dress to wear to a dance
   c. A secretary who is trying to find the most appropriate dress to wear on her first day at work in a new job
3. You are visiting an art museum. First you look at the exhibition as:
   a. An artist who knows the painter whose work is on display
   b. A woman who thinks she should go to museums but does not appreciate the pictures
   c. An elderly man who has been ill and is enjoying visiting his favorite museum for the first time in many months
4. You are exercising in a gymnasium. Do the exercises first as:
   a. A young woman who loves all athletics
   b. A fat man whose doctor has advised him to exercise to lose weight
   c. A child who has never seen gymnasium equipment before

For each of these exercises, consider what does each participant do and how does he or she feel about it?

Pantomime Suggested by Other Means

Some exercises are fun to do and stimulate inventiveness, but they have nothing to do with familiar actions, mood, or characters. These are good as a change and may be introduced any time the leader feels the group needs a new type of stimulation. Some ideas are:

1. Beat a drum and ask the group to move in any way the drumbeat suggests.
2. Ask each person in the class to represent a mechanical appliance. He does not operate it, he *becomes* it. Some very imaginative representations may be expected, such as: a pencil sharpener, an egg beater, a lawnmower, a hair drier, a record player, etc. This is a challenging exercise, guaranteed to break down all inhibitions.
3. Give each person a color and ask that she suggest it by means of movement, attitude, or characterization. This incidentally, may be followed up with an improvisation in which the color becomes a person. For example: Mr. White, Mrs. Black, Mrs. Blue, Mr. Green, Mr. Red, and Mrs. Yellow might be people at a tea. What are they like? How do they talk? How can we distinguish one from another?
4. Each person selects a property and acts according to what it suggests to him. The following are usually good for stimulating imaginative reactions: a gnarled stick, a ruler, a gold bracelet, a broken dish, a sponge. Again the players do not use the properties; they become characters suggested by their qualities.
5. Be puppets. Try to imagine what it feels like to be controlled by strings. Imagine that you are being controlled, then dropped by the puppeteer. While there is an element of characterization involved, it is the feeling of the inanimate object being manipulated that interests us.
6. Have the group listen to orchestral music. Suggest that they try to identify the various instruments. Then have the children *be* the instruments—not the musicians playing them but the instruments themselves. If they are enjoying the exercise, suggest that each child select a different instrument to be until a whole orchestra has been assembled. This particular activity will probably not last longer than one session, but it is fun and a means of stretching the imagination.
7. Put up a sheet at one end of the room with a light behind it. Have the children pantomime something behind it. See what happens. The

Pantomime suggested by other means such as a drumbeat. (*Courtesy of Rachel Carr; photograph Edward Kimball.*)

magic quality of a silhouette never fails to stimulate an immediate desire to try out ideas. This particular activity, incidentally, is an excellent one for the timid child who feels less exposed behind a sheet than he does out in the open. Practice in acting behind the sheet leads to inventiveness: What happens when the actor is close to the sheet? Far from it? Approaches or leaves it? How can a figure be exaggerated? Enlarged? How is humor obtained? Then try acting out nursery rhymes and stories in shadow.

8. The leader discusses growth and growing. It is suggested that the group conceive of themselves as seeds, buried deep in the earth. It is dark and they are quiet. Then spring arrives with rain, sun, and wind. What happens to the seeds? Do they break through the earth? Can we feel them push and grow? As summer comes, the plants grow taller. What are they going to be—flowers or trees? Tall, short, bushy, weak, or strong? Feel the warm rain, the hot sun, the breeze blowing, the

good to do in spring time

final push to maturity. Poetry written about the springtime ties in well with this exercise.

9. Either the teacher or the class composes a story in which a variety of sounds are listed and described. It is great fun to act out the sounds and/or what is making them. For example, one child wrote the following narration for the others to act.

> I woke up in the morning to the sound of my ALARM CLOCK going off. I opened my CLOSET DOOR, which squeaked. Then I turned on the FAUCET and the water made a rushing sound in the sink. After that I ran downstairs to breakfast. The coffee was PERKING in the pot. The BACON was frying in a pan. The TOAST popped up in the toaster. The RADIO was playing but the MUSIC was drowned out by the STATIC.
>
> Outside I heard my father MOWING the lawn and an AIRPLANE was flying low overhead. It was going to be hot and my mother turned on the FAN. Suddenly down the street I heard the noise of the SCHOOL BUS, its engine chugging. I ran out the front DOOR, which slammed and I ran down the walk, my SHOES clattering. My DOG barked as I climbed aboard a very noisy BUS.

Such an exercise as this stimulates awareness as well as imagination in the attempt to suggest or reproduce sounds and the objects making them.

10. Mirror images are popular and great fun for actors of all ages. Two players face each other, one being herself and the other her mirror image. Whatever the person does, her image must reproduce precisely. With practice this can become a skilled performance, challenging to the players and fascinating to those watching. Greater awareness as well as the ability to work together are developed in the process. Older groups may ask to repeat this exercise from time to time, realizing the possibilities for technical improvement.

11. Older players often find the following exercise rewarding. Imagine yourself shut up in a box. How large is it? Can you stand up? Move around? Get out? Let us see the box—its sides, floor, top. Suppose the box becomes larger? What do you do? It grows smaller. What happens to you then?

This is an exercise which may be repeated many times with the players improving their technique as they try to imagine and suggest in every way possible the experience of being encased in a box.

12. The following exercise is for older children or adults. Each member of the group writes a letter of apology for something he has done or

[handwritten margin note: Stare at the eyes - 1st graders can't do it that well concentration]

might have done. Then the leader asks two players to go to the telephone. One gives the apology and the other whatever response he feels is appropriate. Next, the first player faces the other person and makes his apology in person. Finally, he reads the original letter aloud, and the group comments on which apology has the greater reality, how the two improvisations have gone, and why. This is an interesting exercise, which may be carried out with each member of the group, time and interest permitting.

As the group progresses, organization improves, and situations often develop into simple plots. The players are learning to use their entire bodies to express ideas and are ready to add dialogue. Although improvisation, or informal dialogue, is the subject of the next chapter, the teacher will want to alternate exercises in pantomime and improvisation. No matter how advanced the group, pantomime is always good to work on from time to time because of the type of practice it offers.

Starting Places

The following *situations* are suggested as starting places to set children thinking. The younger or less experienced the group, the more preliminary work in the form of pantomime and discussion is needed. Group pantomimes related to the situation will stimulate movement; whereas discussing the topic and asking questions about it helps to stir the imagination. When all seem to be ready, divide the class into several small groups to develop simple narratives. Each group will come up with its own ideas as to plot and characters. This can be a one-time activity or the beginning of a creative play done entirely in pantomime.

> a beggar comes to the door
> a house is for sale
> the tallest sunflower in town
> a magic sandal
> a bracelet in an alley
> a puppy in a box left in a doorway

Starting places may also be *locations*. See what the class can do with some of these, again beginning with pantomimes as warm-ups and discussion questions to start the flow of ideas. When everyone is ready to begin work, divide the class into groups to develop narratives to be told through mime.

Making a Machine

There are many variations on this exercise, which has great appeal for older students. One way of beginning is for the leader to start a regular beat and ask one person to come into the center of the room and begin a movement. When the movement has been stabilized, a second person comes forward with another movement that relates to the first. This continues until as many as a dozen players become parts of a machine, each one contributing a movement that is coordinated with the rest. The effect can be interesting and dynamic when all players are working together.

This exercise may be made more interesting by adding sounds. Each player makes a noise appropriate to her movement. When all parts of the machine are moving rhythmically together, the sounds enhance the effect. This exercise requires imagination, inventiveness, concentration, cooperation, and the ability to sustain both sound and movement until the mechanical quality is established. The machine can run indefinitely, or it can break down, either stopping or falling apart.

The group may also start with a particular machine in mind (threshing machine, wrecking equipment, ice cream machine, sewing machine, etc.); or a machine may develop from the activity of the players. As a group gains experience, the results will become more precise and sophisticated. Incidentally, this is a technique that can be incorporated effectively into an improvisation, and it is often far more interesting than the use of conventional props.

Some teachers find that acting a story while it is read aloud is a good transition from pantomime to dramatization. Many stories can be done in this way, though some lend themselves to it better than others. One story, which has met with success with more than one group, is included here as an illustration. It is *The Little Scarecrow Boy*.[2]

THE LITTLE SCARECROW BOY
Arranged for Creative Playing by Aurand Harris
MARGARET WISE BROWN

Once upon a time, in a cornfield, there lived a scarecrow (he enters and takes his place), and his scarecrow wife (she enters and takes her place beside

2. From *Fun and Frolic* (New York: D.C. Heath, 1955).

him), and their little scarecrow boy (he enters and joins his mother and father).

Every day of the world old man scarecrow would go out into the cornfield to make faces at the crows. (He crosses the room and takes up his position in the cornfield.) And every day of the world little scarecrow boy would want to come, too. (He goes to his father and pulls at his coat.) And every day of the world, old man scarecrow would say:

> No!
> No, little boy,
> You can't go.
> You're not fierce enough to scare a crow.
> Wait until you grow.

(He shows how high little scarecrow boy will have to grow. The little boy is discouraged and returns to his mother.)

So, little scarecrow boy would have to stay home all day and just grow. (His mother holds up her hand to the height he will have to grow. First he stretches his neck, then he stands on his toes and finally he jumps but he does not reach her hand.) Every morning when the sun came up (the sun crosses the room, smiling happily), old man scarecrow went out to the cornfield. He waved his arms and made terrible faces. Every day the crows cried, "Caw! Caw! Caw!" (The crows fly in and circle around the corn, then one by one each crow sees old man scarecrow, screams, and flies away.) He made such terrible faces that the crows would fly far, far away.

Every night, when the sun went down (the sun walks back across the playing space, smiling happily) old man scarecrow would go home (he goes to the mother and the little boy), and there he would teach little scarecrow boy how to make fierce faces. (He makes a face and the little boy imitates it.) One—two—three—four—five—six. Old lady scarecrow would clap her hands and whistle through her teeth at the looks of them.

One day after the little boy knew all six of his father's terrible faces so that he could make them one after the other, he decided to go out into the cornfield by himself and frighten a crow. (The scarecrows have closed their eyes in sleep.) So the next morning, before the sun was up, or old man scarecrow was up, or old lady scarecrow was up, little scarecrow boy got out of bed. (He steps forward cautiously.) He dressed and went quietly ... (he takes one step) ... quietly ... quietly ... quietly out of the house and over to the cornfield. He stood in his father's place. (He takes his father's position in the cornfield.)

It was a fine morning and the sun came up. (The sun crosses the stage, smiling.) Far away over the trees, crows flew around and around. Little scarecrow boy waved his arms through the air. He had never felt fiercer in all his life. (The little boy waves his arms and makes faces.) In the distance the "caws" of the crows were heard. (The leader enters and all of the crows fly in, circling the corn. One crow at a times sees the little boy, screams and flies off. Only the leader is left and he is not afraid. He starts toward the little scarecrow boy.)

"Oh!" said little scarecrow boy, and he made his first fierce face. Still came flying the big crow.

"Oh, Oh!" said little scarecrow boy and he made his second fierce face. Still came flying the big crow. He made his third fierce face. "Oh, oh, oh!" It was time to go. (He jumps down and runs in a circle, covering very little ground but running hard. The crow flies after him.)

So, little scarecrow boy ran and ran. Then he stopped. He made his fourth fierce face. Still came flying the big old crow. He ran and he ran and he made his fifth fierce face. Still came flying the big old crow. Little scarecrow boy had only one face left now. So he stopped. He held his arms wide above his head and he made his sixth fierce face. (As he makes his sixth face, the old crow stops, backs up, then turns and flies off.)

Whoa! The old crow stopped and then flew backwards through the air, feathers flying everywhere, until there wasn't even the shadow of a crow in the cornfield. A scarecrow at last!

(Meanwhile, old man scarecrow walks to his side.) Then little scarecrow boy saw a shadow in front of him and he looked around. There beside him stood his father. Old man scarecrow was proud of his little boy and shook his scarecrow hand. (They shake hands.) Old lady scarecrow was proud of her little boy, who could make all six fierce faces. (She pats him fondly.) And when little scarecrow boy grew up, he was the fiercest scarecrow in all the cornfields in all the world.

This is a somewhat shortened version of the story, with action suggested by one group of children. All took turns playing the different parts and had a grand time creating fierce faces. One child read the story while the others acted in pantomime. The scarecrow offered an opportunity to experiment with physical movement in addition to simple characterizations. Stories read while acted help the more timid or inexperienced children to follow the plot and feel the sense of accomplishment that comes from successful dramatization.

Performing a story in mime as it is read by the teacher or single reader is, however, not restricted to younger children; it can be a challenging assignment for the older ones, whose skills are more developed. Whereas short exercises in pantomime are good practice, most students welcome an opportunity to try something longer and more demanding. There is much excellent material available to enact in this way, but the following story has a number of features that make it an especially interesting and moving experience. First of all, *The Snow Walker* is a beautiful piece of literature that provides the player with much more than a gripping narrative. In order to tell it with clarity and compassion, believable characters must be developed and a picture of life in the frozen North created as a background.

The Snow Walker is a story that will gain richness through discussion and further reading of the author's work.[3] Reading other Eskimo stories will build understanding, just as pictures of the desolate northern landscape with its igloos and frozen rivers will help players visualize the long trip over the icy tundra. An entire class can participate in the action with frequent changing of parts so that all who want to try the longer roles will have an opportunity to do so.

THE SNOW WALKER
FARLEY MOWAT

I am Ootek, and my people are the people of the River of Men. Once they were many and the land was good to them, but now it is my time and we have almost forgotten how it was in the old days when the deer flooded the tundra and gave us life. Hunger comes often now, and the deer but seldom. No one now lives by the big lakes to the north although when my father was young the tents of the people stood everywhere along those shores. I have travelled down the River to the big lakes but when I reached them I turned back from an empty land.

Only the spirits who remain in those places remember the times when a man might stand on a hill as the deer passed by and though he looked to the east or the west, the south or the north, he would see only their brown backs and hear only the clicking of antlers and the grumbling of their full bellies.

The great herds have gone . . . and so we who lived by the deer must follow the Snow Walker even as my father followed him in the spring of the year. After the ice had grown thick on the lakes last winter there came a time of storms and for many days we stayed in our igloos. The children grew quiet and did not play and the old people sometimes looked toward the door tunnels with shadowed eyes. The snows mounted over the top of the igloos until we could not even venture out to look for willow twigs to burn. The igloos were cold and dark for we had long since eaten the deer fat that should

3. From *The Snow Walker* (Toronto: McClelland and Stewart, Ltd., 1975), pp. 131–142.

have been burned in the lamps. So little food remained to us from the few southbound deer we had been able to kill in the autumn that the dogs were beginning to starve, and we ourselves were not much better off. . . .

After a long time the blizzards ended and the weather grew calm and cold. All the people had survived though some of the old ones could hardly stir from the sleeping ledges. We younger men took the few remaining dogs and went searching for meat we had cached on the Flat Country. We found only a little because most of the caches were buried under hard drifts that had mounted so high they had covered the markers.

The women and children helped to keep famine at bay by digging under the drifts near the igloos for fish bones and scraps of old hides with which to make soup. By such means we hoped to cling to our lives until the warm winds and the lengthening days might bring the deer back to our country from the forested lands in the south.

But long after the time when the ice should have started to rot, it still lay heavy and hard on the rivers and lakes, and the days seemed to grow colder again until we wondered if winter would ever come to an end. We ate all the food we had, and the deer did not come. We waited . . . for there was nothing else we could do. We ate the last of our dogs, and still the deer did not come.

One day the men gathered in Owliktuk's snowhouse. His wife, Kunee, sat on the ledge with her child in her arms, and the child was dead. We knew it could not be very long before many of the women were nursing such sorrow. My cousin, Ohoto, put some thoughts into words.

"Perhaps people should go away from this place now. Perhaps they might go south to the place where the white man has come to live. It might happen that he would have food he would give us."

The white man had only recently come to live on the edge of our country, to trade with us for foxes. It was a long way to his place and only Ohoto had been there before. Since we had no dogs, we knew we would have to carry everything on our backs, and the children and old people would not be able to ride on the sleds as they should. We knew some of them would not see the white man's place . . . but the child of Owliktuk and Kunee was dead. We decided to go.

The women rolled up a few skins to use for tent shelters and sleeping robes; the children carried whatever they could, and we men slung our packs on our shoulders and we left our camp by the River and set out into the south.

Soon after we started, the sun turned warm and for five days we walked up to our knees in melting snow. My wife's mother had lost count of the years she had lived, yet she walked with the rest and still helped to pitch camp at the end of each day. But on the fifth night she did not offer to help. She sat by herself with her back to a rock and spoke to none except Ilupalee, my daughter. She called the child to her.

From a distance I watched and listened as the old woman put her bony hands on my daughter's head. I heard her softly singing her spirit song to the child, the secret song she had received from her mother's mother and with which she could summon her helping spirit. Then I knew she had made up her mind what she must do.

It was her choice, and my wife and I could say nothing about it, not even tell her of the sorrow we felt. During the night, she went from camp. None saw her go. We did not speak her name after that for one may not use the name of a person who has gone out on the land to seek the Snow Walker until the name and the spirit it bears can be given again to a newly born child.

The next day we reached the Little Stick country which borders the forests. Here there was plenty of wood so we could at least have fires where we could warm ourselves. Toward evening we overtook Ohoto's family squatted beside a fire, melting water to drink since there was no food. Ohoto told me his daughter had fallen and could not rise again so they had to make camp. When the rest of the people came up, it was clear that many, both young and old, could not go on; and Ohoto thought we were still two or three days distant from the home of the white man.

I had been carrying Ilupalee on my shoulders most of the day and was so tired I could not think. I lay down by the fire and shut my eyes. Ilupalee lay beside me and whispered in my ear:

"A white hare is sitting behind the little trees over there."

I thought this was only a dream born out of hunger so I did not open my eyes. But she whispered again:

"It's a big, fat hare. She Who Walked said it was there."

This time I opened my eyes and got to my knees, I looked where she pointed and could see nothing except a patch of dwarf spruce. All the same I unslung the rifle from my pack and walked toward the trees.

Indeed it was there!

But one hare does not provide more than a mouthful of food for twenty-five people so we had to think carefully what should be done. It was decided that the three strongest men—Alekahaw, Ohoto and I—would eat the hare and thereby gain strength to go on to the white man's place. My wife built a fire apart from the camp so the others would not have to endure the smell of meat cooking. She boiled the hare and we three men shared it; but we left the guts, bones, skin and the head to make soup for the children.

We walked away from the camp along a frozen stream so we would not have to wade through the soft snow. My skin boots were thin and torn and my feet were soon numb because at each step we broke through the thin crust above the thaw water. I did not mind because my stomach was warm.

It was growing dark on the second day when we came to a clearing in a spruce woods on the shore of a lake where the white man had his house. His dogs heard us and howled and when we came near he opened the door and waited with the bright light of a lamp shining behind him. We stopped and stood where we were because he was a stranger, and a white man, and we had met very few white men. He spoke to us, but not in our language, so we could not reply. When he spoke again, very loudly, and still we did not reply, he went back into his house.

It grew cold as the darkness settled around us, and our wet boots became stiff as they froze. I thought of Ilupalee and wanted very much to do something, but did not know what we should do.

After a long time the door opened again and the white man came out. He was wiping his beard. We smelled hot fat from his house but he shut the door behind him and motioned us to follow him to another small cabin.

He unlocked the door and we went in. He lit a lamp and hung it on a rafter so we could see that the walls were piled high with boxes, but we looked hardest at the many bags of flour sacked in front of a table. We started to smile for we believed the white man understood our needs and would help us. We stood under the lamp watching the flame reflect light from the beads of cold fat still clinging to the white man's beard, and we gave ourselves up to the joy growing within us.

The white man opened a drawer in the table and took out a handful of small sticks of the kind used to show how much a trapper can have in exchange for the fox pelts he brings. Holding these sticks in his hand he spoke sharply in his own tongue. When we did not reply he went to a wall of the cabin, took down a fox pelt and laid it before us; then he pointed to the carrying bags which were slung on our shoulders.

The joy went out of us then. I made signs to show we had no fox pelts to trade, and Alekahaw opened his bag to show how empty it was. The white man's eyes were of a strange green colour and I could not look into them. I looked at his forehead instead while I waited for whatever must happen. Slowly his face grew red with anger, then he threw the sticks back in the drawer and began to shout at us.

Anger is something we fear since an angry man may do foolish and dangerous things. When I saw the anger in this man's face, I backed to the door. I wanted to go from that place but Alekahaw was braver than me. He stood where he was and tried to explain to the white man how it was at the camp where the rest of the people were starving. He pulled up his *holiktu* so the man could see for himself how Alekahaw's ribs stuck out from his body.

Alekahaw touched his own face to show how tightly the skin was stretched over the bones.

The white man shrugged his shoulders. Perhaps he did not understand. He began turning down the flame in the lamp and we knew he would soon go back to his house, then the door would be shut against the needs of the people. Quickly Ohoto pulled two boxes of shells out of his bag. These were the last bullets he had and he had been saving them against the time when the deer would return. Now he put them on the table and pointed to the flour.

The white man shook his head. He was still angry. He picked up the lamp and started to go to the door. Alekahaw and Ohoto stepped out of his way, but something happened inside me and although I was frightened I would not let him pass.

He kept his eyes on me but he stretched out one hand behind him until it came to rest on a rifle hung on the wall. I could not make way for him then because I was afraid to move while he had his hand on that gun.

So we all stood still for a while. At last he picked up a small sack of flour and threw it over the table to fall at Ohoto's feet. Then he took the rifle, shoved me aside with the barrel, pushed the door open and told us to leave. We went outside and watched as he locked the door. We watched as he went back into the house.

A little while later we saw him looking out of his window. He still had the rifle in his hand so we knew there was no use remaining. We walked away into the darkness.

Day was breaking when we got back to the camp. Those who were still able to stand gathered in front of Owliktuk's tent and we told what we had to tell. We showed them the sack of flour which was so small a child could easily lift it.

Owliktuk spoke against us, blaming us because we had not taken the food that was needed. He said we could have repaid the white man next winter when the foxes were again good. But if we had tried to take food from the white man there would have been killing. Perhaps Owliktuk only spoke as he did because his second child was now going from him. The rest of the people said nothing but returned to their families with the small portion of flour which were their shares.

I carried my father's share to his tent. Although he had once been the best hunter among us and only the previous year had fathered a child on his third wife, he had aged very much during the winter and his legs had weakened until he could barely walk. When I told him what had happened and gave him the flour for himself, my stepmother and the small child, he smiled and said, "One has a son who knows what may be done and what may not be done. One is glad no blood was shed. It may be that things will get better."

It did not seem he was right about that. We had made the journey to the white man's place and it had come to so little. Now we were too weak to go back to our own land. And on the second day after we three men returned to the camp, the Snow Walker came to the children Aljut and Uktilohik. There was no mourning for them because those who still lived had no sorrow to spend on the dead.

Each day thereafter the sun shone more brightly. Spring was upon us and still the deer had not returned. One day I tried to visit my father to see how it was with him but I was unable to walk that short distance. I crawled back into my own tent where my wife sat rocking herself with her eyes closed and her mouth wide and gasping. Beside her my daughter sometimes wailed in the thin, dry voice of an old woman. I lay down on some brush inside the flap and together we waited.

Perhaps it was the next day when I awakened to hear someone shout. The shout came again and the voice seemed familiar and the words set my heart racing.

"Here is a deer!"

I caught my rifle by the muzzle and crawled into the morning sunlight. At first I was blinded but after a moment I saw a fine buck standing a little way off with his head high, watching the camp.

I raised my rifle with hands that could not seem to hold it. The sights wavered and the deer seemed to slide up and down the barrel. Clutching it tight, I took aim and fired. The buck flung up his forefeet and leapt toward the sheltering trees. I fired again and again until the rifle was empty but the shots all went wide. I could see them kicking up little spouts of snow but I could not hear the hard thud that tells a hunter when he has hit.

The deer ran away ... but just when it was about to disappear in the trees it stumbled and fell. With all my strength I willed it not to get up. The deer's spirit struggled with mine until slowly the buck sank on his side.

Some of the people had come out into the sunlight and with weak voices were asking each other who had been shooting.

"Get out your knives!" I cried as loud as I could. "One has killed a fat deer!"

At my words even those who could not walk found enough strength. People wept as they stumbled and staggered toward the deer carcass. The first ones to reach it clung to it like flies, sucking the blood that still bubbled out of its wound. They moved away after a while to make room for others, sobbing with pain and holding their hands to their bellies.

The women sliced into the carcass with their round knives and tore out the entrails, snatching at the little scraps of white fat that clung to the guts. The men cut off the legs at the lower joints and cracked the bones to get at the marrow. In only a short time the buck was changed into a pile of bones, steaming meat and red snow.

It grew warm under the sun and some people began returning to the shelters with meat for those who were too weak to move. Then I remembered that I had seen no one from the tent of my father, so I made my way there dragging part of a forequarter. The flap was down over the door but I pushed it aside and crawled in. My stepmother was lying under a piece of hairless old hide and she was holding her child. Although they scarcely breathed they were both still alive. But of my father there was no sign.

I cut off a piece of meat, chewed it soft then pushed it into my stepmother's mouth and rubbed her neck till she swallowed. Then I took my little stepbrother to Ohoto's shelter, which was not far away, and Ohoto's wife made blood soup and fed the child with it while I went back to my father's place and chewed more meat for my stepmother. Before I left here, she was able to eat by herself but she could not yet talk so I did not know where my father had gone.

When I returned to my own place, I found my wife had roasted some ribs and boiled the deer's tongue. Ilupalee lay wrapped in a fresh piece of deerskin and it was good to hear her whimper with the pain of a full belly. That whole night we passed in eating and by the next day nothing of the buck remained for the ravens and foxes. The bones had been crushed and boiled for their fat, the skull had been opened and cleaned, and even the hooves had been made into soup. The strength of the buck had passed into the people and we were ready to return to our country.

Next day when I went to my father's tent my stepmother was able to stand. I told her that she and the child would now come and live in my tent, then I said, "One looks about but does not see one's father."

"*Eeee,*" she replied. "He would not eat the flour you brought. He gave it to me and the child. Afterwards he went on the land to meet the Snow Walker."

A little while later I told Ohoto about the voice I had heard. No one else had heard it and none of the people in the camp except me had known there was a deer nearby. Together Ohoto and I followed the marks where my father had stumbled down to the river, then crawled north on the ice. His tracks disappeared at a bend where the current had opened in a hole, but close by we found the tracks of a deer. We followed the tracks until they circled back to the camp and came to an end at the place where I had killed the big buck. Neither Ohoto nor I said anything but we both knew whose voice I heard.

In the autumn my wife will give birth to another child, and then the name of him who went to meet the Snow Walker that we might continue to live will surely be spoken again by the River of Men.

I have seen some superb work done in pantomime by high school students, who loved the medium as an art form and whose disciplined study of it made good theatre. Few groups can or will carry it that far, but working in mime with good literature as a base benefits players and spectators alike.

Although *The Snow Walker* is suggested here as rich material for pantomime, there is no reason why it cannot also be used for improvisation. The many scenes and characters offer opportunities for a large group of children; the locale and way of life call for considerable background study. However, one does not want to lose the literary value of the story, which was the reason for its inclusion in this chapter and which can best be realized if it could be read aloud. In view of the content, however, it is suggested that creating dialogue will add depth to understanding. Most children are fascinated with the way of life of people living in the frozen North; a study of the geography, customs, occupations, hardships, and beliefs of the region will heighten this interest. What does the title *The Snow Walker* mean? There is as much material here for discussion as there is for enactment.

Summary

Pantomime, while good practice at any time, is usually the most satisfactory way of beginning work in creative drama. Although it is not necessary to follow a prescribed program of exercises, it is easier for many groups to begin with familiar activities and then move on to mood or feeling, and finally characterization. By starting with movement and then pantomime, the players learn to express themselves through bodily action, without the additional problem of dialogue. Younger children accept this as a natural means of expression, and older children and adults find it easier to begin with pantomime than with improvisation or formal acting. Pantomime sharpens perception and stimulates the imagination as the players try to remember how actions are done and what objects are really like, as to size, weight, and shape. Recalling emotion demands concentration and involvement: How do you feel when you are happy, tired, angry, excited, anxious, etc.? Close observation of people is a means of developing believable characters whose bearing, movement, and gestures belong to them and whose behavior seems appropriate. Although pantomime is considered here as a medium of expression, it may become an art form in itself. Mimes like Marcel Marceau have demonstrated its power to communicate with people of all ages and backgrounds, when a high level of artistry is achieved.

5
Improvisation: Characters Move and Speak

*I*mprovisation is difficult at first. Dialogue does not flow easily, even when it has been preceded by much work in pantomime and a thorough understanding of the situation or story. With practice, however, words do begin to come, and the players discover the possibilities of character development when oral language is added. Dialogue is apt to be brief and scanty at first, but usually begins to flow rapidly once the children become accustomed to it. Players aged seven and older enjoy the opportunity of using words to further a story and more fully describe the characters they are portraying. It is a good idea to begin with simple situations so as to get accustomed to using dialogue before attempting more ambitious material.

Many of the situations suggested in the previous chapter on pantomime can be used, although they were designed with movement in mind. Frequently, children

94

Children improvise. (*Courtesy of Coleman Jennings and Alan Smith, University of Texas in Austin.*)

will begin to add dialogue of their own free will, as they feel the need of expressing ideas in words. When this happens, the leader accepts it as a natural progression from one step to the next. Younger children, players for whom English is a second language, or older students who lack self-confidence, will usually wait until they are urged to try adding dialogue. The teacher will not expect too much and will accept whatever is offered, knowing that more will be forthcoming the next time. The author recalls a sixth-grade class that was acting *The Story of Roland*. Although fond of the story and well oriented to the background, the first time it was played, one scene went like this: "Hello, Roland."—"Will you marry me?"—"Why, Roland, I'd love to." The final playing, after several had tried and discussed it, was a charming scene with all the necessary exposition and appropriate vocabulary.

Since even the simplest stories present complications for the beginner, some preliminary exercises are suggested. The purpose here is to give emphasis to dialogue rather than to the memorization or plot. Sometimes just one scene of a story can be improvised to advantage. The teacher will feel his way, and if interest is sustained better with excerpts from favorite stories, he may prefer them to exercises.

Sounds, incidentally, can stimulate imagination and lead the listener to the creation of an improvisation. For example, the teacher can beat a drum or tambourine, knock, ring bells, or make any other kind of sound. This works particularly well with younger children, but is also a good exercise to use from time to time with those who are older.

Simple Improvisations Based on Situations

The following improvisations may be done with various age levels, although the backgrounds of the players will determine the appropriateness. In some cases, the situations are better for older players.

1. You are a group of people in a subway station. It is six o'clock in the evening. In the center is a newsstand, at which newspapers, magazines, and candy are sold. It is run by a woman who has been there for many years. She knows the passengers who ride regularly, and is interested in them and all the details of their daily lives. Decide on who you are going to be—a secretary, an actress, a businessman, a cleaning woman, a shopper, a policeman, a teenager, a stranger in town, etc. Then let us know all about you through your conversation with the proprietor of the newsstand, while you are waiting for your train.

2. The scene is a toyshop on Christmas Eve. It is midnight, and the owner has just closed the door and gone home. At the stroke of twelve the toys come alive and talk together. They may consist of a toy soldier, a rag doll, a beautiful doll, a clown, a teddy bear, a jack-in-the-box, etc. Let us know by your conversation and movements who you are and why you were not sold.

3. You are a committee from your school, assigned the job of selecting a gift for your teacher, who is retiring. Each of you has an idea of what you think is appropriate, and you have only a certain amount of money to spend. The scene takes place in a large gift shop. Let us know who you are and what you want to buy. What is the decision you finally make?

4. This improvisation is good on a high school or college level. The scene is a meeting of the student council. You have the job of questioning a student who is reported to have stolen the examination questions for a history class. He is brought before you, and you ask him questions. What is each one of you like? How do you handle the situation? Is he guilty or not? What is your final decision and what do you do about it?

5. This improvisation is also probably better for older students, although it has been done by ten- and eleven-year-olds. You are a group of people returning for your thirty-fifth reunion from high school or college. Who are you? What has happened to you since you last saw each other? Have you been happy, successful, or unsuccessful? Let us know all about you through your conversation.

6. You are a group of young women in a suburban community. One of you has invited the new neighbor in to meet the rest of the group. Coffee is served and you talk together. All seems to be going well when the hostess notices that an expensive silver tray is missing from her coffee table. One by one, you begin to suspect the newcomer. Why do you suspect her? Did she take it? Is it found? Where? If she took it, why did she? Let us know what each one of you is like by your reaction to this situation. How does it turn out?

7. This improvisation is good with children. You are a group of children in an apartment house. It is Valentine's Day, and you are gathered in the front hall to look at and count your valentines. You see one child in the building going to her mailbox, and you notice that she did not receive any. How do you feel about this? What is each one of you like? Do you decide to do anything about it? If so, what do you do?

8. You are a group of children who live near a very cross, elderly woman. She chases you away from her property whenever you come near it. This particular morning, you see that someone has broken her fence

and ruined many of her flowers. For the first time you feel sorry for her. What do you do? How does she react to you? Do you all agree as to whether you should help her? Do your actions change her attitude toward children?

9. A new child has entered your class at school. He does not speak English, and some of the children laugh at him. When recess comes, you all go out to the playground. How does each of you treat him? How does he react to you? You are all different so you will each feel differently toward him. Do you finally take him in, or do you exclude him? Try changing roles so that different players have the experience of trying the part of the new child. Does the improvisation change as you all think more about the situation?

10. The scene is a small bakery. One of you is the owner, one of you a child who helps him on Saturdays, and another is a beggar. It is not busy this particular morning so the owner goes out for coffee. While he is gone, a beggar comes into the shop and asks for some bread. The girl (or boy) knows that she should not give away the bread but she feels sorry for the old man. What do they say to each other? What does the owner say when he comes back? Try changing parts in this improvisation to see if it will turn out differently.

Improvisations Suggested by Objects

Not only situations and stories motivate improvisation; some very imaginative results can be obtained by the use of objects or properties. Try some of the following suggestions as springboards.

1. An object (any object) is put in the center of the circle where all the players can see it. Look at it, without speaking, for three or four minutes. Try to think of a story about it. Where might it have come from? How did it get here? What does it make *you* think of? Each of you will have an original story to tell; tell it.

2. This time, divide the class into groups of three or four. An object is presented, and each group is asked to make up an improvisation about it. Perhaps the property is a wooden spoon. When used with one class, the following ideas were suggested and these situations improvised.

   a. The scene was a settler's cabin over one hundred years ago. The family had very few household items and so they prized each one. Among them was a wooden spoon. In this scene it was used to stir batter for cornbread, and then washed and put carefully away.

   b. The scene was a museum and the spoon, a relic from the Indians who once inhabited the region. The characters were the curator of the museum and two children who were visiting it. The curator answered their questions by telling the history of the spoon.

c. The scene was a cave. Three boys were hiking and found the spoon. They used it to dig, and discovered an old box of coins that had been buried there. They took the old spoon home with them for good luck.

d. The scene was an industrial arts class. The boys were making things of wood, and a blind boy carved the spoon. It was so well done that the teacher said she would display it as one of the best things made in her class that year.

e. The scene was a dump. The old wooden spoon was the speaker as he told the other pieces of trash how he had been used and handed down from one generation to the next. Finally his family became rich and threw him away because they considered him too old and ugly to be of further use to them.

Any object can function as a springboard, and no two groups will see it in exactly the same way. Among the kinds of properties that suggest ideas are:

a velvet jewelry box   an old hat
an artificial rose   a cane
a foreign coin   a quill pen
a feather duster   an old dog leash
a bell

An improvisation with unusual interest was developed from a whistle by a very imaginative group of ten-year-olds. They decided that it was a policeman's whistle, made of silver and bearing an inscription. They laid the scene in his home on the day of his retirement from the force; the characters were the policeman, his wife, and his grandson. The policeman came in that evening, took off his whistle, looked at it nostalgically a long time, then laid it on the supper table. His grandson, coming into the room at that point, begged him to tell the story again of how he had received it. As the story began, there was a throwback scene, in which the policeman was rescuing a child from burning in a bonfire many years before. He was honored for his bravery and given an inscribed silver whistle, which he treasured for the rest of his life. At the finish of the story, the throwback scene faded and some neighbors came in with a cake and presents for him. The improvisation was effective both in its good dramatic structure and the reality of the characterizations.

Not every group is able to develop an improvisation to this degree, but occasionally one will, and when it happens, it is an inspiration to the rest of the class. Incidentally, it is nearly always the result of the play's having been based on familiar material so that the players are sure of the dialogue and can identify easily with the characters. Again, respect for their background and acceptance of the ideas that come out of it not only make for comfort but also bring forth ideas that the teacher probably would not have thought of. Children of foreign background have a wealth of material on which to draw, but too often it remains an untapped source because they have been made to feel that it is unworthy of consideration. Both the stories they have been told and the details of their everyday life contain the basic ingredients of drama. For example, one group of boys, who lived in a housing project, played a scene in an elevator. The situation was simple but had reality. Two boys, having nothing to do, decided to ride up and down in the elevator, angering the tenants and almost causing a tragedy because one man on a high floor was ill and waiting for the doctor. Whether or not this had been an actual experience the teacher did not know, but the situation contained reality, humor, and drama, with characters who were believable.

One final example of the use of properties was an improvisation done by a group of high school girls. They had been asked by the teacher to empty their purses and select the six most unusual or interesting objects. The objects they finally chose were a newspaper clipping, a snapshot, a lipstick in a Japanese case, a key ring with a red charm, a pocket knife, and a purse flashlight. Within minutes they had created a mystery, prompted by and making use of every one of the properties they selected. There were six players, and their preparation time was approximately ten minutes.

Improvisations from Costumes

Similar to the use of objects or props, and equally effective in stimulating ideas, are pieces of costume. Such garments as hats, capes, aprons, shawls, tailcoats, and jewelry will suggest different kinds of characters. Innumerable examples could be given of situations that grew from characters developed this way. For example, to one boy, a tailcoat suggested a musician, down on his luck and playing his violin on a street corner for pennies. A feathered hat helped a little girl create a lady of fashionable pretensions and become a comic character in her extravagant dress and poor taste. A shawl suggested witches, grandmothers, people in disguise, or a scene laid in very cold weather.

It is wise for the teacher on any level, working anywhere, to keep a supply of simple and sturdy costumes available for this kind of use. If children experience difficulty in getting into character, a piece of a costume may sometimes be all that is needed to provide the necessary incentive. Costume used in this way is not dressing the part, but an aid to more imaginative thinking.

Improvisations from Characters

In an earlier chapter, an illustration was given of an improvisation created from a character. This is a successful method of starting, as well as a way of encouraging, observation. If the group is small and has had some experience, original monologues are good practice and fun for the players. If the class is large, however, this is probably not a wise assignment, unless the monologues are kept short.

To create from a character, the teacher can ask each member of the class to think of a particularly interesting person she has noticed that day, or sometime during the week. This is followed by questions as to:

who was he?
what was he doing?
did he have anything to say?
how did he dress?
how old was he?
what special thing about him attracted your attention?

One girl offered as a character a woman who served the hot vegetables in her school cafeteria. Although the woman was bad-tempered, the girl had observed that she was always extremely generous in her servings and did her job more efficiently than anyone else. The group, which chose her as a heroine for their story, decided that she might have been a refugee. Because she had experienced hunger during that period in her life, she was determined that all plates would be generously filled, now that food was available. Her irritability they attributed to her own unhappy experiences and her separation from her family. The scene that the children improvised, using this particular character as an inspiration, was thoughtful, sympathetic, and interesting to the class.

Another improvisation based on an actual person was the story of an elderly woman whom one child noticed every day, sitting on the front porch of her house. The group, which chose her for a heroine, decided that she was really very rich but miserly, and was saving her money for the day when her son came home. They agreed that he had gone into the army several years before and had not returned. Although he had been reported missing, his mother clung to the hope that he would come back some day, and so she sat on the porch—waiting by day, and counting her money by night. The group decided to have him return, so the story had a happy ending.

A fantasy was the result of another character study. Two of the children described a well-dressed old man whom they saw coming home every morning around eight o'clock. They decided that he must have an interesting occupation and so made him a wizard, who helped the good people and punished the evil through the power of his magic cane. This became a modern fairy tale filled with highly imaginative incidents.

Improvisations from Clues

Older players enjoy creating improvisations from clues. The following exercises can be done to build characters. With these clues, what kinds of persons do you imagine? In an improvisation, create a character who is suggested by:

raw vegetables	hat
cane	fur piece
book	checkbook
Coca-Cola	belt
hair dryer	stick
television	bag

The following exercise is good for experienced players. Select a place where a number of strangers might gather. This could be an air terminal, a bus stop, a grocery store in the morning before it opens, a parking lot, a picket line. One person enters and is soon joined by another. They get into a conversation. Another comes in and then another, until a large group has assembled. The class can decide in advance who each will be; or, what is harder, come into the group as the character, making those already there decide who he is. This has wonderful possibilities for character study and simple plot development.

Biography

This exercise is suggested for older players. The leader chooses a character (real or fictional) and describes her briefly. After some general discussion, the class is divided into five or six small groups, each representing a period in the character's life. Each group then plans its interpretation of the character at a given point in time. The periods could be:

birth to age six
six to twelve years
the teens
the twenties
the thirties or forties
later life
old age

Obviously, the persons in the first scene would have to be members of the family, neighbors, or others. The character about whom the scenes are built need not actually appear in each one, but the scenes must be related in some way to her life. This is an excellent way to study a character; if an historical person is used, it will lead to research. If it is not a real person, it is a challenge to the imagination. "Biography" implies not only representing the character but other significant persons in her life.

Improvisations for Two

Try to imagine yourself in the following situations:

1. You receive a letter in the mail, telling you that you have won first prize in a poster contest. Tell your mother the good news.
2. Your dog has been hit by a car. When you come home from school, your mother meets you and tells you what has happened.
3. You have been warned not to go down a dark street by yourself at night. This evening, however, you are in a hurry and decide to go anyway because it is a shortcut. About halfway down the block you hear footsteps behind you. You look over your shoulder and see someone hurrying toward you. You hurry also; so does the other person. You decide to slow up; so does the person who is following you. By this time you are frightened, but it is too late to turn back. You start to run and so does he. You run faster; so does he. Finally, you reach the corner, but the light has turned red. As you stand there alone waiting for it to change, a friend comes up. It was the friend who was following you, but neither of you recognized the other, and both of you had been running to get to the brightly lit corner. You have a good laugh when you discover each other.
4. You are trying on shoes to take to camp. The clerk does not have what you want and tries to sell you something else. Should you take her suggestion?
5. You are moving to a new neighborhood today. Your best friend comes around to say good-bye to you. Although you are looking forward to your new home, you are sad to leave the old neighborhood. What do you say?
6. Your aunt, whom you have never met, has come for a visit. You answer the door. What is she like? What do you say to each other?
7. You have found a kitten that you want very much to keep, but your mother has said you cannot have a pet. Try to persuade her that the kitten needs a home.

Boys in New Canaan Country School improvise a story. (*Courtesy of Mary Perrine.*)

8. A salesman comes to the door. He insists on demonstrating a vacuum cleaner, although you tell him you have one. How do you handle the situation?
9. You have been wanting ice skates for your birthday. Your grandmother, who always selects the right presents, comes to the door with a box in her hands. When you open it, you find it contains stationery. What do you say to each other?
10. You wore your sister's bracelet on a picnic, and when you get home, discover you have lost it. Now you must tell her what happened.

Improvisations for Three

1. You and your friend are going to the playground. Your little sister wants to go with you, but if she does, you cannot go into the area reserved for older children. What do you do?
2. You are delivering papers. You throw one toward a house, but instead of landing on the porch, it breaks a window. Both the man and his wife come to see what has happened.
3. You and your friend find a five dollar bill on the sidewalk. You want to keep it, but at this moment a woman comes down the street looking for something. You are certain she has lost it. What do you do?
4. You tried out for a leading part in a play but were put in the chorus. You try to be a good sport when you talk to the teacher and to the girl who was cast in the part you wanted.
5. Your mother has just given your old rag doll to your younger cousin, who is visiting you. Neither of them knows how much the doll means to you. You try to pretend it is all right.
6. You see the girl across the aisle cheat on a test when the teacher steps out of the room. He suspects that there has been cheating and asks you and the girl to stay after class so he can find out about it. What does each one of you say and do?
7. You are delivering flowers for a neighborhood florist. On this particular day you are carrying a very large plant, and you lose the address. You think you remember it, however, so you go to what you hope is the right door. It is the wrong address, but the person who answers the door accepts the plant, then discovers the mistake. You have left by that time. How do all three of you work things out?
8. Three of you are getting refreshments ready for a party. It is said that "too many cooks spoil the broth." This happens when all of you put salt in the chocolate pudding, thinking that it is sugar and needs sweetening. This can be a very funny situation. How do you handle it?

9. You are falsely accused of cheating on an examination. You are angry and upset. The three persons involved are your teacher, the principal of the school, and you.

10. Your two best friends are running for president of your class. You meet on the playground. What do you say? How do you handle the situation?

11. You are in a laundromat, waiting for a washing machine. One is ready, except that the person who put the clothes in it has not returned for them. One woman tells you that you have a right to remove the clothes and use the machine. Another says that you should wait, because the owner is coming back in a few minutes. Meanwhile, you are in a hurry. What do you decide to do? Does the person who left the clothes return soon? How does the situation turn out? (This has several possible endings.)

12. You are at the checkout counter of a supermarket. The cashier is checking off your items when you realize that you forgot to get the milk. You run back for it. This annoys the person behind you. Then you discover that you don't have enough money to pay the bill so you have to return some items. By this time the cashier and two people behind you are annoyed. You put the things back on the shelves and return, but when you pick up your shopping bag, which the cashier has packed for you, it splits open. Now you are angry, too. This makes everyone laugh, including you; suddenly the annoying situation becomes funny!

Other Suggestions

Unfinished stories can also be used to stimulate thinking. If the teacher introduces a character and sets the scene, the group is given the problem of completing the story. Although this is more an exercise in plotting than in character, the action is motivated by the character: an interesting character makes for an interesting plot.

One club group showed an unusual interest in holidays, so the teacher used this as a springboard for the entire year. She brought in stories about Hallowe'en, Thanksgiving, Christmas, New Year's Day, Valentine's Day, St. Patrick's Day, April Fool's Day, Memorial Day, and the Fourth of July. Sometimes the group acted out the stories she read to them; sometimes they made up stories of their own, suggested by the occasion. One day they observed that there was no holiday in August. The result was an original play, which they called *A Holiday for August.* It was to be a festival of children's games, which developed into a particularly attractive summer pageant. August was the narrator, who began by telling of his disappointment that no one had ever thought to put a holiday in his month. At the conclusion, he expressed his joy that the children had made him special with a festival of games played in his honor.

Television, films, and open discussion of heretofore taboo topics have affected the subject matter that has come into creative drama sessions in recent years. While most children still enjoy working on the material the teacher brings in, their own experiences and problems often surface when they are given a chance to express their own ideas. Broken homes, divorce, racial discrimination, illness and death, values, and social issues of all kinds can be disturbing problems to children, problems the leader must be prepared to deal with if or when they come up. The following improvisations are purposely open-ended in order to allow for the players' interpretations.

"You End It!" Improvisations

1. The personnel officer in a store is faced with a difficult decision. Business has been poor lately and the president of the company has said that two employees must be let go. The personnel officer calls in the last three people he hired and discusses the problem with them. After they leave, he must decide which two will go and which one to keep. The three are then called back into the office and told. The decision has been made on the basis of what has been said, the quality of the work, and what was expected of them.

2. The scene is a courtroom. A woman has been apprehended for selling on a street corner what is suspected of being stolen jewelry. Two or three witnesses are called up front to tell what they have seen or know. Then the woman is called up to give her explanation of how she came by the articles she was offering for sale. The judge decides whether or not she is guilty of having stolen property.

3. Take a well-known story and instead of ending it as written, stop before the final action and end it differently. For example, take *Rumplestiltskin*. Imagine that the miller's daughter does not spin straw into gold. How would you end the story?

4. A small group of people are hiking in a national park. It is a beautiful day and they go farther into the forest than they had intended. Suddenly they realize that is it growing dark. They turn to go back, but discover there are two paths and they cannot remember which one they had been following to arrive at their present location. A decision must be made quickly: one path will lead them back to their campsite; the other may be fraught with danger and they will be hopelessly lost. What will they decide to do? Why do they make this decision?

5. The scene is a country fair. A raffle is being held and the person calling

the winning numbers announces the number for the grand prize. Two people rush forward and claim to be the winners. When they show their tickets, however, the two tickets are identical. The person in charge calls a stranger from the crowd (in this case, from the class) and asks him or her to make the decision. This is to be done by pulling one of the tickets from a hat.

All of the above situations are open-ended. They are to be played as regular improvisations until the end, when someone or the group itself must make an important decision. Players may use details they observe, information they gather, or intuition in arriving at the decision; there is no right answer because each time the situation is improvised, it will be done differently and the variations will affect the decision.

The leader can make up other situations if the group enjoys the open-ended format. If the group is composed of very young children, simpler situations can be created for them, including nursery rhymes. For example, suppose you stopped "Humpty Dumpty" before the last line:

> **Humpty Dumpty sat on a wall,**
> **Humpty Dumpty had a great fall;**
> **All the king's horses and all the king's men . . .**

Can they put him together again or not? If so, how do they do it? The players make the decision.

Here are some other ideas:

1. Arrange furniture and props so as to create an environment or setting. What does it suggest to the players? Create an improvisation which might take place in this setting.
2. Divide the group into two subgroups, representing opposite sides of an idea or issue. Improvise in individual groups first; then bring the two groups together with the aim of reaching a solution.
3. Create a plot from one of the following phrases:
   a. "Can you spare a dime?"
   b. "Got a cigarette?"
   c. "May I have a cup of coffee?"
   d. "Do you have the time?"
   e. "Which way to Main Street?" (or any familiar street)
4. Tell or read the group a short story. Then have them improvise it. Next, create a scene that might take place *after* the ending of the original story.

5. Two friends meet after many years. One, who was once very attractive, is now greatly changed; she is obviously down on her luck. The other, who had been plain, has been successful.

Improvisations with Problems for Discussion

The following situations involve problems. Older players may enjoy first improvising them, then discussing the options with the rest of the class.

1. You are in a gift shop in a terminal. Over the glass and china counter there is a sign that says if you break anything, you will have to pay for it. Your sweater sleeve accidentally catches a glass dish, and it falls to the floor and breaks. It is so noisy in the terminal that no one sees or hears it. What are you going to do?
   a. Go to the clerk with the broken pieces and explain what happened.
   b. Decide to do nothing, hoping you can get away with it.
2. Your class is competing in a play festival. The group about to go on is very good. Suddenly you see their most important prop lying on the floor outside the stage door. You realize that if they lose it they won't be able to replace it, and any substitute prop will probably upset the actors. What are you going to do?
   a. Pick up the prop and give it to the stage manager.
   b. Hide the prop in a trash basket, in an effort to make them do less than their best.
3. You are invited to a party in a very beautiful home. Your mother says you should dress up, but your friends say they are going to wear blue jeans. One of them says she has no dress clothes. What will you do?
   a. Try to persuade your friends to dress up.
   b. Dress up; then change into blue jeans at the last minute.
   c. Wear your best clothes and find that everyone else is dressed casually.
   d. Try to help the one who has nothing dressy to wear.
4. You are buying a birthday present for your sister or brother. You know exactly what she or he wants. You find two different gifts, one cheap and the other expensive. You also see something you want for yourself. If you buy the expensive item, it will take all your money. If you buy the cheap item, there will be enough money left for you to get what you want too.
   a. You decide on the expensive gift.
   b. You decide on the cheap gift and get yourself what you want as well.

5. Just before a game you fall and hurt your knee. You don't know whether it is going to ruin your playing or not. What do you do?
   a. Say nothing about it and play. The knee lets you down.
   b. Explain and stay out of the game. The team is angry and upset.
6. There has been a bad flood in your neighborhood, and many families have had to leave their homes quickly. Your mother invites some people to stay in your house till the crisis is over.
   a. One of them is a boy or girl you dislike.
   b. You have to give up your room to a family.
   c. You decide to help in any way you can.

Improvisations for Older Players

The following improvisations are suggested for older players. In working on them, ask the following questions: Who am I? Where does the scene take place? What has preceded it both recently and earlier in the life of the character? Where does the action take place? You won't have all the answers, so in order to start you will have to think the situation through carefully. Next come these questions: What is the action? What is the problem? What is the conflict that follows? How is the conflict resolved?

Staying Out Too Late

Characters:
Mother
Father
Daughter
Grandmother

Time: midnight on a school night
Place: the family's living room

The daughter, who is in high school, has repeatedly stayed out too late at night. This particular evening she agreed to be home by eleven o'clock and it is now approaching midnight. The family is waiting for her, each reacting to the situation in his or her own way. Think through each character, deciding on the motivation for attitude and action.

The Shopping Center

Characters:
Several residents of the town opposed to a shopping center

Several residents in favor of it
Developer, who is eager to start the project
Owner of the meadow, who sees two sides of the situation

Time: 8:00 P.M.
Place: Town Hall of a very small town

A developer wants to buy a beautiful meadow on the edge of a small town and put up a shopping center and parking lot. Some of the residents think it a good idea but others are violently opposed. For one thing, it will mean destroying a lovely meadow and razing three nineteenth-century farmhouses that are the pride of the town. The owner of the land is not sure which way to go. Decide who you are and how you feel. Then, according to the questions asked above and the information you have about the situation, you will find your motivation and will act on the proposal.

The Playground or a Gym?

Characters:
Group of neighborhood children
Playground director
Community leader

Time: a summer morning
Place: the playground

A new gymnasium is being proposed for the site of a children's playground. The children have just heard about it and most of them are upset. The playground director is not sure where he or she stands but tries to comfort them by talking about it. The community leader comes along and is very enthusiastic about the idea. He offers strong arguments in favor of it. Decide who you are, how you feel about the proposal, and why you feel as you do. The more you know about yourself, your past use of the playground, and your fear or interest in the new gym will help you discuss the proposal.

Make up other situations in which there are conflicts and characters caught up in them. A strong situation could become the plot for a play. Situations such as these offer excellent opportunities for developing dialogue. Arguments must be clear, well presented, and motivated by the interests, needs, and values of the characters stating them. Most players like the challenge of controversial real-life situations.

One particularly effective exercise for older players makes use of suspense stories as a springboard. After the class has heard or read the story, there is a discussion of plot, characters, motivation. Some of the more suspenseful phrases are written on the board. These might be:

the howling wind
creaking stairs
screeching owl
rapid footsteps
dark, lonely street
squeaking hinges

Then the class puts the phrases into sentences. (For example: "The frightened boy walked down the dark, lonely street." "He heard squeaking hinges.") Next, extend the sentences into stories. Finally the class selects one story to enact.

This exercise can be further extended by discussing the improvisation and offering suggestions as to how it might be done differently or even changed. One way to change an improvisation would be to tell the story from the viewpoint of another character (e.g., to tell the story of *Hansel and Gretel* from the witch's point of view or "Humpty Dumpty" from the standpoint of the King's men). This is a challenging assignment, which can be used in the teaching of the language arts as well as serving as an exercise in creative drama.

Improvisations Based on Stories

The most popular and, in many ways, most satisfactory form of improvisation for children is based on good stories. While making up original stories is a creative exercise, a group endeavor rarely achieves the excellence of a story that has stood the test of time or has been written by a fine author. Improvising from a story is a way of introducing literature, and when a story is well-chosen it offers good opportunities for acting. Chapters 8 and 9 illustrate the ways in which both simple and more complicated stories have been approached.

Good stories on any level should have literary quality, worthwhile ideas, correct information, and dramatic values. Children up to the age of ten and eleven like fairy tales and legends. Older children may still enjoy these but tend to prefer adventure, biography, and stories of real life. Frequently the latter, because of their length, will have to be cut or the incidents rearranged. This is a learning experience which, if the group has had some experience, should not be too difficult.

Sometimes groups will want to act plays they have seen. This can be a worthwhile activity, though the tendency is to try to do it exactly as it was presented on the stage. Nevertheless, working on reenactment of a play can be a valuable period of time spent with a good piece of literature and is to be preferred to the reproduction of television shows or enactment of stories from comic books.

In order to present the right story, the leader must, first of all, know the group well. One leader, who was later to achieve remarkable success, told of her first experience as a young teacher at a settlement house in a disadvantaged urban area. Nothing she brought to the children in her drama group captured their interest. Improvisation seemed an impossible goal, though the group was alert and lively when she saw them on the street. Finally she hit upon the idea of asking them to tell her stories they knew. Hesitantly at first, then willingly, legends and family anecdotes came. She tried them. Not only was the material a success—the group doubled in size. Parents began to look in. Before the end of the year, an activity that had seemed doomed to failure became the most popular in the settlement. Some years later, the drama department was to achieve nationwide recognition as an arts center. The search for material had led to the children themselves. Their cultural heritage, and their creative use of it under intelligent and sensitive guidance, was the first step.

Improvisation in Kendall Demonstration Elementary School for the Deaf at Gallaudet College. (*Courtesy of Victoria Brown.*)

The leader should prepare in advance for improvisation of the story, but avoid any preconceived ideas as to how it should be done. Improvisation is a group project with ideas contributed by both children and leader. The teacher is ready to offer suggestions but must be equally receptive to those of the players.

He should not expect the product to be perfect. Improvisation is never twice the same, and while repetition usually leads to greater fluency and richness of detail, each performance does not necessarily "top" the preceding one.

Role Playing

Although it was stated in the first chapter that role playing as therapy is not the job of the creative drama teacher or the classroom teacher using creative drama techniques, some teachers have tried it with reported success. The purpose is educative rather than therapeutic, and the situations examined are common to all. Human conflicts and the ways in which problems are solved can promote social growth. Family scenes, school situations, and playground incidents give opportunity for interaction and group discussion. Discussion is the most important aspect of role playing, according to some teachers, for it is during these periods that various points of view are presented and attitudes clarified. The teacher must accept all ideas, giving the boys and girls a chance to express themselves without fear of disapproval. He will pose such questions as: How do you think the father felt? The brother? The mother? What did the man next door think when you broke his window? How do you think he felt the third time it happened? If you were he, how would you feel?

Exchanging roles is a good way to put oneself in the shoes of another, in order to understand him. One teacher gave a demonstration of role playing done with her group of junior high school girls, who lived in a neighborhood with a growing Puerto Rican population. The girls had had difficulty in accepting the newcomers, and the teacher's introduction of role playing, as a way of helping them understand the problem, led to the following improvisation. The scene was the planning of a school dance by a small clique. The committee wished to exclude the newcomers but could accomplish the exclusion only by making them feel unwelcome. This led to a serious breakdown in group relations. The period spent in playing the situation reportedly did much to restore peace and communication. The problem was faced squarely, and the girls were able to discuss their own attitudes and feelings. Later on, when the improvisation was done as a demonstration for a university class, it made a tremendous impression. The insights expressed through the honesty of the players proved the value of the experiment. The teacher did not claim to be a therapist but was an intelligent and experienced classroom teacher who was deeply troubled about a condition that was interfering with the work of the class.

Peter Slade, in *Child Drama,* summarizes the use of role playing in this way: "I would go so far as to say that one of the most important reasons for developing child drama in schools generally is not actually a therapeutic one but the even more constructive one of prevention."[1]

It must be pointed out that playing the part of a fictional character also demands identification with her and her problems. Exchange of parts gives all of the players a chance to experience both sides of a conflict. Obviously, the real-life conflict that the group itself experiences is stronger than the fictional one, and the solution, if found, is of practical benefit.

Summary

In summary, improvisation is the creation of a situation in which characters speak spontaneously. There are many ways of introducing improvisation, but some groundwork in pantomime is the best preparation. Once the players have achieved a sense of security in movement, they are ready to add dialogue. Dialogue does not come easily at first, but continued practice on familiar material usually induces the flow. There are many points of departure and some of the most successful are those described in this chapter: improvisation from situations; objects or properties; sounds; characters; ideas and stories. A good program is one that makes use of all, though the teacher will be flexible in his approach, using those methods that lead to the greatest success for the group. Stories should be chosen with care and include both familiar and new material. Although the leader will probably want to start with the known, he will find this an excellent opportunity to widen horizons by bringing in good literature with dramatic content.

Role playing is a kind of improvisation, which has as its specific objective the social growth of the individuals involved. There may well be a place for it in the school or club program, but it must not be confused with creative dramatics as art. Both, however, are participant centered and in that respect differ from theatre. When observed by others, improvised drama of any kind should be considered as demonstration and not as performance.

There is a great interest in improvisation today, and several professional theatre groups specialize in it. This, like the commedia dell'arte of the sixteenth

---

1. Peter Slade, *Child Drama* (London: University of London Press, 1954), p. 119.

century, is the development of improvisational theatre by adult actors to a high level of artistry. While older boys and girls are able to become skilled improvisational actors, the purpose of improvisation with children is not to entertain others, but rather to provide the children with a medium of self-expression. The leader or teacher, whether working in school, camp, or club program, tries to stimulate the imagination, free the individual to create, guide the group, and build confidence. Evaluating the results with the group ultimately leads to richer performance and personal growth.

Improvisation, as the student progresses, generally moves in the direction of product or theatre art. The beginning level is creative drama, with an emphasis on personal and group development. The second level, as described by Margaret Faulkes-Jendyk, is an awareness of the dramatic art form. It is still process and "personal development continues with special emphasis on expansion of experiences."[2] The final level is improvisational theatre art and is achieved by only the few. There is a natural progression from one level to the next, though not all students are equally interested in going on to develop the skills demanded of the serious theatre artist.

A final word of warning: theatre games and warm-ups are fine but they can be carried to extremes. A group needs to advance and will become bored when there is a continued absence of substance with no obvious long-range goals. A perceptive graduate student, after observing four different groups of children for several months, recently remarked: ". . . on a physical level the work was good but the mental content was lacking. They did nothing for the entire semester but movement and games."

While most children enjoy impromptu activities, they tire of repeating them indefinitely and want to get on to something more demanding and ambitious. Whether this be story dramatization, original plays, or integrated projects, there comes a time when the group must progress or lose interest. It cannot remain on one level. Ideally, the move will be gradual as the participants grow in confidence, self-control, the ability to work together, appreciation, and the development of their skills. By making use of theatre games and exercises, which become increasingly difficult (always planned carefully in advance), they are able to handle longer assignments and a culminating project of which they can be proud.

One good way of proceeding is to begin a session with a group game while the children assemble—almost in the nature of a ritual involving everyone. When all have arrived, have them do some physical activity as a warm-up, then a game or two. By this time they will be ready to start or resume

---

2. Margaret Faulkes-Jendyk, "Creative Drama—Improvisation—Theatre," in *Children and Drama*, 2nd ed., edited by Nellie McCaslin (New York: Longman, 1981).

work on a major project. Any falling-off in attendance is always a warning: pay attention to it. A group must respect its work, and in order to accomplish this, the work cannot be too easy or too repetitious.

6
Puppets and Masks

Puppets and masks are an important part of
theatre history, predating the play as we know it by centuries. In many countries of the world puppetry enjoys
the status of a fine art, designed and performed for adults,
whereas in our country it is generally regarded as children's entertainment. In recent years, however, there has
been an awakened interest in puppetry as an art form,
resulting in a new popularity, and its value as a teaching
tool has been recognized. Besides providing an alternative
or an adjunct activity, to creative drama, puppetry and
mask making each offer wonderful incentives for
improvisation.

One could say that puppetry starts with dramatic play,
when dolls and toys are manipulated to perform various
roles and actions. The young child's game of "Peek-a-
Boo," with the hands hiding the face, illustrates an early
concept of the mask. As children grow older, they assign

Poko puppets presents *The Boy Who Could Swallow the
Ocean*. (*Courtesy of Larry Engler.*)

both mask and puppet more specific functions and handle them with greater dexterity. A child's first awareness of the mask as a mask, however, probably occurs at about the age of four or five, when he wears it as part of a Hallowe'en costume. Children of that age put on masks, confident that they are hidden from view and disguised as ghosts, witches, or monsters. Puppets and masks have much in common; in fact, at times they are indistinguishable from each other. In this chapter some of the ways in which both can be made and combined with creative drama will be discussed. Although each form merits a book in itself, the limitations of space and content preclude more than the most elementary discussion. There are, however, a number of excellent texts concerning both forms on the market; and it is hoped that the teacher interested in incorporating puppets and masks into her curriculum will investigate those texts listed in the bibliography.

Puppets

In the minds of many persons puppetry is associated with the field of entertainment, although it is equally at home in the classroom. Today, with the popularity of the Muppets and other puppet characters on television, children learn about puppets at an early age and become acquainted with some of the techniques of handling them. This familiarity suggests to the teacher ways in which he can include puppets either as special craft projects or as tools for teaching other subjects. A further, and particularly valuable use, is the social or therapeutic one: through the puppet a shy or troubled child is often able to express what she cannot state as herself. Best of all, perhaps, because these engaging little creatures are such fun to make and manipulate, they capture the child's attention and hold it in a variety of situations.

What is a puppet? Contrary to what many think, puppets are not dolls, although they often resemble them. Puppets are "actors" who come to life with the help of a puppeteer. Almost any object can be a puppet: a toy, a tool, a hairbrush, a lollipop, a spoon, a broom. Even the hand can be a puppet, if you move it and speak so that the hand appears to be doing the walking and talking. Just to prove it, try out a few things. Kneel behind a table and move an object along the edge of it. Keep moving. Here are a few things that can be used.

A wooden spoon. Make it walk, run, jump, disappear.

A toy. A teddy bear or a rag doll will do. They are soft and move in different ways from the spoon. Sometimes toys make fine puppets but it is not a good idea to depend on them. The puppets you make yourself will almost always be better.

A pencil. A ruler. A lollipop. An artificial flower. They will all become

different characters when you start moving them. Now try holding one
in each hand. What happens when a pencil and a ruler meet?
   Your own hands. What can they do that the other things couldn't do?
Hands make wonderful movements. Let them walk, dance, jump, fight,
bow, march off.

   Look around for some other objects that have not been mentioned. Invent
actions for them and decide what kinds of characters they seem to be.
Remember that *you* make the puppet. It is not alive until you move it.

Making Puppets

   There are many different kinds of puppets. Some hang from strings; some
are fastened to sticks called rods. Others slip over the hand like gloves. Some
puppets are as tall as a person and must be pushed or moved from inside.
Because the string puppet is the most complicated to make and manipulate, it is
not recommended for the beginner or for the elementary school classroom.
The hand puppet with its many variations is the most satisfactory for any age
level, and the classroom teacher will find it within his or her capabilities,
regardless of previous experience. The hand puppet includes the bandana
puppet, the finger puppet, the paper bag puppet, the flat puppet, the shadow
puppet, the sock puppet, and the glove puppet.

Bandana Puppets
   The easiest one to begin with is the bandana puppet. Put a bandana or
cloth over the hand. Let the first and middle fingers be the head of the puppet
and put a rubber band around them for the neck. The thumb and little finger
are the arms. Put rubber bands around them in order to hold the cloth in place.
Imagine that the hand is the actor. Have the puppet you have made clap its
hands, shake its head, and fall down.
   There are many more things you can do in making a bandana puppet. For
instance, try cutting a hole in the middle of the bandana and poking the first
finger through it. Next, take a styrofoam ball with a hole scooped out for your
finger and use it for a head. Heads can be made out of many different things: a
small paper cup, an apple (after cutting out the core), or a ball. The bandana
puppet can be quickly made by the teacher, but making one is also within the
capability of young children.

Finger Puppets
   Finger puppets are the smallest of all puppets. They slip on the fingers and
can be played with as they are or used with larger hand puppets to show

different sized characters. For instance, a finger puppet might be an elf, with a hand puppet as a human being. One way to make a finger puppet is to sew it of felt. First, make a pattern. Put the hand down flat on a piece of paper and draw around the fingers with a pencil. Be sure to add a little extra material all the way around to allow for the sewing. Next, cut out the paper patterns and pin them on a piece of felt. You will have to cut two shapes for each puppet. Put the two shapes together and sew around the edges. Leave the bottom open for your finger.

Another way to make finger puppets is to cut the fingers off an old glove. White gloves are the best because you can put faces on them. Slip the glove fingers over your own and you will have five little puppets! you can cut circles and paint faces on them; when the paint is dry, they can be pasted on the puppets.

Paper Bag Puppets

The paper bag puppet is one of the best puppets with which to begin because bags come in all sizes and are easily obtained. Also, if you happen to tear the bag, there are many more around. Adults, children, giants, and elves can all be suggested with different sizes of paper bag. Small bags fit on the hands, whereas big bags will go over the head. If a bag is worn on the head, holes will have to be cut out for the eyes and mouth. Next, paint or draw a face on the bag. You can use your hands, your head, or even your feet for puppets. Hands work best, however, because you can do so many more things with them. You can paint and paste on paper bags and, if the paper is strong enough, you can sew through them. A bag can be just a head or a whole puppet.

Flat Puppets

Flat puppets are also often called rod puppets and are included here because they are easy to handle and can be used with other kinds of puppets. Flat puppets are a little like paper dolls. They can be cut out of lightweight cardboard, colored, and pasted-on tongue depressors or sticks. When the puppet is firmly attached to the stick, hold it in your hand just below the edge of the stage or table top. As it is moved, it will seem to be walking by itself. Animals make good flat puppets because you only have to draw the side view. Incidentally, if you would like to show your puppet moving in both directions, cut out two shapes and paste them together with the stick in between. Color both sides and your animal can be moved from either left or right. One more advantage to flat puppets: they are easy to keep in good condition as they don't take up much space when put away in neat piles.

Shadow Puppets

Flat puppets can be used for shadow shows also. In order to give a shadow show, all you need are some flat puppets, a sheet, and a lamp placed behind the

Shadow puppet of a clown in *Circus Home* by Joanna Kraus. (*Photograph courtesy of Educational Communications Center State University College, Brockport, N.Y.*)

sheet. When you move the puppets behind the sheet, they cast shadows on it. The closer they are to the sheet, the stronger the shadow, or silhouette, will be. Shadow puppets may be made more exciting if parts of them within the outside boundaries are cut out and backed by colored gelatins. Stores that handle stage lighting equipment carry relatively inexpensive gelatins in a variety of colors. Older children love the challenge of making these puppets which in some ways resemble stained glass windows. The strong light shining through the gelatin brings out the richness of the color and creates a magical effect. In the Oriental theatre, where shadow plays originated, one can still see performances using puppets made of wood or hide decorated with elaborate openwork patterns. Older students enjoy making puppets of this kind with colored gelatin pasted over the open areas. The stylized result can be quite beautiful and effective.

Sock Puppets

A sock makes a very good puppet because it stretches, yet won't slip off the hand. You can do many things with a sock puppet, such as making it into a mouth. Take one of your own old socks and put your hand inside it. Put your fingers into the toe and your thumb into the heel. You now have the upper and lower jaws of a mouth. Bring them together in a big bite. By adding eyes and

The mouth. Photograph By David Attie from *Making Puppets Come Alive: A Method of Learning and Teaching Hand Puppetry* by Larry Engler and Carol Fijan (New York: Taplinger, 1973). © 1973 by Larry Engler and Carol Fijan. Reproduced by permission.

other markings, you can create a bird, a wolf, a crocodile, or a dragon. You can make a puppet mouth more exciting by sewing a piece of red felt inside it and adding another piece for a tongue. So many children's stories have animal characters that the "mouth" is a useful puppet to have on hand.

Glove Puppets

The glove puppet needs more sewing than the other types. It has to be cut out of two pieces of cloth sewn together. It may also have a separate head. First, take a piece of strong cotton cloth and double it. Felt is good, if you have it, because it won't ravel. Other fabrics will do, however, so use what you have on hand, provided they are sturdy.

Cut a pattern of newspaper for your puppet. There should be a head and two arms, and the pattern must be large enough to fit the hand. Pin the pattern to the material and trace around it. Then remove the pattern and cut out the puppet. Keep the two pieces of cloth together and sew around the edges, remembering to leave the bottom open for your hand to go through. A felt puppet is ready to use as it is. A puppet made of softer material should be turned inside out to keep it from raveling.

Children will want to put a face on the puppet. Eyes, nose, and mouth can be drawn or embroidered on it. Buttons make excellent eyes and yarn makes good hair. A little stuffing makes the head rounder. If you want to make a separate head, a lightweight material such as styrofoam or papier-mâché, for instance, works well. It is a good idea to decorate the head first, then slip it over your first and second fingers, or just your first. Although it is harder to handle a puppet with a separate head than a puppet that is all in one piece, most children learn how to manage it with practice.

Giant Puppets

Some puppeteers use puppets as tall as they are or even taller. These giant puppets must be made of lightweight material so they can be pushed from behind or inside, or carried. Unless you have a large area in which to perform, you probably will not be making life-sized puppets; for those who want to try, however, here are some suggestions. An easy way is to put a paper bag or papier-mâché head on a broomstick or pole. Then hang a blanket or cape on the broomstick and have the manipulator hide inside the covering. He can then carry the stick as he, in fact, "merges" with the puppet.

Another way to make a giant puppet is to use a tall, narrow cardboard box. A face and clothes can be painted on the box, which the puppeteer pushes from behind. A variation of this, and one which can be very effective, is to take a piece of cardboard decorated on one side and manipulate it from behind.

Materials

Just as a costume closet or box is handy to have for creative drama, so is a supply of scrap materials necessary for making puppets. You probably will not have to purchase anything because most of what you need will be in your own or the children's homes, or in the school. Scraps of paper and fabrics, boxes of all sizes, sticks, styrofoam, lollipops, apples, balls, and paper bags are all useable. Ribbons, yarns, sewing materials, paper cups, paper napkins, discarded decorations, old socks, and gloves will all find a use as somebody's puppet.

Holding the Puppet

There are different ways of holding puppets, so it is suggested that you use the one that works best for you. Because younger children have short fingers

Giant puppets. (*Courtesy of Carol Sterling, New York.*)

they will have to experiment to find a comfortable way to hold the puppet. Some puppeteers put their first and second fingers in the neck, their fourth and fifth fingers in one arm, and their thumb in the other. Puppets can be held either in front of you or over your head. Again, use whichever way is easier for you. If you are playing for a long time, it is usually more comfortable to work the puppet in front of your face.

If you decide to hold your puppet that way, you will be seen by the audience. This doesn't matter. The audience, if you have one, will soon forget you are there. If you want to hang a curtain between you and your puppets, you will need a stage. A dark, lightweight piece of cloth at the back of the stage will hide you and make your puppets stand out. If the cloth is semitransparent, you can see through it without being seen by the audience.

Some Basic Actions

Moving the puppet's head up and down means "yes." Shaking it from side to side means "no." When the puppet's hands point to itself, it means "me" or "mine." Moving one of its hands toward its body means "come here." Waving its hand may mean either "hello" or "goodbye."

Walking, running, and jumping can be suggested by the way you move the puppet across the stage. Try not to lift it up in the air. You will soon get the knack of holding it down, so that it seems to be doing all the moving.

When two persons are puppeteering together, the chances are they will each be holding a puppet. This is more difficult than playing alone but it is also more fun. Each has to watch out that the puppets don't bump into each other. Also, when one puppet is speaking, the other one should remember to listen. Occasionally there will be a scene for three puppets. This takes some doing, for three people will have to work together backstage, or one person will have to handle two puppets. It is a good idea at first to use stories that have no more than two characters on the stage at one time.

The Puppet Stage

In the first place, it is not necessary to have a stage, for puppets can act anywhere. All you need is a smooth surface about three feet long. A table, a coffee table, a bench, or a box will do. In a setting with windows opening on a porch, one group of children used the windowsill for the stage. Another idea for a stage is a cardboard box with the front and back cut off. Making such a stage takes some work, as well as requiring a place to store it when not in use. But a stage with a lamp placed in front of the box to light it adds a professional touch.

Scenery

You do not need scenery any more than you need a stage, but sometimes you may want it. If you do, make it of cardboard or stiff paper and be sure to fasten it securely so that it won't fall down. Doll furniture can be used if it is the right size, but a simple background is usually all you will want. You don't even need that if the puppets tell the audience where the story takes place.

Stories for Puppet Plays

It is a good idea to work without scripts because you have your hands full just moving the puppets. If you know the story you are presenting very well, you can make up the dialogue as you go along, just as you do in creative drama. Besides, it will sound more natural if you do. While many stories that are good for creative playing are also good with puppets, not all work well. One thing must be kept in mind: there is very little room backstage. Therefore, stick to stories in which no more than two or three characters are on stage at the same time. Often you can arrange the scenes so as to have no more than two, but some stories will of course lend themselves to the puppet theatre better than others. Here are three examples.

LITTLE INDIAN TWO FEET'S HORSE

This story can be played just as it is, or it can be made longer by adding adventures. Since Indian Two Feet is a little boy who talks to himself, we know what is happening. You can make the horse move by bending your hand so that the arm of the puppet becomes its front legs. Try out some movements until you find the ones that are right. The horse may be a flat puppet instead of a glove puppet, if you wish.

Characters:
Little Indian Two Feet
His Horse

Little Indian Two Feet wants a horse more than anything else in the world. He often walks on the prairie, dreaming of the horse he will someday own. His father has told him that he can have a horse when he is older. That seems far away to a boy of ten! So one morning Little Indian Two Feet decides to go out to see if he can find a horse. Perhaps if he hunts long enough he'll see one on the prairie, a horse that no one owns. He walks and he walks. He calls and calls, but no horse answers. He climbs a hill, he looks over it, and he calls again. Still no horse comes to him.

He manages to cross a wide stream by a meadow. Two Feet walks in the tall grass until he is tired, but there are no horses grazing anywhere. Finally he decides to lie down and rest before starting home. In no time at all Two Feet falls fast asleep. While he is sleeping, a pony appears. It is a colt, one of the wild ponies that run loose on the prairie. In fact, it is so young that it knows no fear. Since it has never seen a boy before, it steps up to look at him. The pony puts his soft nose against Two Feet's cheek and rubs against it. Two Feet awakens

Hand puppet with stuffed muslin head. (*Courtesy of George Latshaw; photograph by Julian Apsel.*)

with a start! He can hardly believe his eyes. He sits up and touches the pony's shoulder. "Did you come to me?" he asks. "Do you want to go home with me?"

The pony nods his head as if to say "yes." Little Two Feet puts his arm on the pony's neck and the two of them go off together. Little Indian Two Feet has found his horse at last.

THE TALKING CAT
(A French Canadian Folktale)

This French Canadian folktale works better for puppets than for human actors. One of the characters is a ventriloquist, which makes it ideal for the puppet stage.

Characters:
Tante Odette, an old woman
Chouchou, her cat
Pierre, a workman
Georges, his friend

There is an old woman, who is fooled into believing that her cat can speak. Tante Odette lives alone on her farm, deep in the Canadian woods. She is careful and thrifty, always keeping a pot of soup on the stove for herself and her old gray cat, Chouchou. She takes good care of her small farm. But as the years go by, she sometimes complains that the work is becoming too much for her. She talks to Chouchou about the chores that have to be done and how she must save her money for later. Often she says to him, "How I wish you could talk, Chouchou. Then I should not be so lonely."

One evening as Tante Odette is sitting by the fire there is a knock at the door. When she opens it, she sees a man in workman's clothes with a red sash tied around his waist.

"I am looking for work," he says politely, "If you can give me some chores, all I ask is a bowl of soup and a night's sleep in your barn."

"Go away," says Tante Odette. "I do not need anyone to help me. Besides, I have only enough soup for myself."

Just as she is about to close the door in his face, an amazing thing happens. Chouchou speaks! "Wait a minute," he says. "You are getting older, and it would be a good idea to have a strong young man on the place."

Tante Odette can't believe her ears. She looks at the man; then she looks at the cat. "Well, if you think so, Chouchou."

"I certainly do," says the cat. "Ask him to come in and join us in a bowl of soup."

The old woman invites the man in and asks him to supper. "It's only cabbage soup and bread, but we like it."

The man thanks her. When he has finished his supper, he tells her tales of his travels and the different places he has worked. But he says that now he would rather stay in one place, even though he wouldn't make any money. He tells her his name is Pierre. As time goes on both the old woman and Chouchou become very fond of him.

One day Chouchou says to Tante Odette, "Why don't you give Pierre meat and cakes? He works hard. I'm sure he gets very hungry."

"But we have no meat," she replies.

"Then let him go to the store in the town and buy some meat. He will not waste your money."

Pierre appears in the doorway. "I heard what your cat said just now. He's very wise. Let me strike a good bargain."

The old woman goes to a chest of drawers and takes out some money. "Mind you don't waste it," she tells Pierre.

When Pierre has gone, she turns to Chouchou. "How is it that you never spoke in all the years that I've had you and now you are giving me advice?"

But as always, when they are alone, Chouchou says nothing.

The next day when they finish their dinner of meat and cakes, Pierre is in a very good mood and Tante Odette says that she has never enjoyed a meal so much! "Why don't you let Pierre move into the house?" asks the cat.

"What?" says the old woman.

"Winter is coming and it will soon be cold in the barn. We have plenty of room inside."

Pierre says that he would like this very much. And so he moves in.

A few weeks later when the old woman is alone in the house, there is a knock at the door. She opens it and to her surprise, she sees a working man standing there. He is wearing a red sash just like Pierre's.

"Have you seen a workman who calls himself Pierre?" the newcomer asks.

"A man by that name works for me," the old woman says.

"Is he a good worker?"

"A very good worker," she says; and she tells of all the things Pierre can do.

"It certainly sounds like the same man. One more thing, can he throw his voice? Is he a ventriloquist?"

"Throw his voice? Oh, no! I could not stand having anyone around who did that."

"Then it can't be the same person," says the man, as he turns to go.

At this moment Pierre comes to the door. "Georges!" he shouts, "My old friend!"

"Pierre! I've been searching for you everywhere. I want you to go with me to get furs. You know they pay good money for furs in the city. How about it?"

Pierre thinks for a moment. "If I go with you, I'll make money, but it will be cold. If I stay here, I have a good job, food, and a warm place to sleep. What shall I do, Chouchou? You're a wise cat."

"Stay here," the cat answers. Then the cat turns to the old woman. "Why don't we pay him some wages? You have money in the chest. Surely he's worth a few pieces of gold."

The old woman doesn't know what to do. Finally she says, "Very well. I can give you a small wage, if you'll stay."

"Good!" says Pierre. "Then I'll stay." He says goodbye to his friend and walks with him down the road.

The old woman looks at Chouchou. "I don't believe he throws his voice, do you?"

There was no answer. She stares at Chouchou, who says nothing as usual.

Just then Pierre returns. "It will be a much better winter for me here than in the north woods. And I can earn money at the same time, thanks to your cat."

The cat bows and speaks.

"That's all right, Pierre. Fair is fair." Then Chouchou looks at the old woman. "Well, we may as well sit down at the table and celebrate the way it has all worked out."

THE FISHERMAN AND HIS WIFE

This is another good story for puppets to play. You don't need any scenery. If you want to show the different houses, you can draw pictures of them and put them up behind the puppets.

Characters:
The Fisherman
His Wife
The Flounder

A poor Fisherman lives with his wife in a cottage by the sea. Every day he goes down to the shore to catch a fish for their supper. When his luck is good, he has enough fish to sell to their neighbors. One morning the Fisherman goes out as usual and sits down in his favorite fishing spot. Suddenly there is a tug on his line. He pulls and he pulls.

"What have I caught?" asks the Fisherman. He gives another tug on his line and up comes the biggest flounder he has ever seen.

Then, to his amazement, the fish speaks. "Please let me go. I have done you no harm."

The Fisherman can't believe his ears. "You can talk? I have never heard of a fish that could talk."

"I was once a prince," says the Flounder sadly. "An evil spell was put on me, and I am doomed to spend the rest of my life as a fish."

"I am sorry if I've hurt you," says the Fisherman, taking the hook from the fish. "Go back to your home in the sea."

"Oh, thank you," the Flounder says. "You have saved my life. If I can ever do anything for you, call on me. I'm never far away."

The Fisherman promises the Flounder that he will do so. Then, eager to tell his wife about his strange adventure, he packs up and goes home. When he has finished his tale, his wife scolds him for his stupidity. "That's just like you! Why didn't you ask him for a nice house and some food for our dinner? He was a magic fish, and you let him go."

"I'm sorry, wife," says the Fisherman. "I didn't think of it."

"Well, go back down to the sea and ask for a house like our neighbor's, with enough food to last us a year."

"Very well," replies the Fisherman. So he goes down to the place where he had caught the Flounder and calls out:

> "Oh, fish of the sea,
> come listen to me.
> For my wife, my wife, the plague of my life,
> Has sent me to ask a boon of thee."

Scarcely does he finish when the Flounder appears.

"What can I do for you?" the fish asks politely.

The Fisherman tells him.

"No sooner asked than granted," says the fish. "Go home and you will find a house like your neighbor's."

The Fisherman hurries home, and there is a beautiful stone house where his little cottage had been. His wife appears at the door, delighted with their good fortune.

For a time the Fisherman and his wife live happily. Then one morning his wife, who is always discontented, says, "I don't know why you asked for this house. I should like a castle with servants to wait on me."

"This house is plenty good enough." says her husband.

"No," she replies, "Go back and tell the fish I must have a castle."

The Fisherman doesn't want to do her bidding, but at last he agrees. He goes down to the sea and again calls out:

> "Oh, fish of the sea,
> come listen to me.
> For my wife, my wife, the plague of my life,
> Has sent me to ask a boon of thee."

In a flash the Flounder appears. "Nothing easier," he says, after the Fisherman explains the matter to him. "Go home to your castle."

Then the Flounder disappears and the Fisherman returns home. Instead of the stone house, there is a great castle with towers and walls surrounding it. His wife is overjoyed. But after a time, she again becomes discontented.

She sends her husband back to the Flounder many times. She wants to be the richest woman in the world. Then a Queen. Next, an Empress. And finally, Goddess of the Universe. Each time her husband begs her to be content with what they have, but she will not listen. And each time the fish grants her wish—until the last one.

"What is it now?" the Flounder asks the Fisherman.

"Oh, gracious Flounder," replies the Fisherman, "my wife wants to be Goddess of the Universe."

"Never!" declares the Flounder angrily. "I will grant no more wishes. Your wife can return to her cottage."

There is a loud noise like a clap of thunder and the fish disappears. Then the Fisherman goes home, where he finds his wife in the doorway of their humble cottage.

Puppets as Teaching Aids

Puppets also make excellent teaching aids because of their power to hold and sustain the attention of a class; and, in doing so, they facilitate learning. Unlike some curricular materials, puppets are not limited to any one area of study. They can be used to teach any subject, ranging from the language arts to science and math. They can be combined with other teaching materials and they can be used alone. Moreover, puppets cost little or nothing to make. As has already been stated, their value lies in their mobility, not in their beauty or complicated construction. Those made by teachers and children are usually more satisfactory than commercial puppets. If puppets are purchased, however—and there are many on the market—they should be selected for their durability, avoiding the nonwashable and perishable.

The degree of sophistication of puppets that students create depends, of course, upon the age and previous experience of the students. While the simple puppets of young children can be wonderfully effective, experienced older groups find a challenge in making more elaborate ones. It cannot be repeated often enough, however, that a good puppet is one that can be manipulated easily; the most beautiful puppet in the world is a failure if it does not move easily and well. Another consideration, and an important one, is the child's perception of his or her work. In other words, "it is not what the puppet looks like that counts but rather how the child feels about the puppet . . . a rabbit puppet made by a child does not have to look like a real rabbit—the child needs only to believe in it. . . ."[1]

1. Tamara Hunt and Nancy Renfro, *Puppetry in Early Childhood* (Austin, Tex.: Nancy Renfro Studios, 1982), p. 24.

Probably the most extensive use made of puppets as a teaching tool is in the area of the language arts. According to John Warren Stewig, "Children generate more verbal language during dramatic play than in any other situation."[2] In both creative drama and puppetry, extemporaneous speaking is involved; use of the puppet has the added advantage, however, of shielding the speaker who may be shy or weak in verbal skills, thus enabling him to communicate through his puppet. A skillful teacher makes use of the opportunity afforded by this communication to open up new areas of learning and tune into a student's thinking. Telling stories with puppets is not only fun but a valuable activity on all levels. The move from storytelling to story dramatization is a natural next step, involving dialogue, character study, play structure, and growth in language competency. The use of puppets in the teaching of poetry has also proved successful in promoting the appreciation and writing of this form of literature.

Some teachers have found puppets invaluable aids in the study of elementary science and environmental education; the writing of original skits on these subjects, later to be enacted by puppets, is strong motivation in two areas that are difficult for many children. Social studies provide a wealth of puppetry opportunities for the study of other people, other countries, historical events, and current problems. "Famous People Puppets"[3] is suggested as an activity for intermediate grades. Puppets provide exercise in bilingual education also; this can be done by way of dramatic sketches or taught directly by a familiar mascot puppet. The mascot, incidentally, is often able to hold the attention of the most restless group, a phenomenon observed by anyone who has ever used puppetry with children. In short, there is no area of the curriculum that cannot be enhanced by these appealing little creatures who come alive in the most inexperienced hands, teaching and entertaining simultaneously. Their popularity with all kinds and ages of groups practically insures success.

Puppets as Therapeutic Tools

Puppets have been used effectively as both diagnostic and therapeutic instruments. It is understood that neither the classroom teacher nor the creative drama specialist is a therapist; nevertheless, the puppet offers insights often undiscernible in other situations and the sensitive teacher will take note of them. For the puppet becomes a nonthreatening little friend in whom a child can confide, entrusting his most private thoughts and feelings without fear of censure. This friend has access to his inner world and is also able to speak to the outer world as an intermediary.

2. John Warren Stewig, *Teaching Language Arts in Early Childhood* (New York: Holt Rinehart and Winston, 1980), p. 123.
3. Bojabi Treehouse, *Puppetry—a Tool for Teaching*, Brochure (New Haven Public Schools, 1973).

Puppetry provides socially accepted avenues for the discovery, expression, and release of emotions and attitudes. Therapists do not aim at well-rehearsed, finished performances; rather, they use puppets to encourage and help motivate patients and students in clinical and educational settings. Some professional puppeteers have engaged in special ongoing programs. George Latshaw, a well-known puppeteer, worked with a group sponsored by the National Committee, Arts for the Handicapped, using puppets with severely handicapped children. Latshaw's puppets played and interacted with children in classrooms, often eliciting response from those who had until then been detached from others or lacked verbal skills.[4] In their use of puppetry the classroom teacher and the therapist share a similar goal. Thus the teacher will find puppetry an exceptionally effective way of drawing out children who are reluctant to participate in creative drama. Here are a few exercises to stimulate expression of strong feelings.

1. Try to find ways of showing that the puppet feels:

   angry
   excited
   shy
   tired
   happy
   curious
   scared
   hungry

2. Next, see if you can put actions with a feeling:

   curious—and looks into a box
   angry—and hits someone
   happy—and claps its hands for joy
   thoughtful—and comes up with an idea

3. Most of us get into trouble at one time or another. Do you remember a particular time when you got into trouble? Was it your fault? Did you think you were punished unfairly? How did you feel about it? Let your glove puppet be the other person in this story and you be the finger puppet. Act it out.
4. Talking with your puppet is fun. Like a conversation with a person, it builds as it goes along.
   a. Imagine that your puppet is mischievous. You ask it to do something and it refuses. It thinks of reasons why it won't do what you ask. How do you handle the puppet? Who wins in the end?
   b. Imagine that your puppet is angry, and try to find out what is wrong.

4. *Puppets—Art and Entertainment* (Washington, D.C.: Puppeteers of America, 1980), p. 9.

    c. Imagine that your puppet can't speak English. Try to make it understand you.

    d. Imagine that your puppet's feelings are hurt. Can you say or do anything to make it feel better?

5. The puppet is *you*. Talk to it, imagining that you are one of the following: your mother, your best friend, the owner of a candy store in your neighborhood, your teacher, a new child on the block.

6. Try out the following verse as you look into your own inner world. Some children are amazingly perceptive in comparing their inner and outer selves.

> I have two Selves or so I'm told,
>   My Outside and my In.
> And if I take a thoughtful look
>   I'll see myself within.
>
> Although I know my Outside Self,
>   I see it every day,
> My Inside Self seems hidden,
>   So neatly tucked away.
>
> It seems so strange I cannot touch
>   Or taste or hear or see. . . .
> I only *feel* all those things
>   That are inside of me.
>
> Both my Selves are special
>   That's what I'm about.
> Feeling on the *Inside*,
>   Showing on the *Out*.
>
>   **Tamara Hunt**

7. Did you ever get a present that you didn't want? Or *not* get one that you wanted more than anything else in the world? Make up a story about what happened and how you felt about it.

8. It is fun to make up stories. Here are a few ideas for starters, but soon everyone in the class will be coming up with other ideas of their own.

A Mistake

Characters:
You
Your family (they talk offstage)

You come to breakfast early one morning and no one is up yet. You call your mother, but she tells you to be quiet; she is trying to sleep. You find some food to eat; then you get your books and pack a lunch. You call to your family and tell them they are all going to be late. You run out of the house but a minute later you come back in. Your father calls to ask who it is. You tell him that the school bus isn't there. He laughs and says, "Of course, not. Did you forget? Daylight Saving Time is over!"

Space Traveler

Characters:
You
A person from another planet

Imagine you are walking in the country, when you meet a person from another planet. The spaceship has landed in a field nearby. He (she) wants to know who you are, where you live, what you do, and what you eat. Then he (she) tells you all about him (her) self. Can you understand each other's language? How do you communicate?

George, the Timid Ghost

Characters:
Father Ghost
George

There was once a timid ghost named George. He lived with his parents at the edge of a cemetery not far from town. He wanted very much to be able to scare people like a proper ghost but every time someone approached him, he ran away. "Someday, "he often said to himself, "I'll be as spooky as the rest of my family. Someday, but not today."

One night George's father decided that it was time to teach his son a lesson. When it was quite dark, George's father showed him how to sneak up behind someone without being heard, and to say "Boo." "Never hurt anyone," his father warned him. "Just give them a little scare."

George was eager to learn all of his father's tricks, so he practiced saying "Boo" in different tones of voice. He jumped out from behind trees and he ran back and forth, waving his arms in the air.

"Good," said his father approvingly. "You're going to be the scariest ghost in town."

George strutted back and forth after his father went into the house. "I'm going to be the scariest ghost in town."

Suddenly he heard the sound of somebody running behind him. He froze in his tracks, determined this time not to run away. This is an unfinished story. What happened next? You make up the ending.

Paper masks (*Courtesy of Arts in Education Program of West Decatur, Pennsylvania.*)

Masks

Closely related to the art of puppetry is the art of mask making. A brief section on masks is included in this chapter because mask can be either part of a puppet project or an extension of creative drama. Interesting experimental work with mixed media is being done these days in which the human actor, often masked, and the puppet are used in the same production. In the case of life-sized puppets, the human body actually merges with that of the puppet in order to move it. When this happens, it is difficult to say which one is the performer: the human being or the puppet. Young children have no problem with this, for in their own play they assume both animate and inanimate roles simultaneously. Older children and adults, however, faced with an inanimate or grotesque character to act, often find that the wearing of a mask helps to stimulate the imagination and free them of their inhibitions. Not that a mask is necessary to performance but the teacher who enjoys arts and crafts may find mask-making a relevant activity.

In one imaginative production given by a small professional group, human actors, puppets, actors wearing masks, and a larger-than-life cardboard figure were used together. In this way the group were able to suggest more characters than they had actors to play and to suggest size differences involving adults, children, a giant, and other fantastic characters. The effect was both childlike and smart, suggesting ways in which a teacher might solve problems otherwise insoluble.

Many persons link the mask with theatre, even though its functions go far beyond costume and performance. The mask is used in a variety of ways, but its four major functions are:

To act as a protective covering for the head or face (ski and fencing masks)
To function as a disguise or concealment
To describe or identify a character (in a play)
To serve as a symbol (religious and ritualistic rites)

In children's theatre the mask is commonly used in costuming an animal or a fantastic creature, though stage makeup is preferred by many directors and costumers.

Background

Historically, masks and makeup have enjoyed wide popularity throughout the world. Tribal societies have worn them in performing religious rites and rituals. The primitive human being thought that by putting on the face of another he gained power over him. For example, if the hunter wore the skin and mask of an animal, he believed it would bring him a good day of hunting. In time the mask or facial paint became stylized and more elaborate, as it was embellished by generations of wearers. The masks of primitive tribes were thought to be potent in other ways as well. They could release the wearer's personality by concealing it; and they became symbols of a universal awareness of gods or a creative force in the universe.

In the ancient Greek theatre the mask served the practical purpose of projecting the actor's features and amplifying his voice. The mask was larger than the human face and was made with protruding lips that created resonance. Thus the masks of comedy and tragedy gave the actor in the huge amphitheatres, where the performance took place, an objective reality larger than life.

In the Oriental theatre, on the other hand, the mask was part of an elaborate costume, designed primarily for its aesthetic appeal rather than its practical use. Japanese masks, familiar to audiences today, are colorful, decorative, and smaller than the human face. While it is true that they suggest the characters in a play, they make no attempt at realistic representation. The audience, knowing the story, recognizes the symbolism in the mask and the actor's movements, and is appreciative of the skill of the highly trained performers.

In the commedia dell'arte, the Italian traveling theatre of the sixteenth and seventeenth centuries, the mask was an essential part of the actor's costume. Special masks represented stock characters and were always associated with them. A character's actions and appearance were thus closely connected; in fact, the covering of the face seemed to have an effect on the actor's body, making it freer and more expressive. An example of this connection may be found in Punch, a descendent of the commedia character, whose flesh-colored face with its great red nose and bulging eyes are as familiar to us as his outrageous behavior. His face and his actions go together in more ways than one.

Clowns, who prefer greasepaint to the mask, observe a unique tradition relating to mask. Each clown creates his own face and is careful never to copy that of another. A clown's face is, therefore, an individual creation to be respected as long as· he or she lives.

Most children are fascinated with these various uses of masks and attitudes toward them, and enjoy inventing masks of their own. One of the most creative projects I have ever seen involved puppets and children wearing paper bag masks, both made by a class studying a unit on North American Indians. Because the mask has been used by so many people at so many different periods in history, it is a valuable resource for the teacher, and a magic prop for the child who makes and wears it.

Types of Masks

The mask may cover the entire head, the face, or the upper part of the face only, leaving the lower part exposed. The simple half-mask, worn on Hallowe'en or at masked balls, is a well-known example. The obvious advantage of the half-mask is its comfort. It is cooler than the mask that covers the entire face and it makes speaking easier. Speaking through the mouth of a mask is difficult and distracting for the inexperienced performer.

Masks may be simple, elaborate, beautiful, and grotesque; but except for the representation of animals, they are rarely realistic. The values of mask making are many and are implicit in this brief discussion. They provide an extension of the drama lesson; they reveal aspects of a culture in which the mask is an important artifact; and they release the wearer from her inhibitions. Many children feel freer when they are shielded from view by even a partial face covering. The child projects her feeling and ideas through the mask, while she, herself, remains hidden. The mask serves the same purpose as the puppet in this respect. In fact, some interesting research has been done on the use of masks and makeup in therapy.

The teacher will be wise to avoid using the commercial masks sold in stores around Hallowe'en, just as he will avoid commercial puppets. One of the values of including the mask in the classroom is the opportunity it offers for imaginative construction and design. This is particularly valuable for a child who is shy about acting, but who has interest and ability in arts and crafts. In using the commercial mask or puppet, the teacher misses a rich opportunity for teaching.

Makeup is another form of mask. It is not the purpose of this text to go into

Masked dancers and actors appear in The Mermaid's Theatre's *Medoonak the Storm-maker*. (*Courtesy of The Mermaid Theatre, Wolfville, Nova Scotia, Sara Lee Lewis, administrator; photograph by Peter Eaton.*)

its application for the stage; however, the makeup that persons create them-selves provides valuable insights for the leader and drama therapist. Nancy Breitenbach, a therapist working in Paris, describes her innovative work with makeup as "a form of free association," helping children through its use to discover who they are, what they want others to believe they are, and whom they would like to be. In an article published in England, she lists the reaction of children of different ages to makeup and describe how it releases them into drama.[5] In her opinion, the eventual removal of makeup, resulting in the reappearance of the child's familiar face, brings an affirmation of personal strength; strong feelings can be expressed and yet the individual will return to his normal state with a greater degree of confidence in his social well-being.

Greasepaint applied to a child's face by an adult, on the contrary, tends to place the emphasis on the outer rather than the inner aspects of character. This is not to say that the formal, scripted play produced with costume and makeup is without value. It is simply not germane to a text on creative drama; and the art of makeup is therefore left until later, when the student is ready for formal play production.

5. Nancy Breitenbach, "Secret Faces," *British Journal of Dramatherapy*, 3, no. 2 (Autumn 1979): 18-23.

Materials

Like puppets, masks can be made of a variety of materials. For very young children the paper bag mask is by far the easiest and cheapest to make. It is also the most satisfying because it can be completed in a single class period. The brown paper bag from the grocery store slips comfortably over the head, and holes can be cut in it for the eyes and mouth. Younger children need help in locating the right places; once the holes are cut out, however, the mask is ready for decoration. Strips of colored paper can be pasted on the bags for hair, moustaches, and even eyelashes. Paint, chalk, and crayons can be used to color them. Older children, studying a particular culture or tribal society, may paste or sew on feathers, cloth, jewelry, buttons, etc.

Cardboard boxes can be used effectively to suggest robots and stylized characters. These are more difficult to work on than bags, and it is often hard to find boxes of the right size and shape. Because both bags and boxes cover the entire head, they muffle speech and limit freedom of movement. As a follow-up activity, however, after a class has worked on material dramatically, masks have value in extending the learnings. When they are incorporated in a project that is further developed for an audience, they offer an added dimension for the observers.

Paper Plate Masks

Masks made of plain white paper plates are recommended for the middle grades because of their shape, toughness, and availability. To make the mask appear three dimensional, cut two slits about two inches deep and about two inches apart on the edge of the plate. By overlapping the sides adjacent to each slit and stapling them back together again, a chin is formed, making the mask fit on the child's face. As with the paper bag mask, holes for eyes, mouth, and nose must be cut in the appropriate places. A nose that protrudes from the face can be made of construction paper and pasted on the plate, further adding to the three-dimensional quality. From here on experimentation with other materials is fun and will make each mask unique.

Papier-Mâché Masks

Papier-mâché is a substance made of pulped paper or paper strips moistened with thin wheat paste (wallpaper paste). The paper used may be newspaper, tissues, napkins, or toweling. Wheat paste may be secured from any hardware store (follow directions on the package).

You will need a form or mold to work on. This may be made of modeling clay, or you may use a wig form or a large round balloon as a foundation. Be sure the mold is lightly greased with oil or cold cream. It may then be covered with strips of *torn* paper (approximately 1″ by 10″) dipped in paste. Apply strips diagonally, bandage fashion, wherever possible, and overlap them. Two layers of paper is usually enough. Paper pulp (soft paper torn into small pieces and soaked in paste, then squeezed out) may be added to build a nose, eyebrows, lips, etc. Allow this to dry for two to three days before removing from form.

When dry, it will be firm and brittle. Holes for the eyes, nose, and mouth may be cut with a razor blade, X-acto, or mat knife. If you use a balloon blown to larger than head size, you can make a whole head mask (e.g., animal). Leave open at the base, and trim so that the form will slip over the head and rest on the shoulders.

Basic forms for whole head coverings may be made of chicken wire, covered with cheesecloth, and then layers of papier-mâché added. This will require tin snips to cut the wire; be careful that all wire ends are bent under and covered with papier-mâché. The dry head or face mask may then be painted or decorated with cut paper. Feathers, yarn, or paper strips may be added for whatever effect you want. If you spray the mask with a lacquer or plastic finish (Krylon), it will add to its durability.

Unless you want to cover the entire head, which is uncomfortable for the wearer, let it be a face mask and fasten it with elastic across the back of the head. A scarf, hat, or wig will complete the disguise.

Activities for Masks

While masks are fun to make just in themselves, they are even more fun and more satisfying when they serve a purpose; for instance, when they are worn in a play or creative drama class, or when they carry out a theme. Sometimes, on the other hand, the mask will suggest an idea to the wearer!

1. *Pandora's Box*

   Pandora's Box contains a variety of evil spirits. Try making masks to represent them. Players who have created movements for the spirits will love adding masks; this is a perfect example of the relationship that exists between mask and movement.

2. *A Circus*

   A circus calls for clowns, animals, a ringmaster, and any number of sideshow characters. Every person in the class can invent a different mask for a circus parade.

3. *Holidays*

   Although Hallowe'en comes to mind first as an occasion for mask making, every holiday contains possibilities. Take Valentine's Day, Fourth of July, or St. Patrick's Day. What about your birthday? Every child in the class might try making a mask of himself or herself. It may look like you, or it may be simply your own invention.

Summary

Puppetry and mask making provide an added dimension to creative drama as well as being arts in their own rights. Although it has been stated repeatedly throughout the chapter that the types of puppets and masks described are simple, requiring no previous experience or special course work, it is always wise to try out an assignment before giving it to a class. In this way you can foresee any problems that might arise and solve them yourself in advance. Gathering materials and providing enough space for construction is important. As in creative drama, the encouragement of original ideas will help to prevent imitation of familiar television characters.

The teacher who includes puppets and masks in the curriculum will find them a rich resource. Regardless of the reasons for including them, the possibilities they offer are limitless. The major values may be summarized as follows.

1. Puppets and masks provide opportunities for developing motor skills. Tools and materials must be handled with care in order to construct puppets and masks that are sturdy and functional.
2. Dressing and decorating puppets requires imagination. Each puppet must become a character, first through its costume, and then in the way in which it is decorated and painted.
3. Puppets require control. It takes controlled fingers to manipulate a puppet so that it can perform as the operator wishes.
4. Puppets and masks offer an avenue of expression. Through them the operator expresses the thoughts and feelings of characters.
5. Both puppets and masks have therapeutic power. Through them, the timid or withdrawn child can find release, whereas the aggressive child learns to subordinate himself to the personality of the character he is presenting.
6. Puppetry demands cooperation. Children learn to make turns and work together for a successful performance.
7. Puppetry and mask making are inexpensive arts. Delightful results may be obtained within the most limited budget. If there is no stage, a box will do until the teacher is able to construct something more permanent.
8. Puppets and masks may be ends in themselves or the means by which other ends are reached.

Given half a chance, the puppet engages the child as performer, playmate, teacher, and alter ego. The mask, though less versatile, is closely related, serving many of the same purposes.

7
Dramatic Structure: The Play Takes Shape

*I*f a creative drama teacher is going to help children create a play, he must know something of the structure and fundamental dramatic elements that distinguish the play from other forms of literature. He will not be expected to become expert at playwriting or dramatic criticism, but his enjoyment will be greater, and his guidance more helpful, if he has a basic understanding of the art form with which he is working. While there is no established formula for writing a play, particularly in this period of experimentation, there are certain elements that are necessary to its existence.

First of all, a play is to be played. Until it finds life upon a stage, it is not a play. Through the process of interpretation by actors, and the mounting by costume and scenic designers, it is born; and it will live or die according to the communication it has for an audience. It is true that some plays have been popular in their own times but

The Wind in the Willows, adapted by Moses Goldberg. (*Courtesy of Tom Behm, University of North Carolina in Greensboro; Photograph by W.C. Burton.*)

have failed to speak to subsequent generations of playgoers. Occasionally, but much less often, a play that is badly received when it opens finds an audience later. All too often, however, the play that fails to please in its first production is discarded before there is another opportunity to tell whether or not it communicates with even a limited audience.

There are plays that are universal and timeless in their appeal; what they have to say is as true today as when they were written, and this truth is understood by persons of all races and national backgrounds. There are other plays, however, whose messages are more temporal. Couched in the language of the day, they speak to the men and women of their own times, presenting problems both serious and comic, to which contemporary audiences respond but to which those of another time or place are indifferent. This is not to discredit such plays, but simply to observe that although they have found success as theatre pieces, they lack the universality and timelessness of the classics. What classics will come out of our own time must be left to future generations of playgoers to decide. The works of George Bernard Shaw, Eugene O'Neill, and Tennessee Williams are among those that have been translated into many languages and produced widely both at home and abroad. It is too soon to tell, however, to whom they will speak in the future.

As to plays for child audiences, there are not many that meet the criteria of good dramatic literature. This is because the field is new and few professional playwrights have been attracted to it. Charlotte Chorpenning, Aurand Harris, Joanna Kraus, Flora Atkin, and Susan Zeder are among our best-known and most-produced American children's playwrights. We are not concerned with formal production or the printed script in this text; we are, however, concerned with the knowledge of drama that older children sometimes want to carry beyond the classroom. It is here where process and product merge, and where knowledge of play structure and elementary theatre techniques are necessary. For this reason some attention is given to terminology and definition in this chapter.

Children are rarely concerned with linear structure. Their dramas may move backward or forward in time; absent characters may appear without explanation; and action in different times and places may take place simultaneously. This is not because children lack a sense of order but because they do not know the conventions of playwriting until they experience them in the theatre or until they are pointed out. Children have a logic of their own but need some help in communicating. Indeed, some of our modern playwrights, in creating new forms, are doing what children do naturally: letting form follow function instead of traditional rules.

The teacher, therefore, should not change children's work; in giving them a concept of structure, she will be helping them to express, improvise, and eventually, perhaps, write plays of their own. Far from stifling their creativity, this knowledge will help to stimulate it. Given boundaries, children are freer to express themselves than they are with no boundaries or form to follow.

One last word: Styles in playwriting change. Both the times and the theatres for which plays are written affect structure; nevertheless, certain elements identify the drama as a specific art form. Whatever our relationship to drama, these are the elements of every play, whether written for adults or children.

Characters

A play involves characters. It is their conflict that holds our attention, and it is through them that the playwright delivers the message. Whether tragic or comic, lovable or despised, a character must be believable and belong to the play. Even in fantasy, a character must have reality; a witch or a ghost, for example, though unrealistic in itself, must compel our belief through the consistency of its behavior.

The hero or heroine should be someone with whom the audience can identify. Whatever his faults or human weaknesses, our sympathy must be aroused, making us care what happens. Whether he should be more good than bad is debatable, but we must accept him as real and his actions as true.

Characters react to each other in a natural way. Though it is clearly established to whom the story belongs, there are other characters in the play who help to advance the plot through their involvement with it and their relationship to the hero, or protagonist. A skillful playwright develops character and situation through this interaction. Sometimes many characters are needed to tell a story; sometimes it is done better with one or two. The fewer there are, the greater the responsibility they have for telling the story, and the more the audience learns about them. The actor, however, must find in the most minor character the answers or clues to such questions as:

1. Age of the character?
2. Education and cultural background?
3. Interests?
4. Occupation or profession?
5. Religion?
6. Members of the family and the character's relationship to them?
7. Social relationships?
8. Physical appearance and health?
9. Dominant mood?
10. Qualities of personality?

Good characters are at all times consistent. If they are not, either through the writing or the actor's interpretation, we cannot believe in them. A believable character, on the other hand, has a reality that exists for the audience long after the final curtain has been drawn. Even when a character is fantastic, he or she must be credible.

Dialogue

Dialogue is the term given to the lines of the play. Good dialogue should belong to the characters, both in content and manner of speech. A noble-woman will not talk like a peasant, nor will a country boy talk like a prince. While dialogue must, of course, be understood, the speech patterns of the characters must not be sacrificed. For example, a character of little education who comes from a particular region will use colloquial speech or appropriate dialect. Poetic dialogue has been employed in the drama during certain periods of history, but even this convention does not obscure the speech patterns and individuality of the characters.

Dialogue advances the plot. The playwright's job is to tell the story as economically as possible through the words of her characters. A soliloquy, in which only one person speaks, is a device used occasionally; but in general it is through conversation between two or more persons that characters are revealed and the plot is unfolded.

Plot

The plot is the story. It may be simple or complex, internal or external, but what happens between the opening scene and the final curtain is the action we call story or plot. While tastes differ and styles change, a good plot holds the interest of the audience and is consistent. The most bizarre events must belong to it; and the outcome, whatever it may be, must seem logical.

Conflict

Conflict is the basis of drama, whether comic or tragic. Without conflict, there is no resolution; with conflict, the interest is sustained to the end. The successful playwright resolves the conflict in a way that is satisfying and acceptable.

Theme

The theme is the underlying thought or basic idea upon which the play rests. Not every play has a well-defined theme; it may, however, be the most

important element. If there is a theme, the story both springs from and
expresses it.

Climax

The climax is the high point of the play. A three- or five-act play will have
more than one climax, but there will always be a point at which the interest is
highest. This scene usually comes somewhere near the end, after which there
is an untangling, or resolution.

Acts

Acts are the major divisions in a play. Short plays are generally written in
one act. Longer plays may be divided into two, three, or even five acts,
depending on the plot and the need to break it into parts. While three acts are
most often used, there is no right or wrong number. Many playwrights today
use the two-act form with one intermission between them.

Scenes

Scenes are divisions within acts and are most often used to indicate a
different time or place. A play does not have to have any particular number of
scenes; the time covered and the locations in which the action takes place
determine them. Many one-act plays are written in a single scene because they
are concerned with a single action or plot.

Subplots

Sometimes longer plays tell two stories: the story of the major characters
and another story of the minor characters. One-act plays rarely have subplots.
Full-length plays frequently do.

Flashback Scenes

These are scenes that are sometimes used to show an important event that
happened at an earlier time, before the play began. The flashback is a device
that helps to explain the behavior or attitudes of characters more dramatically
than merely telling about them.

Denouement

This is the portion of the play that follows the climax. It may be long or short, depending upon the number of situations that need straightening out. In a children's play, the denouement and climax are often one, since children are satisfied once the conflict is settled, and long explanations at this point do not interest them.

Unity

This is the overall term applied to the integration of the various parts of the drama, making a smooth and consistent whole. Unity may be achieved in a number of ways, such as the creation of: a single hero, a single action, a single idea, a single mood. On the other hand, a good play, no matter how many characters or episodes, can also be unified through the sensitive arrangement and organization of the various parts.

Dramatic Irony

Dramatic irony is the term used for letting the audience in on a secret. Suspense is usually greater when it is employed, and many comedy scenes are funnier because of it.

Structure

Plays are described as long or short, depending on whether they are a full evening's entertainment or consist of merely one act. The number of acts in a long play varies. Though many playwrights have used the three-act form, some prefer four or five, or a series of episodes, rather than the conventional division between acts. Scenes are the divisions within acts and usually occur when the time or place changes.

Comedy

Comedy is defined as a play that ends satisfactorily for the hero or heroine. Comedy may be funny, but this is not essential according to this definition. Many comedies are serious or satiric.

Tragedy

Tragedy is defined as a play that ends with the death or defeat of the leading character. Though fashions in playwriting change according to the times and public taste, the downfall of the protagonist places a play in the category of tragedy.

Prologue and Epilogue

These are the portions of the play sometimes placed at the beginning and end, to introduce the play or to establish atmosphere. Such scenes are not an integral part of the play, though a narrator may appear in the prologue and also be involved in the play. Many children's plays employ narrators or are written with prologues as a means of imparting necessary information to an audience composed of different age levels and theatre experience.

Narrator

The narrator is a person who tells or reads an exposition that ties the incidents together. It is a useful device when an extended period of time or a variety of scenes are included, and is also a way of bridging the distance between actors and audience.

Theatre for Children

Children's theatre is first and foremost good theatre. In this respect, it does not differ from theatre for adults. There are, however, special requirements that must be met if the children's play is to hold their interest as well as be worthy of their time and attention. The script contains the same basic elements—characters, dialogue, plot—but not all material appropriate to the adult audience is suitable for children. Action, for example, is particularly important: the playwright writing for children must remember that it is more important to "show" than to "tell." Speeches should be short; long, talky dialogue is lost on the audience. Though vocabulary is necessarily adapted to the age level of the audience, it should not be oversimplified but should rather add enrichment and an opportunity for learning new words.

In writing an adaptation of a classic or well-known story, the playwright must make every effort to retain the essential elements of the source material so as not to disappoint or offend the audience. Characters must be believable.

Children on the Salt River Indian Reservation enjoy a performance. (*Courtesy of Lin Wright, Arizona State University; photograph by John Barnard.*)

Fantasy and fairy stories comprise a large segment of plays written for children; nevertheless, the characters in such plays must be endowed with credibility, exhibiting a pattern of behavior that is consistent.

If the playwright has suggested difficult technical problems, she must ask herself whether they can be carried out successfully or whether any modification of the effect will damage the play. By "technical problems" are meant such things as blackouts; characters who fly, disappear, or change into birds or animals; or unusual lighting and sound effects. What might be easily solved in the professional theatre can often pose an insoluble problem on the school stage, where equipment, budget, and technical assistance are limited.

Children's theatre, like adult theatre, should not depend on extravagant effects or gimmicks to stimulate interest; if such scenes are essential to the plot, however, and can be executed artistically, they will certainly add to the effectiveness of the play. Children do not demand theatricality, but there is no question that their enjoyment is enhanced by scenes that offer excitement and color. Many children's plays call for music and dance. Therefore, the actor in children's theatre should study both so as to be able to sing, dance, fence, and master any other performance skills demanded by the play.

Values

Much has been said about the values of theatre for children, and basic to this subject is, of course, the script. The children's playwright has a special and difficult task, since he cannot anticipate the age level of the audience. The chances are that those who will be attending the play will range in age from five to twelve, perhaps a span even greater. Efforts have been made in some communities to try to control the age of the audience, either by a statement in the publicity or by two series of plays. Age-level programming is controversial and exists as a problem with which the playwright is faced.

Children's interests change, as has been mentioned. While fairy and animal tales are popular with younger children, the eleven- or twelve-year-old prefers adventure, history, biography, and stories of real life. The attention span of the older child is longer, hence he can be absorbed for as long as two hours, in contrast to the younger child, who can probably not give full attention for more than an hour.

To the younger child, a character is all good or all bad. As she grows older, the child begins to comprehend motives and can see a combination of faults and virtues, or weakness and strength, in a single person. Children identify with characters of high motives and brave deeds. Through this experience they grow, gaining appreciation for the ideals and standards by which people live. Values, therefore, are important to both young and old. Material that confirms such values as honesty, integrity, and social concern holds the interest of all and may be presented without condescension.

In our preoccupation with ideals and values, we sometimes forget the appeal that comedy holds. Children of all ages love humor, though what is funny to the younger child—riddles, jokes, repetition, slapstick, the chase—does not appeal to his older brother or sister. Comical characters, ridiculous situations, and amusing lines are the materials of comedy and may even teach more effectively than the serious play. Some of our social critics have used comedy to point up the defects and flaws of society.

Some criticism has been directed at those playwrights and producers who give children only the musical play. This seems to be a trend of the times, with the adult theatre having an equally large portion. However, whatever the medium, if the ingredients of taste and credibility are combined with a worthwhile idea, a hero with whom the audience can identify, action, poetic justice, substance, and literary quality, the playwright will have accomplished her purpose. Children today are exposed to so much television that they come to expect technical expertise and take spectacular effects for granted. In spite of this, however, they can be absorbed in honest work, well done and simply staged.

The following script of *The Three Wishes* is included as an illustration of a well-known children's story that contains the basic elements of a play:

a worthwhile and relevant theme
a plot that holds interest
plenty of action
characters who motivate the action
conflict
humor
a definite climax and satisfactory end

Like most folktales, *The Three Wishes* may be enjoyed by a wide age range, though it is most popular with children under twelve. Despite the magic, it can be produced simply in classroom, club room, or camp. This is not to advocate formal productions by children of that age (the memorization of a script, long rehearsals, and performances for outside audiences); but an older group interested in giving plays for younger children would find this and other folktales worthwhile and fun to do. Should a younger group want to perform for other classes or friends, it is more desirable for them to create a play themselves than to use a printed script. It takes longer but is well worth the time and effort. Through the process of developing a play, they will have an experience in creative writing and working with others in a variety of ways. The actual performance should be low key, ragarded more as a sharing than a showing.

On the other hand, the theatre is a performing art, and children today see so many shows on television that they accept performance as a usual, rather than an unusual, occurrence. The teacher or leader should emphasize process and discourage production; nevertheless, a sincere desire to perform, on the part of the children, should be respected. "To withhold the experience," as one young teacher observed, "is like refusing them the game after they have practiced for it." According to another teacher, the most serious drawback to performance by children is the adult. Whether it is the teacher who works for a perfect product, featuring some children at the expense of others, or the adult in the audience who gives excessive praise, laughs in the wrong places, or is insensitive to the children's efforts, it adds up to exploitation. And exploitation, pressure, and boredom are destructive both to children and theatre. An occasional show need be none of these, if the adults involved handle the situation judiciously. As John Allen says of drama in schools, ". . . a school does not exist to create beautiful works of child art: what matters is the growth of the child and his ability to express himself in a variety of media."[1]

1. John Allen, *Drama in Schools* (London: Heinemann Educational Books, 1979), p. 23.

THE THREE WISHES
(An Old Tale)
DRAMATIZED BY NELLIE MCCASLIN

JOANNA, *an old peasant woman*
PETER, *her husband*
A STRANGER, *a young man with an air of mystery about him*

The scene is a small cottage. In the room are a table, chairs, a cupboard, and a fireplace. Down right there is a door leading to the outside. As the curtain rises, JOANNA, *an old woman with a discontented expression on her face, is sweeping the hearth.*

JOANNA: As if I could ever sweep all the dust and dirt from the hearth with this broom. (*She examines it.*) As many twigs fall from it as I have swept up. The old man will have to make me another, if he expects me to keep the house clean. (*She sweeps again for a moment, then stops and leans on the broom.*) Or better yet, if we had a servant girl, she could do all the cleaning. Think how that would be! To do nothing all day like our neighbor but sit in a chair by the fire and watch someone else do the work. Oh, why has the old man never earned enough to keep just one servant girl? Not five like the Duke. Nor four like our neighbor. Not even two like the simplest farmer. But one. Just one servant girl would be all I'd ask. (*She sighs.*) Oh, well, if the good man has not made his fortune yet he never will now. And we'll end our lives just as we began them— poor peasants in a cottage. (*She puts the broom in a corner and begins to set the table for supper. While she is doing this,* PETER, *her husband, comes in. He steps wearily through the doorway, then stops, leaning on a stout stick.*)
PETER: (*sniffs*) What! Supper not on the table? What have you been doing all day while I worked in the fields?
JOANNA: What do you expect with no one to help me? If we had a servant girl now, the supper would be ready and waiting.
PETER: And if I had a donkey to carry the plough, I'd not be so tired. I could climb on his back when the day's work was done and ride home in comfort.
JOANNA: A donkey? Why not wish for a horse? We could get a cart then and both of us drive out together on Sunday.
PETER: (*sitting by the hearth and continuing eagerly*) Yes, a strong brown horse like our neighbor's. I'd want one like his. Then I could plant a garden that brought in some money. In time I could buy

another horse. With a team there's no telling how much we could earn.

JOANNA: Well, we haven't even one donkey. So pull up your chair and I'll have supper on the table in a minute.

PETER: (*sitting at the table*) Cabbage soup again?

JOANNA: (*bringing the pot to the table and ladling out the soup*) What did you expect? Meat and white bread like the Duke? Cabbage is the only thing in the garden.

PETER: (*eating it hungrily*) It's good. Though it would be better if you'd had a bone to cook with it.

JOANNA: A bone means meat. When have we had a roast with a bone left to flavor the soup? (*She sits down and tastes her soup. Then she takes a piece of bread.*) White bread now, instead of black. That would help.

PETER: White bread with butter, eh, wife?

JOANNA: (*eagerly*) When I stopped at our neighbor's today with the basket of cabbages to sell, I caught a glimpse of the kitchen. Such things as they were fixing for dinner! Cakes, butter, cream, and a goose roasting on the spit.

PETER: Ah, well, we are poor folk, Joanna. We could wish till the end of our days and nothing would come of it. (*At this moment a voice is heard from the fireplace.*)

STRANGER: Nothing would come of it? Are you sure, Peter? Are you sure, Joanna?

PETER: Who was that?

JOANNA: Was that you, Peter?

PETER: (*getting up*) I'd swear I heard a voice.

STRANGER: (*coming out of the fireplace*) And so you did. (*He brushes off his clothes.*) Now, then, what was that you were saying?

PETER: (*startled.*) Oh, nothing. Nothing important.

STRANGER: Come, now, Peter, Joanna. You were wishing for a well stocked larder, I think.

JOANNA: Well, yes, we were.

STRANGER: Are you sure that's all that you wish for?

PETER: (*eagerly*) Oh no. If I had a donkey now—

JOANNA: Not a donkey, Peter, a horse. So we could ride in a carriage together.

PETER: And plough a garden that went from here to that forest.

STRANGER: I'll tell you what. I've been listening to the two of you for some time and I'm about to make you a gift.

PETER: What kind of a gift?

JOANNA: Who are you? And how did you come here?

STRANGER: Let's say I'm a stranger who heard you in passing.
(*He walks around the table and they look at him in wonder.*)
Oh, I'm not a rich man, if that's what you're thinking.
Though I do have strange powers.

PETER: What kind of powers?

STRANGER: I'll show you. Yes, I'm going to give you three wishes.

PETER: (*repeating the words after him, stupidly*) Three wishes?

STRANGER: Yes. But I must warn you, you'll have only three wishes between you. So watch out you don't waste them.

PETER: (*joyfully*) You mean, if I wished for a donkey, I'd get one?

JOANNA: No, Peter, a horse, not a donkey.

STRANGER: Sh! That's what I mean. Be careful. When you've used the three
wishes up, there'll be no more of them. Think of what you want
most.

PETER: And they'll be granted, no matter how great the request?

STRANGER: They'll be granted, never fear. But only the three. So watch out,
Peter.
(*The* STRANGER *moves back to the hearth and disappears as the old
couple talk excitedly together.*)

PETER: Did you hear that, Joanna? Why, I can wish for a team of horses
with a carriage to boot!

JOANNA: And a house!

PETER: Or a castle! With a kitchen as big as this room.

JOANNA: Filled with all sorts of good things to eat. (*She turns to speak to
the* STRANGER.) Must we use all three wishes at once or can we save
one for—Why, where has he gone? He's not here, Peter.

PETER: (*rubbing his eyes*) Vanished as suddenly as he appeared. Do you
suppose we just dreamed this?

JOANNA: No, of course not. How could we both dream the same thing?
And at the same time? He must have gone out the door while we
were talking. Let's go after him.
(*The two old people go quickly to the door but do not see him.*)

JOANNA: He's nowhere in sight. You go down the road, Peter. He may
have gone round the bend.

PETER: All right. (*He disappears from sight, calling.*) Hey, hey, there!

JOANNA: Gone before we even had a chance to thank him. He was standing right here. (*Puzzled, she stands in the middle of the room for a
moment.*) We might have asked him to supper. I wish we'd—(*She
claps her hands over her mouth.*) Just in time. Now, then, what to
wish for?
(PETER *comes in the door and goes to his chair.*)

PETER: Not a sign of him anywhere. You don't think, wife—

JOANNA: That we only imagined him? No, I don't. He said he had magic

powers. Therefore, why couldn't he disappear like smoke in the breeze? (*She has an idea.*) Up the chimney, perhaps?
(*She goes to the hearth and looks up the chimney.*)

JOANNA: Not there, either. Come, Peter. Let's sit down and think of three things to wish for.

PETER: Well, I still think a horse would be—

JOANNA: Sh! Remember what he said. Don't wish till we've thought of everything we need. I'd say a house, instead of this cottage.

PETER: Or a castle with barns—

JOANNA: And servants—

PETER: And fine dresses for you—

JOANNA: And a gold-headed cane for you to lean on when you're tired.

PETER: Wait! We can't waste a wish on a cane. Why not wish me young and strong again? Then I'd have no use for a cane.

JOANNA: (*excited*) Both of us young again, Peter! As we were when we first moved into this cottage. My hair would be black. And when I put on my fine clothes, I'd be as beautiful as the Duke's daughter.

PETER: We mustn't be hasty. Let's eat our soup and then after supper, we'll decide. (*He takes a spoonful of soup.*) It's cold.

JOANNA: And why shouldn't it be? Sitting out in these bowls. (*She takes a spoonful.*) Oh, I wish we had sausage to go with it.
(*No sooner has she said the words than a sausage is on her plate.*)

PETER: Oh, Joanna, see what you've done! Only two wishes left!

JOANNA: I didn't mean to do it.

PETER: (*angrily*) You've thrown away one third of our fortune, Joanna. I wish that sausage were on the end of your nose!
(*At once the sausage is hanging from her nose. She puts her hands up and feels it.*)

JOANNA: Peter!

PETER: I'm sorry, Joanna. I was angry. I didn't think. Here, let me pull it off.

JOANNA: It's stuck tight. I'm trying.

PETER: (*Going over to her, he pulls and pulls.*) It certainly seems to be stuck there. Come, let's both pull.
(*They both pull but the sausage refuses to budge.*)
It seems as if the harder we pull, the faster it sticks. I have it! I'll cut it off.

JOANNA: No, Peter. You might cut my nose.
(*PETER gets a huge knife and comes toward her.*)

PETER: I'll be careful. Let me try.

JOANNA: (*running away from him*) No, no. Leave me alone.

PETER: Perhaps if I cut it off just below—about here?

JOANNA: I don't want even half a sausage on the end of my nose. (*Wailing.*) Oh, Peter, what shall I do?

PETER: Just one wish left. Shall it be a house or the horses and carriage?

JOANNA: I can't go about with a sausage hanging on my nose. No matter how rich we were, people would laugh.

PETER: We could tie a scarf over your face.

JOANNA: Every time I stepped out of the house?

PETER: Perhaps no one would notice—

JOANNA: Oh, Peter, how would you like to have a sausage hanging down over your chin?

PETER: It may go away.

JOANNA: It won't, I know. Oh, Peter, there's just one thing to do.

PETER: You mean—

JOANNA: Yes. To wish it off. Are you willing?

PETER: I guess you're right. (*They look at each other.*) We were both foolish.

PETER
JOANNA: (*together*) We wish the sausage off her/my nose. (*Miraculously the sausage comes off in* JOANNA'S *hand.*)

JOANNA: There. (*Sadly.*) All three wishes gone. And we're no better off than we were.

PETER: Except, perhaps—Come, wife, let us eat our supper and be grateful that no more harm was done. After all, we do have soup in our bowls—

JOANNA: And a roof over our heads—

PETER: And strength enough to work in the fields.

JOANNA: And each other.

PETER: And, who knows, perhaps some day he will come again. The next time—(*He and* JOANNA *look at each other and laugh.*) (*The curtain falls.*)

The business of the sausages, incidentally, provides excellent material for pantomime, and it is suggested that this part be improvised by itself.

Where does one go to find good stories for creative playing? There are a number of sources. The children's room of the public library is usually the best, and the creative drama teacher will be wise to familiarize herself with its shelves. She will also go to the children themselves. What are their favorite books and stories? What are their interests? Have any of them stories of their own to share? Family stories, stories with ethnic backgrounds, stories no one else knows? There is a creative writing contest held every two or three years in New York City entitled "Stories My Grandparents Told Me," which could be a

Making plans—children in public elementary school in class led by Creative Arts Team of New York University. (*Courtesy of C.A.T.*)

rich resource for dramatization.[2] Lively characters, amusing and touching anecdotes, customs of other lands, and experiences of immigrants in America are all fodder for the playwright and actor. And, incidentally, they help build respect for the cultural backgrounds of both self and others.

As to the criteria one looks for in stories for dramatization, the following are generally agreed to be most important:

> believable and interesting characters
>
> a clear story line or plot
>
> a good protagonist (hero or heroine) with whom the children can identify and for whom they can care
>
> material that is worth spending time on, that makes demands on the reader
>
> a story that is geared to the children's interests, needs, and age level, taking into account their concerns and idea of humor
>
> a story with a number of characters rather than two or three, thus giving everyone in the class a chance to try on the parts
>
> variety in the selections during the course of the year

Dramatizing Legendary Material

Myths, legends, and folktales are particularly good for creative playing. In the first place, these stories have been told and retold over the years so that the story line is clear and easily followed. Characters are generally well defined; have complete relevance to the plot; and, even in the case of the supernatural, have credibility. The theme is usually strong, for one generation has passed the tale along to the next, carefully, if unconsciously, preserving the values of the culture. Primitive creation myths, explaining natural phenomena, are particularly good today in the face of our expanding body of information about the universe and the new kinds of questions we are asking.

A group might dramatize a well-known myth or legend, or, through the study of legendary material, develop a play of its own. A holiday, for instance, often has an interesting origin, which would make good material with which to construct a play. Hallowe'en is a good example.

Hallowe'en

Of all the holidays, Hallowe'en must certainly be one of the top favorites of children. Their fascination with the supernatural, the dressing up in fanciful and grotesque costumes, the parties, games, tricks, and treats (all to be forgiven in the spirit of the occasion) make for a holiday with appeal for every age. Even

2. Conducted by the Police Athletic League of New York; Kitty Kirby, director of Performing Arts.

the commercialization of Hallowe'en in the form of ready-made costumes, masks, crepe paper decorations, and packages of candy corn in the supermarket have not spoiled its appeal, though it has perhaps shifted the emphasis. At any rate, Hallowe'en as a suggestion for dramatizing is guaranteed to elicit an enthusiastic response from the most resistant group. Let's take a look at Hallowe'en to see what some of the possibilities are.

Its roots go back to antiquity, thus providing a rich source of information for playmaking as well as the fun and the social activities associated with its celebration. As a holiday, therefore, Hallowe'en enjoys great popularity because it offers interesting content, action, and an opportunity for dressing up. Fifth and sixth graders, with the help of the teacher, can learn about play structure through the process of building a creative drama from source material concerning this holiday.

The customs associated with Hallowe'en spring mostly from three distinct sources: pagan, Roman, and Christian. The strongest influence was probably the pagan. Each year the Druids of Northern and Western Europe celebrated two feasts—Beltane, on the first of May, and Samhain, on the thirty-first of October. The latter was a fall festival, held after the harvest had been gathered, thus marking the end of summer and the beginning of winter. Their new year began on November first, so that Hallowe'en was actually New Year's Eve. Fortune-telling was a popular custom on this holiday, as people were eager to learn what the new year held.

The Druids believed that the spirits of persons who had died the previous year walked the earth on this night. They lighted bonfires in order to frighten away the evil spirits. It is thought that the candle in a pumpkin is a descendent of this custom. One legend has it that a rogue named Jack was caught playing tricks on the devil. As punishment, Jack was doomed to walk the earth forever, carrying a pumpkin lantern to light his way.

In order to ward off evil spirits and also to imitate them and so frighten others, many persons took to the wearing of costumes and masks. This led to playing tricks, mixing fun with fear and superstition.

In Rome the festivities were mainly in the form of feasts honoring the goddess of fruits, Pomona. When the Romans invaded Britain, they took their customs with them. The traditional use of fruits and vegetables (apples, corn, nuts) may be derived from this intermingling of celebrations.

During the Middle Ages the Christians observed All Saints' Day, which fell on November first. The eve of that day was October thirty-first, which became known as Hallowe'en, or hallowed evening. There is little, if any, Christian significance left; for most people it is a secular celebration, retaining only the outward trappings of ancient customs and rituals. Witches, ghosts, goblins, cats, bats, and pumpkins come to mind when we hear the word Hallowe'en. (Recently, collecting money for UNICEF has replaced the traditional "treats" in many communities.) Because so much information is available and much of it not generally known, Hallowe'en is a good choice for a program that can be researched, improvised, written, and, if desired, performed for the enjoyment of others. The tasks involved would be:

1. Looking up information about Hallowe'en (the amount dependent on the age of the group and the time that can be devoted to it).
2. Improvising legendary material with the greatest appeal for the children.
3. Developing a program or play by the group based on the information found.
4. (Optional) Writing a script that has come out of the research and improvisation.

Should this prove to be something the children want to perform for others, it will lead naturally into the next stage: a play for an audience. What we are concerned with here, however, is an understanding of dramatic structure, obtained through the process of creating an original play or group project. Later, if the group so desires, it might try creating a myth of its own. Children enjoy thinking of ways to explain phenomena, sayings, or chracters for which they have no ready answers. Because an activity of this sort invoves creative writing as well as creative playing, it is a way in which drama can be integrated naturally into the curriculum. Younger children might want to find their own explanations for such things as the Man in the Moon, Groundhog Day, Jack Frost, candles on a birthday cake, or perhaps local jokes and customs. Older children find intellectual stimulation in the study and dramatization of myths and legends. They may also want to try their hands at the writing of original science fiction. Our space age, far more familiar and acceptable to young people than we often realize, can be a powerful force for imaginative writing. The study of dramatic structure, through the creation of an original plot, is a sound and rewarding experience.

Summary

Although the study of dramatic structure belongs to the upper rather than the lower grades, it is a part of playmaking on any level. The advancement of plot and the development of character depend on a structure of some sort. Younger players, unfamiliar with theatre conventions, often invent highly imaginative forms and this is not to be discouraged. The main thing to keep in mind is that structure is necessary to create order out of the profusion of ideas that a lively group offers. Breaking a story into scenes, finding the climax, listing the necessary characters, seeing where additional characters can be added or where extraneous material can be cut, all develop critical judgment and a sense of organization in young players.

Whether performing or writing, the student needs boundaries within which to work. Too rigid a boundary stifles creativity whereas its lack often causes good ideas to become dissipated. Form and content are of equal importance; creative drama offers a superb opportunity to shape material into a form that communicates with the spectator as well as expresses the thoughts and feelings of the player.

The dramatization of a favorite story, on the other hand, makes different demands on the group and is, in many respects, much easier to write than an original play. To begin with, there is a plot which supplies the basic structure. Characters are clearly defined but must be given appropriate dialogue. In a play, dialogue serves three major functions: to describe the characters; to further the action; and to help show the time, place, and circumstances in which the story takes place. Because the players do not have to create an original narrative, they can focus their attention on characterization and believable dialogue. Time spent on improvisation before the actual writing is time well spent; then, when the group is ready to write the play, it will have a much clearer idea of what to include in each scene and how the characters

Creating characters in a jersey tube. (*Courtesy of C.A.T.*)

would react in the light of their circumstances, interpersonal relationships, and the period in which they lived.

Often new characters have to be added to flesh out parts of the story that the author has told through simple exposition. Sometimes characters and scenes need to be cut, if the plot is too long or too complicated for dramatic presentation. When such additions or deletions have to be made, young players need our help. Children are usually quick to find solutions, however, when a discussion is held as to how best to solve the problems. Such questions as "how do we know that . . . ," or "what can we do to show . . . ," or "can we think of a way to explain . . . " will elicit suggestions.

Whereas there are many values in the writing of an original script, most teachers find it more satisfactory to start with an adaptation of a well-known story. The players have the experience of working with a good piece of literature and from it will be better able to handle the additional problems that a totally original project presents, if or when they want to try one. Again, it must be emphasized that creative drama is participant-centered. Product can never be totally separated from process, however; therefore, when a class is ready for the next step—the writing of a play or dramatization of a story for an audience—some knowledge of dramatic structure is necessary. This knowledge can be learned through improvisation or through the development of a script, or, ideally, through a combination of both.

8
Building Plays from Simple Stories

When the group has had some experience with pantomime and improvisation, it will be ready to attempt to act a story. Groups of all ages welcome this next step and often have suggestions of their own to offer regarding favorite stories or material from other classes that they want to dramatize. Regardless of how well they may know the story, there is still some preliminary work to be done before improvisation begins. The teacher, well acquainted with the group by this time, knows the kind of material that will have an appeal and present the fewest difficulties. Success is important to future work, and the leader will want to select a story that he is relatively sure the group can handle.

There is a wealth of good literature readily available, which both group and leader can enjoy and find worthy of their efforts. The stories and poems included in this and the two following chapters are illustrative of the kinds

Fifth graders enjoy a creative drama class. (*Courtesy of Coleman Jennings, University of Texas at Austin.*)

of material groups of all ages have used successfully. Suggestions are offered as to ways in which material may be presented and handled. It should not be inferred that these are the only or even the best ways of using the material; they are merely illustrations of the thinking done by some groups.

Folktales, legends, and fables are recommended material for use on all levels, though different age groups will view them according to their own maturity and experience. For younger children, stories should be simplified in the telling, whereas in working with older children, greater emphasis can be given to characterization. Meanings and insights come with experience as well as age; hence a really good story spans many age levels.

When the teacher has decided upon an appropriate story, she must decide whether it is better told or read. In general, telling the story is preferable because it establishes a closer rapport with the audience and gives the leader a chance to observe the listeners' reactions and to clarify, as she goes along, any points that appear to puzzle them. This means that she must be thoroughly familiar with the material; in fact, the beginning teacher will do well to practice telling the story aloud before she presents it to the group. This will add to her own self-confidence and help her develop greater variety and color in her presentation. A good voice and clear diction are certainly assets, but even more important is the teacher's ability to involve herself in the material so that the story comes alive to the listeners. She will probably find it easier to establish contact if she sits down, with her audience gathered closely around her.

Experience in telling stories helps the teacher to avoid such pitfalls as forgetting parts and having to return to them out of sequence. He will soon learn to proceed in order, holding the climax until the end, including as many details as his listeners are able to handle, and as are necessary to the story. He will avoid condescension and will adapt his vocabulary to the age and background of the group, taking advantage, at the same time, of opportunities to introduce new words and explain ideas that are strange or foreign. With a little practice, most leaders can develop an effective storytelling technique that stimulates enthusiasm for dramatization.

After the story has been told, and all questions answered, the children are ready to begin planning how they will handle it. A discussion should include a review of the plot and descriptions of the characters. When the leader feels that the group has the details well in mind, she will suggest that they try playing it. Asking for volunteers is a good way of starting: this gives the stronger ones a chance to try it first and the more timid an opportunity to become better acquainted with it before taking their turns. Casting is done on a voluntary basis the first two or three times. Later on, the leader may suggest that other children try various parts. For instance, she might say, "Lynne hasn't had a chance yet. How would you like to try the princess this time, Lynne?" Or, "John has been the cobbler. Let's give Alan a chance to play it. And you, John, be one of the townsfolk." Or, "I know David has a strong voice. How about letting him be the giant?"

In other words, it is the development of each participant that concerns us. Later on, when the group is ready to play the story for the last time, the leader might suggest those children who have brought the greatest reality to each part, but this is as close as we come to type casting.

The situation may be played any number of times, but the replaying should not be interpreted as rehearsal. It is hoped, of course, that with each playing, the story will gain in substance and depth; that there will be deeper insights; and that the participants will develop greater freedom and self-confidence. The discussions preceding and following each playing are important aspects of creative dramatics, for it is during these periods that some of the most creative thinking takes place. Some questions that might precede the first playing are:

1. What do we want to tell?
2. Who are the people?
3. What are these people really like?
4. What are they doing when we first meet them?
5. Where does the first scene take place?
6. What kind of a house do they live in?

After the scene has been played once, more specific questions can guide the discussion. These might be:

1. Did they tell the story?
2. What did you like about the opening scene?
3. Did the people show that they were excited? (Angry, unhappy, etc.)
4. When we play it again, can you think of anything that would improve it?
5. Was anything important left out?

In the course of a year, there are often delightful results, and both the leader and group may honestly wish to share them with others. There is no reason why this should not be done, provided public performance was not the original intention. More often, however, the initial results will be crude and superficial. Dialogue will be scanty, despite the most careful planning. To the experienced leader, this does not represent failure. It is an early stage in the development of the group and may, at that point, indicate real progress. Acceptance of the effort, therefore, does not mean that the leader is satisfied to remain at this level but, rather, that he recognizes the efforts that have been made and is aware of the values to those who have taken part. As he works with the group, he will become more selective in what he accepts, but in the beginning he will accept all ideas because they have been offered. It is important for every member to feel that her ideas are worthy of consideration. In time, even eight- and nine-year-olds will learn to distinguish between contributions that advance the play and those that distract or have little to do with it.

The following stories have been chosen for inclusion here because of their simplicity. Most groups are familiar with them and like them, and need only to be refreshed as to the details. The first, *Caps for Sale,* is popular with younger children but equally interesting to older children, and even adults, because of the underlying theme. Very young children enjoy being monkeys and like to take turns acting the Peddler. Older children, however, quickly see a parallel between human behavior and the behavior of monkeys, hence find in this simple tale a meaning worthy of their thought and effort. Although *Caps for Sale,* or *The Peddler and His Caps,* is very well known, a brief synopsis of the story is included.

CAPS FOR SALE

There was once a little old man who made caps. All year long he worked at them: red caps, pink caps, yellow caps, blue, green, and purple caps, caps with feathers and caps without. Every so often, when he had made a large enough number of caps to sell, he would put them in his pack and take them around to the villages. This particular morning he decided that he had plenty of caps to peddle, and since it was a very fine summer day, he took himself off. His cries of "Caps for sale" roused the townsfolk, and soon many of them were trying on caps and selecting the ones they wanted to buy. Butchers, bakers, shoemakers, mothers, children, and even the mayor himself, gathered around the little Peddler, trying on caps and admiring their appearances. Finally, the mayor, who had found nothing to his liking, took off his cap and tossed it back to the Peddler, suggesting that he come again some other day. "Not today, Peddler. Come back another time."

Reluctantly, all of the townsfolk followed his example, echoing the mayor's words that he return another day. Realizing that he could sell no caps in this village, the little Peddler departed. Before long, he passed by the edge of a woods and, feeling very sleepy, decided to lie down and rest. Soon, however, he fell fast asleep, his hats lying on the grass beside him. Now it happened that this part of the woods was inhabited by a band of monkeys. Monkeys are curious little fellows, and finding the Peddler asleep under a tree, they decided to investigate the contents of his pack. First one, then another, cautiously approached. When they saw that the Peddler was wearing a cap on his head, the monkeys tried the caps on their own little heads. Then they scampered a distance away, chattering excitedly, for they were very

Children in Hokulani School playing the story of *The Peddler and His Caps.* (*Courtesy of Tamara Hunt, University of Hawaii.*)

much pleased with themselves. The sound of the chattering soon awakened the Peddler. He reached for his pack and was astonished to find it empty. Greatly puzzled, he looked about him to see where the caps might have gone. Suddenly he saw the monkeys. He called to them, pleasantly at first, and asked them to give back his caps. They only chattered, "Chee, chee, chee," pleasantly, in reply.

Then he shook his fist at them and demanded his caps, but they just shook their fists back. Angrily he stamped his foot at them but they only stamped their little monkey feet at him in return. He begged, and they begged; he moved a few steps away, and they moved a few steps away. Suddenly it occurred to him that the monkeys were doing everything he did. With a sweeping gesture, he removed his own cap and tossed it to the ground at his feet. Immediately all of the monkeys removed their caps and threw them down to the Peddler. He gathered his caps up as quickly as possible, then made a low bow and thanked the monkeys for returning them. Chattering happily, the monkeys also bowed; each was pleased with the trick he thought he had played on the other.

When the leader has finished telling the story, she will be wise to review the plot to make certain that it is clearly understood. From here on, there are many ways of proceeding. She may ask where the story begins and how many scenes the group sees in it. They may suggest two, three, four, or even five, though they usually come to the conclusion that three main scenes are necessary. These are:

1. The Peddler starts out on his travels.
2. He arrives in the village.
3. He stops to rest in the forest.

Some groups imagine a road running all around the room, with the three scenes laid in different areas. This enables the Peddler to move from one place to another and gives him an opportunity to talk to himself as he walks along. Since no scenery is used in creative dramatics, such an arrangement is perfectly feasible. Incidentally, one advantage of a large room in dramatizing this story is the amount of freedom it provides the players: they are not limited by the rows of seats or traditional stage area. When playing in an auditorium, however, the succession of scenes will follow a more conventional pattern, unless there is an apron (area in front of the curtain) to accommodate some of the action.

In discussing how the Peddler's occupation might be introduced, one group may suggest that he have a wife with whom he can talk over his plans for the day at breakfast. Another group may give him a helper; another, a son; and still another may insist that he lives alone and so, has him talk to himself.

Whether or not his trip down the road is considered a separate scene depends on the importance the group attaches to it, but the next major scene is certainly the village in which the Peddler attempts to sell his caps. One of the advantages of a story of this sort is the opportunity for characterization afforded by the villagers. As any number of villagers may be included, there is an opportunity for many children to take part. The mayor is always a favorite, though other delightful characters may be created; a shoemaker, a mother, a small boy, a farmer, a young girl, and a milliner are examples. The playing of this scene will be long or short, depending upon the characterizations and the fun the children have with it. Again, if a road is used to suggest the Peddler's travels, he will move along to a place designated as a part of the forest. If the group is small, the same children who were villagers can be monkeys. If the group is large, however, there is ample opportunity for others to play the monkeys. One of the best features of this particular story is the flexibility of the cast: whatever its size, the entire group can take part in it.

Regardless of age, children always respond to the monkeys, and the activity demanded by their antics is conducive to bodily freedom. There is such great opportunity for pantomime in the final scene that the leader might do well to begin with it, as a means of relaxing the group. By the time all have been monkeys, they are better prepared to begin on the story.

In this, and, indeed, in any story selected for dramatization, it is a good idea to work on small portions first rather than to attempt the entire story at once. No matter how well the children may know the material, it is quite another thing to improvise the scenes. Therefore, working on short bits, not necessarily in sequence, makes for more successful playing. In this respect, it is similar to rehearsing a play: the director does not attempt to run through the complete script until he has rehearsed each individual scene.

A word is in order here regarding the use of folk and fairy tales in creative drama. At one time these were the exclusive fare for dramatization and children's theatre. The reaction against them was based in part on a need for more diversified material and contemporary themes and in part on a question as to whether modern children were interested in fantasy. Bruno Bettelheim's book *The Uses of Enchantment* has caused us to take a second look at traditional material. Yes, we do want to introduce new stories, but in seeking them we must take care not to discard the rich resources of the past. The psychological values of the fairy tale and the cultural insights offered by folktales are important aspects of a child's experience. For this reason, as well as for the imaginative possibilities they offer, a number of folk and fairy tales are included in this and the next chapter. It is further hoped that the leader, in planning a unit or season, will offer material from both the old and the new, the fantastic and the real, the amusing and the serious. Variety and quality capture and hold the interest. Fantasy is not necessarily escape from reality; it can also be an instrument for the analysis of reality.

THE FIR TREE WHO WANTED LEAVES

The German tale of the little fir tree who wanted leaves is a good choice for young children. Although it concerns an individual, it can be played by the group. No dialogue is necessary, but it may be added, if and when the children want to use words. Music to create mood and suggest the changes will help the children play the story.

There was once a little fir tree who grew tired of his needles and wanted leaves like the other trees in the forest. One day, while he was complaining, a voice answered him, asking what kind of leaves he would like. "Oh, green leaves like the other trees," said the little fir. "I want leaves that are green in summer and change to red in the fall."

No sooner had he asked for them, than his needles changed into smooth, bright green leaves. The little fir tree thought he looked very fine indeed. All that morning he moved his branches and admired his appearance. Then, about noon, along came some goats. Seeing the fresh green leaves, they lifted their heads and greedily began to eat them. The poor little tree could do nothing to stop them, and soon all his leaves were gone.

He felt very bad. Finally he said, "I wish I had glass leaves. They would be pretty and no one would want to eat them."

Again, no sooner had he said the words than he found himself covered with sparkling glass. He was greatly pleased. "These leaves are much better than the others."

He moved his branches and watched them sparkle in the sunshine. About noon, however, a storm came up. The wind blew and the leaves hit against each other. They were so brittle that as the storm grew worse, all the glass was broken and fell to the ground.

The little fir was discouraged but not for long. "I know," he said, "I'd like gold leaves. They will sparkle, but the goats will not eat them and they cannot break."

Suddenly he was covered with yellow gold that gleamed in the sunlight. Surely he was the most beautiful tree in the forest! All day long he admired his leaves. Then, as night fell, he saw some robbers approaching. When they saw the little fir tree, they could hardly believe their eyes. "A gold tree," they said, "there's enough gold here to last us the rest of our lives!"

They began picking off the leaves and putting them in sacks on their backs. In no time at all, every leaf was gone. The little tree stood cold and miserable in the forest.

"I wish," he began, "I wish I had my needles back again. They were the best of all."

Quick as a flash his branches were covered with long, dark green needles. And he never wished for leaves again.

The theme of dissatisfaction with one's lot runs through folklore, and it is understood by quite young children. There are many ways in which this particular story can be handled. If the group is small, it can be played by individuals. Better, however, is group playing with some children being the leaves, others the goats, the wind, and the robbers. In this way the imagination is stretched as the players experiment with different ways to show how leaves, glass, and gold might look and move.

The story lends itself to movement as well as to improvisation and offers rich possibilities for discussion and expressive playing.

Fables are popular with some groups, though the obvious moral does not appeal to others. One advantage of a fable is its brevity. There is action as well as a quick and satisfying ending. There is little opportunity for character development, however, though some groups will fill in the plot with delightful and imaginative dialogue. The following is one fable that boys particularly enjoy.

THE BOY WHO CRIED WOLF

There was once a shepherd lad who went out to the fields each day with his flock. One day, growing tired of his lonely life, he decided to create some excitement. And so, when he was a distance from the village, he cried, "Wolf! Wolf!" The townsfolk, hearing his cries, dropped their chores and ran up the mountainside to help him. When they got there, however, the shepherd boy only laughed, and they realized the trick that had been played on them.

The following morning, the boy did the same thing again, and again the townsfolk ran to his rescue. Discovering that he had fooled them a second time, they returned to their work, angrily vowing that they would not be taken in by this trick again. On the third morning, when the boy was high up on the mountain, he heard a disturbance among the sheep. Seeing a wolf attacking them, he called out in terror. "Wolf! Wolf!" No one came. Again he called, "Wolf! Wolf! A wolf is attacking my sheep!"

The townsfolk heard his cries, but thinking it to be only a joke, did not go to his aid. The shepherd lad learned a lesson that day: if one cries "Wolf!" too often, no one comes when there really is danger.

The leader will not want to spend a great deal of time on this story since there is only one major character. On the other hand, the townsfolk offer opportunities for creating a variety of persons. Who are they? What is each doing when he hears the boy's cries, and what is his reaction when he discovers the trick? Who starts up the mountainside first? How would an old man feel if he climbed up a steep hillside for nothing? How does each one respond the second day? What does each say to his neighbor on the third morning? Such questions as these help the group create individual characters of the crowd.

Because the story is so short, every child can have a chance to try the part of the shepherd. What is he like? How do we know he is lonely and restless? Where are his sheep? How does he hit on the trick he plays? How does he feel when he sees the wolf? What does he do when the people fail to come to his rescue? Does he learn a lesson?

If there is a stage in the room, it may be used as the mountain where the sheep are grazing. If there is no stage, the boy can be at one end of the room so as to suggest the distance between him and the village. There is excitement in this story and the kind of action that appeals to younger children. The lesson, incidentally, is one that all are able to understand and appreciate.

THE TORTOISE AND THE HARE

Here is another fable that has great appeal and may be played without much time spent in preparation. Although the characters are animals, children enjoy discovering what they can do to suggest their characteristics and give them reality.

There was once a Hare who was forever boasting of his great speed. In fact, whenever more than two animals gathered together in the forest, he would

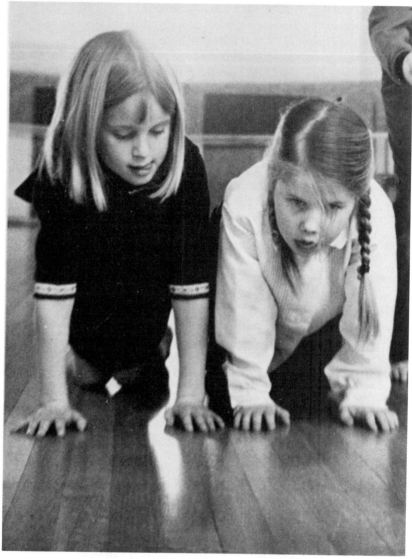

The Tortoise and the Hare. (Courtesy of the New Canaan Country School.)

appear and then take the opportunity of telling them that he could outstrip the best of them. Stretching his long legs proudly, he would declare, "No one has ever beaten me. When I race at full speed, there is no one who can pass me."

The other animals said nothing, for there was no one who wished to dispute him. One day, the Tortoise, who had been listening quietly, replied, "I accept your challenge. I will race you."

"That is a good joke," laughed the Hare. "I could go to the goalpost and back before you had passed the first marker."

"Save your breath until you've won," said the Tortoise. "I'm willing to race you."

The other animals, who were mighty tired of listening to the Hare's boasts, were only too glad to hear someone speak up, though they secretly wished it had been an animal with a greater chance of winning. Nevertheless, they cheered the little Tortoise on and helped draw up a course. Then they lined up on each side and the Cock called the start of the race: 1—2—3—GO!

The Hare was gone and out of sight in a flash as his white cottontail disappeared through the bushes. The Tortoise kept his eyes straight ahead and never varied his pace. Presently, the Hare returned and danced around him, laughing at his slow progress. The Tortoise didn't say a word. Then, to show his scorn for the Tortoise he lay down under a tree. He yawned, shut his eyes, and finally curled up and took his afternoon nap. The Tortoise only smiled and plodded on. After a while, the Hare awoke from his sleep. He opened his eyes just in time to see the Tortoise crawl past the winning post. As fast as he could make his legs go, he could not get there in time to save the race. The Tortoise, slow as he was, had crawled steadily forward while the Hare had spent his time running in circles and taking a nap. "I've learned a lesson today," said the Hare, ashamed of himself for having made so much fun of his opponent. "It's hard work, and not speed, that wins the race."

After the leader has told the fable, there is a good opportunity for total group participation: all can be hares, then tortoises. Younger children particularly enjoy the physical movement of this story. After some preliminary pantomime, it can be played in its entirety, since it is so short. A large room lends itself to the race, which may be run in a wide circle or in repeated circling of the space. Unless the group is very large, all may take turns playing the two parts, with the rest participating as the other animals watching the contest. This is a highly satisfying story for use in a single period or as a change from a more ambitious undertaking. Discussion brings out the moral, which children of ages eight to ten comprehend easily.

The Sun and the Wind and *The Country Mouse and the City Mouse* are favorite fables with many children. They also provide excellent opportunities for pantomime, as well as ideas for discussion. A group of fables, incidentally, makes a good program without taxing either teacher or players.

The stories that follow are longer than the Aesop fables but they have the same advantages of a simple story line based on an amusing or intriguing idea. When a group has mastered the fable, it is ready to take on a longer and more detailed story. The following were selected for characterization, theme, ethnic background and opportunities offered for group discussion.

THE TWO FOOLISH CATS

The following fable comes from Japan. It can be enjoyed by all ages, though I have found it to have particular appeal for younger children. The idea of fair play is well understood by even the youngest, and the trickster is always a popular character. The simplicity of the story precludes depth so far as character study is concerned but there is a lesson in it, if the leader wants to pursue it. The Two Foolish Cats is fun, and for that reason alone, worth doing.

There were once two cats who lived together in peace and harmony. They were good friends, sharing food and shelter. One day, however, each of them came upon a fresh, sweet rice cake on a path leading into a woods. Delighted with their discoveries, they showed their cakes to each other, comparing them for size and freshness. Now it happened that the larger of the two cats had picked up the smaller rice cake. "This is not fair," he said, "I am larger than you and therefore I should have the larger cake. Come, let us trade."

But the smaller cat refused. "No, I am smaller than you and I need more food so I can grow to your size. I wouldn't think of trading."

Well, this led to an argument, each cat insisting that he should have the larger of the two cakes. They accused each other of greediness and as they grew angrier they began to growl and spit. The argument went on for some time, neither one willing to give in to the other. Finally the bigger cat said, "Let us stop. We will get nowhere fighting like this. Let us go find the wise monkey who lives in the forest. If we ask him to divide our cakes equally, we shall each have our fair share and our argument will be over."

The smaller cat agreed, for he was hungry and wanted to eat his cake. So the two took themselves off to the forest to find the wise monkey. They looked in the bushes and tree tops, around rocks and behind the trunks of the trees, until at last they found him. They explained what they wanted but the old monkey replied that he must hear each side of the argument. The bigger cat began. Then the wise monkey said, "Stop. Let me hear the other."

The smaller cat spoke up. When he had finished, the old monkey nodded his head gravely. "I think I can solve your problem. Give me the rice cakes."

The cats handed them over eagerly. The monkey took one in each hand and weighed them with care. "Yes," he said, "this one is heavier. Let me take a bite out of it. Then they will be the same size."

But he took a very big bite and what had been the larger cake now became the smaller. "Dear, dear," said the monkey, "I shall have to take a bite out of *this* cake to even things up."

As you can imagine, he again took a large bite and the first cake became the larger. Paying no attention to the cats, who were anxiously watching their cakes disappear, the old monkey went from one to the other until both cakes were gone.

"Well," he said, "You asked me to solve your problem and I have done it. Without the cakes you have nothing to quarrel about." Whereupon he went off, leaving the two cats hungry and feeling very foolish indeed. But never did they quarrel again!

A discussion of greed and fair play is bound to follow. A small group will be able to play all three parts because of the brevity of the story. After playing and replaying the monkey, most children are ready to talk about his way of handling the problem. The humor must not be sacrificed for the moral, however; the value of the fable is its ability to convey a lesson in a humorous anecdote, usually told through animals.

BREAD AND HONEY
FRANK ASCH

This is a delightful little story for small children.[1] They will probably enjoy hearing it read several times before wanting to act it. Except for Ben, all the parts are short. It is suggested that several children play Ben, shifting with each encounter. If the children are very young, the teacher may have the entire class play each animal before trying it individually. Older children might want to play it for younger ones, in which case props will enhance the humor.

One morning when Ben was getting ready for school, his mother took a loaf of fresh bread out of the oven.

"Can I have a piece?" asked Ben.

"The bread is too hot now," said his mother. "But you can have some when you get home."

"With honey on top?" asked Ben.

"Yes," said his mother, "with lots of honey on top."

"Okay," said Ben and he hurried off to school.

That day, Ben painted a picture of his mother. When the bell rang, he decided to take it home. On the way, he stopped to show the picture to Owl.

"I love it," said Owl. "But you made the eyes too small."

"I have my paintbox with me," said Ben. "Maybe I can fix that."

"Fine work!" said the Owl when he had finished.

At the riverbank, Ben showed the picture to Alligator.

1. From *Bread and Honey* (New York: Parents Magazine Press, 1981).

"I just love it!" said Alligator. "But the mouth needs to be much, much bigger!"

"How's that?" asked Ben.

"Much better!" said Alligator.

A little way down the path, Ben met Rabbit and showed her the picture. "I love it!" said Rabbit. "But the ears are too short."

"Oh, that's easy to fix," said Ben.

"How's that?" asked Ben.

"Wonderful," said Rabbit.

When Ben showed Elephant his picture, Elephant said, "I love it, but the nose is too small."

Once again, Ben took out his paints.

"How's that?" asked Ben.

"Unforgettable!" said Elephant.

Then Ben showed his picture to Lion. "I love it," said Lion, "but you forgot a fluffy mane."

"How's that?" asked Ben, when he had added the mane.

"A picture to be proud of," said Lion.

When Ben was almost home, he saw Giraffe and showed him his picture. "I just love it," said Giraffe. "But the neck is too short."

"How's that?" asked Ben.

"Perfect," said Giraffe.

Ben ran the rest of the way home. When he got there he said to his mother, "Look what I made—a picture of you!"

"I love it!" said his mother.

"Just the way it is?" asked Ben.

"Just the way it is," said his mother. And she hung it on the refrigerator. Then she gave Ben a thick slice of homemade bread with lots of honey on top.

THE SHINING FISH

The following Italian folktale is particularly appealing to younger children, and while it is brief, it has more substance than many other simple stories of magic. The three main parts can be alternated so as to give everyone in the group a chance to play them; meanwhile, the rest of the class can be the sailors so that they also are involved in the action.

An old peasant went out into the woods one morning to gather firewood. He was very poor and he wondered how much longer he and his wife could manage to keep soul and body together. He was growing too old to do the hard work of his younger days and they had no children to help them eke out an existence. They had no near neighbors and saw no one but the fishermen who passed their cottage each night with the day's catch. Rarely did the old couple have the price of a fish for their dinner. It was on this particular morning, as the old man stopped to pick up some twigs, that a stranger came toward him. He said that he knew of the old couple's poverty and wanted to help them. So saying, he handed the old man a purse containing one hundred ducats. Before the peasant could pull his wits together, the stranger disappeared as suddenly as he had appeared.

Now the old man was afraid that his wife might spend the money foolishly if he told her about it, so he hid it under a bale of straw behind their hut. The following evening when he came home with his armful of twigs, he found a sumptuous meal spread out on the table.

"Where did you get the money to pay for all this?" he asked.

"I sold the bale of straw," replied his wife, "and I was paid a good price for it."

Well, the old man was mightily upset when he heard what had happened to the hundred ducats, but there was nothing to be done about it now. The next day, when he went into the forest to gather more wood, the stranger appeared again. "I know what happened," he said sympathetically, "but don't fret, for here is another purse. Mind what you do with it."

The old man thanked him and hurried home. "Where shall I hide them this time?" he said to himself. "I know—at the bottom of the ash pile. She will never think of going there."

But, alas, when he came home the next night, what did he behold but another feast on the table. "Where did this come from?" he demanded of his wife.

"You will be pleased," she replied. "I sold the ash pile for enough money to buy us a meal. Fish and cakes!"

"Oh, what have I done!" groaned her husband and he proceeded to tell her about the stranger and the two bags of ducats.

The following day, when he went into the forest, he once more met the stranger. This time, however, his benefactor said, "I will give you no more money. What I will give you instead is a bag of frogs. Sell them and buy yourself the biggest fish you can find. Hang it by your window each night and see what happens."

Obediently, the old man did as he was told. That night, when he hung up the fish, he saw that it gleamed like a lantern in the darkness. When the fishermen at sea saw it, they used its light to guide them safely to shore. To show their gratitude, they gave the old peasants half their catch. What is more, the fishermen made a bargain with them; if the old man would hang the fish by the window every evening at dusk, they would always divide their night's catch. And so, from then on the fishermen found their way safely to shore and the old couple never knew hunger again.

DARBY AND JOAN

This story appeals to both boys and girls, and is easy to play in a small area. There are only three characters but the story is so short that, unless a group is large, every boy and girl may have a chance to try one of the parts.

Have you ever seen a little house about the size of a birdhouse, with two doors in front marked "Fair" and "Rain"? And have you ever noticed that a little woman stands in the doorway marked "Fair," and a little man in the doorway marked "Rain"? And, depending on the weather, that one is always out while the other is in? Well, this little man and woman are known as Darby and Joan, and the following story is told of how they came to be there.

Many years ago Darby and Joan lived happily in a little cottage together. As time went on, however, they began to quarrel. Regardless of how peaceably the day had begun, before long they were disagreeing and finding fault with one another. And so a spell was put on them: from that day forth, one must be out while the other was in, depending on the weather. Our story begins many years later. The day has been fair but the weather is beginning to change, and Darby is about to come out, allowing Joan to go inside and finish her housework. As they talk together, not seeing each other, they regret the quarreling that led to their punishment.

"How I wish I could see you, Joan. Do you realize it has been ten years since we sat down at the table together?"

"I know, Darby. I'm sure if we could be released from this spell, we should never quarrel again."

"Imagine not seeing one's own wife for ten years. It was too cruel a punishment."

As they are talking together, Darby notices someone approaching the cottage. He calls out, "It's beginning to rain. Won't you stop and rest here for a bit?"

The stranger, who is a Fairy in disguise, comes to the doorway and asks Darby why it is he is standing out in the rain while his wife stays in the house. He explains and sighs over their misfortune. The Fairy then tells him who she is and offers to release them from their spell, but only on one condition that they never quarrel again. They agree joyfully and the Fairy goes off; but not without warning them that if they do quarrel, they will be put under the spell again, and this time it will be forever.

The old couple can scarcely believe their good fortune as they move their arms and legs stiffly and venture outside together. The rain is clearing, and they decide to have supper in front of the cottage. Darby brings out the table and chairs while Joan gets the food. Scarcely have they sat down to eat, however, when Darby criticizes the way Joan slices the bread. Joan replies with annoyance that if he objects, he can cut it himself. Furthermore, she notices that he is wearing his hat at the table. Before they know it, they are quarreling furiously.

Suddenly, the Fairy appears. The old people are stricken. They beg the Fairy for one more chance to try getting along, but she replies, "It is too late. You knew the condition and should have thought of the consequences."

Darby and Joan feel the spell coming on, and slowly move back into their old positions. The Fairy disappears with the old couple once more back in their doorways marked "Fair" and "Rain."

Children of all ages enjoy this story and have a grand time with the quarrel. First, playing the puppetlike figures while under a spell is a good pantomime for the entire group. Release from the spell gives practice in making the transition from a stiff, controlled stance to free movement. After all have tried it in pantomime, they will be ready to add dialogue. *Darby and Joan* is a delightful little story that calls for strong feeling and changes of mood.

THE BAT'S CHOICE
A Tale from India

This legend comes from India and offers various possibilities for creative playing.

In India they tell why the bat hides by day and comes out only at night. Many, many years ago there was a war between the birds and the animals. The bat, who had wings like a bird but a body like an animal, watched them fight but could not make up his mind which side to join. Finally, he decided he would go to the winning side. That appeared to be the animals, so he went over to them, declaring his everlasting loyalty.

Then suddenly things changed. With the help of the eagle, the birds began to overcome the animals. Now the bat wondered whether he had made a mistake; perhaps he would be better off with the birds. Until he could be sure, however, he hid in a tree and watched. When peace was finally reached, the bat found himself unpopular with both sides. And so it is to this day that he hides in a tree by day and comes out at night, when the birds and most of the animals are asleep.

This simple legend lends itself equally well to dance, mime, or dramatization. The birds and animals suggest movement, whereas the plot is so simple that it can be easily told without words. There is plenty of action to make it interesting. If the group prefers to use dialogue, however, the story can be improvised. Another way would be to have a narrator tell it, while the group pantomimes the action. In a story of this kind, any number can play. It is included to show the possibilities in a simple tale with a strong conflict and minimal characterization.

THE MIRROR

This legend comes from the Japanese. It is a delightful story for creative playing and is simple enough for quite young or inexperienced actors. It can be used in connection with a unit on Japan or played for the opportunities it offers for characterization and dialogue. The humor of the situation is particularly appealing to children.

A grand lady is traveling with her maid in a carriage down a country road. Along the way the carriage breaks down, and the coachman says it will take him some time to repair it; therefore he suggests that the travelers may want to get out and enjoy the countryside. The two women do so. After walking about for a few minutes, the lady sits down on a rock so that her maid can comb her hair. She looks at herself in a small mirror, which the maid carries in her bag. Just then the coachman tells them that he has finished the repair and that they can continue the journey. They forget, however, to pick up the mirror, and it is left behind on the rock.

In a little while two young women come by. They soon discover the mirror, which neither of them has ever seen before, and they think it is the picture of a pretty young girl. They wonder if either of their husbands could have left it here. At this moment the husband of the first young woman comes down the road and his wife shows him the mirror. He picks it up and looks at it, but he sees the face of a young man. He accuses his wife of being unfaithul to him. She, in turn, becomes angry.

Other persons come along, and each is asked what he or she sees in the mirror. Each one insists that it is a *man* or a *woman*, depending, of course, upon who is looking into it. The argument grows more and more heated as it cannot be resolved.

Finally, a priest comes along, and the people rush to ask him to settle the argument. He looks into the mirror long and hard; then he says he sees the face of a very old holy man. As they stand there, perplexed at this reply, the lady's maid returns, asking if anyone has seen a mirror.

One of the advantages of this kind of story is that it offers an opportunity for any number of players and no parts are, or need be, any larger than another. Children think of different kinds of people who might be walking down the road and then create them. Who are they? Why are they there? What work do they do? How old are they?

The situation builds in intensity and humor until it is finally resolved. There is also a possibility, imbedded in the story, for discussion of *appearance* and what a mirror tells us. Older players may find the legend a springboard to an original improvisation on mirrors and reflections. What *does* a glass reveal? Is it a truthful image? What is the relationship between surface and inner beauty? Is the latter seen in one's face?

THE PEASANT WHO DINED WITH A LORD
A *Ukrainian Folktale*

Once in a small Ukrainian village there was a rich lord who would have nothing to do with the common folk. As a matter of fact, he was so proud and so greedy that he had little to do with anyone, save his servants. He had no family, and this gave rise to curiosity on the part of the villagers. Whenever a group of them gathered, their conversation was apt to be about the great lord: who had seen him pass by in his carriage, what he looked like, what clothing he wore. Some, who had never seen him, wondered what his servants had bought in the market that day.

One afternoon a poor peasant, overhearing one of these conversations, said laughingly, "Why spend time asking questions? You can find out by simply climbing over the wall and looking into the kitchen."

"When have you done that?" demanded one of the old men, who had dwelt in the village longer than any of the rest of them.

"Yes," said the others, "have you been inside those gates? Has the master asked you to dinner?"

The group laughed uproariously at the young peasant in his ragged clothes, but he answered impudently, "I could dine with him before the week is out, if I wished."

"Dine with a lord? You?" said one of them; then they all laughed again. "Why, if you so much as put one foot inside the courtyard in those clothes, he would have you thrown off the place!"

"Will you make a bargain with me?" asked the young peasant.

All nodded vigorously in agreement.

"Very well. If I dine with him, then will you each give me a sack of your best wheat and a bullock? If I do not dine with him, I will be your servant and do everything that you ask for one month."

All agreed to the bargain, certain that they would get the better of it. Whereupon the young man walked boldly into the courtyard of the great lord. As had been predicted, he was met at the gate by two servants, who started to chase him out. "Wait a minute," said the peasant. "I have good news for your master, but I can tell it only to him."

The lord, being told of the promised message, was curious about it, and asked that the bearer of good news be shown into the house. The peasant said that what he had to say must be said in private, so the lord ordered his servants to leave. "Now, what is it that is meant for my ears alone?"

"What," whispered the young man, looking cautiously about, "is the cost of a piece of gold the size of a horse's head?"

The lord could not believe his ears and asked that the question be repeated. He was sure that the peasant must have found a great treasure. He tried to discover why such a poor man would want to know the value of so much gold. But the peasant, who was far more clever than he appeared, simply said that if the lord did not wish to tell him, he would be on his way and find someone else who would. The lord, afraid that a great treasure was about to slip out of reach, said, "Why not stay and have dinner with me? We can talk while we eat."

He called his servants and ordered them to bring bread, fruit, meat, and cheese as quickly as possible. Then the two sat down at the table together. When they had eaten their fill, the lord said, "And now, tell me where is your gold the size of a horse's head?"

"I have no gold," replied the young man.

"You have no gold?" the lord repeated after him. "Then why did you ask what it was worth?"

"I just wanted to know, my lord. And it was a kind of bet."

The lord was very angry when he heard this, and he ordered the peasant out of the house.

"I am not as stupid as you think me," said the young man, courteously. "I have had a very good dinner and I have won a bet besides. Now I must go and claim my sacks of wheat and my bullocks."

And bowing low, the clever peasant left, chuckling all the while at the way he had outwitted both the villagers and the lord.

Folktales telling of cleverness, especially on the part of ones who are young and poor, are popular with most people. Children love the double trick played in this story and are always eager to take turns being the peasant. Although there are only two major roles as the story is told, there is no reason why the villagers cannot be fleshed out, giving each of them his own motives and personal qualities.

The story can be played just as it is, or additional scenes can be added. It can lead to deeper character analysis or a study of the kind of society that is represented by the master and the peasants. Children are quick to detect greed, vanity, arrogance, and scorn; and they like to participate in a discussion of what they are and how they are found in our lives today. The humor amuses them because it functions on two levels.

JACK AND THE HAINTED HOUSE
R. REX STEPHENSON

Most children love ghost stories. The following tale from the Blue Ridge Mountains[2] *is simple in structure, yet it has all the elements of a good ghost story for creative playing: a hero with whom children can identify, a scary situation which is resolved in the end, and strong dramatic action. It is told here in the dialect of the region.*

This is a story about a boy named Jack. Now Jack is a boy who lives way up in the Blue Ridge Mountains of Virginia. Old Jack, why, he is always getting himself into a fix. This tale is called *Jack and the Hainted House.* "Hainted" is what mountain folks say when they mean haunted. So this tale is gonna find Jack meetin' some ghosts and the like.

Well, one day Jack was walkin' in the woods and it commenced to get dark. Jack was lookin' for a good place to spend the night. Finally he came upon this house with a light in the window and he went up and knocked on the door.

When the door opened, an old man stepped out carryin' a candle. He had about the wildest bunch of hair that Jack had ever seen on anybody's head.

"What can I do for ya, boy?" the old man asked.

"I'm lookin' for a place to spend the night and maybe get something to eat," answered Jack.

"Afraid I have no room here. Too crowded," the old man said, all the time studyin' Jack real careful with his candle.

"I'm awful hungry, too," Jack said.

"Well, I have a goose that I'll give ya. But you'll have to cook hit. Now then, a place to sleep. I got a little house over there you can stay in . . . if'n you want to." With that the old man handed Jack the goose and slammed the door in his face.

Jack took that goose and moved purty slow to the house. When he got there, Jack opened the door and went inside. But before he knew what was happenin' that door shut fast and he was trapped. Try as he would, Jack couldn't get that door open.

Well, all that work tryin' to get that door opened left Jack plumb tuckered out, so he looked around for a place to sleep. He spied a bed over in the corner, picked up a quilt, spread it over himself, and before a cat could of blinked twice, he was fast asleep.

Jack was just beginnin' to dream about bein' home and eatin' ash cakes and sorghum, when he felt this tuggin'-pull on that quilt. Well, the harder Jack pulled, the harder that tuggin'-pull was from the other end. Finally old Jack

2. Published for the first time in this book.

gave up and tore that quilt half-in-two and said, "I don't know who you are or what you are, but I guess I'll have to give ye half of this quilt if'n I'm gonna get any sleep tonight."

After Jack tore that quilt half-in-two, he went right back to sleep, but it wasn't long before he felt that tuggin'-pull on the quilt again. Jack pulled, but the other thing pulled harder and finally Jack fell on the floor. So Jack just gave that quilt to whatever it was and went someplace else to sleep.

Well, it wasn't long before Jack was fast asleep again, dreamin' of his maw's ash cakes and sorghum, when he heard these strange sounds. When Jack looked up, he saw these seven witches comin' in the room! Well, they surrounded Jack, but when they went to grab him, Jack jumped out of the way and all them witches bumped into one another. Well, old Jack, he jumped up and started yellin', "Get out of here, 'fore I beat the Devil out of ye!"

Well, to old Jack's surprise, those witches left. Jack went over to another corner of the room and decided he'd stay awake, to see if there was any other strange critters in that hainted house.

Hit wasn't long till these seven witches returned, not only makin' those scary sounds but carryin' a dead body. The witches left the body and disappeared again.

Well, Jack remembered something his grandpaw had told him. If you speak to a haint using the Lord's name, hit will talk back to you.

So Jack walked over to that haint and said, "What in the Lord's name are you doin' here?" That haint told Jack that he had been killed in this house many years ago by a robber, who was after his gold. The haint told Jack to go find the gold, which was hid in the fireplace, and to give one-third each to the haint's two sons, and, for doin' that, Jack could keep one-third for himself.

Well, Jack did just what that haint said, and you know Jack took the money and bought him a little piece of ground up on the mountain, and today he's got seven sons, jist as ornery as he was. And that's the story of Jack and the Hainted House.

The leader might begin by having all the children be witches. How do witches move, speak, carry the body, disappear? What makes them scary? Many children will want to try the parts of Jack, the old man, and the haint. When all have had a chance to try their favorite parts, the group will be thoroughly familiar with the story. The mountain dialect provides a special quality of authenticity and distinguishes it from other ghost stories that may be more familiar. Older children will appreciate the humor.

Summary

The preceding stories were selected for inclusion because of their simplicity and successful use with beginning groups of all ages. Though children's stories, each one has been used with both children and adults, and each age brings its own insights, meanings, and humor to the playing of the stories. There are many excellent stories just as suitable for beginning creative playing, and the interested leader will have no difficulty finding them. Tastes and interests of the group will guide the selection, though one of the values in creative drama is the opportunity it offers for introducing new material and good literature. One thing the leader will discover is that no two groups ever handle a story in quite the same way; if he is able to present it without a preconceived plan as to how it should be done, he will find that every group brings original ideas to its playing.

The procedures suggested are essentially the same, regardless of age level:

1. Presentation of the story
2. Organization of the material
3. Improvisation
4. Evaluation
5. Replaying

Evaluation is an important aspect of creative drama and leads into the replaying, which should acquire new depth and richer detail. Changing parts with each playing may not always make for a better performance, but it does give each participant a chance to play the part of his choice at least once. When the leader feels that the group has gone as far as it can with the story, she may suggest that the group cast it for final playing. This usually makes for a successful conclusion: the group has created something of its own and has found the last playing to be the most rewarding.

The older the participants, the more preliminary planning the leader can expect. Children, on the other hand, tend to move quickly into improvisation. Their dialogue will be brief, and the scenes shorter than planned, but their attack is direct. Children, less conditioned to the conventions of the proscenium stage, are likewise freer in their use of space, planning scenes in various parts of the room simultaneously. When the class is held in a room with a stage at one end, they are likely to use it as a particular place—perhaps a mountaintop or a distant land—rather than considering it as the central playing area. For every age group there are fewer inhibitions if a large room, instead of a stage, is used. Playing in the round reduces self-consciousness and is conducive to freer movement, since the scattered observers do not seem so like an audience.

When the group has shown that it can handle the problems of simple fables and stories, it is ready to move on to more demanding material. In the next chapter, longer stories are included, illustrating the possibilities offered for characterization and multiple-scene planning.

9
Building Plays from Longer Stories

*I*n this chapter several longer stories are included, with descriptions of some of the ways in which groups have used them for building plays. Again, let it be emphasized that there is no right way to dramatize the material. There are as many ways as there are groups, and the illustrations given here merely describe what some groups have done with longer stories. Not only are the plots of these stories more detailed, but the characters are complex and therefore require more experience to develop than those in the preceding chapter. The stories have been chosen for the possibilities they offer to the group ready to undertake them.

Dramatizing a longer story. (*Courtesy of the New Canaan Country School.*)

PROMETHEUS

Greek mythology is a rich and generally untapped source of material that can be successfully dramatized. One myth, which has been used many times with success, is the story of Prometheus, who stole fire from the gods. Basic human emotions and a dramatic story make it particularly appealing to children from seven to twelve. The idea of a formless earth stirs their imagination and provides an unusual opportunity for creativity. The story must be told carefully and in considerable detail, since not all children will be familiar with it. Although Greek myths are readily available, a brief synopsis of Prometheus is given here, with suggestions as to ways in which the leader may handle it.

The Greek gods and goddesses were believed to have dwelt on Mount Olympus, high above the earth. Ruling over them was the mighty Zeus. Among the young gods, most in favor with Zeus for his bravery in helping defeat the Titans, was Prometheus. One day Zeus and Athena, Goddess of Wisdom, were walking in the garden. They caught sight of Prometheus in the distance, looking down toward the earth. Zeus called to him and asked him what interested him, for he had often seen the young god staring down at the forests and mountains below.

Prometheus replied that he was troubled because the earth was so empty and silent, with no one moving about its surface. Zeus smiled, and said that for some time he had been considering a reward for the young god. "Prometheus," he suggested, "perhaps you would like to descend to the earth and fashion human beings out of soil." Prometheus was overjoyed.

"You are wise and kind," added Athena. "When you create them remember to give them strong bodies, keen minds, and tender hearts. Let them also see that there is a need for beauty as well as for the necessities of life."

"You may give them any gifts you wish except the gift of fire," continued Zeus. "That alone belongs to the gods and must remain on Olympus. When you have fashioned and are satisfied with your work, I will come down to earth and blow the breath of life into their bodies."

Prometheus was eager to begin and went off swiftly. Working with power and skill, he modeled his first human being upright and powerful, and called him "the Builder." Then he took more soil and made a second person, who was likewise tall and strong. Putting a few grains of corn in his hand, he named him "the Sower and Reaper." The third he pronounced "the Hunter," and to that one he gave a stone. The fourth he called "the Musician." Finally, he finished his fifth whom he proclaimed "the Thinker."

Scarcely had he stepped back to admire his efforts when the deep voice of Zeus was heard from Olympus. "We are pleased with your people, Prometheus. I shall now come down to blow life into them."

Miraculously, each statue came to life and breathed, and moved, and walked. As the days passed, Prometheus cared for his people and worked with them, teaching them to do the special jobs for which they had been created. They learned quickly and worked happily. One day, however, the seasons changed. The warm air was replaced by cold winds and snowy weather. The people were cold, and Prometheus was deeply disturbed as he watched them huddling together, trying to keep warm. Finally, he could bear it no longer. He knew he must give them fire.

When he called to Athena for help, she asked, "Do you care so much about your people, Prometheus?"

Prometheus declared that he did.

"Enough to risk the wrath of Zeus!" continued Athena. "He will surely punish you. The one thing he has forbidden them is fire."

"I have made my people, and I must help them, even though I suffer for it," replied Prometheus.

"Very well, then," said Athena. "I will help you find the fire to give them."

As swiftly as he had gone down to earth, Prometheus returned to Olympus to get the fire that he was determined his men and women should have. Then he called the five together and told them not to be frightened, but to learn to use their new gift. Just as he had taught them other things, he taught them how to use a fire for warmth and for the cooking of food. He warned them never to let the fire go out. The people were fascinated with the many possibilities of fire, and were soon warm and comfortable again.

It was not long, however, before Zeus learned what had happened. Angrily he told Prometheus that he had disobeyed, and must be punished for his act.

"I am ready to accept my punishment, great Zeus," Prometheus replied, "for I cannot let my people suffer from the wind and cold."

"A gift that has been given cannot be recalled," continued the god. "Human beings now possess fire, but you must pay the price. I shall have you bound by chains to yonder mountain. There you must remain forever and serve as an example to those who dare to disobey my laws."

So saying, Zeus sent his messenger, Hephaestus, down to seize Prometheus and put him in chains. The people were grieved when they saw the dreadful thing that happened to their creator and teacher, but their hearts were filled with gratitude for his great gift to human kind.

The discussion preceding the story can take many directions. It may begin with a consideration of human qualities and feelings. It may, on the other hand, begin with occupations and some pantomime suggesting them. It may begin with an analysis of the characters in the story and their conflicts. Eventually, in whatever way the story is introduced, there must be a focus on the characters, their behavior, and the consequences of Prometheus' act.

As in the other stories, the myth should be broken down into scenes before it is acted. Work in pantomime can easily be done with the whole group, for there is rich opportunity here. Together, the children can do the following actions: build a hut, hunt for food, plant a field, make a musical instrument (drum or pipe) and discover how to play it, suggest the beginning of human thought processes. Each activity gives scope for imaginative pantomime. Music may be helpful in stimulating movement, though it is not necessary. Children love playing the statues who come to life and learn to do the things for which they were intended. One whole period may easily be given over to these pantomime activities.

When the players are ready to begin on the story, they may wish to take turns playing gods and people. If playing in a large room, the children may conceive of one end of it as Olympus and the other end as earth. Or, if there is a platform, they may decide to locate Olympus on a higher level. The plot calls for at least three scenes, though some groups may see it in five or six. More than one group has played it with use of a simultaneous setting, with Zeus and Athena observing and commenting, while Prometheus works. When this approach is used, the scenes may move back and forth without a break or scene division.

Prometheus is a story strong enough to hold the interest for three or four class sessions, with constructive discussion preceding and following each playing. If the group enjoys the story, other myths may be introduced, for there are many with fine dramatic action, and values that children comprehend. Like the other stories in this chapter, *Prometheus* gains depth and detail with each new playing. The young god's sense of responsibility and compassion for his people begins to emerge, adding another dimension to the character. The conflict between the law of Zeus, and Prometheus' moral courage as he begins to feel for his men and women makes for powerful drama. The final playing can be most rewarding, as theme, story, character, and action are unified. The group that has become really involved in Prometheus' dilemma will have had a rich experience. This is a story better suited to an older group though even seven- and eight-year-olds can understand and play a simplified version.

BLUE BONNETS

This Indian legend, telling how the first blue bonnet flowers appeared on the earth, is a story that appeals to children of middle and upper grades. Many Indian legends are excellent for improvisation, but this one has a special appeal since it is the story of a child and her sacrifice.

Yellow Star is a little Indian girl who lives with her father and mother in a village belonging to the Comanche tribe. As the story begins, the Chief calls his people together. He describes the trouble that has come to their village after many weeks without rain. The long drought has caused the brooks to dry up; vegetation is dying; and animals have left the parched plains in search of food. The people sit quietly in a circle around the campfire as they listen to their leader. Then they beat the drums and dance, praying to the Great Spirit for rain. At first, nothing happens. Then, suddenly, they hear the voice of the Great Spirit far in the distance. They stop, put down the drums, and listen: "You are being punished for your selfishness and greed. You have lived in a land of plenty for many years, but your people have not shared with their brothers."

The Chief begs for mercy, but the Great Spirit replies, "I will forgive your tribe and send you the water you need only when one among you sacrifices on the campfire that which is dearest to his heart."

Excitedly, the braves talk together. They suggest that one give his horse, another his jewelry, and still another offer his beautiful young squaw to the Great Spirit. No one, however, is willing to make a sacrifice for the sake of his brothers, and so they move from the campfire and start slowly off toward their homes. The Chief calls them. "Come to this place again in the morning. By that time one among you may have found the gift that will bring us all forgiveness."

The people slowly disappear, each hoping that someone will think of a way to save them. Only little Yellow Star remains. In her arms she carries her fawn-skin doll with its bonnet of blue jay feathers. The doll is her dearest possession. She realizes that she must throw it into the fire to please the Great Spirit, but it is not easy to part with her only toy. Finally, she reaches her decision, as night falls on the village, and she tells the Great Spirit that she is ready to give that which is dearest to her heart. She watches the doll burn slowly, then, seeing the blue feather bonnet lying in the ashes, she picks it up and throws it into the flames. To her amazement, the feathers do not burn, but become small blue flowers. Yellow Star knows, then, that the Great Spirit has accepted her gift, and with a light heart she runs home.

The next morning, all the Indians gather together as their Chief has commanded, but where only last night there was a campfire, there is now a huge bed of blue flowers. The people are mystified, for they cannot understand how flowers could have sprung up in the hard, dry earth.

Yellow Star's mother tells the Chief about the doll. "Surely," she says, "it must be a sign. Hundreds of flowers now grow on ground that was trampled and dry."

The people, however, are unwilling to believe her story, for why should the Great Spirit be satisfied with so small a gift as a child's fawn-skin doll? At that moment, there is a roll of thunder in the distance. The Chief knows now that the Great Spirit has accepted Yellow Star's offering. Again, he asks his people to beat their drums and give thanks that they have at last been forgiven. The first raindrops fall.

This charming legend gives an opportunity for total group participation. Since movement is an important element, a good beginning can be made with a dance around the campfire. The use of a drum aids enormously in building rhythms, as the Indians move and dance and pray. The leader can, of course, begin with the story, but before dialogue is attempted, practice in rhythmic movement helps the players to become involved.

Discussion of the story and its theme should precede the playing, inasmuch as this will deepen the understanding of a people different in custom, yet like us in their human strengths and weaknesses. When the group is ready to begin, it is again suggested that short scenes, rather than the whole story, be played first. For example, the opening scene, in which the Chief calls his people together and explains the seriousness of their situation, is quite enough for one sequence. Yellow Star's sacrifice is another. The players conceive of the story as taking place in one act, with a break to indicate passage of time, or they may see it as a play in two or three scenes. Because it is a story in which any number may participate, playing it in the round is desirable, if possible. Players and observers are one, and are, therefore, involved to an unusual degree.

The part of Yellow Star is a favorite, but the Chief, the mother, and the selfish braves and squaws can all be built into characters who are believable and interesting. If this story finds favor, the leader may wish to bring other Indian legends to class. Most of them require little more than space for playing, since they are concerned with human beings in conflict with nature and with human weaknesses familiar to all.

A LEGEND OF SPRING

Another Indian legend that has proved extremely successful for creative playing is A Legend of Spring. *It is simple in plot but provides a wonderful opportunity for group pantomime and movement. Players of all ages find it appealing and develop it in proportion to their experience and the time that is given them.*

The Indians of the Great Plains had suffered through a long winter, but this year no sign of spring had appeared. Neither sun nor wind nor warm rains had come to awaken the seeds or bring the wild animals out of their winter hiding. One day, the Chief of the tribe called all the braves and squaws together. He explained to them that unless food were found soon, they would have to abandon their village and seek a home elsewhere. There was silence. The people looked up at the cold, gray sky, and down at the hard frozen earth. They knew the Chief was right, yet no one wanted to leave the pleasant valley in which they had dwelt for so many years. Finally White Cloud, youngest and strongest of the braves, spoke out. "I will go into the forest in search of food.

An African folktale. (*Courtesy of Rachel Carr; photograph by Edward Kimball.*)

With my strong bow and arrows, surely I can find food to bring back to my people."

"I will go with you," cried a second, then a third and a fourth. Others rose from the campfire, where they had been sitting, and joined him. The old Chief smiled. "Go," he said. "Perhaps if you hunt deep enough in the forest you will find the deer and rabbits to provide food until the spring comes to our land. While you are absent, we shall pray to the Great Spirit to make the sun shine again and the clouds empty warm rain on our fields."

The young men ran out as the drums beat a farewell. Then the old Chief called to the Great Spirit for help. The people danced around the fire, asking for sun, rain, and wind for their planting, and game for their hunters. When they finally dropped to their knees, exhausted, there was a rustle in the bushes. Looking up, they beheld a large golden bird flying toward the clearing. Scarcely had it appeared when White Cloud and his band of hunters broke through the underbrush. Two or three of the men had already raised their bows when White Cloud spoke.

"Do not shoot the golden bird. Perhaps it has come from the Great Spirit. It may be a sign for us if we wait to see what it wants. Hold your arrows. Do not shoot!"

The braves put down their bows and waited. Then the golden bird, seeing that the people meant her no harm, glided gracefully into their midst. Suddenly, she was transformed into a lovely young maiden with a golden bow and arrow.

"I have come from the Great Spirit," she said. "Listen to me carefully. Here is an arrow which one of you must shoot straight into the dark cloud overhead. If the cloud is pierced, the rains will begin, and winter will leave your valley. If he who shoots the arrow does not succeed, you must prepare to leave your homes, for spring will not come this year."

So saying, she handed the bow to the Chief, asking him to select the brave who could shoot the straightest arrow. "You choose, golden maiden," he said. "It is your arrow. You choose the one who will send it from the bow."

Slowly the maiden circled the campfire, first looking at one, then another. Finally she stopped before White Cloud and handed him the golden bow and arrow. He took it from her silently, aimed at the cloud, and released the arrow. Up and up it went until it was lost from sight. Then, suddenly, a crack appeared in the sky. The sun came out and the warm spring rain began to fall. The drum beat joyously as the people danced again, this time in thanks to the Great Spirit, who had answered their prayers.

Like the Indian legend Blue Bonnets, this one is best begun with movement. Pantomime and dance, expressing the people's need for rain, wind, and sun, help the group get into the story. Hunting, fishing, planting, eating, and moving camp are activities that may also be expressed in pantomime by each member of the group. If a sufficiently long time is spent on movement and pantomime, many ideas will come that can later be incorporated into the story. Children love to think of as many ways as possible to show how the Indians lived and how they expressed their needs to the Great Spirit. Actually, the whole story can be played without words, although most groups will want to invent some dialogue. A drum is a valuable property for the leader at first, but she will want to pass it along to one of the participants later. Some groups see the story in a single scene; others may wish to break it into several. However it is handled, *A Legend of Spring* is a strong story for creative playing. A drum and plenty of space in which to move freely are the only requirements.

THE COINS OF LIN FOO

The following legend, which comes from the Chinese, is particularly good for dramatization. Younger groups will enjoy playing the story; older groups may wish to try it in the Chinese manner. It is included because of its flexibility, its many characters, and its engrossing story.

There was once in a small village in the State of Tsin a lad named Lin Foo, who lived with his widowed mother, Wing Soong. After the father's death hard times had come upon them, and they had been forced to leave their home and sell their plot of land. Wing Soong, in order to earn a living for herself and her son, made fritters each week, which Lin Foo took to the market to sell. How his mother wished that she might someday earn enough money to educate Lin Foo, for he was as bright as he was industrious!

On this particular morning, when Wing Soong handed him the basket of fritters, the boy asked if he might stay longer in the village, for there was to be a fair and he wanted to join his friends and look around. "I should like to see the wares in the booths, the flags, and the little carved dragons and birds."

"Of course," said his mother. "Just mind you keep the money safe and do not stay so long that it grows dark before you reach home. You'd better be off now, for the way is long and already the village will be crowded with the farmers and their carts."

Lin Foo spent a happy and profitable day in the village. First he sold his basket of fritters and put the money in his pocket. Indeed, he had no trouble at all in selling the fritters, for the humble Wing Soong was known throughout the village for her fine cooking and fair bargains. The lad went from booth to booth, finally deciding that the safest place for his money was under a stone near the entrance to the fairgrounds. If he did this, he thought to himself, he could move among the crowds to his heart's content, with no fear of the coins slipping out of his pocket and rolling away in the dust. Carefully he placed the money under the stone and went off to join some village boys he knew.

Finally, it was time to start for home. He bade his friends farewell and went to the stone under which he had hidden his money. But to his dismay, when he lifted it up, there was nothing there. Lin Foo was sure that someone must have stolen it. Disconsolate, he sat down at the edge of the road, wondering what he would tell his mother and what they would do without money for the coming week. While he was sitting there An Li, the magistrate, came along; seeing the boy, he asked what was troubling him.

"Oh, master, I am a poor boy, whose mother makes fritters to sell on market day. She entrusted me to bring home the money, which I hid under this stone for safekeeping. When I came back just now to get it, I found it had been taken. And so I have neither money or fritters to take home with me."

"Have you a father, my boy?" asked the magistrate.

The lad replied that he had not and that he lived alone with his mother, Wing Soong. He told the kindly man that all the money they had was what he got for the fritters. The magistrate questioned him further. "Did you put the money well out of sight?"

"Oh, yes, honored sir. No one could possibly have seen it."

"Is this the stone?"

The boy nodded his head.

Then An Li said, "I shall arrest this stone. You, boy, go on home. But return with your mother tomorrow morning at ten o'clock. I shall try to get your money back for you."

Lin Foo went home. After he had gone, the magistrate had his attendants summon all the villagers who were at the fair that day and order them to be present the next morning for the trial of the stone. He requested that the magistrate's table and chair, two stout bamboo sticks, and a large jar full of water be brought to the spot for the trial.

The following day, Lin Foo and his mother set out for the village. A crowd was already there by the time they arrived. Many of the people thought that An Li lost his wits from too much study of the law. Some were willing to wait to see what the wise man had in mind. At length An Li appeared with his attendants. He asked if the boy, Lin Foo, were present. Lin Foo stepped forward. Then he asked if the boy's mother were there also. Wing Soong bowed humbly. Finally, he asked if this were the stone that had stolen the coins. When the boy, mystified, replied that it was, An Li ordered his attendants to strike the stone fifty times with the bamboo sticks. Many people laughed and some tapped their heads in ridicule. Angrily, An Li shouted, "Silence! You are showing contempt for this court. Each one of you shall be fined twenty li, which you will toss into this jar."

Soberly the people filed past the jar in a circle and dropped in their coins. As the last man contributed his coin, the magistrate jumped up and shouted, "Arrest this man! He is the thief."

There was a murmur of excitement and bewilderment in the crowd. They asked each other how the magistrate could know that this man was the thief or if, indeed, he was. Finally, An Li picked up the jar, which he showed to the crowd.

"Do you see here? When this man dropped his coin, these streaks of grease appeared on the surface of the water. Only that coin could have come from the basket that carried the fritters." Then he turned to the thief. "Where is the rest of the money?"

The thief pulled it unwillingly from his pocket. "Here it is, Your Honor."

An Li asked that the money be put in the jar with the rest, and then he announced that the court was dismissed. The villagers began to leave but not without expressing their amazement and respect for the magistrate's wisdom. When they had all gone, An Li handed the jar to Wing Soong. "There you are, my good woman. Your money is restored to you. I hope your son has learned his lesson—never to leave things of value foolishly in such a spot as this, thus tempting the dishonest folk who are watching to steal them."

Wing Soong took the coins gratefully. She thanked the wise magistrate for what he had done and for giving her twice the money the fritters had brought.

If the group is inexperienced, it will be wise to play the story just as it is, with no attempt made at doing it in the Chinese manner. Any number of children can take part, for although there are only a few main characters, there is great opportunity to add any number of villagers, farmers, and merchants at the fair. This will give everyone in the class a chance to work on pantomime and characterization and will also help to set the mood. The magistrate's trick to discover the thief is enjoyed by children of every age, and a trial scene always makes for good drama.

Older and more experienced groups may want to play the story in the style of the Chinese theatre, adding to the cast a narrator and a property man. A study of the Chinese theatre should precede any attempt at dramatization. This legend ties in well with a unit on China, should a class be studying it in social studies. If the children want to share their work with another class, it is suggested that simple properties and possibly a panel or backdrop would be fun to make and would also enhance the presentation.

THE MAGIC STONES
Arranged for Creative Playing by Nellie McCaslin
AVIVA LAYTON

The following story[1] can be enjoyed for its simple story line, played in connection with a music theory class, or used as a springboard to another activity or project.

1. From *Magook* #5 (Toronto: Magook Publishers Ltd., 1977).

A long time ago, in a little village which has long since disappeared, there lived a boy named David.

"He's an odd one," the villagers said. "Always mooning and humming to himself. Never know what the lad is thinking."

And it was true. Often David would leave the village and go into the hills where he gathered wild flowers. He listened to bird calls. Sometimes he just lay on his back looking at the sky.

One evening when David was returning from one of his trips to the hills, he heard a great commotion in the village square. All the villagers were gathered in a circle around something that was making the most peculiar wailing sounds David had ever heard. Quickly David pushed his way through the crowd. There to his surprise he saw that the wails were coming from five little black stones lying on the ground. David stared at them, fascinated. As he listened to their strange wails he had a feeling that they were trying to say something important to him.

Meanwhile, the village was in an uproar. What were the stones? What did the wailing mean? Finally the elders decided to call a meeting.

"Silence, good people," commanded the eldest of the elders. "It is obvious that evil spirits are at work. We must rid our village of these stones as soon as possible."

He looked at the crowd. "Who will volunteer to put the stones in a sack, carry them to the river and throw them in, so that they never disturb us again?"

No one spoke. Everyone was afraid. Then a small voice piped up from the back. "Must the stones be thrown away? I have a strange feeling that they have something wonderful to tell, if only we can find some way to stop their wailing."

There were angry murmurs from the crowd. A woman called out, "That's just what David would say. Everyone knows that he's an idle, good-for-nothing boy, wandering around all day instead of doing honest work."

"I wouldn't be surprised if he were in league with the evil spirits who have brought these wailing stones to us," said a man.

The crowd grew louder and louder and angrier and angrier. Then the eldest elder had an idea. He held up his hand for silence. "David," he said, "since you are the only one who wants the stones, I appoint you to take them away. I will give you a choice. You can throw them in the river. Or you can keep them. But if you decide to keep them, you must never return to the village."

David did not hesitate a moment. Running to where the stones were lying, he scooped them into a sack.

"I shall ask the wisest man in all the land to find out what is troubling you," he said to the stones. "I am sure you are trying to tell us something wonderful."

The first wise man whom David visited was a hermit who lived on the top of a mountain. When David explained what he wanted, the hermit told him to leave the sack and return in seven days for his answer. David agreed, and returned when the time was up. But all the hermit would tell him was that he was wasting time. "I have waved my hand over these stones every seventh minute of every seventh hour," he said, "but I can still make no sense out of their wailing."

David thanked the hermit politely and set off again. This time he went to a great scholar. When he had explained what he wanted, the scholar said to him, "You have come to the right person. Just let me have three days in which to consult my books. Then you will have your answer."

At the end of three days David returned. But the scholar could not solve the mystery, for the answer was not in any of his books. So David thanked him and continued on his way. At last he came to the palace of the king. Now the king kept a court jester who was said to be wiser than all the wise men put together. When the king heard David's story, he clapped his hands and commanded that the jester be brought before him.

"Wise jester," said David, "I have brought these wailing stones to you so that you may tell me what they are trying to say."

"A jester, wise?" said the jester. "That's the best joke of all!" Then he turned to the king. "I am a fool, but if you command it, I shall listen to this terrible noise and see if I can tell you what it means."

"Of course, I command it," said the king.

The jester cocked his head to one side and listened. Then he jumped up and said, "They are wailing because *I* should be king and *you* should be jester!"

"Silence," thundered the king. Then he turned to David. "You will never find your answer here, so be off with you."

Poor David. There was nowhere else to go. In despair he wandered into a field to look for a place to rest. There he found a wooden fence with five wooden rails. He leaned against it wearily.

"The villagers were right," he said, looking at the stones. "I should have thrown them into the river a long time ago."

Idly, he took the stones out of the sack and set them on the wooden rails. He put the second stone above the first, the third above the second, and so on. Suddenly David heard a new sound. It was the sweetest sound he had ever heard. But where was it coming from? Could it be from the stones?

All the rest of the day David stood by the fence, arranging and rearranging the little black stones. He found that he could make many kinds of singing sounds by putting the stones in different places.

"I was right about you all along," he said. "You do have something wonderful to say. But I must not keep you to myself. The whole world must hear you singing."

David put the stones back in the sack. Now they were quiet, because their secret had been unlocked. Once again David set out, but this time it was to his own village. When the villagers heard the beautiful sounds that came from the singing stones, David became a hero.

The eldest elder boasted that he was the one who had appointed David the keeper of the stones. And the villagers whispered that they had known all along that David would do something great and special. As news of the singing stones spread, people came from far corners of the world to hear the wonderful sounds. There was only one thing they wanted to do. They could try to make something that would have the same sounds. Many different people from many different countries set to work. One young man drew a bow across a tight string and said, "This is the exact sound."

Another blew through a reed and he said, "No, *this* is the exact sound."

Still another tapped a piece of tightly stretched skin with a little hammer and said, "Both of you are wrong. This is the exact sound."

"Let us consult David," the first young man replied. "He will decide which one of us has captured the exact sound of the singing stones."

David listened carefully. But instead of choosing one, he said, "Each of you has made the sound in your own special way. You should all play together."

And so they did.

This simple tale of a dreamer and his discovery of musical sounds and notes offers a rich opportunity for characterization and conflict. There can be as many or as few characters as desired, which makes it good material for classroom use. *The Magic Stones* also brings up questions regarding superstition, self-confidence, and social attitudes toward the person who dares to be different from the rest of the crowd. Obviously, this can lead to much more than a superficial discussion.

The arrangement of stones on the fence suggest notes and staff and might be a way of showing how music is written and read. This story can be simplified or expanded according to the age and interest of the children.

THE OLD MAN AND THE GOOMBAY CAT
KITTY KIRBY

Stories and legends of the Bahamas are almost unknown in this country. Yet, like all places where people have lived, worked, played, and worshipped, a rich store of folklore exists. It waits only to be discovered. The following tale from the Bahamas[2] makes wonderful material for creative playing.

2. Published for the first time in this book.

Cat Island was home to William T. His father and grandfather were born there. William's father had sold fish by day and had given organ lessons to the island children by night. He had been a "church-going" man. And, like his father, William T. was also a fisherman and gave organ lessons; but now he was getting old and could no longer see the notes.

His wife was dead, and his two sons and daughter had left the island. His only companion was a parrot named Penny. Penny had flown into the old wooden house one day after a tropical storm had swept over the island. She had just flown through the window and adopted old William T. Many afternoons the children would stop by the old man's house to say hello to Penny. The children called William T. Cousin Will-Yum, and loved to listen to stories of his boyhood. They would sit on the old wooden porch and listen attentively as William T. swung in his wornout hammock and drew in long breaths of smoke from his pipe. Then he would begin:

"When I was about sixteen, I was one of the best sea divers on the island. My father used to take me out in his small boat to the coral reefs. There we would dive down into the clear, blue-green water into a sea-garden. It was still—so still—we would swim through coral caves with plants all around us. There were hornlike plants and sea fans that looked like feathers. Pink plumeworms with spindly flower petals danced like angels. And bright, jewel-like fish were swimming all around us: red parrot fish, blue parrot fish, and silvery grunts."

As he spoke little girls' eyes would shine brightly as they listened, but the boys would be fidgety and impatient.

"Tell us about the sea monsters and how you set yourself loose from the water octopus," the little boys would beg.

Penny knew these stories well, and would interrupt William T. each time he spoke of the sea fans, the grunts, and the parrot fish. Still, the children would never leave until the old man had finished his stories. Then, after picking some tamarinds from the century-old tamarind tree which shaded the old man's hut, the children would say good-bye to Cousin Will-Yum and Penny and leave.

William T. never needed a clock to wake him up in the mornings because every morning when the rooster crowed he knew it was time to get up and go fishing.

"Breakfast, Will-Yum Tee. Breakfast!" Penny squawked.

"Come, come, Penny. Give me some time to get hold of myself," answered the old man.

William T. fed Penny and fixed himself a bowl of hominy grits. Penny not only ate her own food, but she helped William T. with his, too.

"Such a glutton," said William T.

"Glutton, glutton!" repeated the parrot. "Yes, you are, but I don't know what I would do without you," said the old man as he put Penny back into her cage.

"Fish biting good today, Will-Yum Tee? Fish biting good today?" chattered Penny.

"Hope so, Penny. You know tomorrow is Goombay Day!" said the old man as he gathered up his fishing pots and said good-bye to the bird.

William T. started down the hilly steps and narrow lanes toward the fishing cove. He hoped that today would bring a good catch. He hadn't had much luck lately. Walking along, he passed barefoot boys and girls on their way to school. They reminded him of when he was a boy. Their faces broke into a smile when they saw him.

"Good morning, Cousin Will-Yum," said the children.

"Morn-in', children. Have a good lesson today and mind the teacher!" answered the old man.

The children giggled. William T. waved good-bye and continued on his way. He walked along the busy waterfront until he came to the edge of Rock Cove. Then he sat down on the warm, pink sand and took his shoes off because he had to wade a little before reaching his rock in the deep water.

"Fish biting good today, mon?" asked William T. as he climbed onto the rock.

"Hope so," answered the other old fishermen.

William T. sat down and began to bait his fishing-pot with pieces of conch.

"Mon, you still using that old fish-pot trap?" teased one of the fishermen.

"Never mind. 'Tis good enough," answered William T.

William T.'s father was known to have made the best triangle fishing-pot traps on the island. The method had been handed down to him from *his* father and he, in time, had taught it to William T. The old man was very proud of the fishing-pot trap and felt it was still good enough to use today. He was just about to lower his pot into the water when the cry of an animal brought him to his feet. The tormented cry grew louder. Leaving his pot behind, William T. went to see what was wrong. He walked to a nearby rock that jutted out into the water. Not too far from there he saw newcomers. They were teenage boys and they were having lots of fun throwing rocks and pebbles at a scrawny, old, black cat.

"Stop it! Can't you see you are hurting a poor, helpless animal?" shouted William T.

"Go 'way, you silly old man!" said the boys as they continued to torment the cat. "This is a fisherman's rock. You can't even bait a catch. You are too old!"

Shoving one of the boys aside with his elbow, William T. butted the other two with his head. The youths were so amazed at the strength of the old man they quickly ran to the other side of the rock. William T. looked down at the cat as it let out a mournful "meo-o-ow."

"They won't hurt you anymore," said the old man as he picked up the cat, and together they went back to his fishing spot.

The old man sat down and dropped his pot into the water. Then he and his newly found friend waited. The fish were not biting, and the old man had grown tired, so he pulled in his pot. The cat jumped into the wet pot and rolled over and over in it.

"Mon, you look like one big cat-ball!" said William T. laughingly. He laughed so loudly that all the other fishermen stopped to see what had happened.

"You catching cat instead of fish?" they teased jovially.

"Haven't seen a cat in a long time on the island," said another fisherman. "How did he get on the rock?"

"Don't know," answered William T. Then, looking at the cat, he kept on laughing as he watched it roll out of the pot.

With his head turning and his tail swishing, the cat pranced lightly over to one of the fisherman's baskets and with one swipe of his paw hooked a small porgy and ran back to William T.

"Tut, tut. That was not nice," said the old man, watching the cat devour its delicious dish. After finishing his meal the cat licked his whiskers and strolled over to William T. Settling himself on the old man's lap, the cat purred and purred and soon fell asleep.

Once more the old man lowered his pot into the water and hooked the ends to the edge of a rock alongside him. He sat there gazing out at the ocean at the hundreds of fishing boats looming over the waters. William T. thought to himself:

"Mon, what big boats! And listen to the sound of those engines and young fishermen singing. Not like the little boats that me and my father used. They even got machines to help catch fish. Look at the haul of Nassau groupers, jack-runners, margaret-fish, and the largest fresh conch that I've ever seen! You've got to be young and strong to carry all that load on your back. Big Goombay Day for them . . . and all that is left for us old fishermen are little fish that got away from the big nets."

He looked further up the rock and saw more newcomers.

"I wonder how long it will be before they take over this rock?" he thought. "My father and grandfather fished here, so in a way I inherited this rock." Then he thought of the young boys telling him he was too old for fishing.

At that moment the cat stirred on the old man's lap. William T. stroked the furry body. Somehow he felt calmer, and as he gazed out into the ocean the ripples of the water made him feel drowsy, and he drifted off to sleep.

Many hours passed. The old man was awakened by the tapping of the cat's paw on his arm. He looked around and saw that everyone had gone.

"I'm glad you woke me," said William T.

The cat pushed the fishing-pot with his two large paws and swung the handle from side to side.

"All right, all right! I'll hurry!" said the old man as he pulled in his meager catch. Showing them to the cat, he said, "I did not catch much fish, but you were good company." The cat blinked his eyes and purred.

With the catch over his shoulder and the cat under his arm, William T. climbed off the rock and waded in the water until he reached the pink, sandy shore. The cat jumped from the old man's arms.

"Don't get lost again," said William T. as he waved good-bye to the cat.

After walking for some time, William T. felt he was being followed.

"Meo-ow, meo-ow."

William T. turned around, and there, nosing into some seashells and fishbone along the road, was the cat!

"You are following me. I'd like to take you home, but I'm a poor fisherman and already have a bird that I can barely feed."

"Meo-o-ow," replied the cat mournfully.

As William T. started to leave, he thought he saw teardrops falling from the cat's eyes, but then he thought of Penny. He was late with her supper. So he hurried on his way.

The sun, shining like a large copper ball, was dropping lower and lower behind the fertile green hills. Tourists riding in bright blue surreys, pulled by horses wearing straw hats, nodded their heads in greeting to the old man as he hurried along. The soft night winds rustled the palm leaves of the coconut trees that stood tall and majestic all over the island. The air was also warm and fragrant with the smell of thousands of hibiscus plants. And lamplighters, flickering in and out of trees, lit up the night with their twinkling lights.

The old man trudged up the rocky steps until he reached his house on the top of the hill. From the porch came the sound of Penny.

"Will-Yum Tee, Penny wants supper! You're late! You're late!" squawked the parrot.

"Just now, Penny. I'm coming," said William T. But the parrot just kept on talking.

"Will-Yum Tee! Will-Yum Tee . . .!"

William T. opened the door, found his oil lamp, and lit it. He then washed his hands and mixed some dilly seeds and pumpkin seeds together. Then he went outside to feed Penny, who was still being talkative. While the old man was feeding Penny, the cat was making his way soft-footed around the side of the house. The cat leaped through an open window and landed silently on the cracked, wooden floor. William T. said good-night to Penny and went inside to prepare his supper.

"MEO-O-OW!"

"My goodness, you followed me. And how did you get in here?" asked the old man.

The cat nodded his head up and down, swished his tail, and turned around. Then before William T. knew what was happening, the cat tore across the kitchen of the two-room house and stopped suddenly in front of the table. Looking up at the bowl of coconut milk, he meowed and meowed.

"So you are still hungry? I will share some of my supper with you," said the old man. He gave the cat some coconut milk, mixed some okra and rice with his meager catch of fish, and went outside to cook it in his coal stove. Finally, William T. and the cat sat down to eat their supper.

After the old man and his little friend had finished eating, the cat stretched his two front paws, brushed his whiskers, blinked a cat blink, and yawned. Then he strolled across the room and curled up in an old, wornout chair. Staring straight at the old man, the pupils of his eyes grew large and bright. His mouth widened into a large grin. The fisherman noticed a strange look on the cat's face. Suddenly the wooden walls began to creak and the sound of bells and drums echoed throughout the room.

"Who's there? Who's there, mon?" he gasped.

William T. tried to get up, but he could not move. There rising up in front of him was an enormous cat of black, shimmering fur. His brilliant eyes, almost blinding the old man, were as green as the ocean. Around his neck he wore a necklace of coral seashells. His silvery whiskers sparkled as he smiled and swayed from side to side to the rhythm of the Goombay. The old man was dumbfounded and his mouth dropped open when the magnificent cat began to sing:

> Goombay fish is very nice.
> Eat it once, you eat it twice.
> Mix it with some okra and rice.
> Goombay fish is very nice.

Finally the fisherman found his voice. "A Goombay Cat!" he cried. "A Goombay Cat! Gracious! Heavens, am I dreaming?"

The singing and music stopped as suddenly as it had begun. William T. rubbed his eyes and looked again at the worn-out chair. There, staring, and smiling, was the scrawny cat. Shaking nervously, William T. got up and went outside to see if Penny had heard the singing and music too, but the parrot was sleeping soundly.

"My mind must be playing tricks," said William T. to himself as he went back into the house. Gazing curiously at the cat, he patted the animal several times and found him a place to sleep. Then he went off to bed muttering to himself.

"I, I, I, must be get-ting old . . . very old."

The next morning William T. was awakened by a light weight on his chest and a tickling on his cheeks. It was the cat sitting there and blinking at him.

"Morn-in'," chuckled the old man as he rubbed his rugged cheeks. "Your whiskers tickled me."

The cat leaped forward, leaped up in the air, turned three somersaults, and landed with a bounce on the old wooden floor.

"Mon, what a cat! You're sure feeling good this morning."

Looking at the cat and studying him for a moment, he remembered last night. Should he tell his friends about what happened? Would they believe him if he told them about the cat? Or might they say: Cousin Will-Yum is getting old . . . very old. Then he thought to himself—how did the cat get on the rock? And why was this island named Cat Island? Did some strange cats live here long ago? He decided to keep all this to himself, but someday he would tell the story to the children.

Bracing his back, he sat up on the edge of the bed. As he went to put on his shoes the cat pounced at them, pulling at the shoestrings.

"Don't tan-ta-lize me, mon. Let me put my shoes on in peace. I gotta hurry 'cause today is Goombay Day!"

But the cat would not let go.

"Don't vex me," said the old man impatiently. Just then a squawk came from the porch.

"Will-Yum Tee! Will-Yum Tee! Don't forget my breakfast! You're late! You're late!" screeched Penny.

The cat let go of the shoestrings and perked his ears toward the sound. Before William T. could stop him, the cat ran to a hole in the screen door and eased himself through the opening onto the porch. Suddenly the cat caught sight of the beautiful red bird with her flowing tail of brilliant green and yellow feathers. His eyes grew wide and bright as he meo-o-owed loudly. Seeing the cat, Penny flapped her wings furiously as she scuttled wildly around in her cage. Her ruby-red eyes glared in panic.

"Will-Yum Tee! Will-Yum Tee! Hurry! Hurry!"

Thinking something horrible had happened to Penny, William T. rushed outside; by now he was out of breath. He calmed down when he saw the cat just sitting there watching the wild performance of the bird.

"Come, come, Penny. He won't hurt you. He wants to be your friend."

Penny looked at William T. and then at the cat. With her beak held high, she moved to the corner of the cage.

"Come, Penny," he pleaded as he opened the cage door. Penny hesitated, then flew onto William T.'s shoulder, keeping an eye on the cat.

William T. was very happy and chuckled to himself as he went inside to prepare breakfast for his two friends. After breakfast was over, Penny quickly flew into her cage. She was very quiet. The cat followed William T. and watched him as he locked the cage door.

"Good-bye Penny. I'll bring you some sweet benny-cake for Goombay."

The cat looked up at Penny and winked his eye, but Penny only flapped her wings. The old man gathered his fishing-pot trap and threw it over his shoulder. He put his last piece of conch, which he had to use as bait, into his pocket; then he and the cat started on their way to Rock Cove.

William T. had seen many a Goombay morning, but somehow there was a strange and happy feeling about this one. The sky was so blue and wide it seemed to run right into the blue-green water. You could not tell where the sky began and the ocean ended. He was so happy that he began to whistle an old familiar tune. Looking down at his little friend, who was strutting gracefully to the rhythm of the tune, he began to sing:

> Got-ta catch fish, before big boats come.
> Got-ta get it done, before the mid-day sun.
> Got-ta catch fish to sell to ev-ry one.
> Got-ta catch fish, before the big boats come.

As he was singing he looked up at the sky. Not a cloud was in sight, and the sky was bluer than he had ever seen it. He could feel the heat from the blazing sun burning through the soles of his shoes. The sweat was running down his face. The old man and his friend stopped to rest a while under a shady silk-cotton tree.

"Good morn-in', Cous-in Will-Yum," said a group of women with shiny faces. They were carrying baskets on their heads filled to the brim with fruits: soursops, saperdilles, Spanish limes, casavas, tamarinds, and sea grapes.

"You are early, Cous-in Hilda, Rebecca, and Cous-in Eunice," said the old man.

"Yes, 'cause it's Goombay Day!" answered the women, swinging their brightly colored, well-starched dresses. Everyone was moving so fast no one noticed Cousin Will-Yum's new friend.

"Come, come let us hurry," said the old man to the cat as they moved along with the crowd. Nearing the waterfront, he and the cat stopped at the Open-Straw Market.

"Big boat in today for Goombay, Cous-in Will-Yum," hollered Auntie Hattie B. from her booth in the Open-Straw Market.

"Yes, child. I seen them big tourist ocean liners down by the Prince Charles stop. Lots of money mak-in' to you."

"We'll set up a table for you right by Cous-in Eunice on the waterfront," she said.

"Where did you get the cat?" asked Cous-in Hilda, noticing the cat for the first time.

"Found him yesterday on top of the rock," answered William T.

Leaving the Open-Straw Market, William T. passed brightly decorated straw booths running along the waterfront. The sun illuminated the blue-green water till it sparkled a jade green. Multicolored seashell beads, big straw pocketbooks, gaily colored straw dolls, and straw hats bedecked with seashells lined the booths.

Suddenly the smell of smothered conch and pigeon peas and rice filled the air. William T. knew he was near the market range with its many booths full of steaming vegetables, sweet fruits, and dazzling pink and white conch shells. Cousin Charlie had his booth here.

Cousin Charlie was busy cooking conch smothered in tomato sauce, and pigeon peas, and rice for the festival. The succulent dish bubbled in a big, cast-iron skillet on an open fire.

The cat ran up to Cousin Charlie's stand, looked up, and meowed and meowed. He licked his tongue and kept his eyes on the smothered conch.

"Mon, where did you find this cat?" asked Cousin Charlie. "Why, I haven't seen one for a long time on this island."

"He found *me*!" laughed William T.

Cousin Charlie fixed a plate of smothered conch and rice and gave it to the old man and the cat.

"Thank you. We will have a good lunch today," said William T. as he and his little friend pushed their way through the Market Range and headed for the waterfront. When William T. and the cat arrived at the fishing rock, he noticed that the cat's back was arched high, his ears were turned up, and he was switching his tail vigorously in signs of anger. It was then that he looked around only to see the young boys who had taunted the cat yesterday. They were fishing not too far from the old man's spot.

"Come, come. They won't bother you," said William T. as he sat down to bait his fishing trap.

The cat flexed his muscles, his tail stood straight up, and his eyes grew large and bright as he watched the fishing trap being lowered into the blue-green waters. William looked at the cat. He gasped when he saw that once more the cat was changing in size. He began to tremble and broke out in a cold sweat as harmonious sounds of bells and drums swelled across the ocean. At that moment a gigantic wave rose up and the great cat leaped into the oncoming billowing waves.

"Help! Help!" cried William T. "My cat is in the water!"

But the other fishermen were so frightened by the crashing of the water against the rocks that they did not hear his cry.

Suddenly the music stopped and the waters were calm again. William T. noticed the fishing-trap was still in place, but there was a heavy tugging on it. He tried to pull the trap up, but it would not give. Again he cried for help. Hearing his call, his fishing companions came to his rescue. Together they grabbed hold of the fishing-trap and began to pull and pull. All at once out of the water came the trap-pot filled with hundreds of beautiful fish shimmering in the sunlight. And there amidst the miraculous catch nestled the cat.

"My *cat*! My *cat*!" cried William T. But the fishermen were so amazed by the miraculous catch they paid no attention to the cat.

"Mon, look at that catch! Biggest I've ever seen!" shouted one of the fishermen.

"Never seen so many fish in one haul," said another.

Tears of joy ran down William T.'s cheeks as he lifted the wet, shivering body out of the trap and cradled it under his tattered old coat.

"Are you all right, mon?" he whispered. The cat looked up at William T. and purred contentedly.

"Old man, how did you catch all those fish?" asked the teenage boys.

It was then that William T. looked at his fishing trap piled high with goggle-eyed fish: margaret fish, jack-runners, grunts, and Nassau groupers. He was so happy that he could not speak for a moment. He just stood there staring at his catch. Then, remembering the boys' question, he looked down at the cat and said:

"Just luck, mon. Just luck."

"Will you sell us some of your catch?" asked one of the boys.

"*No*! I will not sell you any of my catch . . . but I will give you some of them." He then shared many of his fish with his companions and the boys. The boys felt ashamed and sorry for the way they had treated the cat and the old man.

"May we help you carry your load off the rock?" asked the boys.

The cat purred; the old man smiled, and said he would like that very much.

News of Cousin William's catch spread all along the waterfront. Auntie Hattie B., Cousins Eunice, Hilda, and Rebecca, and all the women left the Goombay tables to see the great haul of fish. Even Cousin Charlie left the Market Range to see Cousin William's big catch. Children came from all over the island when they heard the news of the old man's catch. Now they danced around him, playing big bass drums and singing a song of the Goombay catch:

> Cous-in Will-Yum caught big catch!
> From the blue-green waters.
> He caught them in his fish-pot trap,
> From the blue-green waters.

While the children sang, the cat swished his tail to the rhythm of the song. William T. was so happy he began to sing too:

> Goombay Cat caught big fish,
> From the island wat-ters
> He caught them with a great big smile,
> From the island wat-ters.

The teenage boys walked tall, their heads held high, as they carried Wiliam T.'s catch to his table. Wiliam T. strutted proudly before them with the cat riding on his arm. It was a grand sight to see the joyous procession marching to their tables to begin the Goombay festival. Tables were quickly filled with fried chicken, sous, coconut cakes, and other delectable dishes.

"Well, mon," said William T., setting the cat by his table. "It's time for us to fix our table."

The old man was about to pick up his fish-pot when he heard the sound of the Goombay song! It lasted for a brief second, and when William T. looked down again the cat was gone! Where his little friend had stood was a shiny, coral, seashell necklace. He picked it up slowly and he knew that his little friend was now gone forever.

However, Wiliam T. was not sad. The beautiful necklace was left by the Goombay Cat to remind him that miracles still happen and that he wasn't so very old after all.

This tale gives information about the Bahamas in its description of the country, the plants, the foods, and the customs, including the legends told by the people. It could, therefore, be used in connection with a social studies unit on the islands. It could also be played purely for the narrative. William T. is an appealing character, but the others can be more fully developed than they are in this account of his strange experience.

After the children have decided which characters are necessary to the telling and which others may be added, they are ready to decide on the scenes. If playing in a large room, one end can be William T.'s cabin; the other, the fishing area. The middle of the room might be the village square. If the space is small, the scenes can follow in sequence. The procession at the end can be handled in a variety of ways. One group had it move around the playing space in a large circle; another had it weave in and out, suggesting that it was going into different parts of the village. Carefully selected music will suggest movement and a mood.

All can try playing William T.—showing how he moves, walks, sits, runs, handles his fishing pots, and rescues the cat. When the class is thoroughly familiar with the story, it will want to go on to the enactment of scenes. Again, by allowing small groups to play bits of the story, each will have an opportunity to contribute dialogue, characterization, and movement. Some groups can be villagers, creating individual characters and showing their love for William T. An experienced group might want to create earlier scenes in William T.'s life, showing what he was like when he was a boy. Groups handle the cat differently. One class wanted to have a child play the part when it became large. Another group used a "prop" cat in the scenes where it was small, but had a large boy play the cat when it grew to enormous proportions. Still another imagined it throughout, using offstage sounds when the cat and the parrot spoke. This last was probably the most satisfactory solution, but it is good to let the class wrestle with the problem and come up with its own solution.

Some children chant the songs, but one group composed its own music to "Goombay fish is very nice." Superstition and the supernatural intrigue most children, so this aspect of the story usually has particular appeal. There is a rich opportunity here for learning and creative playing. The results will be as simple or as detailed as the children are able to make them.

THE CLEVER LAD FROM SKYE

The following story comes from the Hebrides, and, like many folktales, tells about the poor boy who outwits a rich lord. Tormod's adventures offer a number of good roles but, in addition, allow for participation on the part of the entire class, if desired. Servants and townsfolk are called for, as well as sound effects.

Tormod MacLeod was a lad belonging to the clan of MacLeods who lived on the Isle of Skye. His father had little money and many mouths to feed, so Tormod decided to seek his fortune on the mainland. He wandered from one town to another until he arrived in Glasgow, and there he found a job with a blacksmith who needed an apprentice. Tormod did well and his master was pleased. In fact, Tormod was so clever and quick that the blacksmith blessed the day he had hired him.

Now there was a man in Glasgow who had a fine horse that he often brought into the smithy to have shod. While Tormod was shoeing it one of these times, the lad said, "That's a fine horse you have there."

"Aye, he is," replied the gentleman.

"What will you take for him?" asked Tormod.

"He's not for sale," the gentleman said. "I'll not part with him for any money."

"Aren't you afraid he will be stolen?" asked Tormod.

The gentleman laughed and said that this could not be done. "Why, I have four stable boys taking care of him and all kinds of bells to sound an alarm, if anyone tried to take him away."

Now Tormod, who was as bold as he was clever, said, "I could steal him, if I wanted to—right out from under the noses of your guards."

The gentleman was very angry at this and said, "If you can do that, you can keep him and one hundred pounds besides!"

Tormod thought about this for a long time. Then, one day as he passed a pub, an idea came to him. He would buy two big bottles of ale and put them in his pockets. He would spill some of the ale on his clothes to make the guards think he had been drinking. Then he would stagger around and fall down on the straw near the horse's stall. Thinking him asleep, the guards would drink the contents of the two bottles, go to sleep themselves, and Tormod would lead the animal safely out of the stable.

The plan worked just as he planned it. The next morning the gentleman came storming into the smithy's shop, demanding the arrest of the boy who had stolen his horse. But the blacksmith, who had overheard the gentleman's bargain, stepped up and reminded him that he had said if Tormod stole the horse, he could keep it. And that, furthermore, he would give Tormod one hundred pounds. Angrily, the gentleman went out, leaving Tormod the horse and the money.

Tormod's next adventure was even bolder than his first. It was said in the village that the old gentleman planned to marry his daughter to a rich, elderly lord, and that her father had locked her in her room to prevent her from escaping. When the gentleman came to the blacksmith's soon after this, Tormod asked him if the gossip was true. Being assured that it was, the young man asked what would happen if he managed to get the bride out of the house. "If you can do that, my lad," said her father, "you may have her and five hundred pounds besides."

Again, an idea came to Tormod. Why not rescue the young woman from her fate? So he went to the home of the seamstress who was making her wedding gown, paid her well for the use of the woman's own clothing, took a large basket, and approached the gentleman's house for a second time. Meanwhile, Tormod had dressed himself in the seamstress's clothes. When he arrived at the door, he said, in the highest voice he could muster, that he had come for a fitting of the young lady's wedding gown. The servant, believing him to be the seamstress, told him to come on upstairs and that he would unlock the door.

When the servant had left, Tormod removed the seamstress's dress and apron and shawl. The young woman was so startled to see a young man standing before her that she was about to scream. But Tormod said quietly, "Please don't be frightened. I have only come to help you escape. If you do as I say, you will be able to leave this house forever and so free yourself from this marriage."

The young woman realized that the speaker seemed honest and, furthermore, that he offered her a means of escape from her prison. So she accepted his offer of help. Tormod explained that if she got into the basket, he would cover it over again, put on the seamstress's clothing, and call the servant to help him carry this heavy load back downstairs. He would take her to the blacksmith's house, where she was welcome to stay as long as she liked.

Again the plan was successful. The next morning the old gentleman was furious when he discovered the trick that had been played on him. Fuming, he hurried to the blacksmith's shop, declaring that he had been robbed and that his daughter had been kidnapped. But the blacksmith, who had again heard the whole conversation, stepped up and said, "What about the five hundred pounds you said you would give to the one who could outwit you?"

Realizing that there was nothing he could do, the old man threw down the gold and declared he would never leave his house again.

Tormod was becoming a very rich man. Moreover, he and the gentleman's daughter had fallen in love, and, in the course of time, were married. Thinking it a pity that his wife and her father never saw each other these days, Tormod invited the old gentleman to visit them. But his father-in-law was still so angry that he said he would not budge until the day he willingly followed the young man out of the house, and that that day would never come.

Tormod thought hard and long about this. Suddenly an idea came to him. He would dress himself in a sheet and go to the gentleman's house that night. He would tell him that the end of the world was at hand and that he had come for him. As before, the scheme worked. The old man was so frightened at being wakened out of a sound sleep by a ghostly stranger that he agreed to go at once. Tormod told him to put on a white garment like his own, covering his body and head, and he would do what he could to save him. Then, taking the old man's hand, he led the white-robed figure out of the house and down to the blacksmith's shop. There Tormod and the smithy made all kinds of noise. With hammers and bells and chains, they suggested purgatory. Tormod asked the old man to repent of his sins. The terrified figure, his eyes still covered, fell to his knees and begged forgiveness, if only his life could be spared. Tormod agreed and pulled the sheet off his head.

Then Tormod explained everything, even calling his wife into the shop. The old man was so overjoyed at finding himself and his daughter alive that he forgot to be angry. Tormod then brought out the horse and all the money he had won and gave it back to its rightful owner. As he explained, he was a fortunate man, with a wife, a wee son, and a good place as the blacksmith's partner. After all, what more would any man want?

This is a complex story, but the fact that it can be handled by scenes puts it within the capabilities of children in middle and upper grades. If the teacher has had any experience with participatory theatre, he will find *The Clever Lad from Skye* a story that can be dramatized in this way. However it is done, the first step is to list the characters, and the seond step is to decide on the number of scenes. Then, depending on the age and the experience of the children, planning can proceed.

It is a good idea to spend some time in a discussion of rural life in Scotland a hundred years or more ago. Pantomimes of the following activities might follow: working in the smith's shop, leading the horses around the courtyard, stealing in and out of the gentleman's house, pretending to be the ghost that the gentleman follows. Making the various sounds that are such an important part of the story also challenge the children's ingenuity. When every child is thoroughly familiar with the details, and the entire class has had a chance to try the different noises, actions, and pantomime, the dramatization can begin. Because of the length of the story, it is wise to play it by scene, using a different Tormod and blacksmith each time. This gives many children an opportunity to play these parts as well as to contribute different ideas about the characters and ways of handling the narrative. This tale, incidentally, is excellent to use in social studies as a part of an integrated project. It reveals the customs and attitudes of a people in a particular time and place.

The Clever Lad from Skye can also lead to a discussion of moral and ethical behavior, human relationships, social codes, and tricks with far-reaching consequences. The denouement is different from most tales of the clever lad in that Tormod returns the horse and the money in an effort to heal the breach and establish a good family relationship. This ending can be compared with other more familiar folktales in which the hero destroys his adversary and keeps the goods he has won in a battle of wits.

THE GREEN BEAN PATCH
Taken from the Play by Jonathan Kariara

The following story[3] comes from East Africa and is recommended for older children or young adults. It takes place in a remote village during a long and devastating famine. The people have been praying for relief and have killed a goat as a sacrifice, but still no rain has come.

The time is early one morning and the scene is the hut of the woman, Njuku. She is building a fire when she hears a noise outside. She rushes to the door quickly but quietly, looks out, then goes to a sleeping form at one side of the room and tries to wake him. It is her son, Njogu, who is first annoyed at being awakened from his sleep at this early hour, then angry when she explains the reason.

"Njogu," she says, "Someone is in the bean patch. He is stealing our beans. They're all we have left to eat. You must go and catch the thief."

Njogu, thoroughly awake by this time, picks up a club and rushes out the door, telling his mother to call Karinka, his brother, to follow and help him. His mother tries to explain that Karinka will not go, but Njogu is already halfway to the bean patch.

Then Njuku goes to her other son, who has heard the commotion; but as she predicted, he refuses to chase after the thief. Karinka is a pacifist, who tries to explain to his mother that he is tired of fighting and killing and that no good will come of it. Njuku argues that he is not tired of eating beans, to

---

3. A longer version of this story appears in Jonathan Kariara's play.

which he replies that that is true but with the famine in their valley, all hope is gone for them and their neighbors. They have lost their cattle; their crops have dried up; the only thing left to do is to leave the village. "How," he says, "can we call the bean patch ours? How can we eat if our neighbors are starving?"

Karinka understands how much his mother loves the bean patch, and he tells her of his memories of her planting it many years ago. He was a small child at the time but sitting on a low branch of the tree at the corner of the garden, he used to watch her as she tended it, watering it from the stream, weeding, and later gathering the beans for their supper. "Now," he says, "the time has come for us to leave the bean patch, for it is only a matter of time before it, like the other crops, will die. Why not go to Ndia in the morning?"

Just at this moment Njogu returns, shouting angrily at the crowd that has gathered outside the door. The people react, angrily crying, "A curse on you, Njogu!"

Njogu turns to his brother, accusing him of cowardice and asking him why he must be a "man of peace" when their garden is being stripped of beans. Karinka tries to explain that all the people are hungry but Njogu slaps his face in fury. Karinka controls his anger, for Njogu is his elder brother. Their mother tries to stop the quarrel between her sons but cannot do so. Finally she says that she can no longer live with this anger, to which Karinka replies that he will leave for Ndia in the morning.

At this moment the noise outside, which abated during the argument, is heard again as a man and woman come to the door.

"Peace be with you, Njuku," says Nai, the man.

Njuku asks why he, whom she has known all her life, approaches her so strangely. Nai explains that he brings a string of black beads to place on Karinka's neck, with a prayer for his safe return. Frightened, Njuku begs to know what he means and why the woman is carrying a spear and shield. Nai explains.

Karinka must go to the only green tree that is left at the corner of their garden. On that tree is a creeping vine called "Sorrow." There a ceremony must be performed. Karinka is to take two of the creepers at a time and tie them in a knot. When he has tied seven knots, he must take the bowl of milk he will find there and dip each knot in the bowl. As the milk is shed, drop by drop, the prayer of "Plenty" must be repeated just as it was taught to him when he was a small boy.

Karinka asks why he was chosen for this task. Njogu, who has been listening, interrupts to say that he is the one who should go, for Karinka hated the bean patch and has refused to protect it. The man and woman step up to Karinka and say softly, "No, it is not hate but pain that we see in his eyes. Pain that Karinka cannot help his suffering neighbors. Now is his chance to save them."

Karinka understands. He says goodbye to his mother and brother, and leaves with the man and woman. With a heavy heart Njuku goes to the door to watch. She reports to Njogu, who has turned his back on the scene, what is happening. As Karinka completes his task, there is a sound of thunder, followed by darkness and rain. Then a group of villagers appear at the door, carrying the limp body of Karinka.

Njogu is bitter that his brother will become a martyr and a hero, whereas he, who tried to defend the bean patch, is ignored. Njuku kneels by her dead son's body.

"Tomorrow I will bury you in the bean patch," she promises. "I will plant the seeds all around you. When my eyes fill with tears, they will not be for the loss of you but for the miracle you have brought through your sacrifice. My son, the black beads you are wearing will remind me of your shining black eyes."

This little tragedy can be played either for the story itself or as a part of a social studies unit on East Africa. There are many learnings embedded in it: the geography, the customs and the beliefs of the people, the family relationships, and the conflict between pacificism and defence of property. It is equally good as an example of drama, for the conflict and characters make a strong situation that can only result in tragedy. Older students find the struggle to be much more than a simple difference of opinion, for attitudes toward war and suffering are universal. The age, background, and previous experience of the group will affect the depth that the story will have for them.

THE WISE OLD WOMAN
YOSHIKO UCHIDA

This version of the Japanese folktale The Wise Old Woman[4] *is included for several reasons. First of all, it is a good story. The narrative holds the interest of the players and provides complications that make demands on them. Also, the characters may be interpreted in considerable depth. The situation, though extreme, can be discussed in relation to our attitude toward older people. How do we feel about them? How do we treat them? What value do older people have in our society? What have we to learn from them? Why do you think we react to them as we do? What has caused our attitude? What are the implications in this story for our own old age? These are some of the questions that might be asked.*

Many long years ago, there lived an arrogant and cruel young lord who ruled over a small village in the western hills of Japan.

4. From *The Sea of Gold and Other Tales* (New York: Charles Scribner's Sons, 1965), pp. 61–71.

"I have no use for old people in my village," he said haughtily. "They are neither useful nor able to work for a living. I therefore decree that anyone over seventy-one must be banished from the village and left in the mountains to die."

"What a dreadful decree! What a cruel and unreasonable lord we have," the people of the village murmured. But the lord punished anyone who disobeyed him, and so villagers who turned seventy-one were tearfully carried into the mountains, never to return.

Gradually there were fewer and fewer old people in the village and soon they disappeared altogether. Then the young lord was pleased.

"What a fine village of young, healthy and hardworking people I have," he bragged. "Soon it will be the finest village in all of Japan."

Now there lived in this village a kind young farmer and his aged mother. They were poor, but the farmer was good to his mother, and the two of them lived happily together. However, as the years went by, the mother grew older, and before long she reached the terrible age of seventy-one.

"If only I could somehow deceive the cruel lord," the farmer thought. But there were records in the village books and every one knew that his mother had turned seventy-one.

Each day the son put off telling his mother that he must take her into the mountains to die, but the people of the village began to talk. The farmer knew that if he did not take his mother away soon, the lord would send his soldiers and throw them both into a dark dungeon to die a terrible death.

"Mother—" he would begin, as he tried to tell her what he must do, but he could not go on.

Then one day the mother herself spoke of the lord's dread decree. "Well, my son," she said, "the time has come for you to take me to the mountains. We must hurry before the lord sends his soldiers for you." And she did not seem worried at all that she must go to the mountains to die.

"Forgive me, dear mother, for what I must do," the farmer said sadly, and the next morning he lifted his mother to his shoulders and set off on the steep path toward the mountains. Up and up he climbed, until the trees clustered close and the path was gone. There was no longer even the sound of birds, and they heard only the soft wail of the wind in the trees. The son walked slowly, for he could not bear to think of leaving his old mother in the mountains. On and on he climbed, not wanting to stop and leave her behind. Soon, he heard his mother breaking off small twigs from the trees that they passed.

"Mother, what are you doing?" he asked.

"Do not worry, my son," she answered gently. "I am just marking the way so you will not get lost returning to the village."

The son stopped. "Even now you are thinking of me?" he asked, wonderingly.

The mother nodded. "Of course, my son," she replied. "You will always be in my thoughts. How could it be otherwise?"

At that, the young farmer could bear it no longer. "Mother, I cannot leave you in the mountains to die all alone," he said. "We are going home and no matter what the lord does to punish me, I will never desert you again."

So they waited until the sun had set and a lone star crept into the silent sky. Then in the dark shadows of night, the farmer carried his mother down the hill and they returned quietly to their little house. The farmer dug a deep hole in the floor of his kitchen and made a small room where he could hide his mother. From that day, she spent all her time in the secret room and the farmer carried meals to her there. The rest of the time, he was careful to work in the fields and act as though he lived alone. In this way, for almost two years, he kept his mother safely hidden and no one in the village knew that she was there.

Then one day there was a terrible commotion among the villagers for Lord Higa of the town beyond the hills threatened to conquer their village and make it his own.

"Only one thing can spare you," Lord Higa announced. "Bring me a box containing one thousand ropes of ash and I will spare your village."

The cruel young lord quickly gathered together all the wise men of his village. "You are men of wisdom," he said. "Surely you can tell me how to meet Lord Higa's demands so our village can be spared."

But the wise men shook their heads. "It is impossible to make even one rope of ash, sire," they answered. "How can we ever make one thousand?"

"Fools!" the lord cried angrily. "What good is your wisdom if you cannot help me now?"

And he posted a notice in the village square offering a great reward of gold to any villager who could help him save their village.

But all the people in the village whispered, "Surely, it is an impossible thing, for ash crumbles at the touch of the finger. How could anyone ever make a rope of ash?" They shook their heads and sighed, "Alas, alas, we must be conquered by yet another cruel lord."

The young farmer, too, supposed that this must be, and he wondered what would happen to his mother if a new lord even more terrible than their own came to rule over them.

When his mother saw the troubled look on his face, she asked, "Why are you so worried, my son?"

So the farmer told her of the impossible demand made by Lord Higa if the village was to be spared, but his mother did not seem troubled at all. Instead she laughed softly and said, "Why, that is not such an impossible task. All one has to do is soak ordinary rope in salt water and dry it well. When it is burned, it will hold its shape and there is your rope of ash! Tell the villagers to hurry and find one thousand pieces of rope."

The farmer shook his head in amazement. "Mother, you are wonderfully wise," he said, and he rushed to tell the young lord what he must do.

"You are wiser than all the wise men of the village," the lord said when he heard the farmer's solution, and he rewarded him with many pieces of gold. The thousand ropes of ash were quickly made and the village was spared.

In a few days, however, there was another great commotion in the village as Lord Higa sent another threat. This time he sent a log with a small hole that curved and bent seven times through its length, and he demanded that a single piece of silk thread be threaded through the hole. "If you cannot perform this task," the lord threatened, "I shall come to conquer your village." The young lord hurried once more to his wise men, but they all shook their heads in bewilderment. "A needle cannot bend its way through such curves," they moaned. "Again we are faced with an impossible demand."

"And again you are stupid fools!" the lord said, stamping his foot impatiently. He then posted a second notice in the village square asking the villagers for their help.

Once more the young farmer hurried with the problem to his mother in her secret room.

"Why, that is not so difficult," his mother said with a quick smile. "Put some sugar at one end of the hole. Then tie an ant to a piece of silk thread and put it in at the other end. He will weave his way in and out of the curves to get to the sugar and he will take the silk thread with him."

"Mother, you are remarkable!" the son cried, and he hurried off to the lord with the solution to the second problem.

Once more the lord commended the young farmer and rewarded him with many pieces of gold. "You are a brilliant man and you have saved our village again," he said gratefully.

But the lord's troubles were not over even then, for a few days later Lord Higa sent still another demand. "This time you will undoubtedly fail and then I shall conquer your village," he threatened. "Bring me a drum that sounds without being beaten."

"But that is not possible," sighed the people of the village. "How can anyone make a drum sound without beating it?"

This time the wise men held their heads in their hands and moaned, "It is hopeless. It is hopeless. This time Lord Higa will conquer us all."

The young farmer hurried home breathlessly. "Mother, Mother, we must solve another terrible problem or Lord Higa will conquer our village!" And he quickly told his mother about the impossible drum.

His mother, however, smiled and answered, "Why, this is the easiest of them all. Make a drum with sides of paper and put a bumblebee inside. As it tries to escape, it will buzz and beat itself against the paper and you will have a drum that sounds without being beaten."

The young farmer was amazed at his mother's wisdom. "You are far wiser than any of the wise men of the village," he said, and he hurried to tell the young lord how to meet Lord Higa's third demand.

When the lord heard the answer, he was greatly impressed. "Surely a young man like you cannot be wiser than all my wise men," he said. "Tell me honestly, who has helped you solve all these difficult problems?"

The young farmer could not lie. "My lord," he began slowly, "for the past two years I have broken the law of the land. I have kept my aged mother hidden beneath the floor of my house, and it is she who solved each of your problems and saved the village from Lord Higa."

He trembled as he spoke, for he feared the lord's displeasure and rage. Surely now the soldiers would be summoned to throw him into the dark dungeon. But when he glanced fearfully at the lord, he saw that the young ruler was not angry at all. Instead, he was silent and thoughtful, for at last he realized how much wisdom and knowledge old people possess.

"I have been very wrong," he said finally. "And I must ask the forgiveness of your mother and of all my people. Never again will I demand that the old people of our village be sent to the mountains to die. Rather, they will be treated with the respect and honor they deserve and share with us the wisdom of their years."

And so it was. From that day, the villagers were no longer forced to abandon their parents in the mountains, and the village became once more a happy, cheerful place in which to live. The terrible Lord Higa stopped sending his impossible demands and no longer threatened to conquer them, for he too was impressed. "Even in such a small village there is much wisdom," he declared, "and its people should be allowed to live in peace."

And that is exactly what the farmer and his mother and all the people of the village did for all the years thereafter.

It is suggested that the major discussion of *The Wise Old Woman* be held after several playings. By that time the story will have had an impact on the group, and the players will be ready to discuss the theme and its modern implications. This can lead into a discussion of stereotyping of age, the meaning of wisdom, and the social values in our society. The depth of perception will affect the playing of the story for as the children discover its meaning, they will find their playing enriched, more serious.

Summary

Because of the greater plot complications and length, all these stories will demand more time in planning than those in the preceding chapter. There is sufficient content to absorb the interest of the average group for several sessions, depending, of course, on the length of the class periods and the age of the participants. Characters are presented in greater depth, hence much more time must be spent on their development. Most groups like to consider such questions as:

1. What is the character really like?
2. Why does the character behave as he/she does?
3. What do others think of him/her? Why?
4. If the character is not like that, why do others think so?
5. How is the character changed, or what has he/she learned as a result of his/her actions?

As the participants grow in experience, they will find new ways of telling the story. Some will want to use narrators; others, many scenes; and some may rearrange the sequence of events altogether. As was said in the previous chapter, every group is unique, and the leader learns to expect an endless variety of ways in which the same material can be handled and interpreted. The growing self-confidence of the players releases ideas, which lead to further thinking and experimentation. Each group, regardless of age, becomes more critical of its efforts as, with the help of the leader, it strives for a higher level of accomplishment.

10

The Possibilities in Poetry

*C*hildren like poetry. They are sensitive to the rhythm of it and enjoy the repetition of sounds, words, and phrases. The direct approach of the poet is not unlike their own; hence poetry, unless it has been spoiled for them, has a special appeal. The music and language, as well as the ideas, feelings, and images of poetry, reach the younger child particularly, capturing and stimulating his imagination. For this reason, poetry can be used in creative dramatics, often with highly successful results.

Many leaders find poetry a more satisfactory spring-board than prose for introducing creative playing to a group. This is probably an individual matter, depending as much on the leader as on the participants. If the leader or teacher enjoys poetry herself, she will find that it provides a rich source of material that can be used at all levels of experience, and with all ages. For children, poetry and play go quite naturally together. "The affinity

Poetry and dance go well together. (*Courtesy of Lucille Pa-olillo, Children's Centre for the Creative Arts, Adelphi University; photograph by George Meyer.*)

between poetry and play is not external only; it is also apparent in the structure of creative imagination itself. In the turning of a poetic phrase, the development of a motif, the expression of a mood, there is always a play element at work."[1]

For these reasons, the possibilities in poetry as motivation are considered. What kinds of poems are usable? How can poetry and movement be combined? Has choral speaking any place in creative dramatics? For the answers to these questions, one has only to go to children themselves, as they engage in their play. Many of their games are accompanied by chants, which are a form of choral speaking. In action games, rhythm is basic, while some games are played to verse with the players often making up their own original stanzas. If we listen, we note the enjoyment of repetition, refrain, and the sounds of words. Only very much later does poetry become a literary form to be taken seriously, and when it does, the element of play is, unfortunately, too often lost.

Choral Speaking *any place in creative drama*

Because poetry lends itself so well to group enjoyment, let us begin with a consideration of choral speaking, its purposes and procedures. Choral reading, or speaking, is simply reading or reciting in unison under the direction of a leader. It is not a new technique, for people have engaged in it for centuries. It antedated the theatre in the presentation of ideas and became an important element of the Greek drama. Evidences of choral speaking have been found in the religious ceremonies and festivals of primitive peoples, while today it is still used for ritualistic purposes in church services and on patriotic occasions. In the early twentieth century, however, it was recognized as one of the most effective methods of teaching the language arts and of improving speech habits.

In the past, choral speaking was used as an important means of communication and communion; today it is an art form as well and is employed both ways by the theatre, the church, and the school. When working with older children or adults, the two major purposes of the activity are:

1. Learning (when the purpose is process and, therefore, participant centered);
2. Performance (when the purpose is program and, therefore, audience centered).

Often the former leads into the latter, but, like creative drama, it does not necessarily follow that practice must result in performance. Practice has values of its own, whether or not the product is shared.

1. J. Huizinga, *Homo Ludens, A Study of the Play Element in Culture* (Boston: Beacon Press, 1955), p. 14.

Values

One of the values of choral speaking is that it can be used successfully regardless of space or class size. While a group of twenty or so is more desirable than one of forty or fifty, the larger number need not be a deterrent.

Many teachers consider the greatest value of choral speaking the opportunity it provides for speech improvement. Pitch, volume, rate, and tone quality are important to the effective interpretation of material. The need for clear diction is apparent when a group is reading aloud, whereas the practicing of speech sounds alone is often a tedious and unrelated exercise. During discussion, even young children will make suggestions as to how a poem should be recited. Vocal expression and the clear enunciation of speech sounds are often acquired more easily and with greater motivation when the group works together on meaning.

A third value, and one shared with creative dramatics, is the opportunity it provides for social cooperation. Choral speaking is a group activity, and by its nature, therefore, directs each individual to a common goal. The child with the strident voice learns to soften his tone, whereas the shy child can work for more volume without feeling self-conscious. Even the speech-handicapped child may recite without embarrassment, because she is not speaking alone and, therefore, is not conspicuous.

A fourth value of choral speaking is its suitability to any age level. It may be introduced in the kindergarten, but is equally effective when used in high school or college classes. Not all material is adapted to choral work, but much of it is, and the major criterion is probably that it be enjoyed and recommended by the readers themselves.

Procedures

There are many ways of beginning choral speaking, but with younger children, it will probably spring from their own enjoyment of a poem and their obvious desire to say it aloud or to the accompaniment of action. With older children who have had no experience in group reading, the teacher will not only select the material with care but will give some thought in advance to its interpretation. Discussion of the meaning, and of the various ways of reading the material so as to bring out the meaning, give the pupils a part in planning the group reading. A second reading will reveal further meaning, as well as difficulties in phrasing and diction.

As the group becomes more experienced, it will offer suggestions as to those lines that may be most effectively taken by the whole group, by part of the group, and by individual voices. Although a structured activity, choral speaking offers a real opportunity for creative thinking, as each group works out its own presentation. The teacher leads, indicating when to start, and watches the phrasing, emphases, and pauses suggested by the readers. The amount of time spent on a poem will vary, but it is more important to keep the enthusiasm alive than it is to work for perfection. With practice, the group will grow increasingly sensitive to the demands of different kinds of material, and their results will improve in proportion to their understanding and enjoyment.

Most authorities on choral speaking suggest dividing the group into light and dark voices. This is not quite the same as a division into high and low, or soprano and alto voices, but has to do with quality and resonance as well as pitch. Some leaders, on the other hand, believe that a division in which there are both light and dark in each group makes for more interesting quality. However it is done, some division is necessary for any group of more than ten. Some poems can be read by three groups if the class is very large. These may include middle voices; though, again, it is the material that will suggest the groupings rather than an arbitrary division.

Ways of Reading

UNISON   The whole group reads together. Though the simplest in one sense, this is the most difficult, since using all voices limits variation. Some poems, particularly short ones, are most effective when read or spoken by the entire class.

ANTIPHONAL   This is a division into two groups with each taking certain parts. Many poems are more effective when read in this way. The poem will dictate the way it may be read.

CUMULATIVE   When this technique is used, it is for the purpose of building toward a climax, or certain high points in the poem. As the term suggests, it is the accumulation of voices, either individually or by groups.

SOLO   Often lines or stanzas call for individual reading. This can be an effective technique, as well as a way of giving an opportunity for individual participation.

LINE-AROUND   This is solo work, in which each line is taken by a different reader. Children enjoy this and are alert to the lines they have been assigned.

As the group progresses and attempts longer and more difficult material, it may suggest using several or all of these techniques in one poem. The results can be remarkably effective, encouraging attentiveness and self-discipline, as well as imaginative planning. Occasionally, sound effects can be added. Music, bells, drums, and vocal sounds, produced by the readers themselves, provide an opportunity for further inventiveness.

Because our primary concern is creative drama, only those poems that suggest movement or pantomime are included here. The following have been used successfully with groups, combining choral speaking and activities suggested by the content or sounds. The first, "Happy New Year," is an old rhyme, suggesting the simplest kind of movement as a beginning:

Happy New Year! Happy New Year!
I've come to wish you a Happy New Year.
I've got a little pocket and it is very thin.
Please give me a penny to put some money in.
If you haven't got a penny, a halfpenny will do.
If you haven't got a halfpenny, well—
God bless you!

In England, children went caroling from house to house on New Year's Day. Their neighbors gave them money, much as we give candy and apples for trick-or-treat on Hallowe'en. Whether they received a contribution or not, they sang or spoke, and this old rhyme has been handed down. The group can say the verse together, with one child acting the part of the caroler; or half of the group can speak, with the other half playing the carolers. Perhaps the entire group will want to speak and move. There are various possibilities in even as short a rhyme as this.

A very simple verse, but one that offers an unusual opportunity for imaginative movement, is "Jump or Jiggle." Not only children but adult students as well get into the spirit of it and have a good time thinking of movements that characterize the animals mentioned.

JUMP AND JIGGLE
EVELYN BEYER

Frogs jump.
Caterpillars hump.
Worms wiggle.
Bugs jiggle.
Rabbits hop.
Horses clop.
Snakes slide.
Sea gulls glide.
Mice creep.
Deer leap.
Puppies bounce.
Lions stalk—
But
I walk.

The next verse suggests the use of sound effects rather than action. Part of the group might say the first and third lines, with the others taking the second and fourth. Or, if two clocks are suggested, a solo voice might take the first and third, with the total group taking the other lines. Even so simple a poem as this provides some opportunity for inventiveness.

> Slowly ticks the big clock:
>   Tick-tock; tick-tock!
> But cuckoo clock ticks a double quick:
>   Tick-a-tock-a, tick-a-tock-a,
>   Tick-a-tock-a, tick!

MERRY-GO-ROUND
DOROTHY BARUCH

> I climbed up on the merry-go-round,
> And it went round and round.
> I climbed up on a big brown horse,
> And it went up and down.
>
> Around and round and up and down.
> Around and round and up and down.
>
> I sat high up on a big brown horse,
> And rode around on the merry-go-round,
> And rode around on the merry-go-round.
> I rode around on the merry-go-round
> Around
> And round
> And
> Round.

This poem is fun for children of all ages because of the action, which requires some coordination. As with the others, half of the group can read it while the other half acts the merry-go-round; or, if the group is small, everyone can do the action while repeating the lines. It is probably more satisfactory handled the first way, with variety achieved by having individual voices take the lines beginning with "I." Sometimes children like to imagine the merry-go-round running down until it comes to a stop.

ECHO
AUTHOR UNKNOWN

> I sometimes wonder where he lives,
> This Echo that I never see.

I heard his voice now in the hedge,
Then down behind the willow tree.

And when I call, "Oh, please come out,"
"Come out," he always quick replies.
"Hello, hello," again I say;
"Hello, hello," he softly cries.

He must be jolly, Echo must,
For when I laugh, "Ho, ho, ho, ho,"
He answers me with "Ho, ho, ho."

I think perhaps he'd like to play;
I know some splendid things to do.
He must be lonely hiding there;
I wouldn't like it. Now, would you?

Echoes are fascinating, and this poem is one that may prompt a group to make up an original story about echoes. It lends itself so well to choral reading that it is suggested the class try it this way first, then discuss whether something else might be done with it. The lines in which the Echo speaks are good solo lines that stimulate speculation as to who the Echo is, what he is like, where he is hiding, and whether or not he is ever discovered. Some groups have made up delightful stories about him after reading the poem together first.

Both younger and older students find enjoyment in simple folk rhymes. The following are included because they can be interpreted in more than one way: literally, telling the stories; and abstractly, dancing the characters caught in amusing situations.

SIMPLE SIMON

Simple Simon met a pieman,
    Going to the fair;
Says Simple Simon to the pieman,
    Let me taste your ware.

Says the pieman to Simple Simon,
    Show me first your penny;
Says Simple Simon to the pieman,
    Indeed I have not any.

Simple Simon went a-fishing,
    For to catch a whale;
All the water he had got
    Was in his mother's pail.

Simple Simon went to look
  If plums grew on a thistle;
He pricked his finger very much,
  Which made poor Simon whistle.

THE QUEEN OF HEARTS

The Queen of Hearts
She made some tarts,
All on a summer's day;
The Knave of Hearts
He stole the tarts,
And took them clean away.
The King of Hearts
Called for the tarts,
And beat the Knave full sore;
The Knave of Hearts
Brought back the tarts,
And vowed he'd steal no more.

Although choral speaking is an effective way to begin pantomime, it is not the only way of using poetry. Often a poem can be introduced by the leader, either before or after improvisation. The poem may serve as a springboard to action in which the whole class participates, but the improvising class does not necessarily repeat or read the verse. One short poem that has proved highly successful with many groups of all ages is "Hallowe'en."

HALLOWE'EN
GERALDINE BRAIN SIKS

Sh! Hst!
Hsst! Shsssssh!
It's Hallowe'en.
Eerie creatures now are seen.
Black, bent witches fly
Like ugly shadows through the sky.
White, stiff ghosts do float
Silently, like mystery smoke.

Lighted pumpkins glow
With crooked eyes and grins to show
It's Hallowe'en
Hssst! Shssh!
Sh! Hst!

The period might start off with a discussion of what we think of when we hear the word *Hallowe'en*. Most groups suggest pumpkins, witches, orange and black, elves, broomsticks, cats, night, ghosts, trick-or-treat, and masks. Some pantomime to music can be introduced here, with the whole class becoming witches, cats, or ghosts. After they are thoroughly in the spirit of Hallowe'en, the poem can be read. When the group is small, all may be eerie creatures, witches, and ghosts. When the group is large, it can be divided into several parts, with each one choosing one idea to pantomime. Pumpkins have been suggested in a variety of ways: rolling about on the floor in rounded shapes, squatting with big smiles, and moving in circles to music. Music is helpful, though not necessary. This poem never fails to arouse a response, and on one occasion led to an informal program of Hallowe'en poems and improvisations.

The next poem is one that has been most successful with both children and adults. The universality of its theme appeals to everyone and stimulates an imaginative response at any time of the year. It was the basis for a delightful improvisation by a group of Puerto Rican teachers, who understood and enjoyed it in English, then improvised it with Spanish dialogue.

SING A SONG OF SEASONS
ALICE ELLISON

It's spring.
Such a hippity, happity, hoppity
First spring day.
Let's play! Let's play! Let's play!

It's summer!
Such a swingy, swazy lazy
First hot day.
Let's play! Let's play! Let's play!

It's fall!
Such a brisky, frisky, crispy
First fall day.
Let's play! Let's play! Let's play!

It's winter!
Such a blowy, snowy joy
First winter day.
Let's play! Let's play! Let's play!

Before reading the poem, there can be pantomimes of simple sports and games. Flying kites, skating, tossing a ball, jumping rope, and playing tennis are familiar activities that serve to get the group moving and break down the barriers of self-consciousness. After perhaps fifteen minutes of this kind of activity, the teacher is ready to read the poem. Discussion as to games and sports appropriate to each season directs the thinking, and often brings some unexpected suggestions. After everyone has had a chance to offer ideas, the teacher can ask how the poem might be played.

If the class is separated into four groups, each group can take a season, showing various games and sports belonging to it. Some groups create situations for each, such as going to the beach in summer, with sunbathing, swimming, picnicking, and the like. More than one group has created a scene with characters for each season, using the poem only as a springboard for an original situation. It is urged that this be done in the round, rather than on a stage or in the front of a room, so as to allow for as much movement as possible and easy passage into the center without breaking the mood.

IMAGININGS
J. PAGET-FREDERICKS

> Imagine!
> A little red door that leads under a hill
> Beneath roots and bright stones and pebbly rill.
>
> Imagine!
> A quaint little knocker and shoe scraper, too—
> A curious carved key
> Is waiting for you.
>
> Imagine!
> Tiptoe on doormat, you're turning the key.
> The red door would open
> And there you'd be.
>
> Imagine!
> Shut the door tightly, so no one could see.
> And no one would know then
> Where you would be.
> Imagine, if you can.

A poem such as "Imaginings" lends itself to all kinds of improvisation. Every age will find an answer to the question: What lies behind the little red door? It is a good idea for the teacher to read the poem aloud two or three times before asking what the group sees in it. If the class is not too large, every child may be given a chance to describe what he sees. Younger children find buried treasure, a forbidden city, thieves, a ghost town. Some may describe a

place they know, with friends or neighbors inhabiting it. This particular poem
is a wonderful springboard for the imagination, since it leads the listener to the
threshold, and then leaves him free to follow his own ideas.

Some groups have been stimulated to plan an original play, involving
several characters. If many good suggestions come out of the discussion, the
leader may want to break the class into small groups of three or four, who will
in turn dramatize their ideas. Occasionally, if a group is very small, or if the
teacher wants to plan an individual lesson, each child may pantomime what she
sees and does behind the red door. The poem can hold a group for two or
three sessions, depending on their readiness to use the material and the
interest it stimulates.

SOME ONE

WALTER DE LA MARE

Some one came knocking
  At my wee, small door;
Some one came knocking,
  I'm sure—sure—sure;
I listened, I opened,
  I looked to left and right,
But nought there was a-stirring
  In the still dark night;
Only the busy beetle
  Tap-tapping in the wall,
Only from the forest
  The screech owl's call
Only the cricket whistling
  While the dewdrops fall,
So I know not who came knocking
  At all, at all, at all.

"Some One" has the same power as the previous poem to evoke an
imaginative response. Though the poem is short, it creates an atmosphere of
mystery and wonder. Who can be knocking? How large is the "wee, small
door"? Who am "I"? Do I ever find out who my mysterious visitor was? How do
I react? Groups of all ages enjoy imagining this situation, and the teacher may
expect a variety of responses and interpretations. Some children have insisted
that the door can be no more than a few inches high, which of course leads into
the question of whose house it is. Fairies, elves, friendly insects, and mice have
all been suggested. Other children have seen it as a cottage door—small
compared to the doors of city buildings. Visitors, in this case, vary from

mysterious strangers with magic powers to actual persons—frightened, and faint with weariness. Indians have been suggested, investigating an early settler's cabin. Because the poet does not say who knocked, the reader is entirely free to create his own situation, and some delightful stories have been inspired as a result.

SEA SHELL
AMY LOWELL

Sea Shell, Sea Shell,
  Sing me a song, O please
A song of ships, and sailor men,
  And parrots, and tropical trees.

Of islands lost in the Spanish Main
Which no man ever may find again,
Of fishes and coral under the waves,
And sea-horses stabled in great green caves.

Sea Shell, Sea Shell,
Sing of the things you know so well.

Although "Sea Shell" offers vivid imagery, it leaves the imagination free to roam tropical isles and savor adventure. Every child responds to the singing of a shell, and most will go on to ideas of their own. Perhaps having the group tell their own stories is a good beginning. What did you hear? Where did you find the shell? What is it like? What did it sing when you listened? Tell us its story.

Having a collection of shells adds to the interest as the children feel and examine them. Elaborate plays set on unknown shores have resulted, with the children responding to the thoughts of sailors, pirates, and treasures buried in the sand.

The poems of Robert Louis Stevenson have long appealed to children, and both their content and the suggestions for action make them especially appropriate for creative drama. The two poems that follow can be used with quite young children, who may already be familiar with them.

MY SHADOW
ROBERT LOUIS STEVENSON

I have a little shadow that goes in and out with me,
And what can be the use of him is more than I can see.
He is very, very like me from the heels up to the head;
And I see him jump before me, when I jump into my bed.

The funniest thing about him is the way he likes to grow—
Not at all like proper children, which is always very slow;
For he sometimes shoots up taller like an India-rubber ball;
And he sometimes gets so little that there's none of him at all.

He hasn't got a notion of how children ought to play,
And can only make a fool of me in every sort of way.
He stays so close beside me, he's a coward, you can see;
I'd think shame to stick to nursie as that shadows sticks to me!

One morning, very early, before the sun was up,
I rose and found the shining dew on every buttercup;
But my lazy little shadow, like an arrant sleepy-head,
had stayed at home behind me and was fast asleep in bed.

The idea of a shadow offers all kinds of possibilities. The group might try
this one all together—half being children; half, shadows. This could also lead
into original stories, with use of shadows as a theme. It could also stimulate the
writing of original verse.

THE WIND
ROBERT LOUIS STEVENSON

I saw you toss the kites on high
And blow the birds about the sky;
And all around I heard you pass,
Like ladies' skirts across the grass—
   O wind a-blowing all day long,
   O wind, that sings so loud a song.

I saw the different things you did,
But always you yourself you hid.
I felt you push, I heard you call,
I could not see yourself at all—
   O wind a-blowing all day long,
   O wind, that sings so loud a song.

O you that are so strong and cold,
O blower, are you young or old?
Are you a beast of field and tree
Or just a stranger child than me?
   O wind a-blowing all day long,
   O wind, that sings so loud a song.

Like the preceding verse, "The Wind" offers a wonderful opportunity for strong movement. The group can divide up in many ways, being everything that is mentioned: the wind, the birds, the kites, the skirts, and other things that the children may suggest. Wind is a good topic for discussion, often suggesting original stories as well as the search for other stories such as Aesop's fable about *The Sun and the Wind.* A whole unit could be developed on the subject or on the natural elements.

Most children at one time or another have made a mobile. Perhaps there is one in the classroom. The following poem describes a mobile, suggesting how it moves and seems to be alive. How can it be used as a springboard to suggest movement and dramatic action? See what it suggests to the class.

MOBILE

DAVID McCORD

Our little mobile hangs and swings
And likes a draft and drafty things:

Half-open doors; wide-window breeze,
All people when they cough or sneeze;

Hot dishes giving off their heat;
Big barking dogs, small running feet.

Our mobile's red and made to look
Like fish about to bite a hook:

Six fishes with a hook in front
Of each. They range in size—the runt,

Or baby, up to papa fish,
With hooks to watch and make them wish

That they could reach the nice blue worms
A-dangle there with swirly squirms;

Six fishy mouths all open wide,
Six sets of teeth all sharp inside,

Six fishy holes where eyes should be,
Six fish to swim on airy sea.

I'm eating breakfast now and they are watching me.
And I must say

That every time I take a bite
I see and feel their sorry plight.

Birds, fish, and sailboats are often used as subjects for mobiles. This is because they all move, dip, turn, and swirl as the air circulates around them. There is almost a magic in the way a mobile moves, even when there appears to be no breeze stirring. Without using words, have the class be a mobile:

moving as separate parts of the mobile
putting the parts together in a formation
moving without touching the other parts of the mobile

Now break the class into small groups, each suggesting in movement the images described in the verse. Try adding the images to the moving mobile.

This may lead to the making of a mobile or the creating of a verse. Or it may lead to an entirely different way of suggesting a mobile. See what it makes the class feel, see, do.

Langston Hughes's poetry is rich in images and rhythms. This particular short work suggests strong movement, which older children enjoy using to create the different rivers.

THE NEGRO SPEAKS OF RIVERS
LANGSTON HUGHES

I've known rivers:
I've known rivers ancient as the world and older than
    the flow of human blood in human veins.
My soul has grown deep like the rivers.
I bathed in the Euphrates when dawns were young.
I built my hut near the Congo and it lulled me to
    sleep.
I looked upon the Nile and raised the pyramids above
    it.
I heard the singing of the Mississippi when Abe Lincoln
    went down to New Orleans, and I've seen its muddy
    bosom turn all golden in the sunset.

I've known rivers:
Ancient, dusky rivers.
My soul has grown deep like the rivers.

After some discussion of the places and the different kinds of rivers described in the poem, the children will be ready to use it as a springboard. Strong movement and use of the whole body are called for; perhaps large groups, moving together, can suggest the vast bodies of water better than one or two persons. What else is there to depict besides the waters? Are there any people? Does anything happen? What does the last line mean? How can this be expressed?

THE OLD WIFE AND THE GHOST
JAMES REEVES

There was an old wife and she lived all alone
In a cottage not far from Hitchin:
And one bright night, by the full moon light,
Comes a ghost right into her kitchen.

About that kitchen neat and clean
The ghost goes pottering round.
But the poor old wife is deaf as a boot
And so hears never a sound

The ghost blows up the kitchen fire,
As bold as bold can be;
He helps himself from the larder shelf,
But never a sound hears she.

He blows on his hands to make them warm,
And whistles aloud "Whee-hee!"
But still as a sack the old soul lies
And never a sound hears she.

From corner to corner he runs about,
And into the cupboard he peeps;
He rattles the door and bumps on the floor,
But still the old wife sleeps.

Jangle and bang go the pots and pans,
As he throws them all around;
And the plates and mugs and dishes and jugs,
He flings them all to the ground.

Madly the ghost tears up and down
And screams like a storm at sea;
At last the old wife stirs in her bed—
And it's "Drat those mice," says she.

Then the first cock crows and morning shows
And the troublesome ghost's away.
But oh! what a pickle the poor wife sees
When she gets up next day.

"Them's tidy big mice," the old wife thinks.
And off she goes to Hitchin.
And a tidy big cat she fetches back
To keep the mice from her kitchen.

This amusing verse should stimulate all kinds of ideas for dramatization, characterization, and movement. It can be done entirely in mime or with improvised dialogue. Why not have the entire group work on the ghost's movement and activities? They will enjoy it, and many ideas will be expressed within the security of the group. Music and sound effect are helpful and add atmosphere. This is a good poem for Hallowe'en, but it has a strong appeal for young children at any time of year.

"The Creation" can be read, acted, or danced. Most young people respond to its power and find in its strong, imaginative style a stimulus for expression of one or another of these dramatic forms. It is suggested that it be read aloud first, then performed both in dance and in mime. Because of the numbers of creatures the poet includes, it is an ideal piece for a large group to work on.

THE CREATION
JAMES WELDON JOHNSON

And God stepped out on space,
And he looked around and said:
I'm lonely—
I'll make me a world.

And as far as the eye of God could see
Darkness covered everything,
Blacker than a hundred midnights
Down in a cypress swamp.

Then God smiled,
And the light broke,
And the darkness rolled up on one side,
And the light stood shining on the other,
And God said: That's good!

Then God reached out and took the light in his hands,
And God rolled the light in his hands
Until he made the sun;
And he set that sun a-blazing in the heavens.
And the light that was left from making the sun
God gathered it up in a shining ball
And flung it against the darkness,

Spangling the night with the moon and stars.
Then down between
The darkness and the light
He hurled the world;
And God said: That's good!

Then God himself stepped down—
And the sun was on his right hand,
And the moon was on his left;
The stars were clustered about his head,
And the earth was under his feet.
And God walked, and where he trod
His footsteps hollowed the valleys out
And bulged the mountains up.

Then he stopped and saw
That the earth was hot and barren.
So God stepped over to the edge of the world
And he spat out the seven seas—
He batted his eyes, and the lightnings flashed—
He clapped his hands, and the thunders rolled—
And the waters above the earth came down,
The cooling waters came down.

Then the green grass sprouted,
And the little red flowers blossomed,
The pine tree pointed his finger to the sky,
And the oak spread out his arms,
The lakes cuddled down in the hollows of the ground,
And the rivers ran down to the sea;
And God smiled again,
And the rainbow appeared,
And curled itself around his shoulder.

Then God raised his arm and waved his hand,
Over the sea and over the land,
And he said; Bring forth! Bring forth!
And quicker than God could drop his hand,
Fishes and fowls
And beasts and birds
Swam the rivers and the seas,
Roamed the forests and the woods,
And split the air with their wings.
And God said: That's good!

Then God walked around,
And God looked around
On all that he had made.
He looked at his sun,
And he looked at his moon,
And he looked at his little stars;
He looked on his world
With all its living things,
And God said; I'm lonely still.

Then God sat down—
On the side of a hill where he could think;
By a deep, wide river he sat down;
With his head in his hands,
God thought and thought,
Till he thought; I'll make me a man!

Up from the bed of the river
God scooped the clay;
And by the bank of the river
He kneeled him down;
And there the great God Almighty
Who lit the sun and fixed it in the sky,
Who flung the stars to the most far corner of the night,
Who rounded the earth in the middle of his hand;
This great God,
Like a mammy bending over her baby,
Kneeled down in the dust
Toiling over a lump of clay
Till he shaped it in his own image;

Then into it he blew the breath of life,
And man became a living soul.
Amen. Amen.

I HEAR AMERICA SINGING
WALT WHITMAN

I hear America singing, the varied carols I hear.
Those of mechanics, each one singing his as it
      should be blithe and strong,
The carpenter singing as he measures his plank
      or beam,

The mason singing his as he makes ready for
    work, or leaves off work.
The boatman singing what belongs to him in his
    boat, the deckhand singing on the steamboat
    deck,
The shoemaker singing as he sits on his bench,
    the hatter singing as he stands,
The wood-cutter's song, the ploughboy's on his
    way in the morning, or at noon intermission or
    at sundown,
The delicious singing of the mother, or of the
    young wife at work, or of the girl sewing or
    washing.
Each singing what belongs to him or her and to
    none else.
The day what belongs to the day—at night the
    party of young fellows, robust, friendly.
Singing with open mouths their strong
    melodious songs.

"I Hear America Singing" is a splendid poem for both choral speaking and dramatization. The various characters and their occupations suggest pantomime to participants of all ages. If playing in a large room, the characters can be scattered about the circle, with any number taking part. Pantomime and speaking may be done simultaneously or separately, as the group prefers. This is a poem that is particularly appealing to older students, who are often stimulated to further reading of the poet's work. The mood is powerful and usually acts as a unifying element.

Puppets and Poetry

An imaginative program combining puppets and poetry was devised by two artist/teachers in New Jersey a few years ago. Its popularity attests the effectiveness of the method, which is described in their brochure as follows:

More and more puppets are used in education to add dimensions to learning. A puppet can add clarity and motion to difficult teaching problems and abstractions, demonstrating to the students a living picture of the offered material.[2]

2. Leila Weisholz and Lois Koenig. *Poetry and Puppets in Education: A Learning Experience in the Language Arts* (Cedar Grove, N.J.).

The artist/teachers make the point that poetry and puppets have certain similarities: the words are the puppets of the poem, just as puppets are the materials of the puppeteer. In each case, total involvement is necessary. The idea is not to be construed as a gimmick but rather as another way of teaching the language arts. Lyric poems are handled with great simplicity in order to deepen emotional involvement and not distract by excessive movement. Narrative poetry, on the other hand, is presented differently; puppets mime the story as the poem is read aloud. Puppets demonstrate the basic exaggerations of poetry, the artists say. Results include not only enjoyment and a better understanding of the poetic form, but also encouragement of the writing of original verse.

Poetry and Dance

Poetry grew out of dance and song, and so these are natural companions. Bringing in a dancer to the class—the dance teacher, perhaps older students who have had more dance experience than the class, or a professional dancer if

A member of the audience meets an actor after a performance of *The Magic Word*. (*Courtesy of Periwinkle Productions, Inc., Monticello, N.Y.*)

one is available—adds another dimension when working with poems. For one thing, dance offers an abstract expression rather than the more literal interpretation of mime and improvisation. Dividing the class, with one half moving to the cadence and meaning of the poem and the other half speaking it, calls for imagination and cooperation. This approach is not suggested for older students only; younger children, though lacking well-developed performance skills, are often freer in interpreting poetry through movement.

Working on poetry first in mime and then in dance helps students to experience it more fully. Lyric verse lends itself best to nonverbal interpretation, whereas narrative and dramatic verse stimulate the improvisation of dialogue. Some groups respond to poetry more readily than others but most will enjoy it, if the leader's approach is positive and enthusiastic.

A poet or professional children's theatre company that performs poetry may inspire children. One such company is The Periwinkle Productions, Inc. of Monticello, New York, who began playing poetry programs over twenty years ago and retain poetry performance as an important emphasis in an expanding theatrical repertory. In addition to poetry reading and performances, the company works in schools with teachers to encourage creative writing, principally poetry. Special classes as well as English classes have responded to the stimulation and have achieved some remarkable results.

Summary

Poetry, in conclusion, is an effective springboard for improvisation and improvisation, for poetry. The directness of verse motivates the players to a response that is direct and imaginative. For this reason, poetry is a good starting point for the beginner, though it can be used at any time with even the most advanced players. Because the sounds of poetry have as great an appeal as the content and mood, it is suggested that poetry be spoken as well as acted.

Choral speaking is a group art and can, therefore, be combined with creative dramatics if the teacher so wishes. Some of the reasons for including choral speaking are as follows:

1. It can be done with groups of any size and age.
2. It emphasizes group rather than individual effort.
3. It provides an opportunity to introduce poetry.
4. It offers the shy or handicapped child an opportunity to speak.
5. It promotes good habits of speech through enjoyable exercise, rather than drill.
6. It is a satisfying activity in itself.
7. It can be combined successfully with rhythmic movement and pantomime.

Just as action songs are used with very young children as an approach to creative rhythms, so may poetry be used with older children, to suggest mood, stimulate ideas and begin the flow of creative energy. Chants and the repetition of words have a natural appeal. Thus poetry and nonsense verse may prove a successful method of introducing creative drama. Skill in movement, rhythms, and pantomime are increased as all children are given opportunities to participate.

11

Speech and Speech-Related Activities

*I*mproved speech is a shared objective of modern educators and teachers of creative drama. Although this book is not primarily directed toward speech and the language arts, but is focused instead upon one aspect of dramatic techniques, the implications for improved speech habits are obvious. As the player, either child or adult, feels the desire to communicate orally with others, she will seek the words she wants and try to pronounce and articulate them clearly. This chapter suggests some speech-related activities that may be carried on in addition to creative drama and may act as an incentive for improving oral expression.

Speech depends upon words. The more words one has at his command, the richer and more precise his communication. Children love words and enjoy learning new ones, given half a chance and some encouragement. Vocabulary building, moreover, is a never-ending pro-

The monologue developed into performance with costume and props. (*Courtesy of Diana Mada Kelly, University of Windsor, Canada.*)

cess. Reading good literature is one of the finest ways of meeting new words, and the improvisation of dialogue offers an opportunity for putting them into practice. Different characters speak in different ways. A person's manner of speech distinguishes him as much as his physical movements and behavior do. In assuming a role, the player learns as much as he can about the character he is playing: age, education, occupation, likes and dislikes, strengths, weaknesses, and other personal qualities. Knowledge of a character will help determine the words he uses, as well as the way in which he says them.

The young or inexperienced player will not be able to delineate character at the outset, but she will slowly develop an awareness of the speech appropriate to a character and in time will be able to handle dialogue that conveys more than rudimentary information. Particularly effective in pointing out individual differences in speech and the possibilities of enriching them, is the discussion held after the first and second playing. The leader may ask the player some questions about her character: Would the character talk that way? Use those words? Use slang? Suggest her occupation by the way she describes it? Then the leader may proceed to some general questions about characters: How would a father speak? A storekeeper? a general? A TV newscaster? Would a child say the same thing in the same words and phrases? Children are quick to discern discrepancies. Moreover, they enjoy finding just the right words for a particular character and delight in using long words. Proof of this can be seen in the way in which very young children memorize repeated phrases and words from favorite stories: any deviation from the text on the part of a reader, in an effort at simplification, will bring an immediate correction from the listening child, who knows and loves the original.

As to clarity and audibility, no activity points up the necessity of being heard and understood any better than taking part in a play. The teacher need not—indeed, should not—stress such failings as indistinct or inaudible speech, but the other players will be aware of it. A far more effective way of telling a player that his voice is too soft is to raise such questions as: Would an angry man sound like that? What kind of voice do you think a giant would have? How do we know that the boy is calling to someone from a distance?

Too much attention to vocal projection and articulation frequently leads to an artificial manner of delivery, but attention to the reasons for a louder voice or clearer speech will accomplish the desired goals, though admittedly this approach takes longer. Observers are quick to comment when they cannot hear or understand a player. Peer criticism is a far more effective way of improving a player's speech than constant nagging by the teacher. If the player really wants to be understood, she will make the necessary effort. Again, she will not accomplish everything in the beginning, but with practice and encouragement as well as criticism, she will show improvement in time. Creative drama offers a unique opportunity to enlarge the vocabulary, promote more audible speech, and improve articulation.

In recent years there has been a conscious effort to improve the self-image of the speaker whose verbal skills are poor or for whom English is a second language. In order to accomplish this, voice and diction have been de-emphasized; in other words, *what* is said is considered of greater importance than *how* it is said. The objectives—encouragement of the speaker and the building of pride in a cultural heritage—have been given a priority. While no one would quarrel with this as the first step in language improvement, it is to be hoped that once a degree of self-confidence has been achieved, the student should be helped to move on to better habits of speech. Clarity, audibility, and a constantly improving vocabulary are still the goals for citizens in a democratic society. Freedom of speech is of little value without the ability to express oneself clearly and effectively. Today that ability affects almost every facet of life and most jobs. Therefore, the speech arts are more important than ever before, and in the opinion of the author it is condescending to demand anything less than the best of students in this area as well as in others. The teacher's acceptance of a patois or a substandard level of English does the speaker a disservice both now and later on. Poor speech, like poor writing, is a handicap which need not exist. What better place than the public school classroom to learn to communicate effectively?

Classroom activities other than improvisation provide work on oral communication. One of the oldest and best of these is storytelling, a favorite pastime in itself as well as a primary step in the preparation of a dramatization.

Storytelling

Storytelling is an ancient art that continues to be loved in spite of, or perhaps because of, our technical advances in communication. Television brings a vast array of entertainment into our homes, but it can no more replace the living storyteller than can film take the place of theatre. The reader-audience relationship depends upon the rapport between the one telling the story and the listeners: their involvement in the material and the way it is presented to them, which varies with each telling. The age, background, and interests of the audience, the physical surroundings, and even the time of day affect the development of that rapport. But the most important factor in storytelling is always the storyteller himself, his sensitivity and enthusiasm. Fortunate the boys and girls who are exposed to a good storyteller; fortunate, also, the one who possesses the skill to choose just the right story for the occasion and make it live again for his listeners.

Traditionally, stories were told for three purposes: to entertain, to teach, and to transmit the culture. These purposes have not changed essentially, though in an era of mass education the storyteller primarily provides entertainment and aesthetic pleasure. Folktales, myths, legends, fables, biography, and

history offer a wealth of storytelling material. A lively tale, believable characters, and a worthwhile theme are the primary requisites; these are also the
requirements for a good play, though not every good story can be adapted to
the stage successfully, for a variety of reasons.

The storyteller has the freedom, however, to tell any tales she considers
worthwhile and appropriate, for she will not have to cope with the problems of
dramatization. A vast supply of good literature is available, but the good
storyteller must first be able to find it. She must select material to which she
responds and which she wants to share with others. She must then decide
whether the story will be better read or told. Perhaps she will feel that the
language and literary style of the author should not be sacrificed by putting
them into the words of another. If this is the case, the story will be better if read.
If, on the other hand, she decides that the material will be more effective told,
the storyteller's preparation will be somewhat different.

The storyteller has already considered the age of the listeners; and he has
thought about both the length of the story and the time at his disposal. Having
satisfied himself that he has made a wise choice, he will familiarize himself
thoroughly with all the details. For the beginning storyteller, making an outline
is a good way to organize the material: the beginning, the action, the climax, the
denouement. He should practice telling the story aloud, considering carefully
the mood as well as the significant details.

Choice of words is important in storytelling. Often, certain words or
phrases are repeated a number of times and are so important that the teller will
wish to use them. She will not otherwise try to memorize the story, for this
invariably leads to a stilted presentation and the risk of forgetting. Knowing a
story so well that it can be told in one's own words is a far more satisfactory way
of sharing it. Descriptive words create vivid pictures; words can suggest seeing,
hearing, tasting, smelling, and touching, and can help the listener become
more deeply interested and involved. Some impersonation makes characters
come alive, though the storyteller's aim is to guide interpretation rather than to
establish patterns for characterization. Facial expressions and gestures add
interest only if they are natural and spontaneous. They should not be
memorized and set, or spontaneity will suffer. Several rehearsals will be
needed, however, for the storyteller to polish her sentences and achieve
fluency.

Sincerity is a basic requirement in storytelling, for the child in the
audience is sensitive to condescension and resents not being taken seriously.
Humor, on the other hand, is enjoyed by everyone. A humorous tale, character,
joke, or witty remark serves to draw teller and audience together. Indeed, one
objective of storytelling is to develop a sense of humor, which is really a sense
of proportion.

A pleasing voice and clear speech are to be cultivated, since the storyteller
depends primarily on his verbal communication, unlike the actor, who uses his

entire body to convey his meaning. He must be able to forget himself in his preoccupation with the material. Rather than wondering how well he is doing, he will be checking constantly to see if the audience hears, understands, and seems to be appreciating the story.

The techniques of storytelling are changing, however; whereas in the earlier editions of this book the point was made that the storyteller is not an actor and must resist the temptation to become one, today some of the most successful storytellers use movement and mime freely. The recent revival of interest in the oral tradition has resulted in new ways of telling stories. Instead of rejecting the actor's techniques, many younger storytellers are making full use of them, including vocal effects, strong facial expression, and physical activities that border on the acrobatic—for a frankly theatrical effect. Many of them memorize their material, wear costumes, or at least garments that are different from ordinary street clothes. Some add musical accompaniment or work with a musician. Who is to say that this is *not* storytelling because it breaks all the rules? Librarians and teachers tend to favor the traditional approach when they tell stories: first, because they are not giving a performance but rather are telling stories in a quiet place or are concerned with creating a quiet atmosphere; and second, because they are not performers. On the other hand, the professional storyteller who comes in for assembly programs or special occasions *is* a performer, educated in the storytelling techniques, and serves quite a different purpose. It is not suggested here that either the teacher or the student must discard the old storytelling conventions to keep up with the times. The point is simply this: that we can no longer lay down ironclad rules regarding any art form and refuse to recognize the changes that artists may make in them.

This brief discusson of some of the aims and techniques of storytelling is directed to the teacher, but telling stories is also a good classroom activity for children. High school and college students not only enjoy the experience but often find use for it in working with camp or play groups. Children in the middle and upper grades take pleasure in sharing their favorite stories; at the same time, they are acquiring new skills in communication. If the group is small, each child may have a chance to tell a story of his own from time to time. If the group is large, then each child may be given a portion of a story to tell, one way of ensuring equal participation for all. Besides practice in recall and organization, storytelling is a splendid opportunity for work on vocabulary, syntax, and diction. Everyone loves a good story. Being able to tell one clearly and well is a way of providing pleasure for others as well as discovering the satisfaction of an attentive audience.

Joanna Kraus has coined the term "sound and motion stories."[1] This is a conscious use of the young child's natural impulse to participate in a story

1. Joanna H. Kraus, *Seven Sound and Motion Stories* (Rowayton, Conn.: New Plays, Inc., 1971).

A sound and motion story. (*Courtesy of Joanna Kraus; Photograph from Educational Communications Center, State University College at Brockport, N.Y.*)

being read or told. Her collection of tales, suggesting places in the text where sounds and actions can be incorporated, is an excellent example of what the teacher can do to involve the group more actively in the experience. It is also a way of beginning a creative drama session or of encouraging participation where time and space is limited. With a little practice, the storyteller can find places in a text where sounds and motions add a dimension and are fun to do.

Incidentally, because words grow out of sounds, this is a valid approach to the teaching of speech. Children enjoy the sounds of words, and this enjoyment of sound for its own sake should be encouraged. Small children love repetition; through correct repetition better speech habits are built. Difficult sounds can be practiced in this way without the dullness of drill.

Sound and Motion Stories

Sound and motion stories provide a technique that can be used when space is limited or when desks are fastened to the floor. At the same time the imagination is stimulated, providing freedom within the boundaries of space, time, or the ability of the students to handle more demanding material. It is especially popular with children in the lower grades. If a class enjoys the participation, the teacher can find other stories that lend themselves to the technique, and mark the participation points accordingly.

The following is a delightful story from Joanna Kraus's collection of tales that children with whom I have worked love. Perhaps because it is modern or a contrast to the folk and fairy tales, they enjoy a situation which they can easily visualize.

THE NIGHT THE ELEPHANTS MARCHED ON NEW YORK
JOANNA KRAUS

There they were, stranded in a railway yard in New Jersey, two hundred animals from Gambelli Brothers Circus.

Thirteen miles away in President Gambelli's New York City office, the phone rang. (S)[2]

"What! What! I can barely hear you," President Gambelli yelled into the telephone.

From the other end of the wire came the sound of nineteen hungry elephants. (S) The chief animal trainer was trying to explain, but President Gambelli could only hear half of what he said.

". . . railway strike . . . in the yard at South Kearney, New Jersey . . . - can't get the animals through to New York City . . . two o'clock opening tomorrow. . . ."

President Gambelli heard the roars of nine lions and fifteen tigers in the background. (S)

"I'll do what I can," called President Gambelli and hung up the receiver. (A)

He paced his office. On the wall was a large poster of a circus elephant which he knew thousands of school children had seen. He knew thousands of mothers, fathers, aunts, and uncles had bought tickets for the two o'clock performance of the Gambelli Brothers Circus.

Violetta, his assistant, rushed in with the morning papers and put them on his desk. He picked up the first newspaper. (A). "Rail Strike," announced the headlines. He picked up the second newspaper. (A) Large black letters spelled out the disaster. "Nationwide Rail Strike. Country Comes to a Halt."

"If the animals don't arrive on time, there won't be a circus," he said to Violetta. "Do you know there are over two hundred animals in the unit stranded in South Kearney, New Jersey!" Luigi Gambelli put his head in his hands. (A) How was he going to move two hundred animals by two o'clock tomorrow?

"We could put the smaller animals in vans, if we can find some," Violetta suggested, "but eight thousand pound elephants . . . I don't know. There won't be a van big enough anywhere."

2. In the story (S) calls for a sound; (A), for an action.

"It sounded like the jungle when the chief trainer telephoned me. We've got to do something fast," answered President Gambelli.

"JUNGLE! That's it. That's where they're from—any kid knows that," said Violetta excitedly. "Well, it's only about thirteen miles from South Kearney to midtown Manhattan. In India the elephants walk further than that."

"But they don't have rush hour traffic in the jungle," he reminded Violetta. Then Luigi Gambelli threw back his shoulders and looked sternly at the pile of newspapers on his desk. (A) "Gambelli Brothers Circus has never missed a performance, and it's not going to now! Get the governor on the phone, and then the mayor! I will *not* disappoint all those children."

The governor found vans to carry the smaller animals. He authorized a yellow permit slip for the larger animals to march to Lincoln Tunnel. (A) The mayor authorized a blue permit slip for the animals to finish their march to Madison Square Garden on the public streets of New York City.

Late that night the gorillas, lions, panthers, and tigers were sent in huge vans across the Hudson River over the George Washington Bridge.

President Gambelli, the chief animal trainer, and his assistants lined up the elephants, trunk to tail, and chained them together. As they worked they fastened each chain carefully. (A) When the elephants moved, you could hear the clinking of the heavy metal chains. (S) At the end of the line was a baby elephant. Tied to her tail were a zebra, a llama, and a Shetland pony.

The chief animal trainer carefully guided the lead elephant by the ear with his bull hook. (A)

A few miles from Lincoln Tunnel, a grocer rushed out to the street. "Luigi Gambelli," he said, "I heard about the animal march on the radio. You and the elephants are invited to have supper in my store." Nineteen elephants flapped their ears happily, as the grocer and his two children fed them thirty-nine cents a pound peanuts and fed carrots to the other animals.

A little later Miss Page, the Lincoln Tunnel toll booth attendant, waved hello to the motorists she recognized who drove through the tunnel every night at that hour. (A)

It was nearly eleven o'clock. Soon she could go home too. At her feet her pet dog, Bouncer, was dozing and dreaming of a bone. (S) For a few minutes there were no cars and she glanced at the new report forms she had to fill out. After "Accidents" she wrote "None." After "Unusual Events" she sighed and wrote "None."

Suddenly Bouncer pricked up his ears and let out a low growl. (S) Miss Page looked up startled. (A) She listened carefully, then looked uncomfortably about. (A) She could not see a car or a person. But way down at the end of the tunnel there was a noise that sounded like a movie she had just seen on television. The movie had been all about the jungle. The sound grew louder ... and louder, as it got nearer and nearer. (S)

A minute later President Gambelli, the chief animal trainer, and his assistants arrived at the toll booth. Miss Page could only stare at them. President Gambelli took off his hat. (A) "Gambelli Brothers Circus," he explained. "They're part of a mixed animal act," the chief animal trainer added.

Miss Page looked quickly through the pages of *Traffic Rules, Regulations and Toll Rates*. There were twelve categories of vehicles in the little green book. "But there's nothing here about elephants," she told them. Then she turned back to the page on Class 2 Vehicles: "Animals, ridden, led or herded, and motorcycles." "Fifty cents an elephant," she said.

President Gambelli counted out nine crisp new dollar bills (A) The chief animal trainer counted out five dimes. (A) "What about the zebra, llama, and the Shetland pony," the animal trainer asked.

Miss Page and Bouncer leaned out of the booth. (A) Neither had ever seen a zebra, a llama, or a Shetland pony before. Timidly, Miss Page put out her hand and patted the pony. (A) "Aw, let them have a free ride," she said. "I know there's nothing in the regulations about zebras, llamas, and Shetland ponies."

After they had thanked her, they marched away. Miss Page could hear the elephants trumpeting at the end of the tunnel. (S) She picked up her report. Next to "Unusual Events," she scratched out the word "None." (A) Miss Page wrote rapidly. (A) She could still hear the sounds of nineteen elephants, one zebra, one llama, and one Shetland pony marching away. (S) "They'll never beieve it," she said to Bouncer.

The next day at two o'clock exactly, Gambelli Brothers Circus opened. There were loud trumpets as the house lights dimmed. (S) The news photographers snapped pictures of Luigi Gambelli standing with the mayor and the governor (A). President Gambelli told the press, "Gambelli Brothers Circus has never missed a performance."

The Night the Elephants Marched on New York could tie in with a circus theme. Or it could, on the other hand, be a stimulus to finding stories and local anecdotes in the news to write or tell, as well as discovering good places for sounds and actions. For myself, I like to use sound and motion stories for "starters," going on to improvisation and a total involvement after the limited participation required by this technique.

Monologues

The monologue, a dramatic form that is less in evidence today than it was a generation or so ago, seems to be regaining some of its lost popularity. Although generally done as performance, it has many educational values when prepared thoughtfully and creatively. Most students find it a challenge and a

An original monologue. (*Courtesy of Diana Mady Kelly, University of Windsor, Canada.*)

change. One class of undergraduates whom I visited did a particularly effective job of monologue preparation, each selecting and observing a character, improvising his or her actions and imagined actions, writing a monologue from the material, and finally performing it for the class. One of the reasons the monologue lost favor was the artificiality that so often characterized the performance. This particular class, however, guided by a gifted and resourceful professor, helped the students to seek out interesting subjects and then develop them in a natural way.[3] The assignment sharpened the students' powers of observation, offered an excellent opportunity for improvisation, and provided them with an exercise in written and oral communication, culminating in performance. The professor's success with her class suggested the value of the assignment for a younger group; for instance, a high school or junior high school class. Prepared as carefully as this assignment was, the monologue can have great value; while not creative drama, it does offer some of the same opportunities and is a change from group work in permitting each student to work on individual projects of choice.

Readers Theatre

Readers theatre, a relatively new concept in the speech arts, is particularly suitable for older children and high school students. The simplicity of production and effectiveness of result make it singularly desirable in schools with inadequate stage facilities and where rehearsal time is at a premium. More than that, it is a way of enjoying good literature through guided study, a mutually agreed-upon interpretation, and clear and expressive oral reading. Readers theatre may be defined as the oral presentation of drama, prose, or poetry by two or more readers, with characterization when necessary, narration if desired, coordination of material to constitute a whole, and the development of a special reader-audience relationship as an objective. Although traditionally a reader has handled a single role, recent performances have permitted one person to read several. Readers theatre is neither lecture nor play; rather, it is a staged program that allows the audience to create its own images through the skilled performance of the readers.

The cast (whether large or small) usually remains onstage or on the designated area throughout, reading the various assigned portions. Generally, readers use little movement, suggesting action instead with simple gestures and facial expression. They must understand what the author has to say, the structure of the piece, and the development of characters; and they must be able to interpret a variety of roles in a matter of minutes, if called upon to do so. I have seen many different types of presentation in readers theatre, ranging from some actual movement on stage to formal positions behind lecterns. Stools and steps are sometimes used to sit on, if an effect of informality is desired or if the leader wishes to have the performers seated when they are not reading. Sometimes readers turn their backs to the audience to indicate their absence from a particular scene. The material, as well as the group's experience and preference, will determine how much or how little movement to include. In general, however, movement is minimal.

---

3. Professor Diana Kelly, University of Windsor, Canada.

Readers theatre has grown in popularity in the past fifteen to twenty years, and with this growth has come experimentation. Some groups have abandoned the lectern entirely and are now fully costumed. They use movement and have gone so far along the continuum that their results are scarcely distinguishable from theatre. Indeed, one of the criticisms of readers theatre is its indulgence in novelty for its own sake. I cannot share this concern because it seems to me that exponents of readers theatre are doing what is being done in all of the arts these days: consciously blending and mixing forms in the search for new ones. Sometimes they are successful; sometimes they are not. But I find experimentation that risks failure more interesting than rigid adherence to rules that were established by the originators.

One brilliant example of this mixing of forms is the New York production of *Colored Girls Who Have Considered Suicide/When the Rainbow is Enuf.* Described as a choreo-poem, it combines the oral presentation of poetry with choreographed movement. Simple but effective costumes are worn by the young actresses in the cast, and stage lighting is an important element of the production. First done experimentally, *Colored Girls* was moved uptown, where it drew large audiences on Broadway.

Although a good deal of readers theatre has been done by adults for adult audiences (e.g., *John Brown's Body, Under Milkwood, Don Juan in Hell, Spoon River*), the Periwinkle Players of Monticello, New York, have for years been presenting highly effective programs in the genre for elementary school children. This company uses simple costumes to suggest character or period, and lighting effects to enrich the performance. With several programs in their repertory, they have proved that poetry—as well as drama and prose—has a strong appeal for children. An awakening interest in words and writing were found to be an additional positive result. While these players are adult professional actors doing a professional job, their kind of program, on a simplified scale, could be done by children.

One particularly effective program was performed by high school students who selected and arranged a script using a group of the world's great love poems to celebrate St. Valentine's Day. In this instance, a narrator introduced each section of the program, giving some background material. A different but equally successful program for children was arranged by college students on the subject of the American West. Prose and poetry that told about the settlers and the frontier were combined with appropriate background music played on the guitar. When transitions were needed, folk songs were introduced. A chronological progression built interest, with the music adding a unifying colorful element. Children doing readers theatre can select material they like and then decide as a group, just as these groups did, the questions of arrangement and sequence. Choral reading is often incorporated, if group speech is considered more effective than solo reading for some selections.

It should be mentioned that other kinds of literature can be used effectively: history, biography, letters, and various documentary materials. More than one program celebrating the bicentennial of American Independence featured American history and American essays. Black history has been the focus of other programs, whereas topics of current social and political interest can offer powerful and dramatic content. Obviously, these materials require much more arranging and editing than do drama and short stories. On the other hand, they bring a new dimension to material that is not usually read aloud.

This brings up the point that selections from separate works can be combined. It is not required that one text only be used. Thus there is a wide range of possibilities from which to choose; and the form is one that teachers should consider rather than thinking always in terms of the play, traditionally staged and mounted. Readers theatre features the text, and, because it does so, can serve as an extremely effective tool for learning.

Stories that are partially narrated, with readers assuming the various roles, comprise another way in which readers theatre makes literature come alive for an audience. Plays and scenes from plays can be performed in this way by students of all ages. For older children particularly, readers theatre is a viable activity for the classroom, as well as an appealing vehicle for public sharing. Important to stress here is the fact that readers theatre does not require an audience beyond the class; indeed, the primary values are derived from the selection and interpretation of the material and the practice in reading aloud. Inasmuch as the result is so often worth sharing, this type of presentation is recommended for the opportunity it offers those engaged in it, an opportunity bearing much pleasure and no problems of production detail and lengthy rehearsals.

The following story of *The Musicians of Bremen* is included as an example of one way in which readers theatre was used by older students for children. If children do it, they should act the story creatively first, then read it aloud from the script, eliminating stage movement and business. Any story may be treated in this manner. Myths and legends, which often depend upon the supernatural, can be handled with ease, whereas difficulties are encountered when they are dramatized in the usual way. Appropriate music may be added, if desired, to suggest the passage of time, the movement from one scene to another, or changes of mood. Music is not necessary to this story, or to readers theatre in general, but it often makes the presentation more effective, just as background music and sound effects lend color and setting to a radio play.

Costumes may be suggested, if desired; but they need not, and, indeed, probably should not, be complete or literal. The same thing is true of settings, which, if merely suggested, make demands on the audience that lead to a clearer and more accurate understanding than any attempt to duplicate a place or scene. Platforms, stools, chairs, ladders, and benches do not connote particular places, which has been one reason for their popularity. Although material may be memorized, books or manuscripts are generally used to let the audience know at once that it is going to share literature, not see a play.

THE MUSICIANS OF BREMEN
A Dramatization for Readers Theatre by Nellie McCaslin

NARRATOR	CAT
DONKEY	COCK
DOG	ROBBER

The six readers may stand throughout, reading from their scripts at lecterns or reading stands. Because the story is so simple and informal, they may prefer to sit on steps instead; they will probably be able to get more into the spirit of it if they are seated informally and close to the audience.

NARRATOR: There was once near the town of Bremen a farmer whose Donkey was growing old and was every day less fit for work. The farmer knew that he should soon have to buy a new donkey and so he began to think of how he could get rid of his faithful old beast. Now the Donkey, who was not as stupid as the farmer thought, decided that he would settle the matter himself. So one day, when the farmer was in the house having his dinner, the Donkey took himself off and started down the road toward the city. "For there," he thought, "I may become a musician." He had a powerful voice which, in spite of his advancing years, could be heard for miles around when he put back his head and brayed. Yes, a musician was what he should be.

　　He had not gone far when he met a Dog lying stretched out by the roadside. The Dog was panting as if he had just run a great distance. The Donkey stopped and greeted him.

DONKEY: Good morning, friend Dog. What may I ask are you doing out here all by yourself? And why are you panting so hard?

DOG: Ah, me. I have run away, but I am an old dog and my strength has all but given out.

DONKEY: Run away? Why should an old fellow like you run away? Pardon me for saying it, but I should think you'd be better off at home where you've someone to care for you than out seeking adventure.

DOG: I agree with you. But the truth of the matter is that my master no longer wants me around. I was a "fine fellow," a "good dog," as long as I was able to work. But now he grows angry when I trail behind and can no longer hunt or herd sheep.

DONKEY: (*sympathetically*) That is too bad.

DOG: That's not the worst of it. He even threatened to knock me on the head and thus be rid of me. Then, with me out of the way, he'll get him a puppy.

DONKEY: Your master is a cruel man, but I can understand how you feel, for the same thing has happened to me. My master is impatient with my slow steps and stiff joints and would replace me with a younger beast.

DOG: It's hard to grow old in this world. I suppose I may as well lie here till I die, for I am of no use to anyone anymore.

DONKEY: Nonsense, my dear friend. Listen, I have an idea. I'm on my way to the city. There I plan to become a musician. Why don't you join me and see what you can do? We may harmonize well together and anyhow, two are always better off than one.

DOG: I have nothing to lose by it. Yes, your words give me courage. I'll go along with you to the city.

NARRATOR: So the two of them set out. Before they had gone very far they came upon a Cat sitting in the middle of the road. They stopped to speak to her.

DONKEY: I beg your pardon, my lady, what is the trouble? You look as unhappy as my friend the Dog did less than an hour ago. Surely life is not all that hard.

CAT: And why shouldn't I look unhappy? You don't know what it is to grow old and no longer be welcome in your very own house.

DONKEY: Indeed? Do tell us what has happened. We, too, have suffered similar misfortunes. Perhaps we can help.

CAT: Very well, I'll tell you, though there's nothing either one of you can do.

DOG: (*sympathetically*) Sometimes it helps just to talk.

CAT: That is true. You see, I used to be loved very much. My mistress thought me the most beautiful cat in the world. She brushed my fur—it was soft and sleek in those days—and gave me cream in a saucer each morning, and meat at night. And she praised me to all the neighbors. She said I kept the place clean of mice.

DOG: Go on.

DONKEY: What happened next?

CAT: You wouldn't believe it! Because I no longer care to run about and catch mice and prefer to curl up by the fire, my mistress has said she would drown me. Is that the way to treat an old friend? I was fortunate enough to escape from her, but how shall I find enough to eat or a warm bed at night, I do not know.

DONKEY: Do not despair, old friend. We share the same sorrow. Instead of sitting here in the road, why not come with us to the city? You are a good musician, I'm sure. Perhaps we can work together. A trio is much more attractive than a duet. Wouldn't you agree, Master Dog?

DOG: Yes, indeed.

CAT: I hadn't thought of being a singer. But it's worth trying and I'm glad to have company, however it turns out.

NARRATOR: So the Cat got up and went with them. The three talked and exchanged stories of their youth and began to feel much better as they got acquainted. Presently they came to a farm yard, where they saw a Cock perched on the gate. He was crowing with all his might.

COCK: Cock-a-doodle-do!

DONKEY: What a fine sound you make, Master Cock. Pray, what great event are you proclaiming?

COCK: Why, that it is a fair day and sunny and my mistress can safely hang out her wash.

DONKEY: She must depend on you very much.

COCK: Indeed she does. She would never know when the sun had come up if it weren't for my crowing.

DOG: You don't looked pleased, somehow. What's the matter?

COCK: I've had a rude shock. Would you believe it, in spite of my years of service to her, I have just heard her say that she plans to cut off my head and roast me for Sunday dinner.

DOG: Oh, that is even worse than what has happened to us, friend Cock. Why don't you leave here at once?

COCK: Where can I go? And how do I know every other farmer's wife might not have the same idea?

CAT: Well, we have a plan. . . .

COCK: What kind of a plan?

CAT: Come along with us and we'll tell you.

COCK: Where are you going?

DONKEY: To the city. We are going to seek our fortune as musicians. With your fine strong voice, I'm sure you will have no trouble finding work.

CAT: And if we practice together, we may work up a concert. four voices—do come along.

COCK: I'll join you. And I thank you with all my heart.

DOG: Anything is better than staying here, and who knows, things may turn out for the best after all.

NARRATOR: And so the four of them walked on together. The day was fair and their hearts were high, for they were certain that good luck was in store for them. As evening approached, they were still a distance from town, so they decided to stop at the edge of the woods for the night. The Donkey and the Dog made a comfortable bed under a tree and the Cat climbed up on a bough where she felt safer. The

Cock, however, who was used to spending the night on a perch, flew up to the very top of the tree and settled himself on a sturdy branch.

COCK: Everyone all right down there?

DONKEY: As right as my old bones can be on this hard ground.

DOG: This is better than being knocked in the head, though I shall be glad when we find proper lodging.

COCK: How about you, Mistress Cat? Are you comfortable?

CAT: Oh, I'm all right. The leaves keep out the draft and anyhow it's not a cold night.

COCK: Well, I'll say goodnight then and I'll wake you up first thing in the morning.

NARRATOR: Before tucking his head under his wing, however, he looked out in all directions, to be sure that nothing was amiss. As he did so, he noticed, not too great a distance anyway, something shining and bright. He called down to the others.

COCK: We can't be as far from the town as we thought. I see lights. There must be a house nearby.

DOG: Are you sure? It looks very dark to me.

CAT: Yes, I see it. It's a house or an inn.

DONKEY: Then perhaps we should push on. I could use a softer bed.

DOG: So could I. And, who knows, the master might throw in a bone and some scraps from his table.

CAT: Yes, indeed. I would willingly exchange this bough for a spot in front of a fire.

COCK: I'm game. Let's find out what it is.

NARRATOR: Having agreed, the four companions got up and followed the Cat, whose eyes served best in the dark. At length they came to a house. It was a very comfortable house, in which there lived a band of robbers. The four stopped outside the door, then the Donkey, who was the tallest, cautiously peered through the window.

COCK: Well, friend Donkey, what do you see? Do they look like kindly folk?

DONKEY: I see an astonishing thing. A table piled with good things to eat and a band of men sitting around it, counting their gold.

CAT: What do you take them to be?

DONKEY: If I'm not mistaken, I'd say they were robbers. This is no farmer's cottage.

COCK: Do you suppose they live here?

DONKEY: Either that or they've taken over the place.

DOG: Perhaps we can scare them away. I used to be good at that years ago. My master always said no robber could get within gunshot when I was around.

CAT: It looks like a fine lodging for us, if we can get in.

DONKEY: Let's think of a way.

DOG: I've got it. I'll get on the Donkey. You, Mistress Cat, jump on my back and the Cock can perch on your shoulders. Then we'll make music.

COCK: A capital idea! Let's do it.

ALL: (*ad lib*) All right—I'm for it—Good idea!

DONKEY: Is everyone in place? Good. Now, altogether. . . . (*Each animal makes his own noise at the same time.*)

DONKEY: Now, then, stand back. I'll put my front feet through the window and we'll all go inside.(*Crash of glass.*)

NARRATOR: The robbers, who had been startled by the concert, were terrified when the four musicians tumbled over the sill into the room. They were out the door in a flash and scattered in all directions. The four old friends watched them go.

DONKEY: Well, it looks as if we have the place to ourselves.

DOG: And the dinner.

CAT: Will you see what's on the table! This is a feast.

COCK: It would be too bad to let so much good food go to waste. What say you? Let's eat.

NARRATOR: So the four gobbled up every crumb. Then, their hunger satisfied, each one sought a bed to his liking. The Donkey found a pile of straw outside the back door and bade the others good night. The Dog stretched out on a rug under the table. The Cat curled up on the hearth; and the Cock, who preferred a higher spot even indoors, perched on a beam in the ceiling. Warm and tired from their travels, they were soon fast asleep.

     Later on that night, however, the robbers, seeing the house dark, and hearing no noise, crept stealthily back. The leader of the band was the first to venture inside. He struck a match on the fireplace and then out of the darkness blazed two bright eyes. The Cat was on her feet in a flash and flew at him and clawed him with all her might. (*Meow.*) The robber yelled in fright more than pain. As he stumbled back he tripped over the Dog who bit him sharply in the leg. (*Bow-wow.*) Running out the back door, he bumped into the Donkey who woke up with a start and kicked him with both feet. (*Hee-haw.*) All this commotion roused the Cock who crowed at the top of his lungs. (*Cock-a-doodle-do.*) This was too much for the robber who ran off to his companions and told them what had befallen him.

ROBBER: A witch has got into the house. I saw her eyes in the dark. First she scratched me with her long nails; next she stabbed me in the leg. Then, when I tried to escape, I was struck with a club from behind and all the while someone on the roof was yelling, "Throw the rascal out! Throw the rascal out!" I tell you, the place is be-witched.

NARRATOR: Well, after that, the robbers never ventured inside the house again. The four musicians were so pleased with their lodging that they stayed right there. And I shouldn't be surprised if they're living there still.

The End

With the Sunrise in His Pocket is an American folk legend with appeal for an older group of children. The storytellers can either read or tell the connecting narration in their own words. Like *The Musicians of Bremen*, it offers an opportunity for participation by the whole class. If children enjoy readers theatre, they may want to create programs of their own based on familiar stories, legends, or materials relating to a particular topic or unit of study. Readers theatre is like improvisation in that it combines reading and speaking, though, admittedly, it is a more formal kind of theatre.

The dramatization of *With the Sunrise in His Pocket* features one of the most delightful personalities to be found in our pre–Civil War South, Davy Crockett. The actual man and his legendary adventures make him a richer character for both storytelling and drama. Hunter, backwoodsman, lover of animals, Indian fighter, and member of Congress, he has an appeal for everyone. His gift for spinning tall tales and his rustic sense of humor have caused some to call him the forerunner of Will Rogers and even Abraham Lincoln. Because his adventures are so fantastic, this play has been put into readers theatre form, in which the imagination can produce the miracles impossible to present on the stage.

WITH THE SUNRISE IN HIS POCKET
A Dramatization for Readers Theatre by Nellie McCaslin

FIRST STORYTELLER	MISSISSIPPI, *his alligator*
SECOND STORYTELLER	A STRANGER, *his political opponent*
DAVY CROCKETT	DEATH HUG, *his bear*
RATTLER, *his dog*	PEOPLE *(for applause and animal sounds)*
	SOUND EFFECTS PERSON

PRODUCTION NOTES: *Sound Effects*—animal noises (to be made by the children); whistle; sound of machinery. *Music*—"Pop Goes the Weasel" or "Turkey in the Straw."

FIRST STORYTELLER: We in America have a great many heroes that we don't know very much about. Of course, we know Abraham Lincoln and George Washington and Thomas Jefferson and we know the things they did are true. On the other hand, we know Paul Bunyan and John Henry and Pecos Bill and we know that most of the stories told about them aren't really true but we like them all the same. Well, about halfway between these two kinds of heroes stands another name—the name of a man who was real enough but the stories they tell about him belong to America's "tall tales." That man was Davy Crockett and he served his country in a great many ways. He was a hunter, a backwoodsman, and an Indian fighter; he was even a member of Congress from 1827 to 1835 and in 1836 he was killed in the defense of the Alamo. Now Mr. Crockett, or Colonel Crockett, as he was known, was born in the hills of Tennessee; but because he went to Washington we think of him as belonging to the whole country instead of just one state. The stories they told about him were so mixed up with the facts that it's pretty hard to tell which is which, but since it doesn't really matter anyhow, we're going to tell them to you just as we heard them.

SECOND STORYTELLER: In a way Davy Crockett was a giant. At least he started out that way. Like all the other giants, he was a most remarkable baby. He himself told how he slept in the shell of a great big snapping turtle instead of a cradle. He had a panther's skin for a cover and a crocodile curled itself right up in a ball to make him a pillow.

FIRST STORYTELLER: I like what he said he ate when he was just a year old.

SECOND STORYTELLER: Yes. He told how he used to get so hungry by eleven o'clock in the morning they'd feed him a sandwich made of a bear's ham and a whole loaf of bread with a few spare ribs thrown in for good measure!

FIRST STORYTELLER: One of the things everybody seemed to remember most about him was his grin. Why, it was famous all over the United States. When he was a boy he used to grin the way other people would shoot a gun—he'd just get what he wanted by grinning at it! They tell how one time he saw a coon up in a tree and since he didn't have his old rifle, Betsy, with him, he just stood there and grinned. Well, after a while, that old coon toppled right off the branch and fell down at his feet. And it was from that coon that he made his famous coonskin cap.

SECOND STORYTELLER: And then there was the other time—later on—he *thought* he saw a coon. He and his hunting dog, Rattler, were out in the forest at night and . . .

CROCKETT: Rattler, old boy, do you see that coon way up there on the top branch of that pine tree?

RATTLER; Arf—arf!

CROCKETT: You don't? Well, you just keep alookin' and pretty soon you'll see him come tumbling down. (*Pause.*) Rattler, what do you mean by layin' down? I know it's night but it ain't time to sleep when we're trying to get that old coon to budge.

RATTLER: Gr-r-r-r.

CROCKETT: What's that you say? You going to sleep anyways? Well, all right but you ain't the hound dog I thought you were—leavin' me grinnin' here in the dark all by myself.

SECOND STORYTELLER: Well, Davy Crockett stood there all night agrinnin' and agrinnin'. And Rattler, he just curled up and went fast asleep. But when morning came Davy made a discovery . . .

CROCKETT: Why, Rattler, that ain't no coon up there! That's just a big knot in the branch of the tree! You were smarter'n me when you went off to sleep.

RATTLER: Gr-r-r-r.

CROCKETT: But you know something? I grinned at it so hard, I grinned the bark right off the limb! And it's left that knot as smooth as a whistle!

FIRST STORYTELLER: Yes, sir, that was a powerful grin all right. And when Davy Crockett began running for office, he could outgrin every other candidate. Why, he used to get votes just as easy as he got coons.

SECOND STORYTELLER: But he didn't just grin to make people do what he wanted. He meant it. Davy Crockett was friendly, and people and animals, too, all loved him.

FIRST STORYTELLER: You know, he always said he had just as many friends among the animals as he did among the people. And they weren't all tame, either; some of them were wild. Some of them were animals he'd rescued when they were in trouble and they never forgot his kindness. Two of his friends, Death Hug, the bear, and Mississippi, his pet alligator, stayed with him all of his life. He brought them up from tiny little critters and there wasn't anything they wouldn't do for him. He used to ride on their backs just like he'd ride his horse and with a bear and a horse and an alligator, there wasn't much territory he couldn't cover.

SECOND STORYTELLER: Maybe they'd like to hear about the time he rode over Niagara Falls?

FIRST STORYTELLER: I'm sure they would. That was exciting. Davy Crockett and Death Hug and Mississippi were all out ice skating that day . . .

CROCKETT: Nice skatin' here on this ice, ain't it, Death Hug?

DEATH HUG: (*With great appreciation.*) Gr-r-r-r.

CROCKETT: What about you, Mississippi? I know you don't like the cold climate much but don't you like skatin' around up here above the falls?

MISSISSIPPI: (*With appreciation.*) Cro-cro-cro.

CROCKETT: Wouldn't be safe down south but up here the ice is so thick you can cut any figures you please. watch out, Mississippi, here I come! (*Pause.*) How's that for a figure eight? Let's see you two do one!

DEATH HUG: (*With great glee as he skates.*) Gr-r-r-r.

MISSISSIPPI: (*With delight, also, as he skates.*) Cro-cro-cro.

CROCKETT: Good! You're both better skaters than most people I know. Now let's all take hands and go around together.

DEATH HUG: (*In sudden excitement and fear.*) Gr-r-r-r.

CROCKETT: What's the matter, Death Hug? You ain't afraid, a big bear like you?

DEATH HUG: (*As if warning of great danger.*) Gr-r-r-r.

CROCKETT: Oh, I see what it's all about! There's a crack in the ice and it's gettin' wider and wider—and why, it's broke off altogether! Now we are in a pickle. We got to do some quick thinking or we'll go right down over the falls!

DEATH HUG: (*In excitement.*) Gr-r-r-r.

CROCKETT: You want me to jump on your back, Death Hug?

DEATH HUG: (*Meaning "yes."*) Gr-r-r.

CROCKETT: All right. I'm aholdin' on so let's go! (*Sound: There is a whistle as they go off together down the falls.*)

CROCKETT: Good for you, Death Hug! Right down over the falls on that old chunk of ice and we didn't even get so much as a ducking!

MISSISSIPPI: Cr-r-r-r.

CROCKETT: What's the matter, Mississippi? You want me to ride down the falls again on *your* back?

MISSISSIPPI: (*Eagerly.*) Cr-r-r-r.

CROCKETT: Well, all right, then. But I got a better idea! You're a good jumper. Instead of going down, we'll just go back up. When I get on your back, you just pick up and JUMP! Now—wait'll I get my arms around you. . . . You all ready, Mississippi?

MISSISSIPPI: Cr-r-r-r.

CROCKETT: All right—here we go! (*Sound: A whistle noise again as they fly right up the falls.*)

CROCKETT: Right up over the topside of the falls in one jump! And we're back where we started from.

FIRST STORYTELLER: Yes, they had lots of fun together and lots of adventures. But one of the best ones came later on when Davy Crockett was running for office. Of course all the animals were there that day as well as all the people who wanted to hear the two candidates speak. Now Davy's opponent was a rich man. He was well-educated, too, and he used a lot of big words when he talked. Davy didn't have any more schooling than he had money but he had good common sense. Well, the people listened in spite of his coonskin cap and his backwoods clothes and they liked what he had to say. But when the stranger began to talk it seemed as if they forgot all about poor Davy Crockett. They flocked around the stranger and the animals began to feel sorry. They didn't like to see their old friend deserted this way for someone so rich and smooth-talking.

STRANGER: (*Orating.*) And so, my friends, a vote for me is a vote for better government. I've been around this great country of ours and . . .

FIRST STORYTELLER: Well, the animals had listened just as long as they were going to. Then Rattler let out a bark.

RATTLER: Arf! Arf!

FIRST STORYTELLER: And Death Hug, he growled.

DEATH HUG: Gr-r-r-r.

FIRST STORYTELLER: And Mississippi, he made all the noise he could.

MISSISSIPPI: Cr-r-r-r.

FIRST STORYTELLER: And then all the other animals—the coons and the woodchucks and the bears—the pigeons and the frogs and the crows—and even the skunks—began to make their own particular noises. But they all sounded like "Crockett."

ANIMALS: (*A great din as they all enter in.*) CR-CR-R-R-R-R-R-CROCKETT.

FIRST STORYTELLER: Now that poor stranger tried harder and harder to speak above the noise but he just couldn't be heard. Every time he'd open his mouth the animals would drown him out.

STRANGER: (*In a louder tone.*) As I said before, I've been all over this great country——

ANIMALS: CR-R-R-CROCKETT! CROCKETT! CROCKETT!

STRANGER: (*Shouting above it and losing his temper.*) All over this great country of ours and I've——

ANIMALS: CROCKETT! CROCKETT! CROCKETT!

FIRST STORYTELLER: Well, it kept up like that. The Stranger trying to make his speech and the animal friends of Davy Crockett keeping him from it. Davy, he just stood on the sidelines and grinned. Well, it worked like a charm. The voters were so tickled that they stopped even trying to listen to the Stranger and they all voted for the man the animals loved—Davy Crockett!

ANIMALS: Crockett! Crockett! Crockett! (*Sound: Great applause.*)

FIRST STORYTELLER: Of course you can imagine how Davy felt about that. He was glad to win the election but he was even more pleased with the loyalty of all his animal friends. And so he decided to give them a party. It was the Fourth of July and Davy started off with a big speech, thanking them for their support.

CROCKETT: . . . and I want to thank you all for the help you gave me in winning this election. There's some folks talks about dumb animals but I know animals are smart. And if it hadn't been for all of you, calling out "Crockett"—"Crockett"—I know I wouldn't be standin' here today as a member of the legislature. it's a great country we have, just like my opponent said, this United States of America. One reason it's great is because a poor man can run for office and get it. You don't have to be rich or well known or even well educated, if you're honest and willing to work. That's democracy and it's something we don't ever want to lose. My opponent has called it "Coon-skin Democracy" and I suppose he was referrin' to my cap. But at this meeting, it don't make any difference how I'm dressed. You're all my friends, same as the people of this state, and I'm proud of it. And now let's give three big cheers for our country, the United States of America! Hip-hip-hooray!

ANIMALS: Hip-hip-hooray!

CROCKETT: HIP-HIP-HOORAY!

ANIMALS: HIP-HIP-HOORAY!

CROCKETT: *HIP-HIP-HOORAY!*

ANIMALS: *HIP HIP HOORAY!*

CROCKETT: And now, if you'll all come over here in the meadow, the dancing will begin. I know some of you don't know how to dance, but Death Hug, here, and Mississippi, they'll teach you. we got some right smart fiddlers, too. Are you ready with the music?

VOICES: (*Off mike.*) Ready.

CROCKETT: All right, then. Let's go! (*Music: "Turkey in the Straw" or "Pop Goes the Weasel."*)

FIRST STORYTELLER: (*With the music in the distance, fading by the end of his speech.*) The dancing went on all night and the animals had a wonderful time. Davy Crockett, he was just as happy as anybody is who has a host of loyal friends and a heart that's in the right place.

SECOND STORYTELLER: Well, Davy Crockett went on through life making friends, winning elections, serving his country, and telling his stories. In fact, his stories are what people remembered best about him after he was gone. The things he told about his early life were nothing, though, compared to the adventures he had later on. The one with the sun was probably the best, and this is the story that places him among America's giants.

FIRST STORYTELLER: One winter morning, when Davy Crockett was getting to be an old man, a strange thing happened. It was so cold in his cabin that morning the old tinder box he'd used all his life wouldn't produce so much as a spark. And the daylight—well, it was so far behind coming that Davy thought all Creation was freezing fast. Like anybody that was as cold as he was, he decided the best thing to do was to start moving and so he went for a walk.

CROCKETT: (*Whistling.*) Can't hardly get my lips to pucker up and whistle.

And that ain't ever happened before. (*He tries again but not very successfully.*) Well, here we are anyway, up to the top of Daybreak Hill and just as cold as when we started. Rattler, what you find over there?

RATTLER: Arf! Arf!

CROCKETT: Well, if it ain't a poor old grizzly bear that just plumb froze to death. I'll hoist him up on my back and take him on home. (*Grunts.*) There we are. Now, then, let's keep awalkin'. (*Whistles in surprise.*) Hello there! Rattler, you see what I see? Why, it's the cause of the whole trouble. The old earth has froze in her axis and can't turn around! Now what do you think of that?

RATTLER: Arf! Arf!

CROCKETT; And that ain't all. The sun's got jammed between two cakes of ice under the wheels! The more he tries to get loose, the stiffer he's friz—

RATTLER: Gr-r-r-r.

CROCKETT: Don't you growl at him. He can't help it no more'n you could. But this is serious. Creation—this is the toughest sort of suspension. It mustn't be endured or human creation is done for! Wait, I got an idea! I'll just squeeze the oil out of this old bear I got on my back (*he grunts*)—and pour it over the sun's face (*grunts*)—and give the cog wheel a kick—and there she goes! (*Sound: There is a sound of machinery beginning to move.*)

CROCKETT: The sun's loose and the earth's begun moving. That's all right, Mr. Earth. I'll just put a piece of the sunrise in my pocket and get along home. I can cook one of my bear steaks with it—and there ain't any doubt now about it's being morning.

FIRST STORYTELLER: No, there wasn't and the poeple all along the way were grateful to Davy Crockett for starting the earth aturning. And Davy, he just went along home, with the sunrise in his pocket.

SECOND STORYTELLER: Well, Davy Crockett didn't live much longer after that, but he left his mark on the people of his time and those that came after him. Sure, he told some tall tales and he was different from the rest. But he never said a mean word and he loved every living creature. His country came first with him always and that's why we list him with our heroes.

Yes, Davy crockett was a great man. Some say, a giant.

Story Theatre

Story theatre is closely related to readers theatre. According to Paul Sills, whose production by the same name, "Story Theatre," captivated audiences of all ages a number of seasons ago, it evolved from readers theatre. Sills had worked in readers theatre, but in his search for a new form of expression, developed a technique that has become a genre in its own right. He defines this form as an oral story rather than as a piece of literature. In dispensing with the narrator, which Sills often does, the exposition is imbedded in the dialogue of the various characters. They may also speak in the third person, as in the short sketch that follows.

Like readers theatre, story theatre is hard to define because of its flexibility and because it is so new that no hard and fast rules apply. Actors are usually costumed and may speak or perform in pantomime, while a narrator tells the story. There may be musical accompaniment throughout, if desired; and the pantomime may approach dance, depending upon the wishes and abilities of the group. When readers theatre is kept motionless, and books and lecterns are used, these may be conceived of as distinct and opposite forms. On the other hand, when performers in readers theatre use stage techniques and story theatre is formalized, the two forms may be quite similar. Inasmuch as both reflect the director's approach rather than any rigid set of rules, one can only enjoy and applaud the results, when they are successful.

The following short play[4] is an illustration of what is usually meant by story theatre.

RIMOUSKI

SHIRLEY PUGH

Music: "Gypsy Rover" melody used throughout.

MARCEL: A peasant named Marcel—

MADELEINE: —lived with his wife Madeleine—(*curtsies*).

JEANETTE: —and their little daughter Jeanette—(*Madeleine cues Jeanette to curtsey.*)

MARCEL: —in the tiny village of St. Fabien. But he had it in his head to travel.

MADELEINE: Oh!

(*A sound of deprecation.*)

St. Fabien is good enough for me.

(*Mimes cooking and stirring.*)

I was born here and I'll die here.

MARCEL: Me. I want to see what is in the world. More than anything else, I want to see Rimouski.

MADELEINE: Rimouski! How can you think of it? So far away!

JEANETTE: Is Papa going to Rimouski?

---

4. From *In One Basket* (New Orleans: Anchorage Press, 1972).

MADELEINE: Papa is going nowhere, Jeanette. Stop pulling at my skirt.

MARCEL: Today I talked to the blacksmith. There's a good fellow—he has seen Rimouski.

MADELEINE: (*adds pepper to the pot*) That's very fine for the blacksmith. (*She readies herself to sneeze—and the sneeze doesn't come.*)

MARCEL: (*sneezes without warning*) Ah-choo!

JEANETTE: Bless you, Papa.

MARCEL: Thank you. listen—Rimouski is a town that could swallow St. Fabien. The blacksmith says that people crowd the streets there. Have you ever seen a crowd in St. Fabien? The blacksmith says—

MADELEINE: Then listen to the blacksmith and be satisfied.

MARCEL: No, listen—he says there are fine shops and large houses in Rimouski. He says—

JEANETTE: When is Papa going to Rimouski?

MADELEINE: Play with your doll, Jeanette. Papa is going nowhere.

MARCEL: No, listen. I am going, me myself, to Rimouski.

MADELEINE; Marcel, you are a peasant. We are poor people. Travel is not for you. So expensive!

MARCEL: I can't rest until I see for myself what is in the world.

MADELEINE: You certainly can't afford to ride such a distance!

MARCEL: Then I will walk.

MADELEINE: What? And wear out your boots? They aren't in good repair anyway.

MARCEL: Then I will walk without my boots.

MADELEINE: Barefooted! Hah! A fine sight he'll be in Rimouski with no boots on his feet.

MARCEL: Then I know what I'll do. I'll carry my boots in my hand. When I see the smoke from the chimneys of Rimouski, I'll put on my boots and go into the town.

JEANETTE: (*weeping*) Why must you go to Rimouski, Papa?

MARCEL: Don't worry, Jeanette. I will return.

MADELEINE: (*mimes packing a basket*) What can be done with such a man? Marcel, do you really want to go to Rimouski?

MARCEL: with all my heart.

MADELEINE: Go, then. Here's a basket with sausage and bread and beer—

MARCEL: Sausage and bread and beer—that will be fine. First I'll take off my boots—

(*Mime.*)

—and I'll be on my way.

(*Mimes taking the basket in one hand and his boots in the other, making ready to leave for Rimouski.*)

MADELEINE: Promise me you will stop to rest, Marcel.

MARCEL: Yes, well, I'll do that all right.

MADELEINE: And take time to eat your sausage and bread.

MARCEL: Sausage and bread. I will, I will.

MADELEINE: And whatever you do, Marcel, don't leave your boots at the side of the road or they'll be stolen.

MARCEL: I'm not a nincompoop. I'll keep them right here in my hand.

JEANETTE: How far is it to Rimouski, Papa?

MARCEL: Jeanette, it is a journey of one entire day.

JEANETTE: Oh, Papa! So far!

MADELEINE: And don't lose your way, Marcel. The road will be confusing.

MARCEL: All right! Jeanette, mind your mama. (*Kisses her.*)

MADELEINE: Oh, Marcel, it is such a distance!

MARCEL: (*He kisses her.*) Don't worry, keep well, and when I return I will tell you about the wonders of Rimouski.

MADELEINE; The wonders of Rimouski! Hah! (*Flounces off with Jeanette.*)

MARCEL: (*Music. He walks.*) What a woman to worry, and the little one will be just like her. Do they think I can't keep my wits about me? She should see me now, on the road, a seasoned traveler.
(*Music.*)
The sun is high in the sky—it's getting hot. A little sausage and bread and a drink of beer will go down well. Here's a spot of shade.
(*Music. Mimes eating.*)
A swallow of beer—ah, that's good!—a bite of sausage—That's not so good—
(*He finishes eating.*)
Maybe now a small nap.
(*He lies down, immediately sits up.*)
But if I sleep, how will I remember which way the road goes?
Ah, that's it! I'll put my boots on the ground—and I'll point the toes of them toward Rimouski.
(*Mimes action.*)
There. When I wake up, my boots will point the way.
(*Lies down and snores gently. Threatening music.*)

THIEF: Now a thief happened along the road. There's a pair of boots with no one's feet in them. I could use an extra pair of boots. He's asleep, all right.
(*to audience*) Should I, or shouldn't I? I'm going to do it anyway.
(*Steals boots.*)
These boots, they aren't much. Not worth the stealing. Full of holes and all run down at the heels. They are no better than my own boots.
(*Puts boots down with toes pointing the wrong way.*)
And he put the boots down with the toes pointing back toward St. Fabien.
(*Music. Thief exits.*)

MARCEL: (*Wakes, yawns, scratches, stretches.*)
And now it's cooler and I'm on my way. But which way does the road go? See? I'm not such a fool. There are my boots, with the toes pointing to Rimouski.
(*Takes boots and basket and follows wrong direction. Music.*)
There's smoke! That smoke comes from the chimneys of Rimouski! Now to put on my boots.
(*Mimes action.*)
Well, so this is Rimouski! Looks a lot like St. Fabien! The blacksmith said it was so miraculous here. Why, this street could be a street in St. Fabien! These shops look no finer than the shops at home. And the houses—they aren't so large. I expected a town that looked better than this. Rimouski is not so grand!
(*Walks.*)
I'm really in Rimouski!
(*Madeleine appears, sweeping the sidewalk.*)
(*Jeanette appears, washing a window.*)
Ah, well, this street could be my own street. As far as that goes, look. This house could be my own house. See—an ordinary wife like my own wife. A little girl like my own daughter. If I didn't know I was in Rimouski, I'd swear I was in St. Fabien!
MADELEINE: Marcel! Come in the house and have your supper.
MARCEL: She calls me by my name!
JEANETTE: Did you bring me something, Papa?
MARCEL: It is exactly like St. Fabien! I've never heard of this, but it's true. Imagine—two places so far apart, yet with streets alike, houses alike—even the people are the same! Aha! Now I see! There is someone just like me who lives in this house, here in Rimouski. Maybe at this moment, he is visiting *my* house at St. Fabien.
MADELEINE: Marcel, stop talking to yourself. Go in and eat your supper.
MARCEL: Yes, I know. I know all about it. Tomorrow he'll come back here. Well, I'll stay in Rimouski and wait until he comes.
(*Goes into house, sits and eats.*)
JEANETTE: (*puzzled*) And he's still waiting.
MADELEINE: And he still thinks he's in Rimouski.
(*A single minor note from the musicians.*)
(BLACKOUT)

One other term should be mentioned in this discussion of speech-related activities: *chamber theatre*. In defining it, Robert Breen, the originator, calls it a method of preparing and presenting undramatized fiction in which changes are made to accommodate time, space, and number of characters.[5] A narrator

5. Robert Breen, *Chamber Theatre* (Englewood Cliffs, N.J.: Prentice-Hall, 1978).

becomes dramatically involved in the story and speaks for the author. Chamber theatre, story theatre, and readers theatre are similar in that the primary virtue is the text. All can be highly successful when used with children, as they offer possibilities for inventive production and nontraditional content.

Summary

The number of activities that can be incorporated into a curriculum to improve speech and teach the language arts are almost limitless. Storytelling, sound and motion stories, group discussion, monologues, improvisation, readers theatre, and story theatre are activities most young people enjoy. We are living in a period of experimentation and change, however; and new forms are being created every day. Hard and fast rules no longer apply. The combining of forms and the use of nondramatic material for oral presentation suggest possibilities to the imaginative teacher and student. Whereas the produced play was once considered the logical outcome of a semester's work or a unit of drama, it is now only one of numerous possibilities. What is more, the loosening of the rules that previously governed form make possible the invention of interesting and often exciting new structures. To be sure, not all of these inventions will be successful but school is a place in which experimentation should be encouraged: the opportunities for learning are enormous, and what better way than through speech?

Speech is our most important means of communication, although the written language often receives the greater emphasis in schools. It is through the oral language, however, that our earliest learnings take place; through it we are able to express our thoughts and feelings, our needs and desires. The actor and public speaker are not necessarily more gifted in its use than the average man or woman; they have simply developed their skill through diligent and daily practice. Good speech is within the reach of everyone, except, perhaps, persons with certain handicapping conditions that speech therapy cannot overcome.

The creative drama class offers a rich opportunity for practice in oral communication. Storytelling, reading aloud, class discussion and planning sessions, participation in plays all demand the ability to use the language and to use it well. Students are motivated to work on voice and diction when they participate in these and other activities. Because drama deals with ideas and literature, vocabularies are enlarged and the ability to express thoughts clearly is strengthened. Interpretation of characters brings color to the voice and melody to the speech as players take a variety of roles.

The student who achieves a good standard of speech does more than present him or herself well; he shows consideration for the listener. Communication, be it oral, written or sign language, is a two-way affair; the speaker and the receiver have a relationship that is strong or weak, depending on their ability to express and comprehend meanings.

12

Drama as a Teaching Tool

Why are the arts an essential element of a complete education? Because they are systems of communication *and teach us about human interaction . . . because they demand* creativity *in problem solving and teach us about coping and growing . . . because they challenge our* perception *and teach us to sense and interpret the world around us . . . because they bring us* pleasure *and teach us to enjoy both learning and living . . . because they employ* metaphor *and teach us to discover likeness among things seemingly unalike . . . because they depend upon* individualism *and teach us to discover and appreciate our strengths and weaknesses . . . because they are the child of* self-discipline *as well as the child of inspiration. Like the sciences in some ways and like sports in others, the arts have a power to train and to motivate. They are fundamental to full human development.*

Education is learning to grow, learning what to grow toward, learning what is desirable and undesirable, learning what to choose and what not to choose. In this realm of intrinsic learning, intrinsic teaching, and intrinsic education I think the arts are so close to our psychological and biological core . . . that rather than think of these courses as a sort of whipped or luxury cream, they must become basic experiences in education.[1]

ABRAHAM H. MASLOW

1. Abraham Maslow, *The Farther Reaches of Human Nature* (New York: Viking Press, 1971), pp. 178–79.

A creative drama session following Theatre-in-Education performance. (*Courtesy of R. Rex Stephenson, Ferrum College, Ferrum, Virginia.*)

The use of drama as a teaching tool is not new; historically, both drama and theatre have long been recognized as potent means of education and indoctrination. The ways in which they are used today, however, are new, and they differ in a number of respects from the ways in which they have been used in the past.

Most familiar to us in the Western world is the theatre of ancient Greece, which developed from celebration and dance into a golden age of theatre. Athenian education in the fifth century B.C. was based on music, literature, and dance. Physical activities were emphasized, whereas music included the study of rhythms and harmony as well as the instruments of the time. As dance was basic to religious festivals, it was stressed, and the chorus of young people received a rigorous training subsidized by wealthy citizens. Dramatists were highly respected, and drama was a major educational force. Plato, in *The Republic*, advocated play as a way of learning. Aristotle urged education in the arts, distinguishing between activities that were means and those that were ends.

The medieval church, in its use of mystery plays, taught through the medium of theatre; and, in so doing, helped to restore theatre to its proper place as a great art form. By the last half of the sixteenth century, drama was an important part of the curriculum of the English boys' schools. Not only the reading but the staging of classic plays flourished. We could go on through the centuries, nation by nation, and culture by culture, finding examples of the various ways in which drama and theatre have been used to inform, inspire, entertain, and indoctrinate.

The United States has only recently discovered the relationship between theatre and school. Indeed, the twentieth century was well advanced before the arts began to have any real impact on public education in this country. Private schools often offered opportunities in the arts, but usually as extracurricular activities or as minor subjects, rarely placed on a par with the so-called solids. On the secondary school level, they were given even less emphasis. All the arts tended to be what the teacher made them; thus they reflected her background, interests, and attitude. In the minds of many, theatre and dance were even questionable as to their inclusion as part of a young person's education. Drama, in fact, followed music, athletics, and the visual arts into the curriculum. Few today would argue against arts education; yet the inclusion, let alone requirement, of drama in the elementary school curriculum is far from widespread. In the high school there is still a greater emphasis on play production as an extracurricular and social activity than there is on drama as a serious subject, though recent publications of the Secondary School Theatre Association show progress in this area.

The first major curricular offerings in child drama and theatre in this country appeared in the twenties. These were the result of Winifred Ward's pioneering efforts at Northwestern University, which brought the public schools of Evanston and the Evanston Children's Theatre into sharp focus. For the first time in this country, creative dramatics, as Ward called it, had a place in the public school curriculum; and plays for children were produced and scheduled on a regular, ongoing basis. Ward's own books were among the first to appear on the subject, becoming landmark texts. College courses and textbooks on drama education and children's theatre followed. Since then there has been a steady increase in the number of colleges and universities offering courses and degrees in the theatre arts and in the teaching of drama and theatre. At the same time, there has been fluctuation in both quantity and quality of drama education in our public schools. Budget cuts and the lack of well-prepared teachers have been the most commonly given reasons for eliminating the arts or curtailing established programs.

Despite progress, however, the dispute regarding the importance and function of drama in education continues. Is it to be included in the curriculum as a means or as an end? Are we primarily concerned with its use as a teaching tool, or do we regard it as a discipline in its own right, to be taught for its own sake? Since the twenties, many of the foremost leaders in the field of drama education have warned against the exploitation of drama/theatre to achieve other ends; that is, making it a "handmaiden" to other subject areas. This exploitation, incidentally, has been of concern to teachers of the other arts as well. Are the visual arts, for instance, to be respected as art, or are they to be utilized for the preparation of school decorations, posters, party invitations, stage sets, etc.? This concern is not to be confused with inclusion of the arts in integrated projects, in which the same activities might be performed, but in which they are related, often brilliantly, to a unit of study.

Integrated Projects

Projects integrating drama, music, dance, creative writing, and the visual arts with social studies and literature have been popular since the early days of the progressive education movement. Even the most traditional schools have found integrated projects an effective way of teaching and learning. Arts educators have generally endorsed them because they placed the arts at the core of the curriculum rather than on the periphery. Accorded an importance equal to the academic subjects, the arts thus became a basic part of the educational system rather than a frill or something of fringe interest. Integrated projects continue to find popularity in schools where staff members are able and willing to work closely together. This is often more easily accomplished in small private schools, where the schedule allows for flexibility and where there is concern for student interest.

The integrated project usually starts in the social studies or English class. With the topic as a base, various aspects of it are explored. Take, for instance, the topic of a foreign country such as Egypt. In the exploration of the topic, Egyptian history, geography, climate, religion, homes, clothing, food, occupations, myths and legends, arts and crafts would all be included; and from this study a project evolves. At the time of the King Tut Exhibition at the Metropolitan Museum in New York, one fifth grade class became so fascinated with the subject that the children made shadow puppets and presented them in a program of short plays based on their favorite Egyptian legends. The project lasted for several weeks and involved the art, music, and social studies teachers; the results showed both interest and understanding.

A project might, on the other hand, start with a question on a more specific topic like the *calendar, time, strip mining,* or *peace.* If the children's interest seems sufficiently strong, this could be a beginning for a class project. The teacher then brings in books, newspapers, and visual aids, thus keeping the study within one class or area, rather than integrating it with other subjects in the curriculum.

Integrated projects such as these tend to be part of school work, done during school time and seen by an audience of school children. Occasionally a project reaches into the community or is of such magnitude that a wider audience is invited to see the work. One program given in New York City early in 1979 celebrated the International Year of the Child. This was an extremely effective project in which performers from Asia, Africa, and Latin America, children from the Third World Institute of Theatre Arts Studies, and children from the United Nations International School worked together on an ecumenical multiethnic pageant. Entitled *A Third World Litany*, it brought dance, chanting, music, and religious rites together, concluding with a pledge to observe the rights of children everywhere. The result was a deeply moving performance given for parents and friends in the community. This program, incidentally, which was conceived by the Childyear Culture Corps, had its beginning in 1978 in San Jose, California; the Pacific Peoples Theatre Arts Festival also brought performers from many lands together to heighten the understanding of our rich cultural diversity in celebration of the International Year of the Child.

Whether drama should be taught as a subject in its own right or employed as a medium for the teaching of other subjects is at the heart of a continuing controversy, and each side of the argument has its proponents. Not that the two points of view are necessarily incompatible; they are not. Many teachers holding both points of view achieve successful results. Where the teacher subscribes strongly to one point of view or the other, however, that separate point of view is given a priority; it is for this reason that drama/theatre as an art and drama/theatre as a learning medium will be examined separately.

Drama as an Art

When drama is taught as an art form the goals are both aesthetic and intrinsic: aesthetic, because product is emphasized; intrinsic, because the child is a major concern. Overall objectives in such teaching include range of perception, sincerity, and the deepening of feeling and thought; for arts education is "education of the senses, of the intuition, not necessarily a cognitive or explicit didactic education."[2]

Drama classes include work on movement and rhythms, pantomime, improvisation, character study, and speech. Teachers help students to develop greater awareness as they create dramatic situations and, later on, rehearse scenes and plays. The problems of structure, organization, unity, and plot are studied through guided improvisation and group discussion. Characters and their relationships to other characters in a situation or play are analyzed for insights into motivation for their actions. Students are encouraged to express their own ideas and interpretations, and to offer suggestions to the group. Indeed, the teacher's first job is to create an atmosphere in which the players feel comfortable and at ease with one another while working together.

The teacher of creative drama on any level usually begins drama instruction with simple group activities and theatre games. As the players develop and grow, they are given longer and more demanding assignments. Folklore and literature that lends itself to dramatization make excellent material for creative playing. Class members plan scenes and try out various roles. The teacher enriches the experience by bringing in appropriate materials: music, pictures, and other visual aids. Properties and bits of colorful costumes help to stimulate the imagination and, if it is available, stage lighting to enhance the mood. A stage, however, is not necessary and is, in fact, undesirable until much later, when students reach the performance level. Even then, performing in an all-purpose room or in a large classroom, arena style, is preferable.

There are no right or wrong answers in creative drama; for imagination, the ability to hold an image long enough to see and use it, honesty, and depth of involvement are the major goals. We are not engaged in the training of professional actors; rather, we are helping children discover their own re-sources, from which their most imaginative ideas and strongest feelings flow. Players gain freedom as self-discipline and the ability to work with others develop. Drama/theatre, more than any of the other arts, offers opportunities for full human expression: physical, mental, emotional, and verbal. When players are stimulated and freed to make full use of their creative powers, they produce work that is not only satisfying to them but communicates to others.

---

2. Robert Landy, *A Handbook of Educational Drama and Theatre* (Westport, Conn.: The Greenwood Press, 1982), p. 260.

Or, as Suzanne Langer puts it, "Art creates perceptible forms expressive of human feeling."[3]

The aesthetic growth of a student has little, if anything, to do with his or her chronological growth, for it is individual and so differs from one person to another. In a sound program of arts education students are encouraged to interpret the world as they see it in their own ways. Far from being an escape from life, art is a deep involvement in life, one that enriches the participant now and afterward. In the lower grades children enjoy the act of creating or pretending. Few little children ask on their own to give plays for an audience. The process of playing itself brings fulfillment. In the middle and upper grades, however, product assumes a greater importance. Performing for an audience carries the experience one step further. It must be emphasized that this is not an essential or automatic outcome of every lesson in creative drama, but older children generally do reach the point where they want a performance. When this happens, the teacher should support the request and help them plan the details, adding the necessary showmanship so that the program or play will be a success. He makes sure, however, that the children's work remains theirs and is not transformed into a show with an adult-imposed structure and style. This turns guidance into exploitation.

In the past few years I have been aware of a slight but visible shift in attitude toward public performance. Most educators since the twenties have shared Winifred Ward's conviction that children under the age of eleven or twelve should not perform for an audience. The reasons were obvious: children's productions were generally wooden and lifeless, teacher dominated, and lacking in imagination. Plays were often of poor quality with too few parts to go around. Adult audiences, not schooled in the values of drama for the child, often responded in inappropriate ways, laughing at mistakes or applauding for the wrong reasons. Because teachers understandably wanted productions to go well, they tended to superimpose their own ideas and to cast the same children repeatedly in leading roles, thus giving a few boys and girls a great deal of experience at the expense of the majority. The rest of the class might be cast as a group of "villagers" or "townsfolk" or, worse yet, might not be in the production at all. Minor roles in themselves should not be scorned. Indeed, they serve a valuable purpose when rotated. It is only when some children seem always destined for crowd scenes that opportunities for learning are lost; and at worst, permanent damage may be done.

If the program or play is developed through an improvisational method, process can be stressed before product. Even though a script will be used for performance, working for meaning before casting or memorization of dialogue puts the emphasis on the play rather than on pleasing an audience. Thus process leads into product, which is the normal result of studying a performing

3. Suzanne Langer, *The Problems of Art* (New York: Charles Scribner's Sons, 1957), p. 80.

art. Performance, to be satisfying to both players and spectators, calls for education of the adults in the audience as well as the children in the cast. Parents, teachers, and administrators need to understand what they are looking for and why: to appreciate the work that has gone into the performance; to perceive the growth and share the excitement of the players; to commend the result but not overpraise individuals, laugh at mistakes, or expect skills that are not yet developed. Performing can be a wonderfully rewarding experience if approached in the right spirit and received in the same way.

It is to be hoped that performances by children are confined to school assemblies, where a sympathetic audience will view the product with knowledge of the process through which the product was developed. Honesty and understanding are important, not technical skills that children do not have and cannot be expected to acquire until bodies and voices have matured.

Except for such assembly programs performed by children, theatre for children generally is experienced through attendance at plays produced by professional touring companies or university students. In the past, children's plays tended to be dramatizations of well-known folk and fairy tales, presented for their entertainment value rather than for any educational purpose. They were brought into schools as special "treats" with little advance preparation or follow-up, except that which an individual teacher might provide. Children living in big cities or towns with good community theatres might have the added advantage of seeing plays given by serious nonprofessional adult actors.

The seventies, which brought new concepts of drama and theatre education to this country, caused some far-reaching changes in these practices and a reexamination of our methods and goals. These concepts will be described later in this chapter; simply stated, however, they represent a shift of emphasis from drama as *end* to drama as *means*. Classroom teachers, more at home with the use of drama as a technique for teaching other subjects than with the production of plays (for which they had little or no background or sufficient time to rehearse), discovered this to be an exciting and useful way of working. Proponents of the new techniques offered the suggestion that administrators might find drama and theatre as an educational medium more acceptable than as aesthetic education and would therefore be willing to lend it support. This argument would be further strengthened, they said, if research could prove that children's learning was enhanced when drama and theatre had been used as teaching tools.

Professional children's theatre companies, influenced by the shift in emphasis, took a look at their offerings, and many of them found that another dimension could be added without changing their work in any substantive way. As a result, many companies prepared study guides and teachers' packets; some offered workshops following their performances in order to extend the experience, thus making theatre more than an engaging hour of entertainment. Some of the newer companies took a frankly educational approach from the start. They developed their own pieces based on curricular units and social issues of concern to children and young people. They realized that scripts would have to hold the attention of an audience if they were to have impact and challenge thought. For there is an inherent risk involved in presenting either strongly didactic plays or material that is too obviously educational. Theatre that lacks human feeling fails as surely as theatre without substance, for in time both bore an audience, though for different reasons. Some companies have been able to combine content related to the curriculum or to children's interests with artistry, achieving brilliant results. This is not easily accomplished, and the most successful companies performing educational theatre are those composed of actor/teachers with experience in both professions. Teachers who prepare their classes for plays through the use of materials sent in advance by the producing companies and who welcome the suggested follow-up activities have found such theatre a stimulus to learning. In whichever context theatre is used—to heighten appreciation and give aesthetic pleasure, or to serve as an aid to learning—good theatre is a rich experience for children.

The other important component of aesthetic education is the experience of seeing good theatre. This is often easier said than done because of the wide variation in both availability and quality of plays for the child audience. Availability depends upon the community and its geographic location; quality, on the standards of the producing groups. There is no single pattern throughout the country. Professional, university, and community theatres all contribute but not all meet the same standard of production. In some areas university theatres offer excellent plays and tour them to nearby villages and towns. In other areas civic or community theatres provide regular and ongoing seasons of plays including one or more for children and youth. In still other communities schools sponsor performances by professional touring companies whose work also varies in quality. Few plays designed for the adult audience are appropriate for elementary school children, though some adult plays hold interest for the high school students.

Good dramatic literature, well performed and artistically costumed and staged, is welcomed by every drama and classroom teacher as the other aspect of aesthetic education. A fine production nourishes as well as gives pleasure and, moreover, holds up a standard of excellence. While the involvement of the spectator is rarely as deep as that of the participant, it can bring a child excitement and make a lasting impression. In addition, it helps build an appreciation of an art form which is different from the response one has to film and television. The live performance, in which the audience plays an integral part, touches the child on a deeper level. Not every community provides theatre for its young people, but concerned parents and teachers, by checking local resources, may discover some first-rate work being done by a nonprofessional company in the region and they may even encourage a university theatre to include a children's play among their departmental offerings. While an occasional mediocre performance certainly does no harm, a diet of poor plays, poorly played with nothing better for comparison, cannot build appreciation. Only the best qualifies as aesthetic education; anything less is unacceptable as a component. Discussion and analysis of the production depend on the teacher and the age of the spectators. A curriculum that includes both drama and theatre is the ideal, though it may take time to build. At the present time there appears to be a growing interest in arts education which includes both the performing and the visual arts, an excellent approach and one that may prove to be stronger than a collection of separate programs.

Drama as a Learning Medium

Drama employed as a specific teaching technique differs primarily in intent from drama taught as an art form or end in itself. Many of the same procedures may be followed, but in the case of drama as a learning medium the teacher is using these procedures to reach certain extrinsic goals: to gain knowledge, arouse interest, solve problems, and change attitudes. Through the process of studying a conflict and the persons involved in it, material is illuminated and interpreted just as it is in the preparation of a play. Occasionally an original play with interesting content and good dramatic structure will result; this is more likely to happen when drama is used in teaching the language arts than in other curricular areas.

The language arts include listening, speaking, reading, and writing. When used in teaching the language arts, drama can further the teacher's goals and strengthen the students' abilities in all of these areas. Most teachers find drama to be a strong motivation for reading and vocabulary building. In addition, interpretation of character is deepened through creating dialogue. As to structure, creating a play demands organization of the various elements of which it is comprised.

Drama-in-Education

Many of the innovations in drama and theatre education since the first edition of this book must be attributed to influences from England, where the Drama-in-Education (DIE) program and several well-known drama education leaders have attracted wide attention. Best known of these British leaders, because of their numerous visits to the United States, are Dorothy Heathcote, Gavin Bolton, and Brian Way. Dorothy Heathcote, who is on the faculty of the University of Newcastle-upon-Tyne, has given workshops and summer sessions in various parts of the country and has been the subject of three films made at Northwestern University.

A second grader making puppet to express emotion becomes happy himself in the process. (*Courtesy of Mary Freericks, Paramus, New Jersey.*)

Mrs. Heathcote's approach to drama has been particularly appealing to classroom teachers, who find in it techniques that they can use in their own teaching. She works, as she says, from the inside out; and her concern is that children use drama to expand their understanding of life experiences, to reflect on a particular circumstance, and to make sense out of their world in a deeper way. Her goal is not the teaching of drama alone but of other subjects as well. In fact, there is no area of the curriculum in which she has not used drama. She begins with process, and in time moves to a product that may take an audience into account, though this is not her major concern. Her intent is always the depth and breadth of learning, which excites the class and brings satisfaction to the teacher. She consciously employs the elements of drama to educate, according to Betty Jane Wagner, and aims "to bring out what children already know but don't yet know they know."[4]

In lieu of putting on plays and dramatizing literature, Heathcote prefers to help children find the dramatic moment in an event or unit of study. She believes in helping the teacher use drama to teach more effectively, not by exploiting it to sugarcoat nondramatic material; and encourages the teacher to work with children as a guide and resource person. Where there is a drama specialist in the school, Heathcote advocates having the classroom teacher, or generalist, follow up the lesson with his suggestions. Where there is no specialist, the classroom teacher must learn how to discover the tension, conflict, or point of greatest interest in a topic; how to collect relevant source materials; and how to guide the class through an original piece of work. This process may last for a few periods or for an entire semester, depending on the scope of the study and the interest of the children.

Dramatizing an event, Heathcote believes, makes it possible to isolate and study it. Like most creative drama teachers, she starts with discussion. She uses the children's ideas and encourages their making decisions. Once the direction is clear, she suggests a choice of procedures: analogy, simulation, and role. Of the three, Heathcote prefers the last because she believes it fixes an emotional reaction. She will, therefore, assume a role. In other words, she takes part as a character in the drama. She frequently steps out of role, stopping the drama where she believes clarification is needed, and taking time for further discussion. She will then resume the improvisation. It is said that this technique most differentiates her work from that of the majority of American creative drama teachers, who rarely take an active part or stop a scene to discuss it. Heathcote's classes, because of their interest in the situation, are able to stop, enter into discussion, and then continue playing.

The teacher following this method collects the best reference materials, literature, and artifacts she can find. The children are encouraged to spend much time studying them in order to build an original drama. Social studies, current events, moral and ethical problems become grist for the mill because Heathcote is concerned with both cognitive and affective learning. Possible topics for drama might be: the study of a particular community, industry, energy, pollution, transportation, immigration, a disaster with social implications, or a great or well-known person like Martin Luther King. The possibilities are endless and may come from any area of the curriculum, but the point is that by employing drama in this way, children are helped to see below the surface of an event or topic and thereby gain a better understanding of it.

4. Betty Jane Wagner, *Dorothy Heathcote—Drama as a Learning Medium* (Washington, D.C.: NEA Press, 1976).

Gavin Bolton of the University of Durham has worked with Dorothy Heathcote in the United States on numerous occasions and has also offered workshops of his own. While they share the same educational philosophy, Bolton's techniques differ in certain respects. His approach is more intellectual and analytical; he spends much time in questioning and discussion. Bolton states his aims in drama education as follows:

1. To help the student understand himself and the world he lives in.
2. To help the student know how and when (and when *not*) to adapt to the world he lives in.
3. To help the student gain understanding of and satisfaction from the medium of drama.[5]

Bolton admits to being primarily concerned with the cognitive aspect of the drama experience. Although he does not recommend neglecting the aesthetic element, he says that he teaches through it rather than for it.

The major difference between creative drama as traditionally taught in this country and drama-in-education as here described, lies in emphasis and techniques. There are, of course, as many different approaches to the teaching of drama as there are teachers, but the Heathcote approach has been discussed because it is the best known of the newer methods and has had the greatest impact to date on American classroom teachers. Betty Jane Wagner's book, *Dorothy Heathcote—Drama as a Learning Medium*, provides the most detailed description available of this dynamic leader's philosophy and methods.

Brian Way, on the other hand, is best known for his textbook, *Development through Drama*, and for his theory of participatory theatre (briefly described in chapter 1). Brian Way shares with Mrs. Heathcote a concern for the participant, making the same point but in different words; he says that he is not interested in training actors but in developing people. Way does not endorse drama as a teaching tool, however; his primary concern is the human being, not education, aesthetic or otherwise. For the past several years he has been giving lectures and workshops of varying lengths throughout the United States on the subjects of creative dramatics and participatory theatre. In both areas he has brought new ideas and ways of working, though it is in the use of audience participation that his most original work has been done. Here formal theatre and creative drama are combined to create a new form, which is being used by a number of children's theatre companies. His years as director of the Theatre Centre in London have given him a wealth of experience, particularly with inner city children. This has won him a ready and receptive following in the United States. Where Heathcote's following includes many classroom teachers, Way tends to attract producing groups, both professional and amateur, who work with children in schools. The changes that have taken place

5. From notes prepared for London Teachers of Drama by Gavin Bolton, 1973.

in England in the past thirty years and are being seen here today, are clearly summarized in the following statement:

> There has been a shift in direction from an interest in the personal development of the individual pupil through the acquiring of theatrical and improvisational skills, to the recognition of drama as a precise teaching instrument, which works best when it is seen as part of the learning process, and when it is embedded firmly within the rest of the school curriculum. Drama is no longer seen only as another branch of art education, but as a unique teaching tool, vital in language development, and invaluable as a method in the exploration of other subject areas.[6]

Except for a few fears regarding the exploitation of drama for the purpose of teaching other subjects, some questions regarding the relevancy of creative drama today, and occasional misunderstandings about the nature and function of audience participation, I believe that there are more similarities than differences between these two approaches. Drama, when it is used in education, is, as opposed to formal theatre, primarily concerned with process and the growth of the individual. Both means and ends are involved, however, because they are inseparable. In the final analysis, we must each discover our own way and create our own teaching methods. We may find imitating the methods of others a necessary and valuable first step, but we are strengthened by trusting ourselves and risking failure in the beginning in our search for success.

Theatre-in-Education

One of the newest types of performing groups is the Theatre-in-Education touring company. The concept of T.I.E. originated in England in the mid-sixties. The first company was established in Coventry and was rapidly followed by a number of other companies of actor/teachers, who took plays based on curricular material or topics of current interest into the schools. Performers were required to have certification as teachers and to hold Actors' Equity cards. T.I.E. companies have several plays for different age levels in their repertories and receive funding from government and local education authorities. The pedagogue is the established link between education and theatre. Although many T.I.E. teams are attached to regional theatres, there are also T.I.E. groups in the academic community, and some grants are available only to academic theatres. Standards and goals vary widely among the teams, and the programs presented reflect the team's perspective. Some teams are highly political; others are not. All, however, research and develop their own material and

6. Cecily O'Neill, Alan Lambert, Rosemary Linnell, Janet Warr-Wood, *Drama Guidelines* (London: Heinemann Educational Books, 1976), p. 7.

create original projects that they consider relevant to young people in school and social situations. At the core of the T.I.E. concept is a concern with learning through experience. Actor/teachers engage the students' interest in a subject, then give them the details necessary to bring the subject to life. Language development is an important objective of T.I.E. The emphasis is on the learning involved, though enjoyment and appreciation of theatre are essential. The classroom teacher is a key person in helping children derive maximal benefit from a T.I.E. visit.

T.I.E. is described as "based on an extension of children's play and a combination of theatricality and classroom techniques to provide an experience in its own right, with the glamour of strangers in dramatic role and costume providing both a stimulus and a context which are not normally available to the teacher."[7]

The children are often expected to enter into the situation and asked to make decisions or to solve problems. In this respect they become much more deeply involved than they do in a production that is merely entertaining. Small audiences and preparation or follow-up work are a part of a T.I.E. presentation. A great variety of plays, designed for different age levels, has been presented since the inception of T.I.E. Some pieces are humorous, some serious; all are thought provoking. A class may even be given an assignment between visits; in this case, the teacher, with the help of the materials prepared by the team, sets the stage for the next meeting. In its use of improvisation, relevant themes, audience involvement, and education rather than entertainment as the major thrust, TIE represents an entirely new concept in drama/theatre as a teaching tool.

The United States has a growing number of such companies, some patterned after the British model. A professional company that has been in existence for a number of years is the Looking Glass Theatre of Providence, Rhode Island. Looking Glass sends educational materials to school in advance of a visit; then, on arrival, members of the cast go into the classrooms individually to prepare the children for the active part they will take in the performance. Participatory theatre techniques are used in the belief that they enhance the experience. The company tours schools in the region during the academic year. Looking Glass states that its plays grow out of improvisation and address themselves to the needs of children, both rural and urban, poor and affluent. The company also provides a summer street theatre, a creative drama library series, a workshop school for children and teenagers, and workshops and consultant service for area teachers.

The Creative Arts Team of New York University, on the other hand, is an example of a professional company of actor/teachers attached to an educational institution. CAT defines itself as a "new kind of provocative and challenging theatre which questions, probes, involves, and finally motivates

7. John O'Toole, *Theatre in Education* (London: Hodder and Stoughton), preface, p. vi.

personal response and action . . . a catalyst for thought on social and curricular issues, enriching the lives of both young people and adults by the vitality, immediacy, and pertinence to the concerns of today's society."

The team does its own research and, through improvisational techniques, develops its own material and teachers' packets. CAT offers workshops for students of all ages, as well as for teachers and community organizations. It has a repertory of several theatre pieces, which it performs in a tri-state area, and farther afield on occasion.

Another use of Theatre-in-Education is to create a bridge between events and the persons involved in or affected by these events. At Emerson College in Boston the play *Cannon Fields* was developed through research into the lives of actual persons, and monologues were written as the first step in the development of a living history play. The research was done on a number of persons who had lived in Concord and were known to have taken part in the events that happened on the night of April 19, 1775, when "the shot that was heard 'round the world" was fired. While only scanty information could be found, there was enough to go on to create dramatic and believable characters. With the monologues forming the basis of *Cannon Fields*, original music and lyrics were also written and added. Performances of the play took place for several weeks during the summer of 1982 at the Visitors' Center in Minuteman Historical Park in Concord.[8] This is an example of theatre for the whole community, but the procedures used and the values derived are the same as those sought by the classroom teacher.

Teachers' study guides vary according to the company, its particular objectives, the program, and the age and needs of the groups to be served. Nevertheless, there are three components that are always included. These are:

Preparatory materials (sent to the school in advance of the team's visit)
The presentation (program or play)
Follow-up activities (for immediate use in a workshop following the
   performance or for use later on with the classroom teacher)

As examples, packets from two quite different productions will be described. The first was prepared by CAT (The Creative Arts Team of New York University), whose production *The Brown Bomber* depicted the life of Joe Louis.

Part One.   *Background material on persons and period in which the play took place.*
   Introduction to real persons mentioned in the play
   Biographical facts about Louis

8. Information from program with notes about *Cannon Fields*, written and directed by John Barbetta of Emerson College (1982).

Background on World War II
Historical vocabulary relevant to the play
Clippings from newspapers of the period (xeroxed)

Part Three. *Activities to extend the experience.*
Questionnaires on the content
Poetry by black poets
Songs sung or composed by black musicians
A radio script
Other well-known sports figures of the time
A bibliography for class use

The overall objectives were to acquaint the student with the accomplishments of Joe Louis and help them realize the difficulties encountered by blacks in American society. An overview of the period puts the play in an historical context. Like *Cannon Fields, The Brown Bomber* is a bridge between events in the life of Louis and the present day; in drama, the facts were more accessible; and the purpose was to challenge rather than simply to present history in dramatic form.

Periwinkle Productions, Inc., prepared a different set of materials for viewers of its production, *America, Yes!* a musical celebrating selected highlights in the history of our country. Patriotic and folk music only were used.

Part One. *Suggestions for the teacher who would like to improvise historical events from the founding of our country to the present time.*

Part Three. *Follow-up activities.*
Listening to music—words and tunes of American folk songs
Background information on the music used in the program
Songs for the class to sing after seeing the performance

This study guide had as its objectives helping students to see that the benefits we enjoy today stem from the efforts made by those who preceded us and that history is a continuing process. Obviously, the appreciation of American folk music is important to the production, but it is used as a way of presenting the material rather than offered for its own sake in this particular program.

Another work developed by Periwinkle Productions, Inc., is of interest because it combines elements of Theatre-in-Education with the company's original thrust, poetry. The poems in this case, however, were written by young people in a drug rehabilitation center. The problem with which the piece deals is drug abuse. The script, *Halfway There*, was written by a young playwright who incorporated the poems in the program during rehearsals with the cast. Teachers' materials were prepared for use on junior and senior high school levels. This is an example of a contemporary problem explored and developed through theatre techniques for a specific purpose: to create understanding of a widespread problem facing adolescents today. It is semidocumentary and, while it completes the story of one group of young people in a rehabilitation center, it leaves many questions open to be discussed by the audience afterward.

Some T.I.E. companies, particularly in the early days, left programs open-ended in a deliberate effort to make the audience think and act. Recently, the complete script has been replacing the open-ended script, leaving the follow-up to the teacher. Both are valid ways of presenting material and stimulating further study; the latter, however, is more economical of the team's time, making it possible for them to cover more schools and reach more children in the course of a season.

Today in many parts of Africa, theatre is reported to be used to teach, entertain, and stimulate discussion. For centuries tribal societies have used narrative and other forms of theatre to pass on tribal history, morality, and religious beliefs. Now, from Nigeria to Swaziland, theatre companies similar in objectives and structure to T.I.E. are presenting programs on such topics as health care, family planning, conservation, sanitation, alcoholism, etc. This is found to be a particularly effective way of reaching country people in areas where there is no electricity to run movie projectors or television sets. The audiences respond to live performances, often joining in the singing and dancing, but also engaging in discussion afterward.

Some of the plays call for audience participation; some are intentionally left open-ended. Most are used for instruction rather than for entertainment. The director of the National Theatre of Zaire describes it as a particularly useful way of informing illiterate people of local issues and ways of solving local problems. The theatre department at Ahmadu Bello University in the northern Nigerian city of Zaria works directly with farmers who develop plays them-selves. The final production is of less importance than the process they undergo in finding answers to some of their problems. Often story lines are selected after polling the people for their suggestions. The government of Mozambique has used theatre to show villagers the serious responsibilities that come with independence. Used with adults as well as with young people, drama and theatre are effective techniques for teaching and consciousness-raising in a developing country.[9]

Artists-in-the-Schools
Another approach to drama/theatre education is the Artists-in-the-Schools program, which brings performers into the classroom for a morning, a day, a week, or sometimes a much longer period of time. Here actors perform, demonstrate, or work directly with the children. This provides an opportunity

9. "Drama in Africa Is Used to Educate Audiences," *The New York Times*, April 4, 1983.

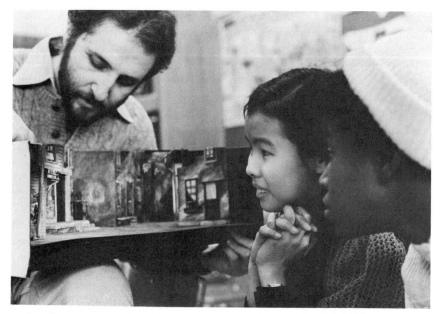

A set designer meets with students in a Manhattan elementary school to discuss *Romeo and Juliet,* which they will see performed by members of the Juilliard Drama Theatre. (*Courtesy of the Lincoln Center for the Performing Arts. Photograph by Susanne Faulkner Stevens.*)

for the teacher to learn new techniques which help her to continue on her own after the actors have gone. It also exposes children to the creative artist, whom they would otherwise probably never meet. Throughout the United States, actors, dancers, musicians, painters, puppeteers, and poets have been brought into schools through funded programs. Information on available artists (both groups and individuals) is available through state arts councils and state departments of education. Although not every school has made use of either the program or the concept, many have, and children have had their education enriched as a result.

The Theatre-in-the-Schools program of the National Endowment for the Arts was described in detail by Sr. Kathryn Martin, the theatre coordinator for the education program in 1979. This report is the last comprehensive documentation of the companies involved in the program and selected as exemplary groups. Inasmuch as there is no longer a theatre coordinator, it is difficult to make a precise statement as to the number of states that currently have a theatre/drama component. According to Sr. Kathryn Martin, however, the probability is that a large majority do have some kind of drama activity within the artist-in-education program. This might be a creative drama specialist, a theatre company in performance or workshop, or a mime and puppetry company. Basic structures vary from state to state because of geographical and educational needs as well as the length of time that such activities have been included.

Playwriting with Young People

Since the last edition of this book there has been a developing interest in playwriting with and by children and young people. It is too soon to tell whether or not this is a trend, but some unusual opportunities have been made available to both elementary and secondary school students and their teachers to learn more about this form of writing. The participation play, by involving the audience in the process as well as in the performance, introduces children to dramatic structure in a way that the formal proscenium production does not do. Whether the idea of bringing a playwright into the classroom is in any way related to participatory theatre is hard to say, but it is obvious to anyone who has ever been in a child audience that children are extremely perceptive regarding character, plot, and motivation. Though children do not necessarily observe a linear pattern in their writing any more than they do in their improvisations, there is a logic in their dramatic writing which, if given encouragement and basic technical help, can lead to some impressive results.

One program that has attracted attention in the New York area is the Young Playwrights' Project, initiated in 1980 by the Dramatists' Guild. To direct it the Guild engaged Gerald Chapman, a young Englishman whose work in playwriting with young people at the Royal Court Theatre in London brought him to their attention. Mr. Chapman launched the project by offering workshops for students and teachers in the New York metropolitan area, and later in other cities. By 1982 the Young Playwrights' Project had become highly successful, with 700 plays submitted that season, ten of which were produced with professional casts. The brochure for the following season announced (1) workshops for young people from fourth through twelfth grades, and (2) a festival in the spring offering professional production of the award-winning scripts at the Circle Repertory Theatre. Critics, educators, and directors have acclaimed the project as "an innovative design for learning" . . . "a bracing theatrical occasion" . . . "an opportunity for children to acquire not only a sensitivity to the art of playwriting and drama but a contribution to their cognitive, social and emotional development." Mr. Chapman elicits the interests and concerns of children, then works with them in their classrooms to help them express these concerns in play form.

A quite different approach is that used by Aurand Harris, a well-known American children's playwright, who has been playwright-in-residence in a number of communities throughout the country. In Cleveland, Ohio, where he spends a month at a time in elementary school classrooms, he works directly with children, stimulating them to writing but without awards or eventual production. His educational objectives are an ongoing interest in the dramatic form and improvement in written communication. The results of his work are reported to be highly successful and, judging from the increasing demands for him to come to other communities, there is little doubt as to the popularity of this new direction in drama/theatre education. According to Elizabeth Flory Kelly, "Mr. Harris not only has developed a creative drama–playwriting formula which can simultaneously inspire the beginning student to write; but he is instructing the teacher in the use of a fresh method of motivating children in the basic skill of writing."[10]

Guided experience in writing plays performs a number of services for the student. Its contribution to the language arts, however, can be summed up in the following simple statement concerning plays as literature: "The important feature is that they [plays] are primarily linguistic, narrative constructs; they are all part of the unique relationship between language and form we call literature."[11]

It is heartening to see that children's plays have finally been recognized as literature and accorded a place in some elementary school textbooks and anthologies of children's literature. Stories, poems, and essays have tradition-ally comprised the contents of these books; today, however, with a growing number of excellent plays by gifted children's playwrights, a new genre of literature has become available, and it is one to which most children respond. It is also interesting to note that the range of subject matter has broadened. Plays with different ethnic and racial backgrounds are being written, and some leaders in the field are also taking an active part in making fine religious dramas available to young people.[12]

A number of colleges and universities now offer courses in playwriting, a few of them in playwriting for the child audience; but the workshops *for* children represent a new direction. Not that some teachers on both elementary and secondary school levels have not included playwriting before now, but the idea of having a professional writer work with the children and the classroom teacher is an innovation.

Child Drama Programs in Colleges and Universities

Since 1950 the Children's Theatre Association of America (CTAA) has undertaken a periodic survey of college and university offerings in child drama. The results of the 1982 survey were reported and tabulated in the 1983 Winter Issue of *The Children's Theatre Review*.[13] The major categories were: (1) graduate programs in child drama; (2) undergraduate programs in child

---

10. Letter from Elizabeth Flory Kelly to the author in January, 1983, following Aurand Harris's second playwriting residency in Cleveland.

11. *Plays Considered as Literature as Well as Theatre for Young People from 8 to 18 to Read and Perform*, compiled and discussed by Aidan Chambers (S. Woodchester, Stroud, England: The Thimble Press, 1982), p. 6.

12. Correspondence with Pamela Barrager and Norman J. Fedder, Kansas State University.

13. Lin Wright and Rosemarie Willenbrink, "Child Drama 1982: A Survey of College and University Programs in the United States," *The Children's Theatre Review* 32, no. 1 (January 1983).

drama; and (3) theatre departments with advanced courses but no declared emphasis on child drama. The 1982 survey, as compared with the four previous surveys, indicated a slow but steady increase in offerings and pointed to four particular trends:

1. The number of college and university theatre departments concerned with child drama or offering course work in it is growing;
2. More comprehensive programs tend to develop once a department offers courses and productions for children;
3. The increase in comprehensive programs indicates the growing depth and breadth of the field;
4. A strong thrust toward touring children's productions throughout the country reveals an interest in taking good theatre to young people, especially in areas where no other live theatre exists.

Special Arts Projects

Supplementing curricular offerings are the many special arts projects that have been funded by the United States Office of Education to promote intercultural and interracial communication for students, teachers, and community members. Although all of the programs fluctuate and are subject to budgetary cuts, some of the areas to which they have contributed are as follows:

1. The artist-in-residence program. Prior to each residency the artist holds a workshop with teachers about his craft. Artists include a poet, a dancer, a media specialist, a visual artist, a dramatist, and a musician.
2. Special series programs. In this area there are performances by actors, orchestras, ballet, mimes, and puppet theatres.
3. Speakers and field trips.
4. Arts camps.
5. Publications.
6. School-community relations. The aim is to involve more parents and community organizations in the purpose and implementation of the special arts projects program.
7. Teacher training. Workshops to help teachers in ongoing arts programs.
8. Project replication. Visits to other school systems and preparation of helpful materials.

What are increasingly evident in education are the strong forces that are attempting to change the direction of education from a purely intellectual emphasis to one that recognizes latent potential and therefore includes the arts as a basic component. What is also apparent is the growing interest of many teachers in using the arts as a tool for teaching, as well as a discipline in its own

A member of the company works with children. (*Courtesy of C.A.T.*)

right—not to sugarcoat other subject areas, but to illuminate and interpret them. This is less a change, however, than it is an expansion of goals. The many and varied approaches to these concepts represent a new vitality.

Circumstances rather than specific methodology, however, should be our guide. Leaders share certain common objectives, but they assign priorities according to their situations, strengths, and needs. In other words, although there have been significant changes in the philosophy and the methods employed by teachers of creative drama, there is perhaps less actual than apparent difference. All subscribe to a primary concern for the child; most place process above product; all hold certain educational goals in common.

Summary

The controversy regarding drama as means or end is not settled, and perhaps never will be. Compelling arguments on both sides press for a curriculum in which there is a place for each. Leading educators have declared drama and speech to be central to a language curriculum. They believe that drama can motivate writing and improve oral skills; they believe that it stimulates reading. Some insist that it can be used to teach any subject effectively.

There is agreement among many educators that study of the arts gives form and expression to human feeling and that attending the theatre as a spectator is a rich experience not found in film and television viewing. In the foreword to a publication released by the State University of New York in 1978, a strong stand is taken regarding the place of the arts in education: "The arts are a means of expressing and interpreting human experience. Quality education of individuals is complete only if the arts are an integral part of the daily teaching and learning process. The integration of the arts in the elementary, secondary and continuing education curriculum is a key to the humanistic development of students."[14]

It is such statements of purpose that distinguish the attitude toward arts education today from that held in the past. The hundreds of agencies and foundations—federal, state, and private—that contribute to the arts are a further expression of support. Though we still have far to go before we can point with pride to a curriculum in which the arts and the academic areas have equal emphasis, progress has been made. In this respect the picture today is brighter than at any other time in the history of American education. Whether or not the progress continues as financial support is reduced will be the proof of its strength and the depth of our commitment.

14. *The Arts as Perception (A Way of Learning)*, Project Search, The University of the State of New York (Albany, N.Y.: The State Department, Division of Humanities and Arts Education, 1978), foreword, p. iii.

13

Creative Drama for the Special Child

Let each become all that he was created capable of being: expand, if possible, to his full growth; and show himself at length in his own shape and stature, be these what they may.

THOMAS CARLYLE

*T*his chapter considers creative drama in one of the newer areas of education: special education, or the education of the exceptional child. Special education may be defined as any program of teaching techniques designed to meet the needs of children whose abilities deviate markedly from those of the majority of boys and girls of their age. Included in this group are the intellectually gifted as well as the mentally retarded, the physically handicapped, the emotionally disturbed, the culturally and economically disadvantaged, children for whom English is a second language, and the underachievers, whose problems may not have been identified.

308

Until recently very little has been done to help these children, whose basic needs are the same as those of so-called normal children but whose individual needs require special educational services. A difference of opinion until recently has existed as to whether, or when, these children should be integrated into regular classrooms; but there is recognition of the fact that their special needs must be met and that they should be helped to take their places with their peers in as many areas as possible, and as soon as they are able to do so. One of the greatest obstacles to this goal has been the widespread notion that these children are "different" from the normal children. Modern educators and psychologists have pointed out the values of getting these boys and girls into regular classrooms while they are receiving remedial help, therapy, or, in the case of the gifted, additional enrichments. The remediation should be an aid to their instruction, rather than a separate program of instruction.

Mainstreaming

This is the term used to define the integration of exceptional children with the so-called normal. The major objective is social: to assist both groups in working and living together. To this end, the following practices may be followed.

Speech therapy, remedial reading, language classes for non-English-speaking children, psychological counseling, and special classes for the partially sighted, blind, or deaf may be included in the school day without removing a child from the group for more than a period or two at a time. Most schools do not have this extensive a program of special services, but many schools have set up some programs to meet the more urgent needs of the school or community. In some instances special activities have been added as enrichment for the culturally disadvantaged as well as for the gifted. In all of these programs there is an opportunity to use creative drama as a therapeutic process. As used here, the term *therapeutic* does not imply psychodrama or sociodrama, but rather points to an aspect of an art form in which children find pleasure, emotional release, mental stimulation, personal satisfaction through success, and, most of all, a chance to use and stretch their imaginations.

The Gifted Child

One group of children that has received very little attention, perhaps because they are able to move ahead on their own, is the intellectually gifted. Only recently have educators and parents taken constructive steps to enrich the curriculum so that these gifted boys and girls may receive the stimulation they need by participating in extra classes and following individual interests. One of the areas that has been used most successfully for enrichment is the arts. This is not to imply that *all* children should not have wide and continued exposure to the arts, but because this is an area with endless possibilities, it has been selected often for use with the gifted. Arts programs have been designed both as afterschool activities and as additional classes during school time. Some programs include field trips to museums, theatres, and concerts, although funds given for this purpose are generally allocated for the use of all children rather than for one specially selected group. Classes in drama, dance, music, and the visual arts offer gifted children a chance to use their abilities in putting on plays—often written by the children themselves—and in designing and making costumes and scenery.

Profiles of gifted children suggest four categories in which such youngsters tend to fall. These are:

The high-achieving studious—Such students work hard in drama as in other subjects, though their work is frequently conventional rather than original. Improvisations are structured and detailed and are likely to be rehearsed and well performed. Their objectives, which they usually succeed in achieving, are a good product, a serious involvement, and better than average performance skills.

The social leaders—They produce superior work in groups. They also work hard but have the additional ability to lead their classmates to desired ends.

The creative intellectuals—These students have originality. They like the freedom to choose situations and they produce work that is original, often humorous.

The rebels—The mavericks in a group who are as likely to be disruptive as to be supportive. With guidance, these students can produce excellent results but they are not always easy for their peers to work with.[1]

Despite these stereotypes, for this is what they are, the gifted student is a challenge, and the results when they are well taught are often brilliant and original. Courses are specifically designed, however, for students of above-average ability; the curriculum of these courses is characterized by intellectual rigor and a challenge to students to make full use of their abilities.

Gifted children have the ability to think of many things at a time; therefore, drama, with its wide range of responsibilities, is an ideal choice. When dealing with gifted children, the leader must always present a challenge. Drama, by its nature, does this.

1. Richard Courtney, *Re-Play: Studies of Human Drama in Education* (Toronto: The Ontario Institute for Studies in Education, 1982), p.106.

Programs outside the school day can be somewhat different from those presented during the school day. One particularly interesting program set up specifically for the gifted was described in the *Children's Theatre Review*.[2] In Pennsylvania the Lackawanna County Schools established a program for sixty fifth- and sixth-grade children whose IQs ranged from 130 to 165. A sixteen-week series of Saturday morning classes was held on the Marywood College campus in Scranton, although funds for the program came from the Pennsylvania Department of Public Instruction in Harrisburg. Believing that all children have creative power, the faculty offered a variety of experiences aimed at stimulating this power and giving the participants a chance to express it. Literature was chosen as the focus of the program. During the eight Saturdays of the fall semester, the accent was on the development of the creative process; during the eight weeks of the spring semester, the accent was on the academic, with each child selecting, as an outgrowth of the first semester's activities, work in special areas in which he was most interested. The central theme, which coordinated all activities of the second eight-weeks' period, was "What kind of world would I like to live in?"

No homework was required, but the Marywood Children's Library facilities were available and the children were encouraged to withdraw books each week. A librarian and three teachers, aided by college students, were responsible for the groups of fifteen children each. Films were shown and specialists in the areas of pantomime, creative drama, dance, and puppetry were engaged to come to Scranton to work directly with the children on ideas sparked by the films selected for the day. Specialists came from the Museum of Natural History in New York City, the Woods Hole Oceanographic Research Center, colleges, and art studies centers. Trips to New York City and the Roberson Arts Center in Binghamton, New York, further enriched the program. The Marywood Readers' Theatre interpreted selections from *Alice in Wonderland* and *The Wind in the Willows*, which the children had read and enjoyed. A documentary film showing each of the children's experiences was made during the first year as a record of the project. Plans for the following year included more subject matter in depth, with particular emphasis on creative drama as one of the most successful means of stimulating creativity.

The Lackawanna County project is not unique; it is cited here because it recognized the needs of the gifted child for opportunities beyond the classroom and because it emphasized creative drama in its program.

Another experiment, designed for a doctoral study, was conducted early in the seventies in La Crosse, Wisconsin.[3] Creative drama classes were held for two semesters in three schools for groups of gifted seventh-graders. The

---

2. Jeanne R. Spillane, "Stimulating Creativity in the Gifted Child," *Children's Theatre Review* 19, no. 1 (1970): 10–13, 18–19.
3. Sister Dorothy Prokes, "Exploring the Relationship Between Participation in Creative Dramatics and Development of the Imaginative Capacities of Gifted Junior High School Students" (Ph.D. dissertation, School of Education, New York University, 1971).

results confirmed the hypothesis that creative drama is an effective learning experience in promoting the growth, development, and functioning ability of the imaginative capacities of gifted junior high school pupils. The favorable results of the research indicated that this approach to education is deserving of far more consideration than it has had in the past.

A different type of program for gifted youth is located at the Hunter College Center for Lifelong Learning in New York City. Here Saturday classes in science, the arts, and social studies are given regularly for young people aged twelve to sixteen who are designated as gifted. Drama workshops are among the offerings, and instruction is by highly qualified and experienced leaders.

A concern for the education of gifted youth in Cleveland, Ohio, led to the formation of a still different type of program designed for both teachers and students. The first such program had been established in the twenties but it was subsequently dropped for budgetary reasons. In 1979 through special funding Dr. Dorothy Sisk, formerly head of the Office of the Gifted and Talented in Washington, D.C., was secured to help establish a series of workshops and seminars. This is cited as yet another example of the awakened interest in one of our most valuable resources, the gifted child, and the ways in which drama can serve his or her interests and needs. Persons wanting to establish similar programs can get help by writing to this government agency, which has publications and a variety of services to aid educators who are working or preparing to work with gifted and talented youth.

The Mentally Retarded Child

Mental retardation describes a condition rather than a disease. Although it can refer to any degree of retarded mental development, the classifications most commonly used are the following: the educable mentally retarded, the trainable mentally retarded, and the dependent mentally retarded. This discussion of creative drama in the education of the mentally retarded child centers on the first category. It is with this group that play can be most rewarding both as a teaching tool and a pleasure. Inasmuch as play constitutes an important role in the all-around development of the child, it has a special significance for the mentally retarded.

According to a survey taken in the early sixties,[4] the major objectives of teachers using creative drama in the education of the mentally retarded child were to stimulate language and to promote social development. The nature of drama makes it a versatile tool in working with these handicapped youngsters. Rhythms, dramatic play, and pantomime are activities that are widely used by many teachers of the educable and trainable mentally retarded. Adaptations of

---

4. Geraldine Brain Siks, *Children's Theatre and Creative Dramatics* (Seattle: University of Washington Press, 1961). chap. 17.

the techniques used with normal children and developed over a longer period of time can bring both immediate satisfaction and lasting benefit. According to one teacher who has used creative drama successfully with mentally retarded groups, some of the best material comes from the very social situations that cause the retarded child to be stared at and shunned: entering a restaurant; ordering food and eating it; going on a bus, train, or plane trip; and dressing— simple daily activities that the average child of his age has mastered.

Like all children, the retarded child wants to be a member of a group, to contribute to it, and to have her contribution accepted. Drama offers this opportunity. One characteristic of the retarded child is her slowness to use her imagination or to deal with abstract ideas. Some teachers believe that the retarded child becomes more imaginative when placed in a class with normal children. Whether she is in a regular classroom or a special class, however, her pace is slow. Recognizing this handicap, the teacher can guide her dramatic play and stimulate her response. Frequently the leader errs in expecting too much too soon. The retarded child needs more help and encouragement than other children; she needs to repeat experiences more often; and finally, she must learn self-confidence and feel the satisfaction of having her contribution, however small, accepted. The game of "pretending" can help her learn to use her imagination, to prepare for new experiences, and to lay a firmer foundation for oral communication. Experienced teachers state that dramatic activities help to develop the skills of listening and looking. In this way, attention is engaged.

Rhythms and movement games are excellent beginning exercises. They aid the development of large muscles while they motivate use of imagination. The acting out of simple stories comes much later. At first, the retarded child will be more comfortable participating in a group than working individually. He has probably experienced frustration and the sense of being different; his need for praise and encouragement, therefore, will be greater than that of a normal child. When he shows an interest in moving out of the group to become a specific character—someone other than himself—he is ready for the next step. Now, instead of general group activities, individual roles may be undertaken. The teacher will need to provide not only stimulation at this stage but must also give clear and simple direction: Who is the character? How does he walk? What is he doing? How does he do it? What does he say?

If social ease and a sense of security are our first consideration, oral expression is the second. Guided dramatic play is a way of introducing oral vocabulary and developing concepts that prepare the child for reading. A variety of experiences will help to provide her with a better understanding of her world, and acting out words that describe this world will give them meaning. Action words such as *jump, run, skip, skate, throw a ball*—teach by doing. Nouns such as *farmer, mailman, mother,* or *grocer* can become the basis for dramatic play and pantomime. Mentally retarded children who have been guided carefully and slowly through dramatic play will eventually be ready to dramatize simple stories. By this time they will have achieved some personal freedom and mastered a functional reading vocabulary. The procedure of planning, playing, and evaluating is the same as that followed in the normal classroom, except that with these children, the task and the process must be simpler and will take longer.

One particularly important point to remember is that adjustments in all activities for the retarded child should be made on the basis of his interests and needs. Stories selected for dramatization should, in addition to being clear and simple, reflect the interests that give meaning to his life. As his interests widen, a greater variety of stories may be introduced, with new words to express and describe them.

Not only literature but other subjects as well can be taught through the medium of improvisation. For example, one teacher had the children in her arithmetic class be plus and minus signs and pieces of fruit; through acting out simple problems of subtraction and addition, the children were able to see the correct answers. So-called creative walks, on which children became trees, flowers, stones, birds, and animals, helped them to observe and recall what they had seen after they returned to the classroom. Such use of creative drama is not generally sanctioned; and, indeed, it was discouraged in an earlier chapter. With these children, however, communication and social development are the primary goals; art is secondary. The potential in drama for motivating and reaching these primary goals validates its use. In time, other objectives can be established, but these are not possible until the child has developed a sense of security, has acquired some freedom of expression, and has mastered a working vocabulary that will enable her to take on the role of another.

Participation by the retarded child in the formal play is to be discouraged. A continuing program of creative drama, on the other hand, offers an opportunity for social growth, emotional release, and a way of learning. As one teacher put it after using creative drama techniques successfully for many years: "These children need to be crawled with first—then they can walk." When they have reached the walking stage, they often astonish us with what they have learned.

The Emotionally Disturbed Child

It is in this area that the classroom teacher must exercise the greatest caution. We know so little about these children and the causes of their problems that the possibility of doing harm is greater than with any group. Indeed, it is often difficult to distinguish between the emotionally disturbed child and the mentally retarded child because of the frequent similarity of behavior. Frequently repeated testing must be done in order to determine the nature of the condition. What might be a rewarding activity for the retarded child might not be good enough for the child who is disturbed. Psychodrama and play therapy are accepted techniques in the treatment of emotionally disturbed children, but they can be damaging in the hands of the lay person, regardless of his background and skill as a teacher of creative drama. The seriously disturbed child will probably not be found in the regular classroom, but will be enrolled in a special class or special school, where he is provided with special services. These services may or may not include psychiatric help and play therapy. Often children in special schools are referred to outside clinics or therapists, and drama may be part of the treatment.

Remedial Drama

Remedial drama is an umbrella term used here to cover several specific techniques. As was stated earlier, drama/theatre has historically been an essential part of human development. In preventive and therapeutic work we are primarily concerned with communication and therefore in helping individuals and groups build better relationships. According to Sue Jennings, author of *Remedial Drama*: "[It] does not differ in content or technique from other types of drama, although great care must be taken in selecting and applying drama techniques to remedial work."[5] Her emphasis is on experience; and the goals of drama, used in this way, are *socialization, creativity*, and *insight*.

Eleanor Irwin, well-known drama therapist, draws a distinction between a therapeutic experience and therapy as a treatment. She says that "any experience which helps an individual to feel a greater sense of competence and well-being may be thought of as therapeutic."[6] This is the sense in which the word *therapy* is used by many persons, and the sense in which it would be most accurately applied to the work of most classroom teachers using drama with the children on a regular basis.

Drama therapy, role playing, psychodrama, and sociodrama are the terms most frequently heard with reference to remedial drama. They differ both as to technique and thrust. David Johnson of Yale University, a leader in this new field, defies drama therapy as "the intentional use of creative drama toward the psychotherapeutic goals of symptom relief, emotional and physical integration, and personal growth."[7] Drama therapy, like the other arts therapies, applies a creative medium and establishes an understanding or contract between the client and the therapist. Thus it is differentiated from creative drama in an educational setting.

Psychodrama is a psychoanalytic approach through drama. It is a struc-

---

5. Sue Jennings, *Remedial Drama* (New York: Theatre Arts Books, 1974), p. 4.
6. Eleanor Irwin, "Drama Therapy with the Handicapped," in *Drama/Theatre and the Handicapped*, ed. Ann Shaw and Cj Stevens (Washington, D.C.: American Theatre Association, 1979), p. 23.
7. David Johnson, unpublished duplicated material, 1978.

Members of the National Theatre Workshop of the Handicapped create a scene in *The Good Times Cafe*. (*Courtesy of Rick Curry, S.J., Director.*)

tured technique that works on the individual and ends in a catharsis. A program of training is required before the therapist is ready to practice. It deals with the real life situations of the participants.

Sociodrama, as the name implies, deals with the group and with group problems or conflicts. A class in creative drama may become a sociodramatic experience when a real life situation is employed, leading to discussion with benefits to all the participants. Classroom teachers and recreation leaders sometimes use sociodrama in a limited way to help solve problems that arise and persist with a damaging effect on the group. Though individuals are involved, it is the group and the group relationships that are the primary concerns.

Indeed, there is a difference of opinion as to the desirability of drama for the emotionally disturbed child. Some teachers believe that role playing is beneficial; others, that the child's problems present difficulties that may make this form of expression less desirable than participation in the other arts. The seriously disturbed child needs to make sense out of her own environment before she can enter another; moreover, until she knows who *she* is, she will have difficulty being someone else. Her greatest needs frequently include the ability to interact and to develop language. Until she can express herself, she will find it difficult, if not impossible, to enter into the simplest form of dramatic play. according to Dr. Haim Ginott: "The playroom behavior of immature and neurotic children is characterized by an excess of inhibition or aggression."[8] Inasmuch as play therapy requires special training techniques, we shall confine ourselves to the consideration of appropriate activities for the child with emotional problems who is to be found in the regular classroom.

The child who functions well enough to be in a class with normal children may derive great benefit from dramatic play and dramatization. Under these circumstances, engaging in creative drama may be both an emotional release and a socializing experience. Bear in mind, however, that because the child's language and speech are frequently poor, he is likely to meet with frustration and difficulty in the oral expression of ideas and the improvisation of dialogue. An inhibited child cannot be expected to function at as high a level as his classmates, and needs much more support and encouragement. The aggressive child, on the other hand, needs to be restrained in his tendency to take over or to distract others. The attention span of children with emotional problems is apt to be shorter than that of other children who have demonstrated poor attention in other classes.

According to some experienced teachers, dramatic play, when first introduced to the child with emotional problems, should include reality-based situations rather than fantasy. Highly imaginative situations may cause young children who are not in touch with reality to meld with the idea or to identify too closely with the characters played. All children tend to become deeply involved in the dramatic play. The normal child can suspend his disbelief for the duration of the period, then return to reality. The disturbed child may not be able to shake off the role so easily, however, and may continue to be the character long after the play period has ended. As said earlier, however, we are dealing here with the child who is able to be in a normal group and therefore may be helped by his more reality-oriented peers.

There is a general agreement that dance, rhythms, and ritual movement are excellent for disturbed children. Physical activity gives them a sense of the body; the large movements, such as skipping, galloping, stretching, and moving the arms, are wonderful exercises for those who are poorly coordinated. "Reaching for the sky or pushing away the clouds," "feeling big," "growing tall"—all are movements that contain an element of drama. The Dance Therapy Center in New York City works for release through the improvisational method, whereby the student is made conscious of new insights through bodily action. The philosophy of this unusual center is based on the "restoration of spontaneous movement to break the tenacity of the neurotic hold of body memory and on the experience of new psychophysical action as health is regained."[9] This is a relatively new field, and it is interesting

---

8. Haim G. Ginott, *Group Psychotherapy with Children* (New York: McGraw-Hill, 1961), p. 40.
    9. Dance Therapy Center brochure, New York, 1972–73.

that it recognizes movement as a specific therapeutic technique in dealing with emotional problems.

Many teachers have reported that the nonverbal child can develop the ability to express feelings and knowledge through the use of movement and pantomime. In this she finds a means of communication, and from it she may find motivation for speech. The teacher may also discover capabilities and awareness that remain hidden in the usual classroom situation.

A good exercise for any group of children but particularly good for the disturbed is the following:

One child begins a pantomime. This might be a man shoveling snow. Another child, who knows what the first child is doing, steps up and joins him. The second child may also shovel snow or do something that relates to it. The pantomime is kept up until the whole group has entered into the activity, one at a time. This is an excellent means of focusing attention and assisting each to "join" the group in a natural and logical way. If the class is large, two smaller groups can be formed, each taking a turn at the same exercise.

Another suggestion is a variation on the old game of "statues." One person comes into the center of the room and strikes a pose. She freezes as another person joins her. Each one stays in a pose until the entire group has come together, forming a large sculpture. This exercise is not drama therapy but is pantomime with possible therapeutic benefits, inasmuch as it encourages both observation of others and movement that relates to them.

Although it is suggested that all groups benefit from starting a session with movement, it is essential for children with problems. Through ritual, they find security; through warm-ups, use of the body; through moving as a group, a lessening of self-consciousness. It is further suggested that dance involving physical touch is often helpful, and patterned dance with its structure is a better starting place for some children than freer dance forms. Under any circumstances, rhythms that involve the whole body, clapping the hands, and making sounds to a beat are all good ways of getting and holding attention. Sue Jennings warns against imposing "end of session" discussions on children with problems. "Let them happen," she advises. The first job is to establish trust and security. Verbalization may be slow, and any analytical discussion should be a future goal.

Both finger puppets and hand puppets have been found to work successfully with children too inhibited to assume roles themselves. Such children usually have a poor self image; thus it takes longer to build interest and ego strength to the point where they are able to move out of the group to assume roles and sustain them through improvised situations. Again, we are speaking of the child with knowledge of himself and his reality. When they reach the point where they can enter into dramatic situations with relative ease, these emotionally disturbed children will begin to derive some of the same benefits found by other children. In terms of objectives, interaction with the group, ability to concentrate, ability to express themselves orally, and ability to take the part of another come first on the list. After these objectives have been met, the child should be able to work with joy, accomplishing as much and sometimes more than the others in the group. His sensitivity, if properly guided, can be an asset to his understanding of a character and creation of a characterization. Drama, because of its total involvement—physical, mental, emotional, and social—offers a wealth of activities, all of which have therapeutic value, if properly handled.

A new professional organization, The National Association for Drama Therapy, was formed in 1978, to set standards and goals. Both specialist and generalist should benefit from this formalization of principals and practices.

The Physically Handicapped Child

In many ways the physically handicapped child presents fewer difficulties to the classroom teacher than the emotionally disturbed or the mentally retarded child. Her handicaps are visible and her limitations obvious. Her problems are easier to identify, and depending upon the seriousness of the disability, decisions have already been made as to whether she can function in a regular classroom or not. As with all exceptional children, the physically handicapped child is thought to be better off in a normal situation rather than segregated; if the disability is so severe that she requires special services, however, she may have to be enrolled, at least for a time, in a special school or in a hospital.

For our purposes we shall consider the physically handicapped to include the deaf, the partially sighted or blind child, as well as the child unable to function normally because of some other physical disability. Frequently the child with physical problems has emotional problems as well; for both of these reasons he will need all the support and encouragement that the teacher can give him as he struggles to reach his goals. Because of the conspicuousness of his handicap, however, he is generally treated with more compassion and understanding than his classmate with emotional problems whose behavior is inappropriate or immature. The person whose psychological problems cause him to behave in a socially unacceptable manner is often criticized or ridiculed, prompting the comment, "Why must he act that way?" The person on crutches, on the other hand, never gets this reaction, for we know he is walking as well as he can. In spite of, or perhaps because of, his physical limitations, the child who cannot hear, see, or speak clearly, or who lacks physical coordination or cannot walk, needs an opportunity to escape the walls of his prison on the wings of his imagination. Creative drama offers this opportunity, though admittedly the goals must be modified for physically handicapped children.

The Little Theatre of the Deaf, which achieved national prominence at the

Members of the Rainbow Company enjoy creative drama class. (*Courtesy of Jody Johnston.*)

end of the sixties, is a shining example of what can be done by actors for children who cannot hear. Because oral communication is emphasized in early education, the deaf child is at a disadvantage when attending theatrical performances, just as she is in ordinary classroom situations. Pantomime is the obvious means of reaching the hard-of-hearing, and it is in this form that The Little Theatre of the Deaf has succeeded so brilliantly. A cue can be taken from this experiment: pantomime is an area of drama in which the child with hearing loss can participate as well as enjoy as a spectator. Incidentally, we have recently become accustomed to seeing interpreters using sign language on television to bring important programs to nonhearing viewers.

Again, movement is an ideal way to begin activities. Large physical movements comes first, then rhythms and dance. Small muscle movements follow. Sensitive to the deaf child's keen visual perception, the leader can move from dance into pantomime. There will be motivation for speech in drama, but the easiest communication will be through pantomime, in which the deaf child can achieve success. Stories may be told in this medium, giving pleasure both to player and observer. My observation of creative drama classes in a school for the deaf revealed remarkable possibilities for learning and emotional release.

Graduate students from the New York University Deafness Center frequently share some of their techniques and experiences with my classes. On a recent occasion, a cast of hearing and nonhearing students, using mime, sign language, and a speech choir, presented a program of unusual artistry. One of the greatest values of the production was the opportunity it offered the actors and the audience to share ideas and insights.

The blind or partially sighted child faces different problems. He is at home with speech, so storytelling is an excellent beginning activity. Choral speaking, like music, is also an art in which he can excel and at the same time find pleasure. Original poetry composed by the group offers him a chance to express feelings and personal responses. Free movement is more difficult for him than for the sighted child, but it is not impossible. Carefully guided improvisation may be attempted, although the formal play, where movement is predetermined and not changed in rehearsal, is by its nature easier. One director who has had great success with a blind drama group stresses the fact that she never moves scenery or props once the placement has been established. A knowledge of where things are enables the players to move freely and easily about the stage. For the blind or partially sighted player, formal drama offers greater security than improvisation.

Children with physical problems that prevent them from running, walking, or even using their arms or legs easily, have also found drama to be within the range of their capabilities. Group participation while the children are seated is an excellent way of involving everyone in pantomime, choral speech, and puppetry. In preparing a dramatization, the roles of narrator and storyteller are highly regarded and can be handled by a child who may not be able to engage in more active participation. The imaginative teacher can find a place for the handicapped child, where she is able to add her bit to the group endeavor, thus enhancing her self-image and giving her a sense of achievement. The philosophy of all therapeutic recreation includes this sense of pride in a job well done and the joy of creative accomplishment.

Physically handicapped persons are able to do and enjoy a much wider range of dramatic activities than was formerly thought possible. Most obvious but little used in the past is puppetry. The puppeteer in a wheelchair is able to run, jump, dance, fly—in short, to perform every physical activity through his puppet. And, in most cases, he is at no disadvantage. There are now a number of theatre groups for the handicapped across the nation. Robert Landy's *Handbook of Educational Drama and Theatre*[10] lists Theatre Unlimited in San Francisco; Process Theatre with the Handicapped of the Alan Short Center in Stockton, California; The San Diego Theatre for the Disabled; and The National Theatre Workshop of the Handicapped in New York. One group that must be given special mention is The Rainbow Company in Las Vegas. Here classes in

10. Robert J. Landy, *A Handbook of Educational Drama and Theatre* (Westport, Conn.: Greenwood Press, 1982).

creative drama, mime, technical theatre, makeup, costuming, and playwriting are held for children from preschool age through high school. The Rainbow Company has received national acclaim for the quality of its work with handicapped performers; in 1982 it was selected as a model site for the fourth consecutive year by the National Committee: Arts for the Handicapped.[11]

The National Theatre Workshop of the Handicapped in New York is an integrated group of physically disabled and ablebodied persons founded by Rick Curry in 1977. Its stated objectives are the same as those of any other drama school. Through training in mime, improvisation, and acting, students develop an appreciation of the theatre arts, learn theatre techniques, and improve their own performance skills; but most important they gain confidence and a better understanding of themselves. Curry believes that the time is coming when physically disabled actors will find employment in the theatre; meanwhile, the theatre is becoming more accessible to them as spectators.

Two other companies, which do not fall precisely in the above categories, merit mention because of the extensive work they are doing for persons with handicapping conditions. They are Facets Performance Ensemble and Imagination Theatre, Inc., both Chicago based. Neither company was originally founded for the purpose of performing for the handicapped, but they have recognized a need and are presently directing a major effort toward these audiences. Facets' statement of purpose differs from the objectives of most T.I.E. companies in its "attempt to increase the ability of elementary school children to learn by confronting the problems of concentration, discipline, and an understanding of communication, through the ability to express thoughts and feelings." Another description states that Facets' "Handicapped Children's Workshop Program gives children a reason to concentrate . . . children learn to hear, see, and act in a unified activity which is simply otherwise unavailable to them."[12] Imagination Theatre, Inc., in adding Specialized Playmaker Programs to its programming, expanded its offerings to include two new types of audiences: physically and mentally handicapped children and young people, and senior adults. Audiences participate and, while the Playmaker Programs are presented as entertainment, they incorporate creative drama techniques that can be used later in follow-up activities. Unlike the other companies described, Imagination Theatre is completely participant centered; however, participants do not give public performances. They are involved in process and what process can do for them. In 1982, Imagination Theatre received the Governor's Award for the Arts in Illinois for its work in providing programs and/or workshops for school children; the mentally, physically, and emotionally handicapped; senior citizens; therapists; teachers; and parents.

11. A brochure of The Rainbow Company, 1982, reports that "This designation has been made to only ten sites in the country and indicates 'exemplary programming in the arts by, with, and for the handicapped.'"
12. Facets Performance Ensemble brochure.

The Kids' Project, a puppet troupe created in 1977 in response to the problems of mainstreaming, has become an effective and growing medium for reaching handicapped school children.[13] The puppets represent a variety of disabling conditions: blindness, deafness, cerebral palsey, mental retardation, and learning disabilities. Two nondisabled puppets are also included in the skits, in which they learn to accept the others. One segment of the performance is devoted to each of the handicapped puppets, followed by a question and answer period. The originator of The Kids' Project, Barbara Aiello, was a special education teacher in Washington, who realized that putting handicapped children into regular classrooms in compliance with The Education for All Handicapped Children Act of 1975 demanded attitudinal changes, if true integration were to take place. After years of separation, both handicapped and nonhandicapped needed to understand each other.

Aiello used the puppets in her own program, "Kids on the Block," but she also made it possible for others to purchase them. Buyers pay a one-time fee, which includes puppets, props, and scripts but they are restricted to nonprofit use. By 1983, 500 groups, including 50 in foreign countries, were reported using the puppets. New York State alone had 16 troupes funded at both state and local levels. Although the New York troupes use the same curriculum, they vary their styles to fit the area in which they are performing. For example, urban children experience problems on the street that are unknown among rural children.

Extensions of the project may be found in some high schools and at the time of this writing are being planned for adults in the workplace. The values of puppets are described in an earlier chapter but the impact of this program demonstrates their effectiveness in reaching youngsters who have trouble relating to others and to nondisabled persons who have trouble establishing a rapport with the handicapped. One of the most remarkable aspects that I have discovered about the years 1968–1984 is the ingenuity teachers and children's theatre directors have shown in finding new ways of reaching young people and of including heretofore excluded populations. The Kids' Project is an example.

In all of these companies and groups the main focus is on giving the disabled person the advantage of the drama/theatre experience rather than preparation for the professional stage. Nevertheless, successful plays featuring the disabled like *Children of a Lesser God*, plays presented by the National Theatre of the Deaf, and a few television productions in which a disabled actor is used, are proof of the unexplored possibilities for employment. Creative drama, however, is not theatre training, and whatever an interested student may wish to pursue professionally later on is not our concern in this text. What is our concern is the added dimension that participation in the performing arts gives the disabled; as educators and community leaders, we have an opportu-

13. "Puppets Depict Life of Disabled." *The New York Times,* July 10, 1983.

Children performing in *Hands, Hands*. (*Courtesy of Milton Polsky; photograph by Ann Raychel.*)

nity through the arts to open doors and expand the horizons of this too-long-neglected population.

There have been some major developments in this country since the publication of the first edition of this book in 1968. One of these was the founding of the National Committee: Arts for the Handicapped. In June 1974 the John F. Kennedy Foundation provided funding for a national conference on arts for the mentally retarded. As a result of the interest engendered by the Alliance for Arts Education, the Department of Health, Education, and Welfare, and the Bureau of Education for the Handicapped, a new national committee was formed. The purpose of this committee was to plan and coordinate an arts program for all handicapped children. The committee's belief in the creative arts experience as a powerful means of bringing joy and beauty into the lives of children burdened by physical, emotional, or mental handicaps has resulted in a strong, ongoing program.

The other and much more comprehensive development that is affecting arts programs, as well as others, inasmuch as educational institutions are involved, is the Rehabilitation Act of 1973 regarding Handicapped Persons. Section 504 of this act states: "No otherwise qualified handicapped individual in the United States . . . shall, solely by reason of his handicap, be excluded from the participation in, be denied the benefits of, or be subjected to discrimination under any program or activity receiving Federal financial assistance."

In 1977 a final Section 504 regulation was issued for all recipients of funds from HEW, including elementary and secondary schools, colleges, social service agencies, and hospitals. Already the results of this legislation have been felt in numerous ways, and they are bound to increase in the future. The arts will be affected as part of the educational system; and, as with any changed condition, so will public attitudes. The concept of "mainstreaming," mentioned earlier, will be strengthened and, it is also to be hoped, the quality as well as the quantity of arts experiences for all children and youth. Indirectly, drama/theatre education will be expanded.

Related but not germane to this text is the current interest in and recent legislation regarding the aged. It is mentioned here only because some creative drama teachers and group leaders have successfully applied the same techniques that they have used in the classroom with senior citizens and nursing home patients. This opens up a new area and one in which very little has been done as yet. Funds are becoming available for programs for the senior adult, however; and it would appear that teachers of the arts, particularly those experienced in working with children and the arts therapies, will have much to offer. Texts and articles dealing with the arts and this population are beginning to appear; meanwhile, the basic principles and practices of creative drama are finding a new use.

Although there is no official certification for drama therapists in the United States at the time of this writing, there are a number of special courses and workshops where one can be trained. Robert Landy, in his *Handbook of Educational Drama and Theatre*, lists the University of Pittsburgh, California State University in Los Angeles, Avila College in Kansas City, Antioch College in San Francisco, Loyola University in New Orleans, and the University of Connecticut in Storrs. He describes New York University as having one of the most comprehensive programs available within its Program in Educational Theatre. There a student can earn either a master's degree or a doctorate with a specialization in drama therapy. Students are required to take work in the related fields of drama/theatre and psychology and to do supervised field work in one of New York's hospitals, special schools, or community institutions that serve disabled persons.

On the undergraduate level there is a unique example to be found in the curriculum of Gallaudet College located in Washington, D.C. This is a well-known institution specializing in the education of deaf and hearing-impaired students. The college theatre arts department at this school recently reviewed its goals and objectives, which resulted in a new program designed to prepare students to work with children in educational, recreational, and social settings, where the arts can be integrated to facilitate learning. The Gallaudet major in "developmental drama," as it is called there, represents a collaboration between the theatre arts department and the departments of psychology, education, and sociology. Theories of dramatic play, creative drama techniques, the use of a visual/gestural approach to working with hearing-impaired children, classes in the theatre arts, and leadership training comprise the major features of the program.

In addition to taking course work in the Gallaudet program, students present plays with and for deaf children. According to the staff, over 4,000 deaf and hearing children from the District of Columbia and surrounding states attend these productions every year. One faculty member reports: "It's an excellent opportunity for hearing children to learn about deafness and for deaf children to be exposed to theatre, many for the first time."[14]

Extensive outreach services for teachers of deaf children are offered by the Gallaudet staff. The college also works closely with the Wolf Trap Foundation in training teachers of Head Start children and their families to use a visual/gestural approach as a more effective way of teaching English as a second language. Improvisation, role playing, movement, puppetry, storytelling, and mime are taught through visual/gestural communication.

Mention must also be made of Sesame in England, a school founded by Marion Lindkvist. Graduates of Sesame are prepared through training in movement and drama to work with mentally, emotionally, and physically disabled persons. Many Americans have visited this well-known institution. The growing interest in this new field is creating a need for special preparation, which will be met as more colleges and universities establish training programs.

The Culturally and Economically Disadvantaged Child

Since the advent of the Head Start program, we have been hearing much about the culturally disadvantaged child, or the child in the disadvantaged urban area. This is not a new problem in our society but one which, for a variety of reasons, is now attracting wide attention, with government and private foundation funds having been allocated for the establishment of educational and recreational programs. The arts, including dramatic play and creative drama, are emphasized in many of these programs. The values cited in chapter 1 have tremendous implications for these children, who have been born into an environment lacking books, playing space, supervision, the arts—and, in many cases, language itself. According to one group of leaders at a conference on the subject of Creative Drama in Special Education, the problems of these children are manifold. For example, poverty may preclude treatment of a physical handicap; the handicap causes feelings of inadequacy; and this results

14. Letter from Vickie Brown, Gallaudet College, March 15, 1983.

in emotional disturbance. Hence, we have a combination of problems requiring understanding and skill beyond the qualifications of the average well-prepared teacher.

The need for special training is recognized, and many universities and organizations are offering courses in this area. Because this is a subject of specialized interest and content, it is beyond the scope of this book; but for those teachers and recreation leaders who are interested in working in disadvantaged areas, let it be said that creative drama and theatre are approved and exciting techniques.

Nevertheless, the classroom teacher can do much for ghetto children. Actually, the first work in children's drama in this country was initiated in the settlement houses of our large cities at the turn of the century. It is significant that the first children's theatre in America was established at the Educational Alliance in New York City in 1903 for the children of immigrant families of the lower East Side. This enterprise attracted wide attention, and in the following twenty-five years many settlement houses and playgrounds introduced story-telling and drama to the children of the poor. Most of the classes were conducted by social workers and Junior League members, some of whom had had theatre training but all of whom realized the potential of drama in teaching the language, brightening the lives of the boys and girls, and bringing strangers together socially in a new land.

Since that time the schools have taken up the challenge, although the social settlements have by no means abdicated their responsibilities. During the sixties and seventies the phenomenon of street theatre began to appear in our cities: free performances of drama, music, and dance in ghetto neighborhoods, where strength is drawn even as it is given. Some of these productions have been subsidized by state arts councils, some by municipalities, others by churches and universities. Some have been part of a two-pronged program, involving both participation and spectator enjoyment. Many school districts have reported pilot projects in the arts for culturally disadvantaged youngsters, and drama is a frequent inclusion.

The schools have been concerned in recent years with bilingual education and the teaching of English as a second language. Particularly in large urban areas has the need been felt for teachers with a knowledge of Spanish and the ability to teach English in the early grades to children who enter school speaking a foreign language. One technique used and discussed today involves movement and pantomime.

For over a century, body movement has been recognized as bearing a relationship to the acquisition of a second language. Indeed, several methods making use of mime, rhythm, and sign language have been devised for teaching foreign languages. Movement is, therefore, not a new technique; rather, it is now recognized as an integral part of the learning process. Movement plus oral activities offer a great variety of opportunities for learning on any level.

The child who is learning a second language is faced with a problem not unlike the others we have discussed. It is therefore suggested that the procedures be much the same. Dance is recommended as a beginning because it forces more concentration than does pure verbal exercise. Folk dances involve a physical response to oral commands. Pantomime makes the spectator guess what the performer is doing and thereby ties the word to the act. Choral speech, on the other hand, has great value because it offers practice in talking, pronunciation, and interpretation. It is, in addition, an enjoyable exercise that does not single out the less able speaker.

A number of experiments have been conducted to determine the value of movement in the learning of language and to create new teaching procedures. One research project conducted at New York University merits special mention, since it revealed that daily participation in oral language activities derived from children's literature expanded skill significantly. The study was conducted with 500 black children in twenty classrooms—kindergarten through third grade—over a period of one year. Selected books were read aloud; this was followed by sessions in creative drama, puppetry, role playing, and storytelling. The objective was to teach standard English without negating the dialect spoken by the children. One important finding was that the earlier the program was begun, the more susceptible children were to language expansion. The research team recognized the importance of self-image to the nonstandard speaker, a point of view which differs from that commonly held a generation ago. The acquisition of language is not an isolated aspect of intellectual development but is rather a part of the process of socialization.

Creative drama with bilingual children does not differ from creative drama with other groups except in the matter of vocabulary. The most common error in dealing with these children is underestimating their ability and overestimating their verbal skill. By giving them very short but interesting activities they can be successful and thus at the same time improve their self-image.

One gifted young drama teacher, whose work with a bilingual sixth grade I observed recently, used television commercials as assignments. Each child wrote and performed a commercial for a well-known product. These were clear, brief, and, in some cases, humorous; in every instance they were within the capabilities of the youngsters, who enjoyed creating and improvising them. An activity of this kind could be done on almost any level and can be assured of being understood. Incidentally, a few bilingual plays have been written and published. The play ¡Zas! by Virginia Boyle incorporates English and Spanish in the dialogue. This is an example of one approach to language learning through theatre.[15]

A particularly interesting experiment was originated by Jearnine Wagner of Trinity University, for nonachieving children in San Antonio. Called Learning

15. Virginias A. Boyle, ¡Zas! (Chicago: Coach House Press, 1980).

about Learning, it is based on a philosophy of the consideration of the whole child—at school, at home, at church, in the neighborhood: his world. Federally funded, a staff of twenty-five worked for two and a half years on a special curriculum directed primarily at the fourth, fifth, and sixth grades. Special books relating to the child's world were written and used to stimulate his interest in himself, his problems, and the people around him. The first objective was to develop a more positive attitude in the child toward himself. This accomplished, the child was free to learn, and an exciting program of community-oriented activities was set up. Creative activities, including drama, formed an important part of this curriculum, which was aimed at helping children discover who they were and to value this discovery.

The need for special training in working with the disadvantaged is widely recognized, and many universities and organizations are offering programs toward this end. Because of the emphasis on the urban child, there has been less recognition of the disadvantaged rural child. In both instances, experienced teachers urge beginning with children's own experiences and interests rather than forcing preconceived ideas on them. Encouragement of their efforts helps build confidence and motivate interest in exploring new ideas and new interests.

Funding programs giving support to professional and community theatre groups benefit the economically deprived by making performances and workshops available. Drama experiences that would otherwise not be available to the inner city child are now possible, if school administrators take advantage of artists-in-the-schools programs, theatre-in-education teams, and professional and highly competent nonprofessional performers in the community. Free and half-price tickets to plays in cities where live theatre exists provide enrichment for older students. CETA money, now cut back, was designed for a different purpose, though audiences were composed of children who would otherwise not have been able to attend the theatre.

It is to be hoped that all the agencies and organizations that have taken such positive action in establishing programs will be able to continue and to expand. Only through ample subsidy can all children be provided with regular arts experiences of quality. *Perspectives: A Handbook in Drama and Theatre*, edited by Ann M. Shaw, Wendy Perks, and Cj Stevens,[16] includes a most useful chapter on grants and proposal writing. Inasmuch as programs for the handicapped generally fall outside established budgets, this information is of special value. The book also carries a section listing resources, a little known but nationwide network among those working to expand opportunities for persons with disabilities. Handicapped children should be enabled to enjoy

---

16. Ann M. Shaw, Wendy Perks, and Cj Stevens, *Perspectives: A Handbook in Drama and Theatre* (Washington, D.C.: American Theatre Association, 1981).

Actress with flute. Drama project for students with special needs. (*Courtesy of C.A.T.*)

participation in the daily activities of life so that they may share the opportunities for self-realization that other persons experience.

Summary

This chapter has dealt with the subject of the special, or exceptional child in the most cursory way, and it is hoped that the leader of any handicapped group, or class in which there is a child with a handicapping condition, will avail himself of the growing literature in the field. Each condition cited merits a book in itself. The purpose of discussing them here is to:

1. Raise the consciousness of the leader in order to make him or her become more aware of the needs of the disabled or special person in the group;

2. Offer encouragement to try creative drama and puppetry with disabled persons;
3. Give an introduction to some of the materials in the field.

A practical starting place for the beginner is with assessment—of oneself, of existing programs, and of the facilities that are available.

The exceptional child, regardless of the condition that sets him or her apart, suffers isolation and unhappiness. Life is said to be dependent on one's social network,[17] which in the case of the exceptional child is all too often lacking. Social isolation is defined as nonparticipation in activities that require interpersonal contact. Drama is an ideal way of meeting and working with others and of establishing interpersonal relationships through a shared interest.

The exceptional child merits individual attention, and each teacher knows the capabilities as well as the disabilities of the various children in the group. We are not here discussing the special services school; we are, rather, concerned with the exceptional child in the regular classroom and the ways in which creative drama techniques can be utilized to meet her needs and potential. Although she cannot do everything that the normal child does, the exceptional child can do some things well, and from this experience she can move forward, thus gaining pleasure and a sense of accomplishment. One successful teacher stresses *listening* as the first and most important element of the teaching process. What is the child trying to tell about herself, her desires, her frustrations? What is unspoken and why? Important cues are there to be picked up by a sensitive ear.

Every teacher recalls with clarity those handicapped children and college students who have been able to meet the challenge of learning and succeed beyond all expectation. The child with muscular dystrophy who participated in the enactment of an Indian legend by sitting around an improvised campfire with the rest of the braves. The boy with the broken leg who beat a drum because he could not walk, yet was able to lead the group. The child labeled "slow," who memorized a lengthy part in a play although she was failing in her academic work; after that, she improved in all areas—was it, perhaps, because of increased self-confidence? The high school stutterer who was able to perform without hesitation in her class play. The college student with an arm partially paralyzed by polio, who not only participated actively in workshop drama but who later went on the professional stage as a singer. Not all will attain this degree of success, but all can achieve in some measure if we hold the belief articulated by the late Emily Gillies in an article describing the Institute of Physical Medicine and Rehabilitation in New York: "Here is a child's world where we can concentrate on the abilities, not the disabilities, which brought

---

17. Joseph Zubin, *Aging, Isolation and Resocialization* (New York: Van Nostrand Reinhold, 1980), p. viii.

him here. Hopefully, if given enough sense of accomplishment, he can come through to a discovery and recognition of himself as a person."[18]

The classroom teacher does not presume to be a therapist, but by knowing the exceptional child in the class—his problems and needs—the teacher may apply the techniques of drama to effect growth, strengthen abilities, and build a more positive self-concept. Moreover, the teacher can work with the therapists to their mutual benefit. These are our goals.

18. Emily Pribble Gillies, "The Katherine Lilly Nursery School," *IMPR* 2, no. 3 (1962): 11.

14
Sharing Work with an Audience

*T*he formal play, in contrast to creative drama, is
primarily audience centered and has, from the beginning,
public performance as its goal. A script is either written
or selected in advance and memorized by the players. It
does not matter whether the lines were written by a playwright or the teacher, or composed by the children themselves. The use of a script distinguishes the formal play
from creative drama and supplies the structure—plot,
theme, characters, dialogue—that will be followed.

It would be unwise to attempt to cover both informal
and formal dramatic techniques in one book, whatever its
length. It is hoped that teachers of young children will
confine their efforts to creative drama exclusively. But for
teachers of older children and junior high school students, who may wish to share their work with others, a
few elementary suggestions are offered as to the smooth-
est way of moving the play to the stage.

Improvisation for an audience in all-purpose room. (*Courtesy
of Milton Polsky; photograph by Tom Fridy.*)

This transition should come easily and naturally to the group that has spent many hours in improvisation. For boys and girls who have played together informally over a period of time, the result is more likely to be one of "sharing" than "showing," and to this end the teacher should be able to help the players achieve their goal—successful communication with an audience. Public performances, regardless of their popularity, should be infrequent, however, and then planned only for other classes or parents. This chapter has been included to help the teacher move, if she must, from informal classroom drama, to the sharing of an experience with others, or to experiencing performance as the natural outcome of creative playing.

Unless the teacher has had some theatre training, directing the formal play can be a difficult experience. That is the reason for emphasizing simplicity: a long script, requiring elaborate scenery and costumes, poses problems for the most seasoned director. The average teacher does not have the background, time, or facilities to cope with such problems, but he can support and help enthusiastic young players prepare and demonstrate their work. In guiding beginners of any age, the most important single element is the approach of the leader. Enthusiasm and guidance help young players to cross the bridge between self-expression and successful communication.

Creativity is less dependent upon training and past experience than it is upon a special way of feeling, thinking, and responding. It is, therefore, quite possible for the teacher to be a highly creative person without having specialized in the theatre arts. Nevertheless, the formal play does make technical demands, which the teacher must realize; an audience is involved, and, therefore, a product. She must be prepared to take an additional step by supplying showmanship and maintaining discipline.

Choosing the Script

It is to be hoped that the play presented by children in the lower and middle grades will be one they have written themselves. When the script comes as the result of enthusiasm over a good story or the culmination of their study of a subject, it is much more likely to have meaning for the class. If, for example, a class has been studying another culture (the American Indian, China, the Middle Ages), and they dramatize material relating to it, the play emerges from this background as a natural result. The class may decide they want to dramatize one of the stories or legends they have read. After playing it creatively a number of times, they will be ready to write, or have the teacher write, the dialogue as they suggest it. The results will be childlike and crude, but the story itself has stood the test of time and, therefore, serves as a good scenario.

Sometimes a group wants to try an original plot. This is infinitely more difficult. Again, if it comes as the result of great interest in a subject the class has been studying, they will know something of the background (time, place, occupations of the people, beliefs, superstitions, education, food, housing, folk or tribal customs). Their very enthusiasm is the primary requisite. Beyond that, they will need the guidance of the teacher in planning a story and developing characters who motivate the action. Inexperienced playwrights of any age cannot be expected to turn out well-made plays. What they *can* do is demonstrate their understanding of the subject matter about which they are writing and show believable characters involved in the story. The play that comes as the result of integrating drama with social studies, music, literature, dance, or art will have its greatest value to the players. Another class will enjoy seeing their work and perhaps will be stimulated to try a play of its own. These are sufficient reasons for deciding to share the project, but unless the children are older and the teacher has had considerable experience in drama, it should probably not go beyond the school-assembly audience.

Occasionally, however, a class of older children will want to do a play that is not related to class work. When this request comes, the problem is somewhat different. There is the question of finding a good script that will offer as many opportunities as possible, without featuring three or four talented players. There is a scarcity of such material, though there are some good short plays available that have been written with the class or drama club group specifically in mind. The values cited in an earlier chapter should be considered when making the decision. Is it worthwhile material? Are the characters believable? Does the dialogue offer enrichment? Is the play interesting to the players? Has it substance? Beyond that, we must ask if it has enough parts to involve the whole group in some way.

The text, by whomever it is written, should be a literate entity. Language should help to create character, provoke action, further plot, offer color and credibility. The construction of the play is of equal importance, for content and form should work together. A good play will offer opportunity for young people to interpret not only its literary content but its production requirements—scenery, costumes, lighting effects. Finally, a good play generates interest beyond itself—beyond its subject matter, ideas, or characters. It should move and stimulate thought in both performers and audience. This is a big order and not all plays meet these demands equally, but material that is worth working on must contain some of them. Students work best when challenged, and tire or become bored when too quickly satisfied.

Within the past few years a number of good collections of plays for children have appeared on the market. Consult the catalogues of publishers who specialize in this area of dramatic literature. Visit bookstores that carry their material. If you have no resources of this kind in your community, write for scripts; most publishers are helpful in supplying information and books for examination.

There are also many short plays by major dramatists that are suitable and challenging for junior and senior high school students. These plays are seldom considered, but they make excellent material on which to work. Moreover, one of these plays will hold the attention of an audience of peers if the cast enjoys the play, and can project its meaning and dramatic value. The choice of play is important because it is the foundation of the production. A play of good quality is worth all the time, effort, and study that will be required in the weeks that follow.

Often a play written expressly for classroom use will have several major characters, and groups of townsfolk or a chorus. This structure gives everyone a chance, makes double casting possible, and may even offer an opportunity to add music or dance. Production problems are another consideration. What are the staging facilities? Or will the play be performed in the classroom? If so, will it be in the round, or in proscenium style? Are scenery and costumes essential, or can the script be simply performed with the tables and chairs that are available?

Sometimes the teacher will find a play based on a favorite story. Other times, the children will want to work on a particular kind of play—for example, a mystery. Whatever the choice, it should be a short script, requiring as little time as possible for rehearsals; long periods spent in rehearsing difficult scenes rarely make for a lively experience. If the group does a play for an audience, the choice of a script is the first important consideration.

Occasionally a junior high school group will want to do a Shakespearean play. This is a challenge to the teacher as well as to the class, but it can be done intelligently and effectively, if approached in the right way. First of all, the play will be far too long as it stands. If the teacher familiarizes the class with the story, has them improvise scenes from the play, then cuts the play to a manageable length, the project will be realistic. Rather than cutting within the play, it is better to select key scenes on which to work. In this way there is no dilution of the literature; what is done has been carefully selected to be performed as written.

Shakespeare requires more time to prepare than a modern play because of the language and the necessary orientation. On the other hand, children who can experience Shakespeare as *theatre* rather than a textbook assignment are amazingly quick to grasp meanings and see its humor. *A Midsummer Night's Dream, Twelfth Night, As You Like It, Julius Caesar*, and *The Merchant of Venice* are among the plays I have seen or have done with seventh and eighth graders; and they have all been successful.

Not only Shakespeare, but Molière, Goldoni, and Rostand as well, have appeal for older children. Again, scenes only should be performed rather than the full-length play; however, the actors must have knowledge of the entire

Children absorbed in performance of *The Magic Word*. (*Courtesy of Periwinkle Productions, Inc.; photograph by Joe Lippincott, Detroit.*)

work. An advantage of working on classics is the fact that scenery is rarely important. Two or three chairs, a bench, a table, perhaps some sturdy boxes, a screen—these are all pieces of furniture and props that schools and community centers have on hand. The classics are certainly not for beginners or for the very young. Still, for children who have had previous work in creative drama, they provide a real challenge and can establish a lifelong love for some of the world's greatest dramatic literature.

Few modern Broadway plays are appropriate for children. Older plays like *Our Town, Abe Lincoln in Illinois,* and some of the comedies of the modern stage are. The big musicals and the ultrasophisticated script should be avoided. Children under high school age rarely suggest doing them; but, in addition to their problematical content, the need for skilled dancers and singers to perform them is another reason for excluding them from consideration.

The Director

The teacher moves from being guide to being director during the rehearsal periods. Some directors are permissive and allow much opportunity for individual interpretation. Others plan action carefully in advance and supervise every detail. The director of inexperienced casts often finds her greatest success in an approach that is somewhere between the two extremes: she gives enough direction to make the cast feel secure but provides enough leeway for individual interpretation and inventiveness. Regardless of method, however, the use of a script and the anticipation of an audience automatically place the emphasis on product rather than process.

Production also implies scenery and costumes; hence time and effort must be given to their design and construction. These need not be elaborate; indeed, they seldom are, in school or club situations, but the mounting is an important aspect of the formal play. When children can assume some responsibility for scenery, costumes, and properties, additional learning experiences are provided, as well as the opportunity for integrating arts and crafts with drama. Cooperation between the players and the backstage crew is essential to success, and is certainly one of the greatest satisfactions a group can experience.

For younger children, however, these values are all too frequently outweighed by anxiety, or boredom, or both; and the results tend to be wooden, lacking freshness and charm. For the child in the middle grades, however, there is occasionally reason for producing a play, provided the script is not too demanding or the direction too rigid. For the older child, on the other hand, the produced play is frequently of great value in teaching dramatic techniques and sharing an art with an audience. For the seventh- or eighth-grader, there are values to be found in the sustained work of production. Older children delight in the sharing of an activity and enjoy the discipline required to bring the performance to a high level.

It is suggested that before any work on the play is begun, the director have the group play the story creatively. Improvisation helps the players become familiar with the plot, get acquainted with the characters, and remain free in their movement. When the cast is thoroughly acquainted with the story, it is a relatively easy matter to rehearse more formally.

Floor Plans

The director should make a floor plan or diagram of the playing space in advance. On this he will sketch in the essential pieces of scenery or furniture and indicate the entrances. This is not a picture of the set, but rather a careful diagram of the floor area, which indicates where each piece of scenery will be placed, its relative size, and the space left on the stage for easy movement. He will be careful to put entrances where the actors can use them most comfortably and effectively. Although the scenery will probably not be available much before final rehearsals, he will try to find pieces of comparable size so that the cast becomes used to the plan and will have as little trouble as possible adjusting to the setting when it appears.

UP RIGHT	UP CENTER	UP LEFT
RIGHT CENTER	CENTER	LEFT CENTER
DOWN RIGHT	DOWN CENTER	DOWN LEFT

WINGS   APRON   WINGS

The areas of the stage. *Left* and *right* always refer to the *actor's* left and right.

The director will also want to list all pieces of scenery so that she can check them off as she collects or makes them. The beginner will find that the simpler the setting, the fewer the problems, and, incidentally, the more effective the stage will probably be. Children can be involved in all the details of the production; they will enjoy it and learn from the experience.

Arena Stage

The term *arena stage* is used to describe a center playing space. Some smaller theatres are built with the playing space in the center and the audience seated on all four sides; others, often called "thrust stages," have seats on only three sides. In either case a different style of acting is demanded from that required by the proscenium stage, but it is one that is often easier for the less experienced player than for the professional adult actor, accustomed to the

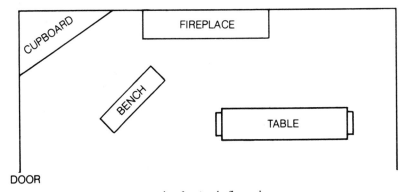

An example of a simple floor plan.

ARENA STYLE

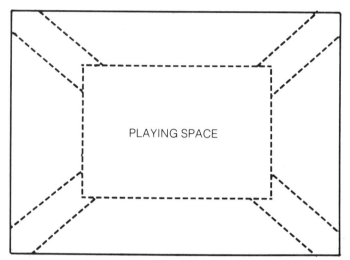

The audience is seated on three or four sides of the indicated playing space.

techniques of the proscenium stage. In schools with an all-purpose room, plays are frequently given in the round. Although such areas lack proper lighting and good acoustics, they have the advantage of being familiar territory to the students and they require little in the way of scenery. What scenery there is should be simple and low so as not to block the view, and so lightweight that it can be carried on- and offstage in front of the audience. Entrances may be indicated by putting masking tape on the floor. The audience must be told when it is seated that the taped-off areas will be used by the actors and must therefore be kept open. If the play calls for audience participation, it is much easier to handle in the round than on an elevated proscenium platform.

Whatever the space, it should be small, with as good acoustics as possible. This will not only put the actors at ease but will help to prevent the constant reminders to "speak up" or "louder, please!" These admonitions all too often lead to a stilted, unnatural performance, with children talking to the audience rather than to the other characters in the play. Large high school auditoriums are probably the worst possible places for children to perform. A small room, on the other hand, de-emphasizes the lack of performance skills and puts the attention where it should be, on the play.

The Stage Manager

This is an important job, and one that a responsible girl or boy can do and enjoy. She should be appointed at the same time the cast is selected and given a script of her own. She attends all scheduled rehearsals and keeps a record of all cuts, action, and business. It is a good idea for her to sit at one side of the stage where she can not only see and hear but also call the actors for their entrances.

Under most circumstances, she will be able to pull the curtains and handle or give cues for the lights. She works closely with the director and assumes as much authority as the director feels she can when the play is presented. The stage manager has a chance to grow in her job, for she is important to every aspect of the production and learns, by doing, the meaning of the word "responsibility."

Casting the Play

This preliminary work done, the director is now ready to give his attention to casting the play. In creative drama the cast changes with every playing. In the formal production, however, there is one cast that rehearses each scene a number of times in preparation for the performance. The matter of casting is therefore, important. The director tries to get the best possible cast together and usually does it by means of tryouts. He is obligated to do a certain amount of typecasting. For example, a giant must be played by a very large child; a dwarf or elf, by a child who is small; other characters who may have certain specified physical characteristics, by children with similar characteristics. To cast for any other reason than theatrical effectiveness is a questionable practice.

The audience must believe in the reality of the characters, and if they are too obviously different from the description or implications in the script, an audience cannot find them acceptable. Likewise, older players will feel uncomfortable if they realize that they are not believable, and so the good that the experience may do them is negated by their own feelings of inadequacy. This, of course, is one of the strong arguments against public performance by children. An actor cannot grow if he is constantly cast in the same type of role; yet he cannot experiment with a part for which he is conspicuously miscast, in front of an audience.

Casting should be done carefully, for a mistake made in the beginning may be fatal later. Some directors like to have two casts. This is a good idea, provided there is sufficient time for a double set of rehearsals. It is a precaution against illness and accidents, and gives the entire group a feeling of security. It also provides twice as many opportunities for participation and should work out well if there is time enough to rehearse both groups equally. It goes without saying that both casts must be given a chance to perform.

Stage Movement

Stage movement is the movement of actors about the stage. The director who plots it in advance will find that she saves valuable time in rehearsal. Writing notations in her script, or even making diagrams, will help her see at a glance where the various characters are. Although most published scripts have action included, it seldom works, for the simple reason that no two stages are alike. For example, an important entrance, which the script indicates should be from the right, may have to be reversed if the wing space in the school auditorium cannot accommodate it.

If the movement is memorized along with the lines and not changed, it is an advantage. Once the general movement is set, the cast is free to develop appropriate business (action) and work on characterization. Early memorization of lines also helps the group move ahead, giving attention to the rhythm of the play, the building of climaxes, projection of voice, and general polishing. Perfection is never the aim when working with children, but their satisfaction will certainly be greater if they can feel well prepared, comfortable, and able to enter into the performance with a sense of security. Encouragement, plus necessary constructive criticism, help to make the rehearsal period one of pleasure and learning.

Scenery

Scenery means the large pieces that suggest the locale of the play. There is always controversy as to the difference between scenery and properties, or "props." Scenery is background, whereas properties are those items used by the actors.

The trend today (and a fortunate trend it is for inexperienced and young groups) is toward curtains rather than box sets, and toward suggested rather than realistic settings. For example, a bench, a table, chairs, stools, perhaps a fireplace or a hutch—if available—will suggest a peasant's cottage, without the necessity of building flats, putting in doors, or painting an elaborate representional background. Some of the most effective modern settings, both on Broadway and off, have been abstract, or so simple as to focus all the attention on the play and the players.

Platforms and steps are helpful in creating different levels, thus adding variety in appearance and making for interesting movement. A bright tablecloth, a few large flowers, two or three benches or stools can often provide all that is needed. Children have wonderfully imaginative ideas for suggesting scenery; what they do need is practical help in constructing it and in supporting the pieces. If the director works closely with the art department of the school, most backstage problems can easily be solved. And, best of all, the stage crew or scenery committee will have an ideal opportunity to learn techniques of painting and handling materials.

Scenery is usually not needed until the final rehearsals. It is suggested that if it can be ready a week in advance of the first dress rehearsal, the players will have a chance to get used to it and not have to add that adjustment to costumes and other last-minute details. A few *dos* and *don'ts* may be helpful:

1. Scenery should enhance, not distract.
2. Scenery should be firm, not flimsy.
3. Scenery should unify the production.
4. Scenery should be in keeping with the mood of the play.
5. Scenery should suggest the time and place of the story, and the circumstances of the. characters.
6. Scenery and costumes should be planned together.
7. Scenery should help the players, not get in their way.

Properties

Very little needs to be said about properties. They are all the objects (usually small) used by the players. If the school has a property closet, many commonly used items can be kept and brought out when needed. Baskets, canes, wooden bowls, china, swords, and the like are basic equipment. Some things must be borrowed, some made. It is a challenge to the ingenuity of the property committee when, for example, such things as a "golden goose," a "snowman," a "roast chicken," or a "birthday cake" are called for. Papier-mâché and styrofoam are excellent materials for the unusual item, but, again, the young or inexperienced committee needs help in construction.

One other word regarding props: The property committee learns through its assignment what responsibility is all about, for objects are often needed at particular moments in the play, and the absence of them can ruin an otherwise excellent scene. Properties should be checked before and after every rehearsal and performance, and if damaged or missing, replaced. It is a good idea to begin gathering the properties as soon as the play goes into rehearsal so as to give the actors ample time to get used to handling them.

Costumes

Costumes, like scenery, can be a source of worry and frustration to the teacher whose group is too young or inexperienced to assume responsibility for them. Sometimes parents take a hand with the costumes, and sometimes the art department offers assistance. The former may be a satisfactory arrangement, but all too often it builds what should have been a simple performance into a major production. Too much emphasis is put on the mounting, and the public performance with adult contributions takes precedence over the learning. The second arrangement—assistance from the art department—is decidedly preferable, since it keeps the play within the framework of the school and may give the class an opportunity to help design or even make some part of the costumes. If neither type of cooperation is available, the teacher should try to solve the matter of clothing by merely suggesting it, or adapting easily obtainable garments to the play.

For example, aprons, hats, vests, capes, boots, and shawls are easily acquired and go a long way toward suggesting various kinds of characters. Children accept simple suggestions readily and do not demand complete or authentic outfits. Blue jeans, tights, and colored T-shirts are in the wardrobes of most children and young people today, regardless of economic circumstances. If these can be chosen with a color scheme in mind, they can be used as costumes for many folk tales, or for plays with historical backgrounds.

Paper shold be avoided. It tears easily and so is hazardous. It is suggested that all good costumes, whether made for a particular occasion or given to the school, be saved and kept in good repair. The collection of basic garments should be a continuing project; as time goes on, it will provide many, sometimes all, of the costumes needed for future productions.

It is generally better not to put old and authentic garments and inexpensive, newly made costumes on the stage at the same time. The effect is usually that of making the old look faded and dirty, and the new—cheap, and too bright. Occasionally the two can be combined, but in general it is better to use one or the other for a unified overall impression.

Here a few suggestions are offered as to the function of costumes:

1. Costumes should suggest the personality, age, occupation, and financial circumstances of the characters.
2. Costumes should belong to the period and setting of the play.
3. Costumes should be appropriate to the season of the year, as suggested by the story.
4. Costumes should help to unify the production.
5. Costumes should be planned with the scenery in mind; they should carry out the color scheme and look well against the background.
6. Costumes should not distract for reasons of brightness, richness, or design, unless of course there is a reason for it.
7. Costumes should fit the wearers and be clean and well pressed.
8. Costumes should be secure, neither carelessly made nor too fragile to be safe.
9. Costumes should make the wearers feel appropriately dressed and comfortable, not self-conscious.

Rehearsals

In the beginning, the director, regardless of the group, will have many decisions to make and many details to organize. Once she has cast the play, decided upon the floor plan, and has made arrangements for settings and costumes, she can get down to the serious business of rehearsing. As stated earlier, time spent on improvisation will be time well spent; the cast will become thoroughly acquainted with the character's and the plot. Better yet is the play that evolves from a comprehensive unit of study. When children have been deeply immersed in a situation, a period, or a place for a long time, the play they build will have much greater meaning for them and for the audience.

The director is now ready to set up a rehearsal schedule. It is hoped that, for the teacher or director of children, this will be an informal procedure. Even though a performance date has been set and the work planned, she must try to avoid the anxiety and boredom that mar rehearsals of so many nonprofessional productions. For this reason, rehearsals should be frequent but short. Scenes, rather than the entire play, should be rehearsed first; complete run-throughs come later.

Early memorization of lines is advocated, since it frees the players to move and develop pertinent business. People memorize at different rates of speed, but the sooner it is done, the more productive the rehearsal periods will become. Most important is probably interpretation. Discussions along the way help the actors to learn who the characters are and why they behave as they do. First of all, there should be an oral reading of the whole play. Then such questions as these should be answered.

1. How would you describe the character you are playing?
2. What does he/she have to say about him/herself?
3. What do others have to say about him/her?
4. What are his/her relationships to other persons in the play?
5. What are his/her aims? Motivations?
6. What are his/her individual qualities? Details that help in understanding him/her (personality, temperament, age, occupation, background, likes, dislikes, education, beliefs)?
7. What are the main events of the play? How does each character fit into them?

It is suggested that improvising scenes from the play precede memorization and blocking. Any misunderstanding or lack of understanding will be cleared up if plays create their own dialogue, characters, and motivations.

One word of caution: The dramatist's intention must be respected in interpreting the play. Altering the meaning is dangerous and disrespectful. If the group does not like the play as written, better give it up and select something else. Changing mood or meaning will throw the play out of focus. Leave the "spoofs" for older and more experienced players, if they wish to tamper; it is a questionable practice at best and not for young players.

Blocking the scenes comes next. If the director plans the movement in advance, he will be able to approach a rehearsal knowing when characters enter and leave, by what door, and where they sit or stand. It is a good idea to note all movements on a master script. Often, when a few days have passed between rehearsals, there is disagreement as to what was done before. A careful record will answer the questions so that the rehearsal can proceed.

Business, which is individual action in keeping with the character, can be developed next. For example, knitting, sweeping, eating, and so on add to the reality of the characters and give young players something definite to do. The more times business is repeated, the more natural it becomes. As was mentioned earlier, if properties are available at the beginning of the rehearsal period, the players grow used to them, and can handle them with ease and naturalness.

Composition, or "stage picture," is another thing for the director to bear in mind. Even an experienced actor cannot see the grouping on the stage when she is part of it; hence the director, who is watching closely from the front, must be aware of the composition. Are the players hiding each other? Can important business be seen? Are entrances blocked? If there are several players together, do they make a pleasing picture? Does one composition flow into another? All of this pertains much more to the play designed for an outside audience; yet, even under the most informal circumstances, it is important that the players be clearly seen and heard.

If dances or songs are included, they should be rehearsed and integrated as early as possible. It is always a temptation to let them go, but the director will find that this makes for a weak spot or a slow transition. Such business should appear to spring from the play and belong to it; it should not be imposed for the purpose of adding more people or relieving monotony.

As with scenery, any cooperation between the drama and music teachers is an advantage. The more a staff can work together on a project, the better the learning and the better the production. If a player is absent, the stage manager or another person should step into the part. When the director reads the lines from out front, the cast is at a disadvantage; for while the lines are delivered the space is empty, and the scene very often breaks down. Incidentally, this is another good reason for double casting. It assures each group of a substitute at a moment's notice.

As the rehearsal period proceeds, the play should grow in feeling, understanding, technical competence, and unity. Smoothness will come as lines are learned, the business perfected, and the actors develop rapport with each other. Rough spots should be ironed out in the beginning, rather than left to the end for polishing. And, finally, if the director can maintain a spirit of fun, the rehearsal period will be a source of pleasure as the cast shares the satisfaction of building something together.

As in creative drama, the director occasionally finds a show-off, or clown, in the cast. He does not want to inhibit inventiveness, but he cannot afford byplay, which disrupts the rehearsal and takes the attention away from the script. Clowning must be stopped at once, for it can jeopardize the entire performance. Most children and young people, if approached constructively, will see that practical and private joking are out of order and, for the good of the production, their energy must be used to build, not break up, a scene. For children of junior and senior high school age, this experience may be the highlight of the year and leave a lasting impression.

Teamwork is both a necessity to a good performance and a source of deep satisfaction to the players. There is probably no experience comparable to the camaraderie that develops during rehearsals. A special feeling binds a group together when it shares the hard work, the creative effort, the interdependence, and the fun of rehearsing and presenting a play.

The Dress Rehearsal

The dress rehearsal can be either a day of confusion or a satisfying culmination of weeks of group effort. When details have been well planned, and the scenery and costumes are ready, there is no reason why it should not be the high point of the rehearsal period. The old adage, "a poor dress rehearsal makes a good show," is fallacious. It is true to a degree only when the dress rehearsal is so bad that the cast makes one last mighty effort to prevent the play from being a disaster. This always involves work that should have been done weeks before; with this work completed, the cast is ready to add the final details with a sense of security.

Two, or even three, dress rehearsals are desirable and should be planned from the beginning. At the first one, the scenery should be finished and in place. At the second and third, costumes should be worn, so that by the time the play goes on, the cast and backstage crew have mastered all the problems. After each dress rehearsal and performance, costumes should be hung up carefully and properties checked. This not only helps to keep things in good order but also instills a sense of responsibility in the players. Even in the most informal of plays, the actors should remain backstage and not mingle with the audience. Food and other refreshments have no place in a dressing room. They are a risk to the costumes and divert the players.

If makeup is used (and with children it is nearly always unnecessary), it should be tried out first for effectiveness. Teenagers like working with makeup; therefore, for them, another learning experience is provided. Again, makeup extends or enhances a character; it does not create one. Sometimes a player will say, "I'll be all right when I'm made up and get into my costume." He will be better, perhaps, but if he has not succeeded in creating a character by that time, costumes and makeup cannot do it for him.

If there is a curtain call, it should be rehearsed so that the players are ready to come out and take a bow to the audience. One curtain call is sufficient for the audience to show its appreciation. Although there is some difference of opinion about this, the curtain call is a convention of the formal theatre, and an audience should be given a chance to observe it.

The Performance

Once again, let it be stated that a performance by beginners or children should be simple and informal. The director has the greatest responsibility here, for his attitude of calm encouragement will be contagious. If he regards the play as a good piece of work which the cast and crew take pleasure in sharing, they will view it much the same way. They will look forward to the performance with anticipation rather than with anxiety. Both excessive criticism and excessive praise are as harmful at this stage as at any other. The most satisfying response a group can be accorded is the appreciation of the audience. The players will know that they have succeeded in achieving their goal: successful communication.

One performance of a play is recommended for younger children, for they plan and anticipate it as a special event. Repeating the experience rarely recaptures the fun; the play lacks the original spontaneity and the players become bored with what was once a lively involvement. Junior and senior high school students, however, can gain a great deal from the experience of giving a play two or three times. As the product assumes more importance, there is the challenge of trying to improve it and discovering in the process the responses of different audiences.

In a children's production the director supplies the necessary showmanship. This does not mean dictating the way lines should be read or imposing a style that is unnatural to young players. It means being sensitive to their ideas and helping them express those ideas most effectively. It means checking costumes and props, watching that the players look and are comfortable in their clothes and that the clothes they wear add to the individual and overall effect. Attention to cleanliness, color, design, and fit need not take up much time; but it is worth every minute spent and will avoid the amateur look of the old-fashioned school play. Simplicity, selectivity, appropriateness will always outweigh elaborate mounting and will be easier for everyone involved.

The Auditorium

One aspect of producing a play that is frequently overlooked is that of the auditorium seating area. Ushers may be members of the class who have worked on play committees and so are free when the dress rehearsals are over. Ushering is an excellent way for them to perform a necessary function. If there

A scene from *Robinson and Friday*. (*Courtesy of Carol Korty, Emerson College, Boston;* *photograph by Jamie Cope.*)

are programs, they may hand them out, though in an informal situation, a narrator is a preferred way of imparting necessary information to the audience.

Attendance should be by invitation only, rather than by ticket. When tickets are sold, there is an added emphasis on perfection, and a felt obligation to make elaborate settings and costumes. Young players feel the strain, and the "sharing with" too often turns into "showing-off." Publicity, also, should be restricted to posters made by the group and oral announcements. The greater the participation of the class in every aspect of the production and the fewer contributions from outside, the more positive values the experience will have.

Summary

The presentation of a play for an audience should be done only when older children are involved, and then infrequently. Informality and simplicity should be stressed if the basic values of communication and sharing are to be realized. There is real difference of opinion as to whether children should ever appear before an audience, for fear of destroying their spontaneity and

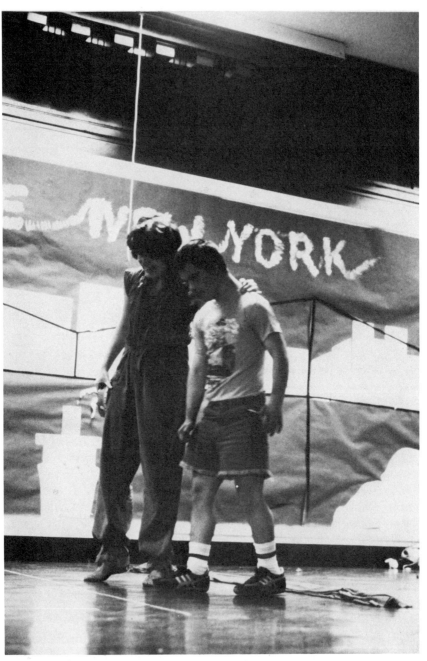

Children design the backdrop for an original play. (*Courtesy of C.A.T.*)

naturalness. This is a valid argument, but the contention here is that performance will do no harm if it is done without pressure, thus avoiding drudgery. The teacher must become director, supplying showmanship, and making certain decisions. As teacher, however, she tries to involve every member of the group so that the procedure is as democratic as possible. Most important, children should not be exploited to show the value of the content or of the instruction.

In the school, club, or camp play, the educational and social values come first. The product will hold interest for the viewers if they are properly oriented and their appreciation is the natural consequence of a successful attempt at communication. If these emphases are preserved, the leader and group will find producing a play a rewarding experience. There is probably nothing that binds a group together more closely than the production of a play; and no joy more lasting than the memory of a play in which all the contributions of all the participants have dovetailed so well that each has had a share in its success. This can and should happen, when exploitation does not enter the picture. If teacher and class work together on a play from the beginning, discussion of costumes, set, and style will expand the learnings. Although the director is the final authority when important decisions are made, showing the cast pictures and photographs; relating costume to period, place, and role; and helping them visualize the scene will provide further opportunities for learning.

Finally, theatre is a performing art. Let us not forget it. The suspicions that have surrounded the theatre in our country from the beginning are still here, if masked. When we cut the arts from the budget in times of depression and de-emphasize *acting* in favor of the word *learning*, we are giving tacit acceptance to an old prejudice. Some funding agencies request a product as proof of the effectiveness of the programs to which they have given financial support. A product need not be interpreted as a full-fledged production, however; in fact, a good demonstration can meet the requirement just as well, often better. You may find a production desirable, but if not, consider a demonstration of creative drama or an open class by showing what it is, what it does, and how it works. If there is one thing that recent experimentation in the arts has shown us, it is that there are few, if any, rules that must be obeyed. Children experiment freely, mixing media, ignoring conventional forms, being "horse and rider" simultaneously, and erasing the line that exists between actor and audience. Therefore, an opportunity to observe children working creatively may satisfy the funding agency and be a far more effective presentation than the traditional school play.

15

Creative Drama in Alternative Spaces

*N*ot all creative drama is taking place in classrooms and community centers. Some very imaginative work is being done in or under the auspices of other social and cultural institutions, and in the streets and playgrounds of the city as well. It is with these alternative locations that this chapter is concerned. The years since the original publication of this textbook have witnessed a dramatic spread of activities and the acceptance of an expanding arena for learning. The open classroom, the magnet schools, the university without walls programs and their various permutations have increased our awareness of the possibilities for learning beyond the boundaries of our public and private educational institutions.

There are many reasons for this phenomenon, and any one answer would be simplistic. Certainly recent budget cuts for the arts is one; this has caused many communities to look elsewhere for places in which to hold

An American company in street theatre for a Spanish-speaking audience. (*Courtesy of FACETS Performance Ensemble, Chicago; photograph by Nicole E. Dreiske, Director.*)

classes in drama, puppetry, dance, music, painting, and pottery, as well as the meetings of special crafts and hobby groups popular in individual neighborhoods. Another reason is the superior facilities of some community centers and civic theatres, and the closely related asset of a central or accessible location that these centers usually offer. Some Y's and community centers have simply continued a long-standing tradition of classes in the visual and performing arts; and as school programs are curtailed or cut altogether, they find themselves again providing an important community service. Still another source of creative energy is to be found in some of the alternative and magnet schools, which came into being during the late sixties and seventies. While not all of these programs have survived, enough of them remain to account for an important contribution to education in the arts.

Obviously the goals and values of drama in alternative spaces do not differ from those of the classroom; therefore the suggestions of literature and other activities in the earlier chapters are still appropriate. There are some differences in the situations, however, and this chapter is concerned with the special environment and features that these outside locations possess, and some of the ways in which to use them. The environment does not alter goals, but it may modify procedures. It may also offer unique resources that the leader can use. Among the more common sites of activities are libraries, churches, and museums. There are also some spacious cultural centers with programs expressly designed for children. Among these are the Minneapolis Children's Theatre, which has become a school; the Nashville Theatre and Academy; the Empire State Institute for the Performing Arts in Albany; Lincoln Center in New York; and the Kennedy Center in Washington, whose programs will be discussed in chapter 16. Each center has developed a format of its own, depending on the interests and needs of the community and the particular resources it has to offer.

Free of board of education guidelines, these alternative sites are able to be flexible regarding organization, schedule, workshops for teachers and students, and programs in general. This is not to say that they have no restrictions; they have. Their programs differ from those of the schools in that the classes are not part of a required curriculum, students are not graded (though they may be evaluated), and the classes fall within the category of leisure time interests.

Let's take a look at some of the institutions in which interesting work is going on.

Drama in Libraries

Not all libraries offer classes in creative drama, but many include storytelling, puppetry, and children's films among their special services. Story dramatization grows naturally from storytelling and librarians who have worked with it

Drama group in a library. (*Courtesy of Magie Dominic, Woodstock, N.Y.; photograph by Susan Kain.*)

report its popularity. Older children are eager to enact favorite stories, whereas little children are drawn to tales they have just heard told and they want to try on the various roles. Surrounded by walls of books, children meeting in libraries have literary resources at their fingertips—an advantage over groups meeting in schoolrooms. Whether the creative drama class is conducted by the children's librarian or by an expert who comes in each week, the environment is conducive to the pursuit of creative drama, particularly story acting.

According to Nancy Pereira, author of *Creative Drama in the Library*, there are benefits to the library as well as to its young patrons. First of all, drama brings children into the library and encourages their returning. Children discover its resources and in the process get acquainted with the staff. They find persons there who will answer their questions, show them film strips and materials, and help them locate periodicals and books. At a time when television viewing is claiming many hours a week in a child's life, a strong connection with the local public library has mutual benefits.

One question that always comes up has to do with noise and space. If there is an activity room, and many libraries have one, this is no problem. Some libraries have more than one room available for storytelling, lectures, and classes. Large urban libraries often have auditoriums with stages, where films are shown and plays can be given. Because of the noise level when a group of children get together, the most soundproof quarters available should be chosen for classes in creative drama. If, on the other hand, the library is small or consists of a single room, the hours for creative drama have to be set when the fewest persons tend to use it. Obviously this will affect the program, but a way can usually be found if drama is really wanted. Storytelling and puppets, which require very little space, make a good beginning. It may be that a simple rearrangement of furniture is all that is necessary to create a larger space for human actors. The cooperation of the staff, however, is essential under any circumstances.

One interesting drama program evolved through the efforts of a librarian in Woodstock, New York. Her interest in history prompted an unusual focus on material relating to a particular person, event, or culture. Calling itself "The Children's History Theatre," the children with whom she works meet on a regular basis during the school year, doing their research on the chosen topic, and rehearsing the play they develop and present as a culmination of their work. Because the project exists outside the classroom, the librarian is free to select a topic that particularly interests the children and, on occasion, to enlist the help of local professional artists, dancers, and musicians. Posters in the library and school inform the public as to when plays are being performed.[1]

Drama in Museums

Museums play a central role in preserving the cultural, artistic, and historical heritage of each generation. Through their education departments they have become more than repositories of treasures; lectures, films, special exhibits, and programs are offered to attract a larger public. Some art museums, in expanding their community services, are providing not only more educational programs than they offered in the past but are providing space for outside groups to use and in which to perform. Some museums now offer classes in the performing as well as the visual arts. One example is the Brooklyn Museum in New York, where a number of years ago an innovative drama program was inaugurated. Paintings and sculpture provide stimulation and inspiration, whereas galleries are used for playing space. Actually, the drama program is one of several offerings of the museum education department. Shrinking funds for community services in the past few years challenged the museum to find new ways to involve and educate children and family audiences. One way that has proved successful is drama/theatre. The visual images and emotional impact of the museum's collections motivate interest and learning. At the Brooklyn Museum, the use of theatre techniques is said to

---

1. Magie Dominic is director of The Children's History Theatre, Woodstock, N.Y.

parallel Piaget's contention that children are motivated to gain a greater understanding of their world and to restructure their knowledge when they encounter experiences that are dissonant with their previous assumptions.

In the museum children find objects removed from their original context. Helped to understand that these objects once belonged to a particular society and were expressive of that society, children recreate a cultural context for dramatization. In this context they explore the environment and the relationship between the objects of art and the people who created them. Aesthetic standards that differ from their own, as well as cognitive learnings, result when children visit the museum in this way. They also view plays as well as create them in a special gallery that seats no more than one hundred persons.

The Brooklyn Museum has several other educational and theatre-related programs. *Museum/School Collaboration* creates an educational experience that meets the needs of both institutions. *Holiday Programs* provide family audiences with programs to stimulate interest in particular collections. *Summer Day Camp Programs* provide activities for ad hoc groups, often representing a wide age range and little past experience of the museum. *Informal Theatre Events for Special Exhibitions* create quick theatrical "happenings" to point up or highlight an exhibit. These vignettes are written and performed by staff members and student actors. Staff involvement in theatre encourages participation on the part of both children and adults. Further, the museum has found that audiences who participate are motivated to return.

Additional programs are also made available to children and planned as field trips for different grade levels. Previsit kits for teachers prepare children coming from schools in school time. "What's Up?" on the other hand, is a free year-round program for elementary school children. Storytelling, drawing, and painting aid participants in learning about a different collection every time they attend. A film entitled "Statues Hardly Ever Smile" was made up of the drama work at the Brooklyn Museum, showing how one museum opened its doors to the children of the community at little cost and with great success.

An example of one of the museum/school collaborations was the Chinese mythology theatre "collage" entitled *Can You Hear the River Calling the Moon?* This piece was created and performed by elementary school children for the general public over the Christmas holidays. A class of school children visited the Brooklyn Museum for ten weekly sessions, during which time Chinese art and culture were the subject of study. The children acted Chinese myths improvisationally, and made their own costumes and props in the museum workshops. The script that evolved was based on the myths and put into written form by the museum instructor. As described in a museum newsletter, the protagonist of the "collage" was a river that flowed from a landscape painting and introduced the various components of the production: a shadow puppet play, showing the creation of the land; large puppets in a morality legend; and a group of children performing a dragon myth.

The play told of the relationship of the people to the land and explained the convention of Chinese landscape painting. A Chinese musician accompanied the performance with music played on traditional instruments. Following each performance the audience was invited to tour the galleries, where they viewed the original paintings of the characters, dragons, waterfalls, and landscapes that they had just seen portrayed. After the weekend performances at the museum the play was given in the school auditorium for the rest of the children. This is an illustration of one way in which school, museum, and community can work together on a project involving all of the arts, with educational and aesthetic values receiving equal emphasis.

The Children's Museum in Boston is another example of a museum with an extensive program of activities including classes in drama and weekly children's theatre performances. Both a Sunday series and a Friday night series of entertainments are open to the public and are held in a small area called the "Sit Around Space." Because the space is small, puppet shows, storytelling, magic shows, and singers are featured, though plays are also offered on occasion.

Classes in creative drama include those held at regular meeting times and in special workshops. Two examples of the latter were conducted in the summer of 1981. Under the direction of Carol Korty, children created plays from folktales, which were then performed in the "Sit Around Space." Advanced drama classes were taught at the museum by the Boston Shakespeare Company. Wheelock College has also held acting workshops and given performances for children at the museum. Brochures from the museum describe teacher workshops as well, and these include drama among a variety of arts and crafts.

Although many museums are serving their communities in similar ways, the Boston Children's Museum is cited for the quantity and quality of its offerings as part of an ongoing program.

Museums are also serving as hosts for theatre performances and workshops. Cleveland's new Museum of Natural History was the principal venue chosen for a children's theatre festival held in that city in the spring of 1982. The imaginative architectural design of the building afforded a variety of playing spaces for performances of plays, dance, and music. Large museums have traditionally offered educational programs for both adults and children, but these informal grassroots programs in which children are active participants define the museum in new terms. The museum, once a hushed and awesome sanctuary, is proving to be a lively and suitable location for classes in drama, movement, and mime.

Bruno Bettelheim, commenting on the value of the museum to the child, said that irrespective of what a museum's content might be, it serves ". . . to stimulate his imagination, to arouse his curiosity so that he wishes to penetrate ever more deeply the meaning of what he is expected to admire in the museum, to give him a chance to admire in his own good time things that are

Creative drama in the park draws a crowd. (*Courtesy of Milton Polsky.*)

beyond his ken, and, most important of all, to give him a feeling of awe for the wonders of the world. Because a world that is not full of wonders is one hardly worth the effort of growing up in."[2] Bettelheim was not writing of drama when he made that statement, but the role of children's drama in the museum serves two of his purposes: to offer an aesthetic experience in a welcoming cultural institution and to bring the child into the museum, which he might otherwise not have entered.

Drama in Parks

Parks and playgrounds since the early part of this century have included drama among their activities for children. In many cases this has meant an informal program of storytelling, improvisation, puppetry, and traveling theatre companies, who performed free of charge in parks. In recent years, however, more structured programs have been designed with well-qualified leaders and better facilities for both classes and performances. An example of the latter is Wolf Trap Farm Park for the Performing Arts in Virginia, where programs for adults and children take place all summer long with children's productions in both indoor and outdoor settings. Drama lends itself to this type

2. Bruno Bettelheim, "Children and Museums," in *Children Today* 9, no. 1 (January-February 1980): 23.

of structure, which combines recreational opportunities, and picnic and sport areas, with performances of drama, mime, dance, and music. Though the emphasis is on performance at Wolf Trap, participation is included. Again, this is not an isolated example, but it is probably one of the better known parks providing excellence in entertainment. On a recent visit to Wolf Trap the author watched a group of students with their professor from Georgetown University giving a performance of a participatory play. The situation was ideal for this kind of production and the director was skilled in handling it. Performing daily had helped the actors to achieve a high level of artistry, which could not normally be expected in an informal activity in a park.

Drama in Churches

The church has historically had a close relationship with the theatre. The medieval theatre was born in the Church, and despite the repudiation theatre has suffered periodically at its hands, an unquestionable connection and acceptance of certain common values and goals exist between them. It is therefore no surprise to discover the growing number of drama and theatre

A church offers a space for drama. "God loved variety; each tree according to its own kind." (*Courtesy of Elizabeth Rike, Knoxville, Tenn.*)

groups that are housed in church buildings of various faiths. Some of these groups are companies that produce plays on religious themes. Others are groups to whom space is given for classes in acting, creative drama, and dance. Many churches support extensive programs in the performing arts, including professional resident companies; and, like museums and libraries, they also offer space to outside groups for whom commercial studios are unavailable or financially beyond their ability to pay. Indeed, one has only to look at a history of the community theatre movement in this country to see how many successful ventures were begun in the church. Large meeting rooms; a stage, if or when one is needed; after school and Saturday morning hours for classes; low rent (or no rent)—these are the services that many churches provide. In large cities, where rents are prohibitive, the church house is often a haven for the performing arts.

In addition, there is now an awakened interest in drama written on religious themes, modern plays posing moral and ethical questions relevant to life today. Both educators and church people are involved in writing, directing, and promoting this new kind of religious drama. Also available is a body of information on choral reading, monologues, clowning, and textbooks on creative drama and improvisation. Successful Broadway plays like *Joseph and the Amazing Technicolor Dreamcoat, Godspell*, and recent productions with religious themes may have been the precursors of this new wave of interest; they may also account for the strengthened relationship between theatre and church. Paralleling this development is the church's receptivity to theatre companies as cited above.

The Children's Theatre Association of America has a Religious Drama Committee, which publishes a newsletter and bibliographies of religious plays for children and books on creative drama in religious education.[3] It also sponsors programs at the annual convention of the organization each August, thus helping other groups initiate programs in their local churches and parishes. While the goal of many of these groups is public performance, often followed by audience discussion, classes in creative drama and mime for children are also popular. These may be taught by staff members, scout leaders, or by experts from outside; and children who attend are not necessarily affiliated with the church.

Other Locations

Classes in creative drama are to be found in a variety of other places as well, both indoors and out. Among them are department stores, shopping centers, parks, playgrounds, hospitals, housing complexes and beaches. In

---

3. Pam W. Barrager, compiler, *Creative Dramatics as a Subject or Method in Religious Education: A Bibliography* (Washington, D.C.: ATA, 1975), and *Religious Plays for Children, Youth and Family Audiences: A Bibliography* (Washington, D.C.: ATA, 1975).

Drama in a shopping mall. (*Courtesy of Eunice Joffe, Imagination Theatre, Inc.*)

some cases they are established, ongoing programs; in others, they are little more than informal play groups to which children may come while parents are shopping. One cannot expect a high level of accomplishment where attendance is irregular or where weather conditions affect the meeting of the class. Nevertheless, these informal drama groups are not to be written off as lacking direction or continuity, for a number of highly successful ventures were begun in playgrounds and parks under skillful leadership. The key to success is the leader: a dedicated, well-prepared man or woman, who is able to work with prevailing conditions while seeking funding and more permanent quarters.

Procedures obviously vary according to place, time, length and frequency of meetings, and the experience of the leader. The suggestion given in earlier chapters for improvisation and mime, and the materials for dramatization may be used under most circumstances, though not all are suitable everywhere. More than one informal program has attracted regional and even national attention for its originality and success. These are what James Reany calls "root ideas that uncurl in a community until you find yourself taking a workshop to a school gym or helping 129 teachers in Niagara Falls improvise a play."[4]

One example of a project which has found a generous sharing of space in several institutions is the Creative Theatre Unlimited of Princeton, New Jersey.

4. James Reany, *Apple Butter and Other Plays for Children* (Vancouver: Talonbooks, 1973), introduction.

Summer class on the church lawn. (*Courtesy of Joan Robinson and Jacqueline Johnson, Creative Theatre Unlimited, Princeton, N.J.*)

The McCarter Theatre, the 150-year-old Trinity Church, and selected historic sites in the area have all contributed to its continuing growth. In 1983–84 public creative drama workshops were funded by the Mercer County Cultural and Heritage Commission. Sites for these workshops were selected on the basis of their relationship to labor and industry. Summer and winter programs make for a year-round community service and illustrate clearly how local facilities can enable a fledgling group to gain a foothold in these precarious times. The availability of a lawn is an attractive feature of the summer program, which culminates in a work-in-progress on the stage of the McCarter.

On the practical side, most leaders recommend charging a fee for the informal drama group, albeit a small one. This payment constitutes a commitment insuring, or at least encouraging, regular attendance. The after-school program is elected by the participants, a feature that has both its positive and negative aspects. The child who *chooses* to attend and becomes an interested member will in all probability stay in the group; the child who is uncommitted is the one who tends to drop out. The leader of a leisure time activity should make a special effort to reach every child in the class in order to build a strong, ongoing group. A modest fee will not affect registration; boredom or casual attitude toward the class will.

Summary

The leader of a group meeting in a nontraditional setting is wise to take stock of its assets: to consider what the facility has, not what it lacks. For instance:

The *library* has rich resources in literature, visual aids, and research materials. Make use of them. In addition to finding favorite stories, you have a unique opportunity at the library to introduce children to new literature and authors they do not know.

The *museum* has collections and special exhibitions, and their education departments can provide a wealth of resources. Discover the possibilities of the museums and how you can work with the staff to add another dimension to the creative drama experience.

The *church* has meeting rooms, often a stage, and access to a piano. Its staff is accustomed to having groups of young people around, and you will probably find more time there in which to work or rehearse.

Other spaces vary so widely that one has to discover their unique advantages. Most will have some positive features. If not, then look for another place in which to hold the class. A room, a leader, a group, imagination, and a regular meeting time: these are the prerequisites. A drama program, unlike all of the other arts, and contrary to public opinion, is the least expensive to launch. One warning: Remember that alternative spaces were not designed for classes in creative drama and will therefore lack some of the features teachers expect. Respect them, use them, but do not abuse the hospitality of the institution. Your successful use of its resources is a measure of your *own* creativity—and perhaps a new program will grow tomorrow from the roots you put down today.

One further suggestion involves the planning of a single workshop in creative drama. So far we have been thinking in terms of a course or series of classes; however, an occasional workshop held in a particular place, or planned for a special occasion, has a unique value that must be mentioned. Obviously, it cannot have the depth of the well-planned sequence of lessons, but it may hold an excitement that the participants will remember for the rest of their lives. The fact that it happens only once sets it apart—much like the experience of going to the theatre.

Workshops of this sort are generally held in places not normally available to students, at least for this purpose. For example, the site might be the location of an historical event; the original house of a well-known person, who once lived in the community; or a landmark building such as a court house, church, or farm museum. An imaginative teacher, seeing the possibilities of extending a field trip to include the dramatizaiton of material at the site might arrange ahead for a full morning or afternoon visit. Museums are generally glad to cooperate with a plan made in advance. Familiarity with the place and, in the case of older children, research into its past, can make a single such workshop an inspiring occasion.

Dramatizing history or taking the roles of real or imagined persons who lived at that time or in that place makes an indelible impression on young participants. Follow-up activities in the classroom afterward (if the workshop is a school event) may include further improvisation, creative writing or arts and crafts. Teachers find these experiences an opportunity for greater enrichment and another dimension in learning. During the bicentennial year both historic sites and significant dates led to imaginative workshops throughout the country. I have heard children and college students recall with pleasure their experiences in both seeing and creating plays arranged by their teachers with local children's theatre companies. Their memories of the learnings that took place during that period are still amazingly vivid.

Creative Theatre Unlimited, described earlier in this chapter, held three workshops, all funded in part by a local cultural commission, held "on location." They included trips in which drama was created on the following sites:

1. The Port Mercer Canal House, where participants would dramatize life along the working Delaware–Raritan Canal at the turn of the century;
2. The Kuser Farm Mansion, where participants might imagine the response to the first movie with sound in the year 1928;
3. The New Jersey State Museum in Trenton, where participants would reenact the Potters' Strike of 1923.

Every community has a multitude of possibilities which an enterprising teacher or theatre company can exploit, often at little or no extra cost. Workshops may be one-time events or represent a high point in the semester; either way, they are examples of the unique value that a special space has to offer.

16
Changes, Challenges, and Choices

*T*he changes that are taking place in creative drama are numerous and perceptible. Whether they indicate a trend is difficult to say, but the fact that they are happening in all parts of the country would suggest that drama education is taking on new aspects in the mideighties. Although many of the changes can be attributed to the economy, there are also other forces at work. The most conspicuous change in the past few years is the introduction of programs for the handicapped, which have grown out of a concerned legislation. We are also seeing better articulated school and community programs, a greater use of artists in the schools, and more well-trained leaders in all areas. Recognition of minorities continues, though much of the funding for programs serving them has been cut. Creative drama programs have suffered similar cutbacks, but as a result we are witnessing some highly imaginative ways of reaching children through the arts.

368   A pumpkin is transformed into a flying coach. (*Courtesy of Empire State Youth Theatre Institute; Photograph by Fred Ricard.*)

Pioneering Programs

The preceding chapters have dealt mainly with creative drama as part of a curriculum or, at least, as an art to be included whenever time and curriculum permit. Although the focus of this text is on the classroom, mention has also been made of some of the other areas where creative drama programs exist. These include museums, libraries, community and recreation centers, and churches. As recreation and leisure time activities, drama classes and clubs have always enjoyed great popularity. These recreational programs are important for a variety of reasons, not the least of them being that they are elected "for fun." Many leaders doing outstanding work today in such programs hold degrees in recreation or theatre; some volunteers are teachers and graduate students who lead workshops in the arts because they, also, enjoy them. The first recognition of drama as an educational and social tool came from such centers as the Educational Alliance, the Henry Street Settlement, Christadora House, and Greenwich House in New York; Hull House in Chicago; Goodrich House and the Karamu Theatre in Cleveland. These centers and many other settlements, from Boston to the West Coast, included classes in storytelling and informal dramatics under the guidance of social workers and the Junior League. Today the American Community Theatre Association and the National Recreation Association, to mention only two national organizations, offer help and support to leaders of leisure time programs in theatre. True, the demand for qualified leaders and directors still exceeds the supply; but with the consciousness of our increasing leisure time, government agencies and universities are endeavoring to help communities set up programs to help people live richer and more satisfying lives, including experiences in the arts.

The little theatre movement of the twenties brought dramatic activities to the children of other communities, but it was not until the forties that the major responsibility for children's dramatic activities was assumed by educational institutions. Notable for its pioneering efforts in this field since 1925 is Northwestern University, which in cooperation with the public schools of Evanston, under the distinguished leadership of Winifred Ward, first demonstrated what town and gown can do working together. There have been other ventures, too numerous to mention, some of which have resulted in permanent programs, contributing both to the children of the community and the training of teachers. Many colleges and universities now offer work in children's drama as a curricular inclusion as well as an extracurricular activity, with touring programs or campus performances of plays for children's audiences.

The Adelphi University Children's Centre for the Creative Arts in Garden City, New York, is a unique program serving both students and area. Founded in 1937 as a community service, it now includes an extensive program of Saturday classes for children aged six to twelve, evening classes for teenagers, and classes for adults. In addition, graduate students may earn a master's degree in speech arts and educational theatre, or in elementary or secondary education with a concentration on aesthetic education, through participation in the activities of the Children's Centre. Throughout, attention is devoted to the process rather than the product and to all the arts instead of drama only. There are many instances of university and community cooperation in this country, but the Adelphi program is cited because it has been in successful operation for over forty years and provides the same strong leadership for both groups of participants, community residents and students.

The Children's Theatre Association of America (CTAA), first established in 1944 as a committee dedicated to the promotion of children's theatre and creative drama, became a full-fledged division of the American Educational Theatre Association in 1951. Its membership, interestingly enough, has always included teachers and leaders from universities, colleges and schools, community theatres, settlement houses, the Association of Junior Leagues of America, the professional theatre, and interested citizens. National conventions of CTAA, held every August, provide programs demonstrating work done in the various regions of the country, as well as talks, symposia, and panel discussions on topics of current interest. Workshops in creative drama and puppetry, under the direction of outstanding leaders, have often been planned prior to the opening of the conference, in response to the members' demand for further training. While the principal interest at the present time is the introduction of creative drama into the school curriculum, there is a growing enthusiasm for its inclusion in camp, hospital, and special education programs. Reports on research in the field indicate the effectiveness of this aspect of drama as a social and educational technique.

During the last two decades a number of experimental and pilot projects have been initiated in the arts. Some of these have been funded by state arts councils, some by private foundations, and some by interested organizations such as PTAs. All have had a common goal: to bring the arts to the children of communities in which little has been done or where more exposure to the arts is desired, and to bring the arts to the handicapped. Such projects have not been confined to any particular regions; they have been nationwide. Nor have they followed identical patterns.

An example of a particularly extensive project was the Arts in General Education program, financed by the John D. Rockefeller III Fund, for the 8,000-pupil school system of University City, a suburb of Saint Louis. In this program, painting, music, photography, dance, poetry, drama, and other visual and performing arts were integrated into the curriculum from kindergarten through the twelfth grade. The major objective of the program was to give children experience in the arts and to increase their knowledge of the arts. In-school participation, field trips, and exhibitions were among the experiences offered. One problem discovered by the evaluators initially was a general feeling of inadequacy on the part of the educators. Because few teachers have had enough training and experience to feel comfortable with the arts, they have not introduced a variety of arts activities into their classrooms on any regular basis. Moreover, arts education, particularly in the upper grades, is often considered a separate area and is segregated from other studies, if not neglected.

Through the financial support of the JDR III Fund, the community support of the University City School Board, and the staff and resources of CEMREL (Central Midwestern Regional Educational Laboratory, Inc.), an extensive educational program was carried on over a three-year period. Both specialists and classroom teachers participated in an effort to realize present and long-term goals, with the result that many of the ideals and objectives of the three-year program have become a part of the University City Arts Program.

CEMREL's long-range curriculum program, including drama/theatre for children, was founded in the hope that its materials and philosophy would have a lasting effect on education throughout the United States. CEMREL is reported to be the first educational laboratory established under the provisions of the Elementary and Secondary Education Act of 1965 (ESEA), which included all the arts in its program.

Examples of many different types of educational drama programs are to be found throughout the United States. This chapter does not purport to enumerate or describe them in detail, but they exist both at state level and in institutions of higher learning. The spread of activity is impressive but there is no single pattern or area of emphasis. *Coming to Our Senses, The Significance of the Arts in American Education*, generally referred to as The Rockefeller Report of 1977 (discussed later in this chapter), indicated a strong desire for the arts on the part of the public, but the present state of the economy does not augur well for their growth in the immediate future. Nevertheless, imaginative steps have been taken, and it is to be hoped that new types of arts programs will be designated if or when present funding for current programs is withdrawn.

While the arts in this country are still not generally included as a significant part of public education, such efforts as these indicate a growing concern for a neglected area and represent positive steps in the direction of constructive change in the curriculum. Drama, a relative newcomer to the schools, is finding recognition as an art that contributes to the emotional, intellectual, and social development of the child, with values to be derived from active participation on all levels.

The Arts-Centered School

The Mead School in Byram, Connecticut, attracted national attention in 1977 when it was featured in an article in the *Saturday Review* entitled "Why Children Should Draw."[1] The unique character of this school lies in its belief in

1. Roger M. Williams, *Saturday Review,* vol. 4, no. 23, Sept. 1977, pp. 10–16.

This story took to the road. (*Courtesy of The National Committee Arts for the Handicapped; photograph by Andrew French, Rockford, Ill.*)

the arts as basic to education. The Mead catalog states that learning is multisensory. "Children need to touch, taste, see, talk," and to that end it is suggested that they should follow a curriculum that gives the arts and traditional subjects equal status. In fact, the arts in a sense are predominant. "Art gets the largest space here," according to Mead's director, who explained that a child uses her mind in concert with hands and eyes. Through experiential learning (the arts), the child reaches the symbolic (traditional). This small private school after fifteen years, is able to point to scores at or above Standard Achievement Test (SAT) averages in every subject.

The *Saturday Review* article also cited some other schools that have embarked on innovative arts programs. Project IMPACT, begun in 1970 and located in five different areas, lasted only a few years but developed into other institutions like the Magnet Arts School in Eugene, Oregon, and The Eastgate School in Columbus, Ohio. In these schools, and in The Magic Mountain School in Berkeley, California, the emphasis is on the role of the arts in the development of human capacities, rather than on arts education as traditionally taught. The magnet schools, with an alternative curriculum, often provide more time for the arts than the more traditional public schools.

Creative Drama in the Camp

Except in the arts camp, drama/theatre is rarely one of the more important activities of the camp program. Camps exist primarily to give city children an experience in group living in an outdoor setting. An opportunity to engage in a variety of sports is provided, with nature study, music, arts and crafts, and drama, as well as other activities from which to choose. Because of this broad emphasis, children should not be expected to spend long hours indoors, in rehearsals, but rather to enjoy drama and share the results of their work in occasional informal programs. Creative drama is actually an ideal activity for campers of all ages and backgrounds. Pantomime, improvisation, and simple, out-of-door pageantry can contribute both to the participants and to those occasions when the group comes together for programs. Full production with scenery and costumes would seem to have no place in the average camp; the drama counselor might better prepare herself by studying creative drama techniques so that she is able to work informally with campers of all ages, rather than formally for an audience. Class periods should be short and flexible. This, however, does not mean that time should be wasted or misspent; quite the contrary. No activity brings satisfaction unless it is looked upon with respect; hence, informal drama, seriously undertaken, has as much to offer the camp as it has the community center or school.

The Retreat

The retreat has become a popular way of studying a subject in depth. A group, in isolating itself for a day or a weekend—sometimes for as long as a week—is able to focus on a topic without interruption or distraction. Improvisation is a useful technique for getting into a subject or for seeing a problem from inside. Whether the purpose of the retreat is religion, some aspect of the arts, or a social issue, improvisation can be a most effective tool for gaining understanding. Lectures, panels, films, and informal discussions are more meaningful when participants are able to become fully involved. Drama heightens involvement. When it is included in a retreat program, students, teachers, and community leaders report the excitement it contributes and that they believe it to be one of the lasting values of the retreat; many of them mention improvisation as one of the most effective techniques employed.

One reportedly successful experiment in creative drama was carried out in a retreat for teachers held at a mountain camp in Switzerland.[2] A leader and twenty-five participants (all kindergarten and elementary school teachers) lived and worked together for a week. The members of the group did not know

2. Fräulein Brigitt Streuli, 2 Hauptlehrerin, Kantonales Kindergartnerinen, Semenar, Umiken, Switzerland.

each other beforehand, but became well acquainted through the close association of informal classes, discussion groups, and meals taken together in the dining hall. The first classes were conducted in a large room, bare except for a carpet on the floor and a piano. Participants wore informal clothing and soft shoes, or rhythm sandals. On the first morning, they were asked to walk around, to get used to the space they would work in. Movement and rhythms followed, with piano accompaniment. Next came simple exercises in pantomime.

The Grimm tale of *Frau Holle* was introduced the next day, but for several sessions only portions of the story were played. The leader then took the group outdoors and had them try the scenes in the woods under the trees. In pairs they enacted the scene of Frau Holle's trying to pull the girl into the cottage. This was followed by the scene in the doorway with the shower of gold and the dripping of tar. By the end of the week, they had played the entire story outdoors, in a setting appropriate to the tale and conducive to physical freedom.

Mornings began with singing, movement, and dance. Evenings included readings from modern literature and group discussion. These, and Bible stories, were enacted by the participants so that they had the experience of approaching material as children might, but making ultimate use of literary works that challenged them on an adult level. According to one member of the group, the greatest values of the workshop were the sense of freedom it engendered, the loss of self-consciousness that ensued, and the concept of creative drama as an art form that emerged by the end of the week. This illustration is cited because of the unusual opportunity it offered for group work in a simple yet ideal setting. While the camp program is filled with a variety of different activities, it does offer the same advantages of plenty of space, an outdoor setting, and freedom from the usual daily distractions.

Workshops and Training

Workshops in creative drama are held in the United States each year under a variety of sponsorships. Some are part of the summer school offerings of universities and colleges. Others are sponsored by such organizations as the Children's Theatre Association of America, the Association for Childhood Education International, and the National Recreation Association. Still others are among the in-service courses for public school teachers held after school or on Saturdays. The Junior League, women's clubs, religious and recreational organizations, as well as individual community theatres and churches have instituted programs for the training of their drama leaders. Although surveys have been made from time to time in an effort to determine the amount and kind of training being offered by educational institutions throughout the country, it would be difficult to list or assess the numbers and types of workshops conducted by the alternative institutions and organizations mentioned. It is significant, however, that they seem to be on the increase, and that hundreds of teachers and leaders take part in them each year for the purpose of broadening their own backgrounds and adding another dimension to their programs.

Most successful seem to be the workshops that include demonstration, actual work with children, and participation in acting on the adult level. Reading, lectures, and discussion are to be taken for granted, but practical laboratory experience is essential for any study of the arts. It has been my experience that the class members most reluctant to participate in drama in the beginning have always mentioned it first when evaluating the course. Only a concentrated workshop, or a semester's class, permits enough hours to include all these activities. The acquisition of fine technical skills should not be expected, for techniques are a developmental process, attained over a much longer period of time spent in practice and study.

The Naropa Institute Teacher Re-Training Program in Boulder, Colorado, is one of a number of recent programs designed to bring the teacher into a closer and more comfortable relationship with the arts. Despite such excellent resources as Young Audiences and Artists-in-the-Schools, the classroom teacher often feels personally alienated and inadequate when it comes to continuing the programs they have initiated. Administrators, farther removed from these programs, have even greater difficulty relating to them; hence, a good start all too often dies out before it has accomplished its purpose. At the Naropa Institute, the objectives are (1) to change the attitudes of non-arts teachers and administrators, and (2) to introduce the arts to this population through direct personal experience. In its first summer session in 1977, eighty-five students from throughout the United States were immersed in the performing arts; during the following summer, the visual arts were added.

The aim is not to provide either "recipes" or workshops in sensitivity training. Rather, it is to try to develop awareness and appreciation of the arts that will enable non-arts teachers to continue on their own after the summer is over. This includes the development of greater self-confidence; a basic understanding of the elements of the arts; an appreciation of the interrelatedness of the arts; a belief in the creative spirit in all human beings, not just the artist; and a desire to relate all of this to education.

A number of American universities have brought visiting lecturers in the arts from abroad and have established overseas study programs for credit. Among the universities that have done extensive work in the area of drama/theatre education are Northwestern University, which has brought Dorothy Heathcote and Gavin Bolton for summer sessions on the Evanston campus; and New York University, which has conducted a program for the past several years at Bretton Hall College of Education in England. In Cleveland, in-service drama/theatre courses for area teachers have been held for the past few winters under a joint sponsorship of Cleveland State University, the Cleveland Playhouse, and the Board of Education. Many other colleges and universities in the West, the South, and in New England have sponsored teacher workshops and exchange programs for students in the field of drama education. Brian Way has spent much of the past several years traveling throughout the United States and Canada, lecturing and giving workshops on creative drama and on participation theatre. In addition to leaders already named, there have been other educators who have come for conferences and short-term engagements. Among them are Donald Baker, formerly of Weymouth College of Education in England, who has also worked closely with the ACEI (Association for Child-hood Education International); Margaret Faulkes-Jendyk, cofounder with Brian Way of the Theatre Centre in London, and now on the faculty of the University of Alberta, Canada; John Hodgson of Bretton Hall; Gerald Tyler, former drama adviser in Yorkshire and a founder of ASSITEJ (discussed later in this chapter); and Marian Lindkvist of Sesame in London. There have been additional programs in other foreign countries, but these are among the very successful and are cited because of their content, common language, and duration.

With improved travel, American teachers have been able to meet with colleagues overseas and, on occasion, to lecture, give workshops, and to attend conferences and festivals—in short, to extend the perimeters of their own experience as no generation of educators has until now been able to do. This appears to be a trend in drama/theatre education, which can only enrich our offerings.

A valuable guide to resources in the field of educational drama is the *Theatre Resources Directory/Handbook*, prepared in 1980 by the Education Division of the National Endowment for the Arts. It was designed to help Artists-in-Schools coordinators for state arts agencies in locating and selecting theatre companies and resource persons that are capable of providing successful in-school theatre residencies. The fourfold purpose of the *Directory/Handbook* is to:

1. Provide descriptive information about those companies who have developed or are willing to develop programs for residencies in schools;
2. Provide lists of individual theatre artists willing to participate in artist-in-residence programs in schools or communities;
3. Provide companies with sample educational materials of a preperformance and postperformance nature;
4. Provide in-school coordinators with examples of schedules for plan-

ning residencies and suggestions for curriculum materials related to
theatre artists and performance groups.

More than mention must be made of the 334-page Rockefeller Report
released in spring 1977. Entitled *Coming to Our Senses: the Significance of the
Arts in American Education*, it is by far the most comprehensive survey of the
subject ever made in this country. A panel of experts, over a period of two years,
studied arts education in elementary schools, secondary schools, and colleges,
with funding provided by the Office of Education, the National Endowment for
the Arts, and several private foundations. Professional organizations assisted in
the research, which revealed a widespread belief in the arts in education,
despite inadequate programs in many areas. Among the ninety-eight recommendations that were made, the panel called for the creation of a National
Center for Arts in Education; a federal agency to coordinate information about
artists, funding, programs, and research; and also recommended that the
existing federal council on the Arts and the Humanities carry out a ten-year
strategy for art in education, in cooperation with states.

The panel also suggested that school districts allow students to earn credit
for work done in community arts programs and that curricula should be
expanded to include dance, film, drama, poetry, and design. In the area of
teacher education and in-service training, the panel urged that all prospective
teachers have experience in a variety of arts and learn how to relate them to
each other and to other disciplines. The reception of the report was generally
favorable, and some results have already taken place. One was the formation, in
1978, of a new organization called Arts, Education, and Americans, Inc., which
has as its aims to:

1. Organize several regional conferences, in which there will be an
   opportunity to discuss the Rockefeller Report, develop specific plans
   for local or regional implementation, and to make recommendations
   toward the national plan;
2. Maintain a speakers' bureau that will include panel members and
   others connected with the report;
3. Establish a central communications center in the New York office;
4. Promote distribution of the report;
5. Participate in developing a national plan for the arts in education.

As a private organization, Arts, Education, and Americans, Inc., was
designed to seek all possible means to foster the development of a national
program for strengthening the role of the arts from kindergarten through
college. One chapter, incidentally, suggests cooperation between schools and
nonacademic institutions as a way of increasing funds that are available for the
arts. In addition, the organization suggests that children's experiences can be

enriched by making use of community resources such as museums, theatres, studios, film libraries, and local artists.

Government Programs

By 1976 the principal programs among which the federal government efforts were divided were:

1. The Alliance for Arts Education
2. The Office of Education Arts in Education Program
3. The Office of Education Special Arts Project
4. The Educational Program of the National Endowment for the Arts
5. The Educational Research and Development Program of the National Institute of Education
6. Educational Innovation and Support Program of the Office of Education's Bureau of School Systems
7. The Division of Education Programs of the National Endowment for the Humanities
8. The National Committee/Arts for the Handicapped.[3]

In addition to the large federal programs, however, smaller state, municipal and community programs may be found in all parts of the country. Many of them are organized by civic-minded community leaders who see needs and get local organizations to work on committees with them to meet these needs. In some instances professional organizations offer guidance; in others, universities supply consultants and resources. Local businesses and foundations can often be persuaded to give financial assistance.

Professional Organizations

The CTAA (Children's Theatre Association of America) has been described earlier as to its purpose and community services. CTAA's expanding list of interests today give it a major role in assisting both professional and amateur groups in a variety of ways: publications, conferences, workshops, showcases of superior productions for children, and consultantships. A placement bureau informs members of jobs, whereas its conventions offer opportunities to meet others in the field.

3. Junius Eddy, *Arts Education 1977 in Prose and Print (An Overview of Nine Significant Publications Affecting The Arts in American Education)* (Washington, D.C.: The Subcommittee on Education in the Arts and the Humanities of the Federal Interagency Committee on Education, 1977).

Festivals of the arts in foreign countries attract visitors from all over the world. (*Courtesy of Sibenik Festival of the Child, Yugoslavia.*)

ACTA (American Community Theatre Association), another division of the American Theatre Association, is an active force in establishing contacts for its members in different parts of the United States and the world. ACTA embraces all areas: children's theatre, high school theatre, and adult theatre. It publishes a calendar listing theatre festivals in the United States and abroad; it assists Americans wanting to attend festivals overseas; and it assumes a responsibility for entertaining out-of-town and foreign visitors and showing them work of interest going on here.

ASSITEJ (Association Internationale de Theatre pour L'Enfance et la Jeunesse) is an international organization for children's theatre. The United States center was established in 1965. ASSITEJ holds a congress in a different country every three years, but American members meet annually during the ATA national convention. Among the values of belonging to ASSITEJ are the opportunity it affords to meet with children's theatre artists in other parts of the world in a spirit of cooperation and sharing, and to see children's theatre productions presented by companies of the member nations. While formal theatre is not the primary concern of the teacher of creative drama, ASSITEJ is mentioned here because it is an important organization to which many American teachers now belong, thus further enriching our field.

One of the most heartening developments in drama education was the position recently taken by ATA; it was reported as follows in *Theatre News:*

The commission on Theatre Education of the American Theatre Association early in 1979 issued the following statement on general education.

That drama/theatre must be an integral part of general education and that at the same time such involvement should affirm the integrity of drama/theatre as an art form.

Any consideration of drama/theatre in general education must:

1. Recognize the arts as fundamental to the learning process;
2. Recognize drama/theatre as a major component of the arts;
3. Acknowledge the values of studying drama/theatre as an art form in its own right as a significant part of general education;
4. Acknowledge the value of drama/theatre processes when skillfully applied as a pedagogical tool to facilitate learning in many areas of the curriculum.[4]

The Arts and the States

Paralleling this statement was the report of the Arts Task Force prepared by the National Conference of State Legislatures in 1981 and recommended for state action. Among the several proposals included in the report were the following:

Basic Education: Amend the state education act to redefine basic education to include arts education at the elementary and secondary levels.

In-Service Teacher Training: Make state funds available to interested school districts to provide in-service arts education training for elementary school teachers. Training programs should emphasize both arts experiences and appreciation, and integration of the arts into the educaional curriculum as a means of teaching math, reading, science, and other basic subjects.

Gifted and Talented: Include children gifted and talented in the arts within categorical state funding of gifted and talented programs.

Schools for the Arts: Consider funding schools for the arts to provide intensive training opportunities for artistically gifted and talented school-age children. The schools may be organized as (1) summer schools for the arts, (2) schools where a substantial portion of the day is devoted to arts instruction, or (3) after-school arts instruction programs.[5]

4. *Theatre News* 15, no. 1 (January/February 1983): 1.

5. *Arts and the States* (A Report of the Arts Task Force, National Conference of State Legislatures), compiled by Larry Briskin (Denver: NCSL, 1981), p. 7.

Community Arts Agencies

Ten years ago there were approximately 200 community arts agencies in the United States. Today there are 2,000. Most of these agencies have been established through local initiative because citizens want arts programs in their own communities. The purpose, regardless of structure, is "mainstreaming the arts into all areas of the community—working with seniors, in the schools, with redevelopment, among many other areas. . . . Community arts agencies can be catalysts for new approaches to problems in urban and rural areas."[6] Rural communities, which heretofore were isolated from the arts, are now bringing in professional artists and nationally known arts companies. Government-supported public television programs, arts periodicals, artists' residency programs, and improved transportation have made the arts accessible to rural citizens. Most encouraging of all has been the encouragement and support of local artists and the increased opportunities for participation in the arts that the community programs provide. While there is great variation in type and quality of programs, this seems to be a grass roots movement supporting the stated belief in the arts as essential to an enlightened and humane society.

Artists-in-Education Program

The Artists-in-Education program is an illustration of a partnership between the National Endowment for the Arts and the state arts agencies. According to a recent report, more than 21,000 artists participated in arts-in-education projects in 42,000 schools and communities across the country during the years between 1969 and 1980; 10.3 million school children and 328,000 teachers were involved in the projects. In a larger context, however, a National Assessment of Educational Progress Study, conducted in 1978–79, showed a disappointing picture. Of the 95,000 students, aged 9–17, who were surveyed, the following results indicated that:

1. Students' knowledge of music had declined since the early seventies;
2. Teenagers were less inclined to pursue arts activities outside school hours;
3. Many students received formal instruction in the arts only in the seventh and eighth grades. Subsequent courses emphasized only the development and refinement of skills;
4. Courses in art history and appreciation were a rarity.

6. Ibid., p. 88.
7. Frank Hodsoll, "Dealing with Reality," excerpts from an address delivered to the National Assembly of State Arts Agencies, October 29, 1982, published in National Endowment for the Arts journal *The Cultural Post* 8, no. 6 (January/February 1983): 3.

As a result of the survey, arts education was declared an important area of concern for the Endowment and the state arts agencies; both realized the need to design a more effective plan for dealing with the situation. The eighties, the report continued, would not be like the seventies, for the factors affecting the arts must be identified and a response made. Enhanced arts education must assume a top priority; the public had expressed a desire for the arts, hence there was an obligation on the part of the established agencies to the taxpayers and to the artists.[7]

Arts Centers

One of the most exciting developments of the past twenty years has been the growth of large cultural centers with programs in the performing arts for young people. Some of these are large arts complexes that have incorporated services for children and youth; others were designed specifically for children and have since extended their services to include workshops and training programs for teachers. Best known among the former is the Kennedy Center for the Performing Arts in Washington, D.C. Here an extensive series is offered to children free of charge under the aegis of its Education Department and CEMREL.

During the construction period of the Kennedy Center the U.S. Office of Education created twenty-two educational research and development laboratories across the country. Two of these laboratories, the South West Regional Laboratory (SWRL) in Los Angeles and the Central Mid-West Regional Educational Laboratory (CEMREL) in St. Louis, involved themselves in teacher training and curriculum development. As CEMREL's interest in arts education and the Kennedy Center's mandate coincided, a collaboration was established between them. In 1976 the National Aesthetic Education Learning Center (NAELC) was opened at the Kennedy Center. From it a model for collaborative programming by educational institutions and arts centers evolved. Twenty years ago the large centralized performing arts center was all but unknown in the United States; today, according to NAELC, many exist.

In New York City, Lincoln Center has developed a somewhat different program. The Lincoln Center Institute is responsible for bringing children to performances and for taking artists into the schools. In addition numerous teacher and student workshops in all of the performing arts supplement and enrich the program.

Each different in inception and program are the Children's Theatre Company and School (CTC) in Minneapolis, Minnesota; the Empire State Institute for the Performing Arts (ESIPA) in Albany, New York; and the Nashville Academy Theatre in Nashville, Tennessee. Though already well-known for its artistry and innovative approach, the Children's Theatre Company and School burst on the scene nationally with the August 1982 issue of the *Smithsonian*. Beautiful color photographs of productions and a description of its program told the story of a successful community institution. Founded in 1961 in humble surroundings, it is now housed in a splendid theatre complex designed especially for children. The building was officially opened in 1974 and today operates both a theatre and a school for children and young adults.

The Empire State Institute for the Performing Arts, officially established in 1974, was the first state-mandated theatre for young people in the United States. It is housed in the "Egg," an imaginative structure in which a series of plays and concerts is offered each season. In addition, and of equal importance, is an extensive touring schedule and teacher education program, including the training of interns.

The Nashville Academy Theatre, on the other hand, has served that city for over fifty years. Its growth and success led to the establishment of a fully accredited theatre school in 1970, in which members of the company teach classes on all age levels. Performances in the theatre, a touring program, and numerous appearances abroad distinguish its work and make it a model for other communities.

A quite unusual center also deserving of mention is the O'Neill Memorial Theatre Center in Waterford, Connecticut. Best known for its Theatre of the Deaf and its Playwrights' Conferences, the O'Neill Center is involved in numerous other programs. The following is a summary of its major areas of activity:

Ensuring that New Voices Are Heard
  National Playwrights' Conference
  Second Step Program
  The O'Neill Playwrights
  Playwrights Catalogue

Developing New Forms and Uses
  National Theatre of the Deaf
  Creative Arts in Education

Training a New Generation
  National Theatre Institute
  Professional School for Deaf Theatre Personnel

Raising the Standards of Appreciation and Judgment
  National Critics Institute
  Children's Theatre Conferences

Reaching Out to Young Audiences
  Showboat
  Little Theatre of the Deaf
  Summer Theatre Camp

Preserving a Heritage
   Eugene O'Neill Theatre Museum
   American Theatre Treasury Recollection Series

Learning About Learning is an educational foundation for research, development, and training at Trinity University in San Antonio, Texas. Established in 1971 as a program for children, it has grown and gained prominence as a resource center for teachers, parents, and community organizations. Books, films, and a variety of attractive curricular materials are available from the foundation, while special interest and after-school workshops are regularly offered for children and adults. Learning About Learning, in meeting area needs, has grown in a special way, different from the other centers cited, and has gained national prominence and prestige.

On the West Coast, the Civic Conservatory of Theatre Arts San Diego Junior Theatre offers instruction for young people from eight to eighteen, in addition to giving five productions a year. Under the sponsorship of the city's Recreation and Parks Department, this thirty-five-year-old institution is among the nation's oldest and largest centers of its kind. It began as a summer project, but its popularity led to a year-round program, a large paid staff, and a home of its own. An estimated 1,500 children and teenagers attend classes which, added to audiences, are reported to total around 35,000 persons served each year.

Although only in its fourth year, the Performing Arts Council Music Center of Los Angeles County has achieved national recognition with its extensive and progressive programs. Best known are:

The Holiday Festival, an annual event in which 16,000 children participate in music, dance, mime, and drama and take part in a performance at the Music Center.

The Very Special Arts Festival, a day-long festival in which handicapped and special education children participate in performing arts workshops, meet film and television actors, display their work, and view performances by special education students.

Music Center on Tour features a roster of twenty artists and performing groups who, during the 1982–83 season, planned 650 performances in a tour of 70 cities.

Workshops for Teachers are held on Saturday mornings at the Music Center. They are offered in a variety of disciplines including drama/theatre techniques and mime.

The Summer Institute for Educators is a three-week period of study offered to teachers and administrators. Learning about different arts includes spending time at various cultural institutions throughout Los Angeles County as well as the Music Center.

The Bravo Award is the newest addition to the program. It applauds educators for their outstanding achievement in arts education.

Attractive brochures describe the various activities held in the Mark Taper Forum, the Music Center, the Ahmanson Theatre, public schools, and local community centers.

Fees are minimal for the programs sponsored by the Performing Arts Council, and some activities and events are free. This unusual structure involves children and adults, school and community, nonprofessional and professional artists, and is an example of the trend toward cooperative, collaborative enterprises. While it is obvious that a large city like Los Angeles is better equipped to launch a comprehensive program of this sort than a small town, it represents a type of organization that seems to be gaining ground and financial support in a number of places. Given continued interest and available artists and locations for activities, we may see more such programs in the future. Certainly, if school budgets suffer further cuts, community programs may be the means whereby youth and the arts are brought together until the time when the arts are again included in the public school curriculum.

Other arts center programs could be described, but these are cited because of the magnitude of their operations, their special services to the community, or the imaginative design of their structure. What is interesting to note is the fact that theatre and education are at last coming together. Today workshops and classes emphasize creative drama and improvisation rather than the production of plays. Encouraging as all of this is, however, there is cause for concern. Funds for the arts at the time of this writing are being cut on all sides, with "back to basics" as the slogan of the day. Of equal concern is the sense of discouragement that prevails. With budget cuts, curtailment of funding programs, and staff reduction, schools and community centers are finding it increasingly difficult to maintain quality programs. It is to be hoped that they may weather these difficult times so as not to lose the remarkable progress that has been made.

Arts centers and educational institutions have special skills and competencies and by working together they can achieve their desired goal of better education in the arts. The arts center has access to the finest performers, contacts in the community, and often special funds at its disposal, whereas the schools and universities have other kinds of resources that complement it. Teacher workshops and seminars were instituted by the arts centers in response to the need of educators to learn more about the arts in order to use the materials that were prepared for them. It is to be hoped that these imaginative programs will not be lost during a temporary period of recession.

One way in which some communities are finding support for the arts is through forming a consortium. The consortium is a group of local organizations that band together in order to pool their resources and approach funding agencies cooperatively. This unified effort is often far more successful than the efforts of a single organization struggling alone toward the same goal.

Young Audiences, Inc.

An organization that does not fit any of the above categories but has been a help and source of inspiration to many communities is Young Audiences, Inc. Founded in 1952 as a national nonprofit organization, it has as its stated purpose to enhance the education and, in doing so, the quality of life for young people by introducing them to the performing arts. In order to achieve this purpose, Young Audiences sponsors professional musicians, dancers, and actors, who present programs in public and private schools. Students learn about the creative process directly from the performers. In 1983, thirty years after its founding, Young Audiences had 38 local chapters throughout the United States with 2,800 professional artists participating. Over 6,000 workshops and 12,000 performances annually were reported with the totals rising. Although music has been emphasized, drama/theatre is included in the offerings, and it is hoped that these offerings will grow as the organization continues to expand. Young Audiences offers:

> *Programs for Students:* Young Audiences offers performances and demonstrations in primary and secondary schools. Workshop and residency programs are also offered to teach students about the arts in a series of presentations, conducted over a longer period of time.

> *Programs for the Education Community:* Young Audiences advocates arts education in education systems of the local, regional, state, and national levels. It encourages the integration of the arts into the training of teachers, as well as students.

> *Programs for Artists:* Young Audiences designs its programs and trains its artists to meet the educational and cultural needs of the individual communities it serves. It provides—and sustains—career opportunities for performing artists.

> *Programs for Growth:* Young Audiences works to expand its representation throughout the United States. It is committed to strengthening affiliations among the [38] chapters in its national network. Young Audiences researches techniques for developing arts education programs and distributes the published results to professionals in the field of arts education.[8]

8. Young Audiences, Inc., brochure, 1982.

One of the benefits of a high quality performance is the stimulation it has on students' own creative work. When the teacher makes use of the excitement engendered by the artist, the results are often imaginative and strong. On occasion when performers come into the classroom, another point is made: that art can be created and enjoyed anywhere; it is not confined to the concert hall. Young children have no problem with this. It is only the adult who thinks in terms of auditoriums, lights, curtains, etc. All of which brings up a point rarely made: that drama is the least expensive of all the arts to implement. It requires no elaborate equipment and no special materials. A room, a leader, and a group of children are all that are needed. A piano and tape recorder are useful but not necessary. Nor is stage lighting, though it adds atmosphere, if it is available. Costumes and props can be supplied by teacher and students, but they act as stimuli rather than as dressing for players or stage. Education of the leader *is* important, however; but the many classes and workshops that are available today in most communities make it relatively easy for the interested teacher to find the help she needs. Pointing out the fact that creative drama is not the production of plays, and therefore does not require a theatre, rules out the first objection of an administration that says "drama is too expensive."

Research

In reviewing the achievements and new directions of drama and theatre in America, I am reminded of a statement made by Professor Judith Kase-Polisini of the University of South Florida at the ATA convention in 1981. She described the leaders of the three periods through which creative drama has passed and is presently engaged as being the *pioneers,* the *practitioners,* and the *researchers.* We are today indeed engaged in a variety of research projects having to do with testing the effectiveness of our work, its impact on learning in other subject areas, and the changes in social attitudes as the result of experience in drama. Some of the research is being done by doctoral students; some, under the auspices of government agencies or universities with government grants. Money is needed for projects of any size extending over a period of time, however; and the reality is that such monies are today in increasingly short supply. One of the largest and possibly the last of the large grants in the foreseeable future was given to the Arts Council of Tampa-Hillsborough County and the University of South Florida department of arts education. Under this grant Professor Kase-Polisini, project director, recently completed two years of work evaluating a school-system-wide Artist-in-Schools program. Included for testing were theatre, dance, music, architecture, sculpture, photography, filmmaking, creative writing, and poetry. The theatre component was one of the largest tested and received over one-fourth of the $150,000 budget. The report included 1,000 on-site observations and interviews; findings were

Alice in Wonderland production by the Children's Theatre Company and School of Minneapolis. (*Photograph by George Heinrich.*)

not available at the time of this writing but will soon be published. A special research portion of the project focused on creative drama (Artist-in-Schools program) and revealed new information to support previous findings that creative drama is a valuable inclusion in the elementary school curriculum.[9]

9. "Florida Survey Studies School Arts Activities," *Theatre News* 14, no. 9 (December 1982): 16.

Most of the changes that have taken place in drama/theatre education are heartening. The greatest challenges we face in the next few years may be finding the monies to finance these programs and overcoming the discouragement that prevails regarding employment. The programs that the pioneers envisioned, the practitioners have created, and the researchers are finding viable and of value are in jeopardy; it is up to us to discover new ways to support and preserve them.

I believe that a third challenge has grown out of our own zeal to make drama/theatre meaningful: to preserve the *fun* of theatre (a word chosen consciously and with care). In our effort to enrich education through drama, and to sponsor theatre with greater substance than it has had in the past, we sometimes lose sight of the *fun* that it brings to our lives. We who have worked to improve the quality of dramatic literature and performance skills risk losing the spirit with which the best theatre is endowed. Fun in this sense is not to be confused with the trivial and banal, or with poorly presented camp; rather, fun may be the joy that comes from creating drama or from watching superb performers in vehicles that may or may not be concerned with a serious subject matter. Not that we should settle for mediocrity; on the contrary, we must continue to strive for excellence but to remember that the spirit is of the utmost importance and fun is a part of it. A good season of children's theatre will contain a variety of plays, including both serious and amusing subject matter, produced equally well. A good class in creative drama will use varied material appropriate to the age, experience, and interests of the children.

The Teacher or Leader

With so much concern for the future of creative drama, is it not appropriate to raise some questions regarding the teacher? What special qualifications should he have? What kind of education best prepares a person to teach creative drama at this point in time? Is a pure theatrical background a disadvantage? Is a workshop experience sufficient preparation? Dare the teacher embark on a program without some specialized training? Is certification necessary?

Without discrediting academic preparation, what seems most important to me are those personal attributes that make him a good teacher. If a person already possesses the qualities of sympathetic leadership, imagination, and respect for the ideas of others, he has the basic requirements. Sensitivity to the individuals in a class is necessary to an activity that is participant centered, with the growth of each child an objective. In other words, although he is teaching an art and should therefore have some knowledge and appreciation of it as a form, a genuine concern for the players is of equal importance.

The successful creative drama teacher guides rather than directs. She is able to work with others, offering and accepting ideas. To her, sharing is more

Creating statues. (*Courtesy of Kelsey E. Collie, Howard University.*)

important than showing; thus her satisfaction will come through the process as well as from the product. When she does show the work of her group, she will be clear as to what is demonstration and what is performance. Unless she is working with groups over the age of ten or eleven, she will avoid the latter, in favor of informal class demonstrations.

The teacher of creative drama finds her own way. No methods courses can prepare her perfectly, for no two groups are alike. What works well with one class does not work with another. Materials and methods that arouse a response in one group may be totally inadequate in a second, whose cultural background, age, and experiences are different. Knowledge of the neighborhood in which she is working is just as important as a knowledge of literature and drama. She must find out for herself what stimulates and what fails to elicit a response. Familiarity with techniques is an invaluable asset, but the imaginative leader will, in the end, create her own methods.

A sense of humor helps him over those periods when nothing goes right. His ability to laugh with the group, as well as at himself, enables him to carry on, in spite of failures and frustrations. Because he is interested in all kinds of things, he will have an expanding background of information on which to draw. He learns constantly from his pupils. He must also learn not to expect good results each time the class meets. Many efforts will be pedestrian and disappointing, but, as Hughes Mearns points out: "Those who work with children creatively are compelled to discard or ignore a hundred attempts while they are getting a mere half-dozen good ones."[10] It is these "good ones" that inspire others and encourage the leader to keep on trying.

He maintains high standards, knowing that what he accepts in the beginning is what the group is capable of at the time, but that he can expect more from them later. By establishing an atmosphere in which all feel important, he will challenge his class to give only their best; the teacher waits for this, without demanding or pushing. For this reason, it is more difficult to teach creative drama than formal theatre. The absence of a basic structure, or script, demands flexibility, judgment, a willingness to accept the efforts of the shy and inarticulate, patience, and the confidence that something of value is eventually forthcoming. This is not easy for the teacher whose only previous experience has been with the formal play or whose theatre background has conditioned him to expect technically perfect results within a stipulated period of time.

The teacher must, at the same time, set limits. The establishment of boundaries does not limit freedom but, rather, gives a sense of security to the young or inexperienced player. As in any class, discipline must be maintained at all times in order to ensure, for each member, the freedom to experiment. In his book *Child Drama*, Peter Slade has observed that "The manner of handling is what matters, and, because of this, some of the best work with children is done by experienced teachers who really understand what they are doing and yet, strangely enough, have very little knowledge of drama."[11]

All of this is not meant to imply that specialized training is unnecessary; what is meant is that the successful teacher of creative drama seems to possess certain attitudes and qualities of personality that distinguish and qualify her. A

10. Hughes Mearns, *Creative Power* (New York: Dover Publications, 1958), p. 33.
11. Peter Slade, *Child Drama* (London: University of London Press, 1954), p. 271.

background that includes both education and theatre is ideal, but the interested leader, whatever her preparation, may acquire, through course work and reading, additional information and techniques. Some knowledge of music and dance is invaluable and should be part of the teacher's preparation. Classroom teachers, professional actors, and social workers have all achieved notable results in creative drama with children. Because of their belief that creative drama has a contribution to make, they have adapted their own individual skills to its use, with intelligence and imagination.

Finally, a successful creative drama leader keeps abreast of the times. The world is changing rapidly. With constant exposure to television, children and adults have access to the same information. Children are no longer excluded from discussion of subjects once considered inappropriate or taboo. In his book *The Disappearance of Childhood*, Neil Postman documents the ways in which modern technology has destroyed the boundaries separating the world of the child from the world of the adult. This has important implications for the teacher, both generalist and specialist. For us to assume, however, that children today "know more" than children of previous generations, is a facile and easy assumption. They no longer inhabit a protected environment, but this does not mean they have a mature understanding of complex social, psychological, and political issues. What it does suggest is that the teacher must be prepared for a variety of new subjects and problems to come up, and he must be ready and able to handle them. Children today are bombarded with sex, violence, and news of crime in high places; many of them experience divorce, drugs, alcoholism, and death in their own homes or neighborhoods. Often they suggest situations dealing with these topics for improvisation. This is where the teacher must be able to accept wht is offered and help the group deal with it. Through drama, some understanding may be reached and relevant information given. It means a greater openness on our part than has been expected of us in the past, and this presents both difficulties and rewards.

Summary

In conclusion, creative drama may be viewed as an art form, a way of learning, a means of self-expression, a leisure time activity, or a therapeutic tool. In each instance, learnings include self-knowledge, knowledge of others, information acquired through the process of drama, and aesthetic appreciation.

Self-Knowledge

Through drama, the player thinks, plans, and organizes. He feels deeply but learns to channel and control his emotions. His communication skills are involved as he speaks and expresses his ideas. Through rhythms and physical movement, he makes use of his body. Working with others teaches him the meaning of cooperation. He comes to understand his own strengths and weaknesses. Benedetti calls acting self-extension rather than self-expression, which describes in a word what we are talking about.

Knowledge of Others

By trying on characters, the player learns about other people. Acting a variety of parts helps her to think and feel like persons different from herself. Being part of a group not only teaches her something of teamwork but sensitizes her to the feelings of those with whom she is working. And, finally, through the material the teacher brings in and that brought in by her classmates, she is exposed to other people's customs, to ideas and values that may be foreign to her own.

Intellectual Development

Play has long been recognized by nursery educators as experimentation that offers unlimited possibilities for learning. Jean Piaget has written extensively on the function of play in the intellectual development of young children. He sees conceptual thinking as originating in spontaneous play through manipulation of objects and social collaboration with other children. Recent research indicates that an appropriate balance between spontaneous and more structured play is desirable.[12] No activity provides a greater variety of opportunities for learning than creative drama, regardless of the level.

Aesthetic Appreciation

The most difficult aspect to assess is aesthetic appreciation. Although it is obvious that the child who has been taken to museums, concerts, and theatres will have the advantage of knowledge as to the nature of these art forms, what meanings they hold for him may not be immediately evident. Research reveals learnings but cannot measure the extent of appreciation. Nevertheless, one can observe involvement through the attention and behavior of children in an audience. Those who are exposed to the best tend to be more deeply engaged, often paint pictures of the experience afterward, speak of it, or use it in creative drama classes as a springboard to further exploration. Erwin Edman describes the aesthetic experience as "reinstating the emotions, clarifying experience, interpreting life and giving pleasure."[13] In an ordered society these opportunities can and should be accessible to all children, regardless of intellectual, social, physical, cultural, or economic differences.

Peter Slade capitalizes the word *Joy* in writing of child drama. This is an

12. Millie Almay, "Spontaneous Play: An Avenue for Intellectual Development"; reprint from the *Bulletin of the Institute of Child Study* 28, no. 2 (University of Toronto, 1966).

13. Erwin Edman, *Arts and the Man* (New York: The New American Library, 1950), p. 25.

emotion we may be overlooking rather than emphasizing in our concern for substance and the social experience a group activity provides. Joy, however, implies another dimension, for it reaches a deeper level of consciousness than enjoyment or fun in providing an ultimate human fulfillment. Let us not forget joy.

Recent research indicates that there may be an important connection between the arts and learning. Dr. Jean Houston, director of the Foundation for Mind Research in Pomona, New York, has produced some new and challenging questions in the past few years. She goes beyond the integration of subject matter into methods of enhancing concentration and freedom from distraction. She advocates a holistic approach to education; in other words, if a start is made from a deep aesthetic base, everything related to the subject at hand can be learned more quickly, easily, and thoroughly. A richer sensory perception, kinesthetic thinking, and the use of rhythms and movement to facilitate learning form an important part of her theory.

Her workshops in discovering latent human capacities are being offered to teachers on elementary and secondary school levels, to religious leaders, and to social workers. Dr. Houston's goal is a fuller development of the human being, and she is convinced of the important role the arts play in this.

Conclusion

A basic requirement of any activity is that it be a satisfying experience for both leader and group. The more successful the project, the greater the degree of satisfaction. As the leader grows in experience, he will recognize the possibilities in a variety of materials and methods, and his group will likewise grow in security and the ability to tackle problems more imaginatively. This is true of the creative drama leader and her group on any age level, whether in a school or recreational setting.

Through the spread of our mass media, we have become known as a "spectator society." Our lives have become increasingly programmed and our experiences packaged. Participation in any of the arts is, therefore, more needed today than at any other period in our history. Drama, of all the arts, demands of the practitioner a total involvement. By offering an opportunity for participation in drama, we are helping to reserve something of the play impulse in all of its joy, freedom, and order.

Educational and social goals are closely related in drama; therefore a climate in which the player feels good about him or herself and others is conducive to learning. At a time when the questions of peace and survival concern us deeply, drama can serve a two-fold purpose in the lives of children: it offers an opportunity to learn more about others, including the values and customs of different racial and ethnic groups, and a place where fears of nuclear war and destruction (often unvoiced) may be relieved and examined. This is not to suggest that drama is a panacea for the world's ills but it has the power to bring people together through cooperative endeavors and mutual understanding. Although the word *child* is used throughout this text, the basic principles apply to all ages, and the concept of a warm and supportive environment as a positive influence is applicable everywhere. It is this kind of environment that we should try to create, an environment in which all persons can grow. Robert Benedetti, in a text written for the adult actor, puts it most succinctly when he says, "Acting is neither seeming nor being; it is becoming."[14]

14. Robert Benedetti, *Seeming, Being and Becoming* (New York: Drama Book Specialists, 1976), p. 87.

A Selected
Bibliography

Creative Drama

Barnfield, Gabriel. *Creative Drama in Schools*. New York: Macmillan, 1971.
A British publication with an emphasis on the secondary school. It gives
ideas that the author has used and found successful. He begins with
movement and rhythm and dance, and describes the use of music as a
technique for encouraging imagination.

Barrager, Pamela. *Spiritual Understanding through Creative Drama*. Valley
Forge: Judson Press, 1981.
An up-to-date text on the use and values of creative drama in religious
education. Written by an experienced teacher and well-known authority
in the field.

Bolton, Reg. *Circus in a Suitcase*. Rowayton, Conn.: New Plays, 1982.
This is a clear and delightful presentation of teaching circus skills to young
people. The author is an English clown and a certified teacher with years
of experience in clowning with and for amateurs. Highly recommended
and the only book of its kind in the field for children and young people.

Burger, Isabel B. *Creative Drama in Religious Education*. Wilton, Conn.:
Morehouse-Barlow, 1976.
One of the few books on the use of creative dramatics in religious
education. Mrs. Burger's years of successful teaching make this a practical
and authoritative text for leaders in this field.

Byers, Ruth. *Creating Theatre*. San Antonio: Trinity University, 1968.
This is a handsome book with a focus on a creative approach to playwriting with children and teenagers. Pantomime and improvisation lead to
exercises in writing. Many beautiful photographs and nine scripts illustrate the work done in classes under the guidance of the author, who is
director of the Teen-Children's Theatre and assistant professor of drama at
Baylor University in the Dallas Theatre Center.

Chambers, Dewey W. *Storytelling and Creative Drama*. Dubuque, Iowa: William C. Brown, 1970.

This is an invaluable little book for the teacher, librarian, or group leader who wants to learn something of the ancient art of storytelling. Clear and succinct, it guides selection of material and offers simple techniques for effective presentation.

Cheifitz, Dan. *Theatre in My Head*. Boston: Little, Brown, 1971.

This book describes an experimental workshop in creative drama conducted by the author in an inner-city New York church. Cheifitz communicates the need to look *into* the child, not merely *at* him, as he reports the successes and failures he met.

Crosscup, Richard. *Children and Dramatics*. New York: Scribner's, 1966.

Mr. Crosscup's book is an autobiographical account of his twenty-seven years' experience in one school. Of greatest value is the view he gives of a gifted teacher, able to stimulate the creativity of his pupils. Social values are stressed.

Ehrlich, Harriett, and Patricia Grastry. *Creative Dramatics Handbook*. Philadelphia: School District of Philadelphia Instructional Services, 1971.

This handbook offers a wealth of ideas for the teacher wishing to include creative drama in the curriculum. Since the material grew directly from the authors' experiences, it is fresh and practical.

Fitzgerald, Burdette. *World Tales for Creative Dramatics and Storytelling*. New York: Prentice-Hall, 1962.

In this book the author introduces a wide variety of stories not usually found in collections of this sort. She has drawn from the folklore of countries rarely represented in anthologies of children's literature, thus making an interesting contribution to the field.

Hagga, Agnes, and Patricia Randles. *Supplementary Material for Use in Creative Dramatics with Younger Children*. Seattle: University of Washington, 1952.

This outline of lessons, planned and evaluated by the authors, is of great practical value to teachers of younger children. It is unique in describing the activities of each session in detail, the music and literature used, and the children's reactions.

Haggerty, Joan. *Please Can I Play God?* Indianapolis: Bobbs-Merrill, 1967.

Mrs. Haggerty's book tells of her first teaching experience in a ghetto school in London. Throughout her account, which is both amusing and touching, runs her concern for these disadvantaged children as she guides them in creative dramatic activities. It is not a textbook but a sympathetic account of a beginning teacher's classroom experiences.

Heinig, Ruth. *Creative Drama for the Classroom Teacher*. Englewood Cliffs, N.J.: Prentice-Hall, 1981.

This is a second edition of a text originally written by two experienced teachers but this time by one, who is well known in the field. Pantomime, improvisation, songs, and games are among the activities suggested. They are arranged so as to guide the classroom teacher through simple to more advanced techniques, and each chapter has suggestions and assignments for the college student.

Hodgson, John, and Ernest Richards. *Improvisation*. London: Methuen, 1967. This book on improvisation is not directed exclusively to work with children. The aim is to utilize two elements from everyday life: spontaneous response to unexpected situations and the employment of this response in controlled conditions. Exercises are given.

Kase, Robert. *Stories for Creative Acting*. New York: Samuel French, 1961. Professor Kase has collected stories recommended to him by experts in the field. All the stories have been used with success, thus making this a valuable addition to any teacher's library.

Keysell, Pat. *Motives for Mime*. London: Evans, 1975. This little paperback is divided into three parts: the first deals with beginning activities for children from five to seven; the second, with development for the seven- to nine-year-olds; and the third, application for those aged nine to twelve. Starting with real objects, the author progresses to mime. She works for awareness of size, weight, shape, and the use of space. Although the material is organized according to age levels, it also follows a logical progression from simple to complicated and is, therefore, a useful text on any level.

Kraus, Joanna Halpert. *Sound and Motion Stories*. Rowayton, Conn.: New Plays, 1971. Although not a textbook, the way in which sounds and actions can be used to capture attention to stimulate the imagination of younger children qualifies it for inclusion in this bibliography. The reader can learn from the author's suggestions how to use other material in this way.

McCaslin, Nellie. *Children and Drama*. 2nd edition. New York: Longman, 1981. This is a collection of essays on creative drama written by twenty different experts in the field. A variety of viewpoints are represented and different methodologies suggested. It is of greater interest to the experienced teacher than to the beginner.

Nobleman, Roberta. *Using Creative Drama Outside the Classroom*. Rowayton, Conn.: New Plays, 1974. In this book the author tells how creative drama may be taught successfully in nontraditional spaces and places. As valuable, however, for the teacher as for the leader in community and camp situations.

Pereira, Nancy. *Creative Dramatics in the Library*. Rowayton, Conn.: New Plays, 1974. While the content is not substantially different from other books on the subject, the consideration of the neighborhood library as a location for dramatic activities is. The author offers suggestions for starting points, games, use of time and space, and handling of groups, visual aids, and culminating activities.

Polsky, Milton. *Let's Improvise*. Englewood Cliffs, N.J.: Prentice-Hall, 1980.
A text crammed with good ideas for improvisation on every age level and level of experience.

Schwartz, Dorothy, and Dorothy Aldrich, eds. *Give Them Roots and Wings*. Washington, D.C.: American Theatre Association, 1972.
This is a guide to drama in the elementary shool, prepared by leaders in the field and edited by Dorothy Schwartz and Dorothy Aldrich as co-chairmen of a project for the Children's Theatre Association. Published in workbook form, it offers the classroom teacher goals and dramatic activities with checklists for rating children's development. Usable and attractively illustrated.

Siks, Geraldine Brain. *Children's Literature for Dramatization*. New York: Harper & Row, 1964.
This is a collection of stories and poems, old and new, for the classroom teacher and group leader. The introductions to the stories make the book particularly valuable to less experienced teachers, but it is useful to anyone working in the field.

Siks, Geraldine Brain. *Drama with Children*. 2nd ed. New York: Harper & Row, 1983.
This latest book by a well-known creative drama leader and author of other texts in the field is of particular interest to the more experienced teacher or graduate student. It is divided into three parts: the philosophy, the teaching of drama, and individual experiences and uses of drama. In this new edition the author expands on what she calls the "process-concept structure approach," and includes a selected bibliography and a few short plays.

Slade, Peter. *Child Drama*. London: University of London, 1954.
Written by an expert in children's dramatics in England, this lengthy book presents a philosophy and way of working. It is detailed and informative and should be of interest to all leaders and teachers of creative dramatics. The author takes an unequivocal stand against children in public performances.

Slade, Peter. *An Introduction to Child Drama*. London and Toronto: Hodder and Stoughton, 1976.
All the fundamental principles of Slade's methods are here. Children, if unhampered by adult imposition, can find self-expression and reach toward full human development. It is simply written, short, and to the point. Highly recommended for the beginner.

Spolin, Viola. *Improvisation for the Theatre*. Evanston: Northwestern University, 1963.

> This is a comprehensive handbook of teaching and directing techniques, not specifically designed for use with children, but nevertheless appropriate and useful to the more experienced teacher. It contains a variety of exercises and theatre games.

Van Tassel, Katrina, and Millie Greimann. *Creative Dramatization*. New York: Threshold Division, Macmillan, 1973.

> Here is a book with special value for the teacher of very young children. Based on sound educational principles, it is a guidebook for the stimulation of creativity through music, mime, movement, and language arts. It is clearly written and presented in an attractive format. Illustrated. Highly recommended.

Wagner, Jearnine, and Kitty Baker. *A Place for Ideas: Our Theatre*. Rev. ed. New Orleans: Anchorage, 1978.

> This is a unique book in that it describes with appreciation and beauty the theatre in which the authors work. It is not a children's theatre in the usual sense but rather a "place for ideas," where the arts can be explored and experienced. Illustrations show children experimenting with color, movement, and music, as well as creative drama. This is less a textbook than an inspiration to others who work with children in the arts.

Ward, Winifred. *Playmaking with Children*. New York: Appleton-Century-Crofts, 1957.

> This book by a distinguished leader is a landmark text. It is arranged both as to age levels and use, including dramatics in school, recreation, religious education, and therapy. Highly readable, it is valuable both for the beginning and the experienced teacher.

Ward, Winifred. *Stories to Dramatize*. Anchorage, Ky.: Anchorage, 1952.

> In this collection, the author includes a rich variety of stories and some poems for use in school and recreation groups. It is arranged for children on various age levels (from six to fourteen) and contains material that the author tested and found rewarding in her many years of teaching.

Way, Brian. *Development through Drama*. New York: Humanities, 1972.

> The development of the whole child is the thesis of this book, directed particularly to teachers of older children. Many practical exercises in improvisational drama are included. Highly recommended.

Wilder, Rosilyn. *A Space Where Anything Can Happen*. Rowayton, Conn.: New Plays, 1977.

> The author brings a wealth of experience to this text, directed to the teacher of older children. Challenges, projects, descriptions of her own classes and students, discipline, and clear guidelines for leading modern youngsters in creative work are the most valuable aspects.

Drama for the Special Child

Creative Dramatics. Washington, D.C.: American Alliance for Health, Physical
Education, and Recreation, 1977.
> Creative drama with handicapped and nonhandicapped children and
> adults is described. Games, activities, story drama, and role playing are
> included for the purpose of expressing one's own feelings and helping
> one to work cooperatively with others.

The Eagle Soars: The Artist, the Teacher, and the Handicapped. Chappaqua,
N.Y.: New York State Poets in the Schools, 1977.
> Activities used in an interdisciplinary arts program with both moderately
> and severely handicapped students are described. Objectives, proce-
> dures, and lesson plans are included.

Gillies, Emily P. *Creative Dramatics for All Children*. Washington, D.C.: Association for Childhood Education International, 1973.
> Mrs. Gillies, whose years of experience qualify her to speak authorita-
> tively, discusses drama for the emotionally disturbed and physically
> handicapped child, as well as its use in the education of children for whom
> English is a second language.

Jennings, Sue. *Remedial Drama*. New York: Theatre Arts, 1974.
> The message in this book is that the experience of drama can enrich
> everyone's life, whether one is mentally or physically handicapped, or
> socially disadvantaged. For nonspecialists. It is clear and easy to read and
> will help the teacher to work with the therapist.

McIntyre, Barbara. *Informal Dramatics: A Language Arts Activity for the Special
Child*. Pittsburgh: Stanwix, 1963.
> This book is a useful guide for teachers of special education and is one of
> the first directed toward this new area.

*Materials on Creative Arts (Arts, Crafts, Dance, Drama, and Music) for Persons
with Handicapping Conditions*. Washington, D.C.: American Alliance for
Health, Physical Education, and Recreation, 1975.
> This guide provides information on resources for use in the arts for
> persons with various handicapping conditions. It suggests activities,
> guidelines, and implications for programming in art, crafts, dance, drama,
> and music; materials, references, and suppliers of equipment add to the
> usefulness.

Prokes, Sr. Dorothy. "Exploring the Relationship between Participation in
Creative Dramatics and Development of the Imaginative Capacities of Gifted
Junior High School Students." Ph.D. dissertation, New York University, 1971.
> This is one of the few studies made in the field of the arts for the gifted
> child and is unique in its focus on creative dramatics. The study is available
> in microfilm and at the New York University Library.

Schattner, Gertrud, and Richard Courtney. *Drama in Therapy*. Vol. 1. New

York: Drama Book Specialists, 1979. Vol. 2. New York: Drama Book Specialists, 1979.

> The editors have collected and assembled two volumes of essays written by a large group of experts in a variety of specialized areas. The first books of their kind, *Drama in Therapy* should be of enormous interest and value to teacher and student, as well as to specialist and generalist in drama education.

Shaw, Ann M., and Cj Stevens. *Drama, Theatre and the Handicapped.* Washington, D.C.: American Theatre Association, 1979.

> This collection of articles is the work of a committee of the American Theatre Association, funded under a Special Project Program Grant of the National Committee: Arts for the Handicapped, and chaired by the editors. Contributors are experienced in their respective areas and address themselves to the potential of the arts for handicapped persons, the removal of barriers, programs that have already been established, and a review of the existing literature. This is recommended reading for all teachers and recreation leaders.

Shaw, Ann M., Wendy Perks and Cj Stevens, eds. *Perspectives: A Handbook in Drama and Theatre by, with and for Handicapped Individuals.* Washington, D.C.: American Theatre Association, 1981.

> An invaluable handbook for persons working with the handicapped. Developed by a committee of the American Theatre Association with support from the National Committee: Arts for the Handicapped, it includes articles and plans from eighteen contributors in all areas: the blind, deaf, retarded, emotionally disturbed, elderly, etc. Although each contributor has a point of view, the collection is practical rather than theoretical. Exercises and resources include proposal and grant writing.

Simos, Jack. *Social Growth through Play Production.* New York: Association Press, 1957.

> The author is a social worker who describes the step-by-step process of producing plays with emotionally disturbed children in a treatment center. Although he deals with teenagers in this book, his observations and techniques are useful on any age level.

Wethered, Audrey G. *Drama and Movement in Therapy.* London: Macdonald and Evans, 1973.

> The therapeutic use of movement, mime, and drama are covered in this short text. It is simple, clear, and should be useful to both nonspecialist and specialist.

Education and the Arts

Allen, John. *Drama in Schools: Its Theory and Practice.* London: Heinemann Educational Books, 1979.

The author of this book is both well known and well qualified to write on drama education. After a brief history of the subject in England, he proceeds to discuss current practices and to take a strong stand on a number of controversial issues. This should be required reading for every specialist and recommended for the generalist.

Baker, Donald. *Understanding the Under Fives*. London: Evans, 1975.
The author combines background and expertise in early childhood education as well as theatre and drama education. It is a unique, practical, and highly readable text.

Behrn, Snyder, and Clopton. *Drama Integrates Basic Skills: Lesson Plans for the Learning Disabled*. Springfield, Ill: Charles C Thomas, 1979.
The material in this book is based on the authors' work at the Kingsbury Laboratory School (for learning disabled children) in Washington, D.C. They present a convincing argument for a drama curriculum to help integrate basic affective and cognitive skills. These include behavioral sensory, motor, verbal, and conceptual skills. This is a practical and unique text for any teacher.

Bolton, Gavin. *Toward a Theory of Drama in Education*. London: Longman, 1979.
Written by one of England's outstanding drama educators, this is a theoretical treatment of the subject. It is of greatest interest to the specialist or experienced classroom teacher.

Cullum, Albert. *Aesop in the Afternoon*. New York: Citation, 1972.
This is a most usable collection of Aesop's fables, which can be played creatively by children of all ages.

Cullum, Albert. *Push Back the Desks*. New York: Citation, 1967.
The author has written an account of some creative projects and techniques he has used in the public school classroom to enhance learning. History, reading, vocabulary, and math are included units of study.

Cullum, Albert. *Shake Hands with Shakespeare*. New York: Citation, 1968.
Eight of Shakespeare's plays are adapted for children. The results are filled with action and are relatively simple to produce. They do require time to prepare but could also be improvised, if desired. The value of using Shakespeare is the richness of the language and is a further recommendation for this text.

Courtney, Richard. *Play, Drama and Thought*. New York: Drama Book Specialists, 1974.
There are many useful sections in this British publication directed toward the philosophy and practice of drama in the school.

Courtney, Richard. *Re-Play: Studies of Human Drama in Education*. Toronto: Ontario Institute for Studies in Education, 1982.
The author deals with the process of education as spontaneous drama. He begins by examining developmental drama and proceeds to the drama of

learning. A rationale for including the arts in education is provided. Detailed and theoretical rather than practical.

Dodd, Nigel, and Winifred Hickson, eds. *Drama and Theatre in Education*. London: Heinemann, 1971.

This is a collection of essays by well-known British experts including Gavin Bolton, Dorothy Heathcote, Veronica Sherbourn, and others. Of interest to the more experienced leader.

Doyle, Donald P. "An Investigation of Elementary Teacher Education Related to the Preparation of Teachers in the Use of Creative Drama in Teaching Language Arts," Ph.D. dissertation, University of Minnesota, 1974.

The findings of this study advocate the use of creative drama as an aid in teaching of language arts in the elementary grades; research showed preparation inadequate and in general not required.

Green, Harriet H., and Sue Martin. *Sprouts*. Carthage, Ill.: Good Apple, 1981.

This is an amply illustrated collection of ideas for use with younger children. Highly recommended.

Hall, Mary Ann, and Pat Hale. *Capture Them with Magic*. Rowayton, Conn.: New Plays, 1982.

A wonderful and useful collection of ideas to help kindergarten and primary school teachers enliven classes in language arts and science, encourage reading, and improve self-esteem. Described by the authors as "real life" lessons, they deal with the magic of everyday experiences and activities.

Kelly, Elizabeth. *Dramatics in the Classroom: Making Lessons Come Alive*. Bloomington, Ind.: Phi Delta Kappa Educational Foundation, 1976.

This small pamphlet gives, in a nutshell, a philosophy of education as well as practical help in showing how drama can be used to teach curricular material effectively. Of greatest value to the beginning or general classroom teacher.

Landy, Robert J. *A Handbook of Educational Drama and Theatre*. Westport, Conn.: Greenwood Press, 1982.

A book based on New York University's Sunrise Semester, in which the various uses of drama and theatre currently found in schools and communities are described. The author describes interviews with experts in all the fields covered.

McGregor, Lynn, Maggie Tate, and Ken Robinson. *Learning through Drama*. London: Heinemann, 1977.

Here is another book for the specialist, particularly if he knows something about drama education in England. It represents a comprehensive survey done by three well-qualified researchers. An important contribution to the field.

Mearns, Hughes. *Creative Power*. 2nd rev. ed. New York: Dover, 1958.

This classic text by the gifted educator offers a philosophy of education in the creative arts and techniques with which to implement it. Long out of print, it was republished in paperback at the instigation of the Children's Theatre Association of America, a strong supporter of his views.

Moffett, James, and Betty Jane Wagner. *Student Centered Language Arts and Reading, K–13.* Boston: Houghton-Mifflin, 1976.

Written by two well-known educators, this book is an argument for the use of drama in language learning and comprehension.

Piaget, Jean. *Play, Dreams and Imitation in Childhood.* New York: W.W. Norton, 1962.

A study of child development in terms of systematic and representative imitation, the structure and symbolism of games and dreams, and the movement from sensory-motor schemas to conceptual schemas. A landmark book.

Shuman, R. Baird, ed. *Educational Drama for Today's Schools.* Metuchen, N.J.: Scarecrow, 1978.

This collection of articles came about as a result of workshops given in this country by Dorothy Heathcote, who has written the lead chapter. Drama in education is defined as "anything which involves persons in active role-taking situations in which attitudes, not characters, are the chief concern . . . at this moment, not memory based." Each chapter, written by a different person, deals with values clarification, language development, moral education, etc.

Stabler, Tom. *Drama in Primary Schools* (Schools Council Drama 5–11 Project). London: Macmillan Education, 1978.

This is a one-year study of forty schools in England, including infant, primary, junior, and middle schools. Objectives are clear, with material for teachers and administrators in areas of language, writing, and literature.

Stewig, John Warren. *Informal Drama in the Elementary Language Arts Program.* New York: Teachers College Press, 1983.

This text focuses on the value of drama in the development of language skills. The author deals with the various ways in which the classroom teacher can use movement and improvisation, and can evaluate sessions in terms of the language arts. Greatest value is for the generalist or classroom teacher.

Stewig, John Warren. *Teaching Language Arts in Early Childhood.* New York: Holt, Rinehart and Winston, 1980.

Although a text on language arts by a specialist in the field, drama is stressed as to its value in English teaching. The author shares his enthusiasm with readers.

Tiedt, Iris M. *Drama in Your Classroom.* Champaign, Ill.: National Council of Teachers of English, 1974.

Written by and for the teacher of English, the text advocates drama as an aid to more effective classroom teaching.

Tynas, Billi. *Child Drama in Action: A Practical Guide for Teachers.* Toronto: Gage, 1971.

This is an instructor's manual, which opens with a brief but clear introduction, then moves directly into a series of lesson plans. Each of these plans follows a theme and gives the activity to be emphasized. This very beautiful book will be of most use to teachers with a background in creative drama rather than to beginners.

Wagner, Betty Jane. *Dorothy Heathcote: Drama as a Learning Medium.* Washington, D.C.: National Education Association, 1976.

The author has done a masterful job of describing the methods of this distinguished English drama teacher. Ms. Wagner explains how Heathcote finds material, helps children build an imagined situation, and leads them to see and feel the elements of human experience. Most important, she shows how the learning takes place. It is apparent from this book why Dorothy Heathcote has so great a following among elementary school teachers.

Watson, Charles M., Editor and Project Supervisor. *Theatre Resources Directory/Handbook.* Washington, D.C.: National Endowment for the Arts, Artists in the Schools, 1980.

Movement and Dance

Barlin, Ann and Paul. *The Art of Learning Through Movement.* New York: Ritchie Ward, 1971.

The authors have had wide experience in public school teaching. They present their material clearly with enthusiasm and practicality.

Blatt, Gloria T., and Jean Cunningham. *It's Your Move.* New York: Teachers College Press, 1981.

The authors' aim is the integration of expressive movement and the language arts. Lessons in movement help the teacher in reaching language and literature.

Carr, Rachel. *See and Be: Yoga and Creative Movement for Children.* Englewood Cliffs, N.J.: Prentice-Hall, 1980.

This beautifully illustrated book shows parents and teachers ways of helping pre-school age children to develop self-awareness and confidence through yoga and creative movement.

Conner, Norma, and Harriet Klebanoff. *And a Time to Dance.* Boston: Beacon, 1967.

This is a sensitively illustrated book that explains, encourages, and shows the reader how to involve children in creative dance. Simply written, it also shows what can be done with the mentally retarded.

Dorian, Margery. *Ethnic Stories for Children to Dance.* San Mateo, Cal.: BBB, 1978.

Here is a second book by the author of *Telling Stories through Movement.*
It includes stories from around the world with suggestions for rhythmic
accompaniment on drums and other instruments. Years of experience as a
dancer and as teacher of dance give the author knowledge and insight.
The choice of material is a valuable addition to the resources available to
teachers in lower grades.

Dorian, Margery, and Frances Gulland. *Telling Stories through Movement.*
Belmont, Cal.: Fearon, 1974.

This is an invaluable little book for creative drama teachers working with
young children. The authors bring a rich background in dance, education,
and drama to the task, and the result is practical and clear. Creative
movement and rhythms are used to tell stories from many lands.

Gray, Vera, and Rachel Percival. *Music, Movement and Mime for Children.*
Oxford: Oxford University, 1962.

The emphases in this book are on music and movement, and the authors
give a good basic introduction to those planning to teach in these areas. It
is clear and concise with many exercises and procedures suggested.

King, Nancy. *The Actor and His Space.* New York: Drama Book Specialists, 1971.

This book explains the importance of movement in an actor's training.
Many exercises are given. It is probably less useful to the elementary and
secondary school teacher than the author's other text, *Giving Form to
Feeling,* but is good material nevertheless.

King, Nancy. *Giving Form to Feeling.* New York: Drama Book Specialists, 1975.

This is a sound and useful handbook with many exercises and ideas. The
author says that it is a book of beginnings. This is true, but it is not
necessarily written for the beginner; the actor, dancer, and teacher on any
level will find help in expressing ideas and feelings through movement,
rhythm, sounds, and words.

King, Nancy. *A Movement Approach to Acting.* Englewood Cliffs, N.J.: Prentice-
Hall, 1981.

A text that goes from breathing and body awareness exercises to circus
skills, stage combat, and nonverbal elements of drama. Written by an
experienced teacher, this book is highly recommended.

La Salle, Dorothy. *Rhythms and Dance for Elementary Schools.* Rev. ed. New
York: Ronald, 1951.

This collection of rhythms and dances should be extremely useful to the
teacher of dramatic play and creative drama, or to the children's theatre
director. It contains movement fundamentals, singing games, and folk
dances, ranging from simple to advanced.

Lowndes, Betty. *Movement and Creative Drama for Children.* Boston: Plays,
1971.

First published in England, this practical and stimulating book should find
enthusiastic readers in the United States as well. The author, an ex-

perienced teacher, explains the value and use of improvised movement and follows with chapters on body awareness, locomotion, mime, sensory awareness, and creative movement.

Maynard, Olga. *Children and Dance and Music.* New York: Scribner's, 1968. This book includes material not usually found in texts on creative drama. A good supplement to any text.

Rowan, Betty. *Learning through Movement Activities for the Preschool and Elementary Grades.* New York: Teachers College Press, 1982. The author suggests ways to use the child's natural movement for the teaching of language, science, numbers, and social studies. Lists of literature and recordings add to its value as a reference book.

Slade, Peter. *Natural Dance.* London: Hodder and Stoughton, 1977. This is particularly recommended for the teacher of creative drama. In it Slade discusses "natural dance," or dance that is improvised, as opposed to formal dance techniques. It deals with all ages, levels of experience, and levels of ability; the therapeutic aspects of dance are also included.

Puppetry and Masks

Alkema, Chester J. *Mask Making.* New York: Sterling, 1981. A variety of masks made from a variety of materials. Beautiful illustrations in both black and white and color, ranging from simple paper bags to elaborately decorated masks.

Boylan, Eleanor. *Puppet Plays for Special Days.* Rowayton, Conn.: New Plays, Inc. 1976. This delightful collection of short plays should prove helpful to classroom teachers and community leaders engaged in puppetry. Focus is on the play rather than on methods of construction.

Brooks, Courtaney. *Plays and Puppets Etcetera.* Claremont, Cal.: Belnice Books, 1981. This book is designed as a starting point for readers who have little or no knowledge of puppets. Written in a conversational style, the text encourages the inexperienced person yet it does not talk down to the reader.

Champlin, John, and Connie Brooks. *Puppets and the Mentally Retarded Student.* Austin, Tex.: Nancy Renfro Studios, 1980. Developing literary comprehension with the mentally retarded child. The text shows how to adapt books for telling stories and offers special techniques for utilizing puppets in programs K–6.

Cole, Nancy. *Puppet Theatre in Performance.* New York: William Morrow, 1978. What distinguishes this book is its emphasis on performance. Whereas many texts on puppetry offer detailed instructions for making puppets,

Nancy Cole gives ideas and clear directions for handling them. An unusually good book for advanced as well as older puppeteers.

Cummings, Richard. *101 Hand Puppets: A Guide for Puppeteers of All Ages.* New York: McKay, 1962.

This is an extremely comprehensive book offering step-by-step instruction for making every conceivable kind of hand puppet, from the simplest to the most elaborate. It includes scripts and has over sixty diagrams and illustrations. For older and more experienced classes.

Dean, Audrey Vincent. *Puppets That Are Different.* New York: Taplinger, 1973.

This book was specially designed to teach beginners how to bring the hand puppet to life and how to develop the skills needed to mount a successful show. Every detail is included in a clear, attractive step-by-step primer.

Engler, Larry, and Carol Fijan. *Making Puppets Come Alive.* New York: Taplinger, 1973.

This is a charming and practical text for the beginner of any age. To be used by the teacher, it offers help in making and handling puppets, including exercises to develop the skills needed to produce a show. Beautifully illustrated.

Freericks, Mary, and Joyce Segal. *Creative Puppets in the Classroom.* Rowayton, Conn.: New Plays, Inc., 1979.

As the title states, this book gives instruction for using puppets in the curriculum. Inexpensive materials and simple techniques add to its value for the teacher.

Hunt, Tamara, and Nancy Renfro. *Puppetry in Early Childhood Education.* Austin, Tex.: Nancy Renfro Studios, 1982.

One of the most comprehensive books on the subject. Teachers, librarians, and recreation leaders will find this enormously helpful. Highly recommended.

Jagendorf, Moritz. *Puppets for Beginners.* Boston: Plays, 1952.

A simple, comprehensive book with attractive illustrations. Recommended for school and community use.

Hanford, Robert Ten Eyck. *The Complete Book of Puppets and Puppeteering.* New York and London: Drake, 1976.

A 157-page paperback concentrating on an overview of puppetry—past, present, and to come; the tools of the trade; the production; and techniques and tips from the pros. An excellent book written in clear, definitive style with simple, yet complete instructions on all aspects of puppets and puppet productions.

Krinsky, Norman, and Bill Berry. *Paper Construction for Children.* New York: Reinhold, 1966.

Masks and puppets are among many projects described in this book. Delightful text with drawings and photographs to illustrate the brief but adequate explanations.

Luskin, Joyce. *Easy to Make Puppets*. Boston: Plays, 1975.

Instructions, patterns, and photographs show how to create twenty-four puppets: hand, glove and marionette. Simple, attractive format.

McCaslin, Nellie. *Puppet Fun: Performance, Production and Plays*. New York: McKay, 1977.

This text, directed to the child from ages seven to ten, can be used equally well by the inexperienced teacher or recreation leader who wants to include puppetry but who has never worked with it. Diagrams and illustrations show the rudiments of making and manipulating hand puppets.

Nobleman, Roberta. *Mime and Masks*. Rowayton, Conn.: New Plays, 1979.

A gifted teacher brings two areas together in this book: mime, which is an actor's tool, and the mask, used for dramatic projection. In this text the performing and visual arts meet.

Peyton, Jeffrey, and Barbara Koenig. *Puppetry: A Tool for Teaching*. New Haven, Conn.: P.O. Box 270, 1973.

Simplicity and economy characterize this 100-page guide to puppetry for the curriculum. Originally prepared for the New Haven Public Schools, it is adaptable to other systems and a variety of subject areas.

Renfro, Nancy. *Puppetry and the Art of Story Creation*. Austin, Tex.: Nancy Renfro Studios, 1979.

A guide to story-creating with simple puppet ideas. There is a special section on puppetry for the disabled.

Ross, Laura. *Scrap Puppets*. New York: Holt, Rinehart and Winston, 1978.

A clearly illustrated book that describes four basic kinds of puppets. A list of materials supplements the directions for making them.

Schmidt, Hans J., and Karl J. Schmidt. *Learning with Puppets*. Chicago: Coach House Press, 1980.

A guide to making and using puppets in the elementary school. Stress on acquisition of academic and social skills, as well as artistic expression.

Sims, Judy. *Puppets for Dreaming and Scheming*. Walnut Creek, Cal.: Early Stages, 1978.

A source book for those using puppetry in the elementary classroom. Especially well suited to the needs of teachers of younger children; many ideas and simple, clear directions.

Related Fields

Aesthetics

Andres, Michael F. *Aesthetic Form and Education*. Syracuse: Syracuse University Press, 1958.

Coming to Our Senses: The Significance of the Arts for American Education. Panel Report, David Rockefeller, Jr., chairman. New York: McGraw-Hill, 1977.

This long-awaited survey of the state of arts education in America is of greatest interest to the specialist and the administrator. It represents years of collecting, compiling, and writing down information gathered from many sources, both persons and organizations.

Edman, Irwin. *Arts and the Man.* New York: The New American Library, Mentor Book, 1950.

Engel, Martin, and Jerome Hausman, eds. *Curriculum and Instruction in Arts and Aesthetic Education.* St. Louis: CEMREL, 1981.

Knieter, Gerard L., and Jane Stallings, eds. *The Teaching Process and Arts and Aesthetics.* St. Louis: CEMREL, 1979.

Langer, Suzanne. *Problems of Art.* New York: Scribner's, 1957.

Linderman, Earl W., and Donald W. Heberholz. *Developing Artistic and Perceptual Awareness.* Dubuque, Iowa: William C. Brown, 1964.

Lowenfield, Viktor. *Creative and Mental Growth.* New York: Macmillan, 1952.

Madeja, Stanley S., ed. *Art and Aesthetics: An Agenda for the Future.* St. Louis: CEMREL, 1977.

Mumford, Lewis. *Art and Technics.* New York: Columbia University Press, 1952.

Choral Speaking

Abney, Louise. *Choral Speaking Arrangements for the Lower Grades.* Boston: Expression, 1937.

Gullan, Marjorie. *The Speech Choir.* New York: Harper & Row, 1937.

Huckleberry, Alan W., and Edward S. Strother. *Speech Education for the Elementary Teacher.* Boston: Allyn & Bacon, 1966. Chapter 6.

Rasmussen, Carrie. *Choral Speaking for Speech Improvement.* Boston: Expression, 1942.

Rasmussen, Carrie. *Let's Say Poetry Together and Have Fun.* Minneapolis: Burgess, 1962.

Government Support for the Arts

ACA Update: News for Arts Leaders. Vol. 3, no. 12. New York: American Council for the Arts, December 23, 1982.

ACA Update: News for Arts Leaders. Vol. 3, no. 2. New York: American Council for the Arts, February 12, 1982.

Annual Report 1975, National Endowment for the Arts, National Council for the Arts. Washington, D.C.: U.S. Government Printing Office, March, 1976.

Briskin, Larry, compiler. *Arts and the States.* A report of the Arts Task Force, National Conference of State Legislatures. Denver, Colorado: National Conference of State Legislatures, 1981.

Fosburg, Linda. "Arts Councils and Arts Education." In *Arts and Aesthetics: An Agenda for the Future.* St. Louis: CEMREL, 1977.

Plowitz, Kathryn A. "Artists-in-Schools: Background Information," mimeographed report. Washington D.C.: National Endowment for the Arts, April 7, 1980.

Porter, Robert. "State Appropriations: Will They Be Enough?" In *ACA Update: News for Arts Leaders.* Vol. 3, no. 2: 10–12. New York: American Council for the Arts, February 12, 1982.

Schiff, Bennett. *Artists-in-Schools.* Washington, D.C.: National Endowment for the Arts, 1973.

Siks, Geraldine Brain. "Drama in Education—A Changing Scene." In *Children and Drama,* edited by Nellie McCaslin. 2nd ed. New York: Longman, 1981.

Media and Music

Aronoff, Frances Webber. *Music and Young Children.* New York: Holt, Rinehart and Winston, 1969.
> A widely used text for music teaching, this book has much to offer both specialist and generalist in drama. Ways in which music can enrich the lives of children are suggested and explained. An excellent resource.

Concannon, Tom. *Using Media for Creative Teaching.* Rowayton, Conn.: New Plays, Inc., 1980.
> A text for today's classroom, in which a media specialist explains how skills may be developed through the use of camera, video tape, tape recorders, and even the human body. Methods and specific suggestions for using media in the curriculum areas from K to 8 are given.

List, Lynne K. *Music, Art, and Drama Experiences for the Elementary Curriculum.* New York: Teachers College Press, 1982.
> This book differs from most in that it focuses on all the arts, showing how they can stimulate learning and enhance teaching. Games and projects are described, as well as suggestions for using them with children who have special problems and needs.

Ravosa, Carmino. *Songs Children Act Up For.* Rowayton, Conn.: New Plays, 1974.
> Twenty-two action songs collected by an experienced teacher and composer for use with children. This is a good and seldom used way of stimulating creative drama.

Play

Hartley, Ruth, Lawrence Frank, and Robert Goldenson. *Understanding Children's Play.* New York: Columbia University, 1964.

Huizinga, Johan. *Homo Ludens.* Boston: Beacon Press, 1950.

Koste, Virginia Glasgow. *Dramatic Play in Childhood: Rehearsal for Life.* New Orleans: Anchorage, 1978.

Piers, Maria W., ed. *Play and Development: A Symposium with Contributions by Piaget and Others.* New York: W. W. Norton, 1972.

Rasmussen, Margaret, ed. *Play.* Washington, D.C.: Association for Childhood Education International, 1963.

Reilly, Mary. *Play as Exploratory Learning: Studies of Curiosity Behavior.* Beverly Hills, Cal.: Sage Publications, 1974.

Schechner, Richard, and Mady Schuman. *Ritual, Play and Performance.* New York: Seabury Press, 1976.

Willeford, William. *A Fool and His Scepter: A Study in Clowns and Jesters and Their Audience.* Evanston, Ill.: Northwestern University Press, 1969.

Storytelling and Reading

Blake, James Neal. *Speech Education Activities for Children.* Springfield, Ill.: Charles C. Thomas, 1970.

Coger, Leslie, and Melvin White. *Readers Theatre Handbook.* Chicago: Scott, Foresman, 1967.
    Here is an excellent text on this new technique written by experts in the field. Directed toward the adult reader, it is nevertheless equally useful to the high school teacher or to any teacher interested in trying this concept of theatre.

Colwell, Eileen. *A Storyteller's Choice.* New York: Henry Z. Walck, 1965.

Maclay, Joanna Hawkins. *Readers Theatre: Toward a Grammar of Practice.* New York: Random House, 1971.
    This is an excellent text on the subject. It covers a definition of readers theatre, gives a selection of material, and also describes performance techniques. It is most useful to teachers of upper grades.

Sawyer, Ruth. *The Way of the Storyteller.* New York: The Viking Press, 1962.

Sloyer, Shirlee Epstein. *Readers Theatre: Story Dramatization in the Classroom.* Champaign, Ill.: National Council of Teachers of English, 1981.

Theatre for Children

Breen, Robert. *Chamber Theatre.* Englewood Cliffs, N.J.: Prentice-Hall, 1978.

Broadman, Muriel. *Understanding Your Child's Entertainment.* New York: Harper & Row, 1977.

Chorpenning, Charlotte. *Twenty-One Years with Children's Theatre.* Anchorage, Ky.: Anchorage, 1955.

Corey, Orlin. *Theatre for Children—Kids' Stuff or Theatre?* Anchorage, Ky.: Anchorage, 1974.

Courtney, Richard. *The School Play.* London: Cassell and Co., 1966.

Davis, Jed, and Mary Jane Evans. *Theatre for Young People.* New Orleans: Anchorage Press, 1982.

Fisher, Caroline, and Hazel Robertson. *Children and the Theatre.* Palo Alto: Stanford University Press, 1950.

Forkert, Maurice. *Children's Theatre that Captures Its Audience.* Chicago: Coach House, 1962.

Goldberg, Moses. *Children's Theatre: A Philosophy and a Method.* Englewood Cliffs, N.J.: Prentice-Hall, 1974.

Hall, Jeanne. "An Analysis of the Content of Selected Children's Plays with Special Reference to the Developmental Values Inherent in Them." Ph.D. dissertation, University of Michigan, 1966.

Healy, Daty. *Dress the Show.* Rowayton, Conn.: New Plays, 1976.

Johnson, Richard. *Producing Plays for Children.* New York: Rosen, 1971.

McCaslin, Nellie. *Children's Theatre in the United States: A History.* Norman: Oklahoma University Press, 1971.

Rosenberg, Helane S., and Christine Prendergast. *Theatre for Young People: A Sense of Occasion.* New York: Holt, Rinehart and Wilson, 1983.

Siks, Geraldine Brain, and Hazel Dunnington, eds. *Children's Theatre and Creative Dramatics: Principles and Practices.* Seattle: University of Washington Press, 1961.

Whitton, Pat Hale. *Participation Theatre for Young Audiences.* Rowayton, Conn.: New Plays, 1972.

Way, Brian. *Audience Participation.* Boston: Baker's Plays, 1981.

Films

Creativity: A Way of Learning.   11 min. color, sound.
    NEA Distribution Center
    The Academic Bldg. Saw Mill Rd.
    West Haven, Conn. 06516
    This film explores creativity, how it is related to life in and out of school, and how it can be encouraged.

Creative Dramatics: The First Steps.   29 min. color, sound.
Northwestern Film Library
614 Davis Street
Evanston, Ill. 60201
This is a vintage film that demonstrates the teaching of creative dramatics
to a group of fourth-grade children. Guided by an experienced teacher,
the group moves from the faltering first steps to the creation of a drama.

Dorothy Heathcote Talks to Teachers—Part I.   30 min. color
Northwestern University Film Library
1735 Benson Avenue
Evanston, Ill. 60201

Dorothy Heathcote Talks to Teachers—Part II.   32 min. color
Northwestern University Film Library
1735 Benson Avenue
Evanston, Ill. 60201

Everyman in the Streets.   30 min. color
Channel 13 NET—New York (no charge)
304 W. 58th Street
New York, N.Y. 10019

Ideas and Me.   17 min. color
Dallas Theatre Center
3636 Turtle Creek Blvd.
Dallas, Tex. 75200
In this film children participate in the various aspects of creative drama.

One of a Kind.   58 min. color, sound.
Phoenix Films, Inc.
470 Park Ave, S.
New York, N.Y. 10016
Intended for audiences of all ages, this powerful film deals with the
relationship between a child and a troubled mother. Through participation in a traveling puppet show, the child is able to express her anguish
and needs. The film can be used effectively for classes in special education, psychology, creative drama, and language arts.

Playing: Pretending Spontaneous Drama with Children.   20 min. b/w
Community Services Department
Pittsburgh Child Guidance Center
201 De Soto Street
Pittsburgh, Pa. 15213
This film, by Eleanor C. Irwin, describes a number of different forms of
spontaneous drama with primary and elementary-age children. Activities
showing creative movement, puppetry, role play, and improvisation are
demonstrated. The nature of creativity; the developmental roots of drama;
the importance of impulse control as well as impulse expression; the

individuality of children and their fantasies; and the value of dramatic play for children in both cognitive and affective learning are discussed.

Statues Hardly Ever Smile.   25 min. color
Brooklyn Museum
Eastern Parkway and Washington Ave.
Brooklyn, N.Y. 11238
This film shows work done at the museum. Though several years old, it is unique in content, form, and approach to creative drama.

Three Looms Waiting.   52 min. color
BBC Production
Time-Life Films, Inc., Distributor
43 W. 16th Street
New York, N.Y. 10016
This film shows Dorothy Heathcote, one of the leading British teachers of creative drama, working with a group of children. An excellent demonstration of her method.

Take 3.   70 min. 16-mm, color, sound
National Audio-Visual Aids Library
Paxton Place, Gipsy Rd.
London SE27 9SR
This English film describes the work of three drama teachers and is intended to provoke thought and raise questions about the nature of drama, assessment, and evaluation. Although not available for rental in the United States at the time of publication of this book, it is recommended because it shows three different teachers at work in three entirely different situations, each using individual techniques.

Why Man Creates.   25 min. color
Pyramid Films
P.O. Box 1048
Santa Monica, Cal. 90406
This is a popular film to be shown more than once. It inquires into the human need to create in an unusual way.

Index

A Note about the Author

Nellie McCaslin is the director of undergraduate studies of the Gallatin Division and teaches in the Program in Educational Theatre at New York University. She began her graduate studies at Case Western Reserve University; later she worked with Madame Maria Ouspenskaya, and went on to earn her Ph.D. from New York University. Then, she taught at the National College of Education in Evanston, Illinois, Teachers College of Columbia University, and Mills College of Education.

Professor McCaslin is a Fellow of the American Theatre Association. The Children's Theatre Association elected her their president in 1973 and she served in that post until 1975. She is frequently invited to participate in international conferences and festivals and she lectures and writes extensively on children's theatre. Her books include a history of the movement in the United States and two books also published by Longman, *Children and Drama* and *Theatre for Young Audiences.* In addition, she is the author of a number of children's plays and three juveniles, *Act Now!*, *Puppet Fun,* and *Shows on a Shoestring.* She has been a guest on CBS educational television, coordinator of children's programs on WABC radio, and producer of two records for children.

Jan-Feb
Feb-mar
mar-apr
apr-may
may-June
June-July
July-Aug
Aug-Sep
Sep-Oct
Oct-Nov
Nov-Dec
Jan-Feb
Feb-mar